Sustainable Fossil Fuels

More and more people believe we must quickly wean ourselves from fossil fuels – oil, natural gas and coal – to save the planet from environmental catastrophe, wars and economic collapse. Professor Jaccard argues that this view is misguided. We have the technological capability to use fossil fuels without emitting climate-threatening greenhouse gases or other pollutants. The transition from conventional oil and gas to unconventional oil, unconventional gas and coal for producing electricity, hydrogen and cleaner-burning fuels will decrease energy dependence on politically unstable regions. In addition, our vast fossil fuel resources will be the cheapest source of clean energy for the next century and perhaps longer, which is critical for the economic and social development of the world's poorer countries. By buying time for increasing energy efficiency, developing renewable energy technologies and making nuclear power more attractive, fossil fuels will play a key role in humanity's quest for a sustainable energy system.

MARK JACCARD is a Professor in the School of Resource and Environmental Management at Simon Fraser University in Vancouver.

"Jaccard's book offers an important perspective on the major challenges posed by conventional energy. CO_2 emissions from fossil fuel burning must be curbed and oil dependence must be reduced to address climate-change and oil-supply-insecurity concerns. Many understand that this implies making energy use more efficient and increasing renewable energy roles. But few realize that fossil energy technologies can be modified at relatively low incremental costs to help address these concerns with CO_2 capture and storage technologies. This book addresses this issue. It is a marvelous primer showing why this option must be taken seriously by policymakers and the general public."

Dr. Robert Williams, Senior Research Scientist, Princeton Environmental Institute, Princeton University

"Mark Jaccard's analysis of the potential contribution of fossil fuels provides a much-needed contrast to the more extreme views of imminent resource exhaustion."

Dr. G. Campbell Watkins, co-editor of The Energy Journal

"This is an optimistic book. It significantly broadens energy perspectives. In the general discourse, energy is often associated with serious challenges: security of supply, peace, climate change, many other environmental issues, and the unfilled needs of energy services for economic growth and poverty alleviation for a majority of the world's population. This book presents new technically and economically feasible options that promise to address these challenges. There is light in the tunnel, and it is now up to all stakeholders, and our political processes, to realize these options! I strongly recommend this book to all concerned about our common future!"

Dr. Thomas Johansson, Professor and Director, International Institute for Industrial Environmental Economics, Lund University – formerly Director of the Energy and Atmosphere Programme of the Bureau for Development Policy in the United Nations Development Programme

"Professor Jaccard's book provides a very important addition to the policy debate over future sources of energy in a climate constrained world that is trying to become environmentally sustainable. At the heart of his book is the idea that 'Renewables and zero-emission fossil fuels will compete for the dominant position in meeting the needs of a sustainable energy system over the coming century'. He finds that zero (carbon) emission fossil fuels are likely to have a cost advantage over renewables and in any event renewables, he argues, 'would be hard pressed to overtake fossil fuels by the end of the century'. Whilst a number of published scenarios challenge this view, particularly for the period beyond the 2050s, he has marshalled a lot of arguments that are worthy of serious debate and further research. Although I am not convinced, I would urge all involved in this debate to read this important book!

Bill Hare, Visiting Scientist, Potsdam Institute for Climate Impact Research – formerly the Greenpeace International work on the Kyoto Protocol

"Professor Jaccard tackles the two key global energy problems, an apparent shortage of oil and a dangerous build up of CO_2 in the atmosphere, and presents an original perspective on how simultaneously to resolve them with such clarity that it appears obvious – after you have read the book! . . . The text provides a balanced mix of serious economics and science, presented in easy-to-understand language and with just the right addition of everyday examples and quiet humor."

Dr. Jon Gibbins, Professor, Energy Technology for Sustainable Development Group, Mechanical Engineering Department, Imperial College

"Mark Jaccard skillfully makes the case that those who leave modifying the way we use fossil fuels out of any plan to achieve 'sustainability' in our energy systems surely confuse means with ends. If our objectives are to improve energy security and protect the environment at reasonable cost, he makes clear that, with a little bit of ingenuity and resolve, our extensive fossil fuel resources could well be our best friend rather than our worst enemy."

Dr. John Weyant, Professor, Department of Management Science and Engineering, Stanford University

"Jaccard's well-researched study injects a much-needed dose of reality into the discussion of a 'sustainable' energy system. It is the voice of the economist tempered by extensive practical experience in the field and an evident concern for the future of our environment."

Dr. H. Jake Jacoby, Professor of Management and Co-Director of the MIT Joint Program on the Science and Policy of Global Change, Massachusetts Institute of Technology

"Discussions of energy options too often oversimplify the world into good guys and bad guys. In his latest book, Mark Jaccard has done us all a service. He has brought cool analysis and common sense to a complex area of public policy fraught with myth and image management. His objective is to consider what might constitute a more sustainable energy system and in this he considers not only the usual suspects (energy efficiency, nuclear and renewables) but the unusual – fossil fuels. In doing so, he moves beyond the simplistic rhetoric and offers us practical policy recommendations that deserve serious consideration."

Milton Catelin, Chief Executive, World Coal Institute

"Does preventing global warming require an end to fossil fuels? Jaccard makes a strong case that significant fossil fuel use and climate protection can co-exist, without harming economic growth. Read the book and decide for yourself."

David Hawkins, Director, Climate Center, Natural Resources Defense Council

Sustainable Fossil Fuels

The Unusual Suspect in the Quest for Clean and Enduring Energy

MARK JACCARD

CAMBRIDGE
UNIVERSITY PRESS

CAMBRIDGE UNIVERSITY PRESS
Cambridge, New York, Melbourne, Madrid, Cape Town, Singapore, São Paulo

Cambridge University Press
40 West 20th Street, New York, NY 10011–4211, USA

www.cambridge.org
Information on this title:www.cambridge.org/9780521679794

First published 2005
Reprinted 2006

Printed in the United States of America

A catalogue record for this book is available from the British Library.

ISBN-13   978-0-521-86179-3 hardback
ISBN-10   0-521-86179-9 hardback

ISBN-13   978-0-521-67979-4 paperback
ISBN-10   0-521-67979-6 paperback

Cambridge University Press has no responsibility for the persistence or accuracy
of URLs for external or third-party Internet Web sites referred to in this publication,
and does not guarantee that any content on such Web sites is, or will remain, accurate
or appropriate.

I dedicate this book to my parents, Doris and Lou.

Contents

Figures

Tables

Preface

The dates on my initial computer files remind me that I first developed the detailed argument and structure of this book in April 2001. I remember being concerned at the time that the book might take two years to write and publish – but I wanted it out more quickly than that. Such optimism.

Various commitments intervened. One was a book on costing greenhouse gas abatement policy that I wrote and published with two co-authors in the period 2001–02. There was also international and national advisory work related to climate change policy as well as my ongoing research, article writing and teaching responsibilities. If a manuscript is incomplete by the end of summer, there is little chance for significant progress during the following eight months of teaching. I finally had a virtually completed draft of the manuscript by mid-2004, but then I consumed almost a year eliciting feedback from various researchers, especially in areas that are peripheral to my expertise. This led to more research and significant rewriting in some sections. I am grateful to the many people who provided this service. Of course, I alone am responsible for remaining errors.

It is difficult to anticipate how this book will be received. I have always seen myself as strongly motivated by a concern for the environment, so I am predisposed to arguments that our economic system is unsustainable and that our policies for environmental protection need to be much stronger. I hope that message is clear in this book. At the same time, I enjoy challenging my and others' assumptions in a spirit of earnest inquiry, and this leads me to question assumptions that some environmentalists may currently take to be incontrovertible. My hope, however, is that even those who cannot agree with the hypothesis I explore in this book will only do so after carefully considering the evidence and arguments I present.

My goal is that the book be of interest to a fairly wide readership. I have tried to avoid technical jargon and excessive technological detail in order to invite non-expert readers. At the same time, I have aimed for a thorough presentation of the evidence that supports my hypothesis so that experts would also find the book to be a useful stimulus for debate and further research.

Because of this, the book is a bit longer than I would have liked. This presents a challenge to senior decision makers who need to review of lot of material in a given month. To accommodate these readers, I provide a synopsis of the book as an appendix. This synopsis includes chapter-specific reading suggestions so that someone can grasp the key evidence and arguments from a selective reading of about one fifth of the book's pages.

The book also has a website at http://www.emrg.sfu.ca/sustainablefossilfuels. This is updated regularly with reviews, comments, debates and updates on critical information.

Acknowledgments

In the early stages of preparing this book, I benefited greatly from discussions with Thomas Johansson and Bob Williams and from comments on early drafts from Trent Berry and Mel Kliman. I want especially to acknowledge the unflagging support of Bryn Sadownik, who edits my writing and whose suggested changes are always right.

In the later stages of the book, I got help from Jon Gibbins, Dominique Finon, Campbell Watkins, Nic Rivers, Chris Bataille, Charlie Wilson, Chris Green, Karin Albert, Rose Murphy and some anonymous reviewers. Others in my research group, including Jacqueline Sharp, Noory Meghji, Paulus Mau and Chris Joseph, helped out with various tasks. In particular, I note the complete support I always get from my close collaborator, John Nyboer. Nothing happens if not for him working quietly away at keeping our research group functioning smoothly.

I thank my editor at Cambridge University Press, Chris Harrison, for his enthusiasm and support from the first time he read my book synopsis. I also thank Lynn Dunlop and Jackie Warren at the Press for carrying us through the final stages of editing and production, and Judith Anderson for the indexing.

I thank my immediate family for their patience and support – Ingram, Kjartan, Torsten, Brit and Ingrid.

If I have forgotten anyone, I will list them on the book's website (http://www.emrg.sfu.ca/sustainablefossilfuels).

Finally, I acknowledge with sadness the contribution to my thinking of two wonderful colleagues who have passed away in the last two years – much too young. Steve Bernow of the Tellus Institute had an infectious passion for the pursuit of a sustainable energy system. I am not sure he would have agreed completely with my hypothesis, but I would love to have had the chance to debate it with him. Campbell Watkins was from the other end of the spectrum, a cautious economist who taught many of us a lot about the good and the bad of energy markets. While he did provide some feedback on my exploration of fossil fuel supplies and substitution potential, I did not get a chance to discuss with him the broader sustainability themes of the book, some of which he may not have agreed with. Disagreeing with Campbell or Steve was one of the pleasures of life, and a great opportunity for learning.

1 | *What is energy sustainability?*

Wᴇ frequently hear that our energy system is not sustainable. This certainly sounds right.

Our economies, especially those of industrialized countries, are completely dependent on fossil fuels – coal, oil and natural gas. These are non-renewable resources that we shall exhaust one day, perhaps soon. Fossil fuels provide energy via combustion and in the process release emissions that are toxic to animals and plants. Some of these emissions may be changing the earth's climate. Indeed, each stage in the exploration, extraction, processing, transportation and consumption of fossil fuels has known impacts and suspected risks for humans and ecosystems.

Surely the solution is to wean ourselves quickly off of fossil fuels – for there are ready alternatives. We can use energy much more efficiently. Reduce our energy consumption and we equally reduce emissions, slowing the depletion of fossil fuels at the same time. We can increase our use of nuclear power. It has negligible emissions and is virtually inexhaustible. We can rekindle our pre-industrial dependence on renewable energy, this time with advanced technologies that meet the needs of the information age for high quality, reliable energy.

In the more than twenty years that I have devoted to researching the relationship between energy, the environment and the economy – first as a graduate student, then combining duties as professor, policy advisor and five years chairing an energy regulatory agency – I have assumed that the shift to a sustainable energy system would entail a transition away from fossil fuels. I have also assumed that I would witness much of this transition during my lifetime.

My basic premise was that the way we consume the earth's fossil fuels must certainly be unsustainable given that fossil fuels are a rich and irreplaceable endowment produced from millennia of biological and geological processes. Consumption of them today leaves nothing for the future. Our appetite is clearly out of control, given that half of the oil consumption throughout human history has occurred since 1980. Moreover, our appetite is highly wasteful. We are unwilling to acquire more energy efficient equipment that should repay its extra up-front cost many times over. We leave the car running while chatting to a friend. We acquire frivolous energy-consuming products whose contribution to our well-being is questionable at best. Then there is the human and ecological mess of our addiction to fossil fuels: oil spills on land and sea, emissions that cause smog, acid rain and perhaps climate change.

I saw the reliance on nuclear energy as no better – and even more disquieting. The accidents at Three Mile Island in the US in 1979 and Chernobyl in the USSR in 1985 occurred during my university studies, leaving an enduring impression – especially when Chernobyl's radioactive cloud settled over the village in France where I lived at the time. The assumption that humans can safely handle radioactive waste seemed arrogant. Leaving a stockpile of such material for others to deal with went completely against my values of taking responsibility for one's impact on the earth and one's obligations to future generations.

To make matters worse, nuclear and fossil fuels fared poorly in the very field where they were expected to excel – financial performance. Almost everywhere, the costs of nuclear power ended up higher than promised, even when these costs failed to include all the up-front development subsidies, the full insurance liability, and the eventual decommissioning of old plants and permanent storage of radioactive fuel, equipment and structures. The initial oil price shocks of the 1970s and early 1980s were followed by price spikes in the 1991 Gulf war and then the 2003 Iraq war. Combined with the high prices of the last few years, these events convinced many experts and non-experts that price volatility is a perpetual threat with fossil fuels, regardless of whether the cause is impending resource depletion or geopolitically created shortages.

In contrast, because renewables rely on the free flows of nature – especially the sun – real or artificial scarcities seemed impossible. I remember a saying from the 1980s: "the oil companies cannot get between us and the sun's rays, but they will keep trying." Efficiency and renewables were associated with the careful husbanding of natural endowments, while harmonizing our lives and our economy at a smaller scale more in tune with the dispersed and unique character

of each renewable energy source. While the initial capital costs of renewable energy might sometimes be high, its operating costs would be stable and predictable, reflecting the continuous and free energy from the sun and other natural sources. Surely a renewables-based economy provided the blueprint for how to live sustainably on this earth.

I therefore focused my career research efforts on the technical and economic analysis of energy efficiency and renewable energy, and the policies needed to foster these two energy alternatives. My longstanding preference for efficiency and renewables is a view that has finally gained support in recent years, usually for reasons that match my own. Today, we often hear these arguments. What is the point of greater dependence on fossil fuels if we must eventually run out? What is the point of trying to clean up fossil fuels when we keep discovering new problems from using them? Shouldn't we save fossil fuels in case we have a special need for them in future? How can nuclear be sustainable with its ongoing risks of catastrophic accidents, on the one hand, and of low-level radiation exposure from generating plants and facilities for waste treatment, transport and storage on the other? How can we feel secure about a dramatic, worldwide expansion of nuclear generation given the threat that such technology will be diverted to military and terrorist ends?

The answer must be to begin immediately the transition away from fossil fuels to a high efficiency, renewables-based energy system, especially before the rapidly growing energy needs of developing countries overwhelm whatever small gains we have made in cleaning up fossil fuels and reducing the risks of the existing nuclear power industry. This position is advocated today not just by environmentalists but also by international agencies, corporations, energy experts and politicians. These recent quotes illustrate this widely held view.

The 2001 report of the Global Environmental Facility states:

A transition to renewables is inevitable, not only because fossil fuel supplies will run out – large reserves of oil, coal and gas remain in the world – but because the costs and risks of using these supplies will continue to increase relative to renewable energy.[1]

L. Brown, in his 2001 book *Eco-Economy*, says:

As the new century begins, the Sun is setting on the fossil fuel era . . . It is this desire for clean, climate-benign fuels – not the depletion of fossil fuels – that is driving the global transition to the solar/hydrogen age.[2]

In his 2001 book *Tomorrow's Energy*, P. Hoffman writes:

Hydrogen could be generated in a fusion reactor itself, providing another pathway toward a sustainable energy future with no environmental damage and virtually unlimited fuel supply. For the moment, however, solar and renewables represent the best complementary energy resource for hydrogen production in terms of environmental benefits.[3]

With the 2001 printing of his book *The Carbon War*, J. Leggett seethes:

Exxon, Mobil, Texaco and the other residually unrepentant thugs of the corporate world look like continuing to sign the cheques that bankroll the carbon club's crimes against humanity, along with their kindred spirits in the auto, coal and utility industries. They may well enjoy minor victories along the way. But they have already lost the pivotal battle in the carbon war. The solar revolution is coming. It is now inevitable.[4]

In describing the transition to a sustainable energy system in their 2002 book *Great Transition*, P. Raskin and co-authors say:

Climate stabilization at safe levels requires transcending the age of fossil fuels. The path to a solar future would be bridged by greater reliance on natural gas, a relatively low-polluting fossil fuel, and modern biomass technologies.[5]

H. Scheer, in his 2002 book *The Solar Economy: Renewable Energy for a Sustainable Global Future*, says:

An energy supply that protects the climate and the environment must necessarily be based on renewable, not fossil or nuclear energy, which means replacing the current system with more efficient energy technology using renewable resources.[6]

In his 2002 book *The Hydrogen Economy*, J. Rifkin states:

If the fossil-fuel era is passing, what can replace it? A new energy regime lies before us whose nature and character are as different from that of fossil fuels as the latter was different from the wood-burning energy that preceded it. Hydrogen is the lightest and most ubiquitous element found in the universe. When harnessed as a form of energy, it becomes the forever fuel. It never runs out, and, because it contains not a single carbon atom, it emits no carbon dioxide.[7]

H. Geller, in his 2003 book *Energy Revolution*, says:

A sustainable energy future is possible through much greater energy efficiency and much greater reliance on renewable energy sources compared to current energy patterns and trends. . . . Shifting from fossil fuels to renewable energy sources in the coming decades would address all the problems associated with a business-as-usual energy future.[8]

Referring to the impact of impending oil scarcity in his 2003 book *The Party's Over*, R. Heinberg says:

The core message of this book is that industrial civilization is based on the consumption of energy resources that are inherently limited in quantity, and that are about to become scarce. When they do, competition for what remains will trigger dramatic economic and geopolitical events; in the end, it may be impossible for even a single nation to sustain industrialism as we have known it during the twentieth century.[9]

On the cover of *The End of Oil*, a 2004 book by P. Roberts, it is stated:

the side effects of an oil-based society – economic volatility, geopolitical conflict, and the climate-changing impact of hydrocarbon pollution – will render fossil fuels an all but unacceptable solution.[10]

Finally, in his 2004 book *Out of Gas: The End of the Age of Oil*, D. Goodstein confidently asserts:

Civilization as we know it will come to an end sometime in this century unless we can find a way to live without fossil fuels.[11]

I found these quotes quickly and easily, and I knew I would because, as an avid follower of both popular and academic writing on energy sustainability, I encounter similar quotes every week. Indeed, I hear this sentiment expressed much more frequently today than I did fifteen or even five years ago.

As an academic researcher and policy advisor, this seems like an ideal time to ride the wave of efficiency and renewables. There is lots of research money available. Industry and environmentalists are starting to say the same things about the need to abandon the fossil fuel ship. Politicians are listening. The media is onside. The public is receptive.

But as is obvious from the title of this book, my research has gone in quite a different direction in the past four years. As I started to look more closely at our global energy options, I began to entertain, and then research more vigorously, a counter-intuitive hypothesis about the future of our energy system. Is it really necessary that we quickly reject fossil fuels? Is it possible that our supplies of fossil fuels are in fact still plentiful even if our production of them in one form – conventional oil – might be reaching its peak? Is it possible that we might develop, at a reasonable cost, ways of extracting useful energy from fossil fuels without causing harm to the biosphere and ourselves? Is it really true that abandoning oil would reduce geopolitical conflict and price volatility in energy markets? Or, do these phenomena happen mostly for other reasons?

What about a critical and popular concept like sustainability? Fossil fuels are a finite resource that we are using up. They cannot be part of a sustainable energy system. Or can they? The more I thought about the issue, and the more I researched it, the more I found myself challenging even my assumption about the elements and character of a sustainable energy system. And as I read more and more books and articles proclaiming the end of the age of fossil fuels, I started to notice more and more unfounded assumptions embedded in these proclamations – assumptions about resource magnitudes, technological potential, the function of markets, substitution between resources, and how one might define and determine the sustainability of a system.

Questioning these assumptions has taken me down an unexpected path indeed. It has led me to develop the hypothesis that fossil fuels can continue to play a significant role in the global energy system in this century, and probably long beyond, even though we might characterize such a system as sustainable. But given how I just described fossil fuels – their non-renewable and polluting character – this seems impossible. This book explores how I arrived at this unexpected conclusion. I begin the exploration at a general level by outlining in this introductory chapter some fundamental concepts: the definition and basic characteristics of a sustainable energy system, our experiences with using fossil fuels, and the major options for our energy system.

1.1 What is the energy system and how do we determine its sustainability?

Energy analysts refer to an energy system as the "combined processes of acquiring and using energy in a given society or economy." Such a system includes therefore sources of *primary energy*, the forms of *secondary energy* that we transform these primary sources into, and the final *energy services* (also known as *tertiary energy* or *energy end-uses*) such as lighting, mobility, space heating and cooling. We receive energy services by using secondary energy in end-use devices (or technologies) like lights, cars, furnaces and fridges.

Primary energy

Although energy appears to us on the earth's surface in different guises, these are all in some way the product of only two primary sources of energy. These are gravitational force and the conversion of mass into energy via nuclear reaction.

The gravitational force of the moon on the earth causes tidal movement of water, and the gravitational force of the earth causes earthward movement of objects, such as the kinetic energy in water flowing downhill. Gravitational forces of accreting mass in the earlier development of our solar system caused the consolidation and compression into larger bodies that eventually led to the creation of the earth. The earth's hot interior is the legacy of these earlier gravitational processes and the radioactive decay of long-lived radioactive elements – notably uranium, thorium and radium – that were incorporated into the earth at the time of its formation. Thus, geothermal energy that is now available near the earth's surface, especially in volcanic zones, might be interpreted as a combined result of gravitational force and nuclear reaction.

Mass is converted into energy either by the nuclear fusion of two light atoms or by the nuclear fission of a heavy atom. Naturally occurring nuclear fission does not provide much energy at the earth's surface, but in nuclear power plants humans have learned to concentrate and control fission processes to split uranium atoms and capture the resulting heat to drive steam turbines that generate electricity. Solar energy, resulting from the nuclear fusion in the sun of hydrogen atoms into helium, is responsible for most forms of energy found naturally at the earth's surface; at 174,000 terawatts (TW), solar radiation dwarfs all other natural energy sources and is 10,000 times greater than the current human use of energy. The sun's heat energy produces wind, waves (from wind), ocean currents and hydropower, as solar thermal energy combines with gravity to produce the hydrological cycle. The sun's light energy drives the growth of plants via photosynthesis, which is therefore responsible for chemical energy from biomass (forest and crop residues, animal and human waste). Humans have also learned to generate electricity directly from solar light energy via photovoltaics – using cells, made from silicon or other materials, whose electrons are released when struck by light energy (photons). Researchers are studying how to mimic the fusion process in the sun in a controlled reaction that they hope will one day produce heat for generating electricity, as we do today with nuclear fission.

Fossil fuels are a byproduct of solar energy. Over millions of years some of the remains of plants and animals have been preserved in sedimentary layers and then eventually transformed and concentrated under tectonic forces that subjected them to higher pressures and temperatures. Coal is mostly the remains of swamp plants that decomposed into peat and were eventually buried and subjected to higher pressure. Oil and natural gas are assumed to originate primarily from plankton that fell to the ocean floor near continental shorelines where it was covered by layers of sediment and eventually transformed into gaseous and liquid hydrocarbons through high pressure and temperature over millions of years.

In discussions over the past few years, I have suggested to my graduate students – environmentally oriented as they are – that fossil fuels are nothing more than solar energy, conveniently concentrated by nature for ease of use. I enjoy the heated discussions that follow. In frustration, one group referred to me as their "fossil fool" – affectionately I like to assume. My retort was that we should actually refer to solar energy as nuclear energy, given the primary energy role of nuclear fusion in the sun. Somehow this made me "a nuclear advocate." My point was that the closer you look at the sources of energy the more difficult it is to stick to simple classifications like fossil fuels, nuclear, and renewables. These sources of energy are more interrelated than many people assume. Maybe it was the need to challenge these comfortable assumptions of my students and myself that eventually made me more receptive to the hypothesis I entertain in this book.

In pre-industrial times there was little processing of primary energy prior to use. The dominant source of energy was heat from wood combustion. Usually, however, we process and transform primary energy in some way to render it easier to use or to remove unpleasant properties. We call the resulting products secondary energy.

Secondary energy

Coal is only slightly transformed before its use in electricity generation and steel production, although we can extract methane (natural gas) directly from it as coal-bed methane, and in the past century (and still in some places today) coal was gasified and distributed as *town gas* in cities. Before the Second World War, Germany's scientists developed ways of producing *synthetic gasoline* from coal as a precaution against wartime disruption of their crude oil imports, and relied on this extensively in the later years of the war. This process is still used in South Africa. Crude oil is transformed at an oil refinery into a range of refined petroleum products including gasoline, diesel, propane, kerosene and heavy heating oil. Raw natural gas requires processing to extract sulphur, liquids, and other gases, and to inject odorous compounds to help consumers detect leaks.

Some forms of secondary energy differ dramatically from the original primary source. Electricity is not available in nature – except during a lightning storm or sometimes when I touch my car door after driving – but it can be produced from uranium via nuclear fission, from fossil fuels and biomass via combustion, from the heat of geothermal energy, from solar light energy via photovoltaics, and from solar heat energy and gravitational force via the resulting wind, waves, hydropower and tides, whose mechanical energy can spin electricity-generating turbines. Hydrogen is another form of secondary energy that is not freely available in nature but can be produced from other primary and secondary forms, including the removal of hydrogen from hydrocarbon compounds (fossil fuels and biomass) or the electrolysis of water (separating oxygen and hydrogen) using electricity. As these last examples suggest, energy systems can get complicated, with several transformations possible prior to providing final energy services to consumers.

Hydrogen and electricity are frequently seen as essential components of a sustainable energy system because both appear to have negligible impacts on people or ecosystems, making them ideal forms of secondary energy for delivery to homes, offices and factories, and for fueling vehicles. The properties of electricity are well known and its risks, like electrocution and fire, are understood and accepted. The properties of hydrogen, in contrast, are not well known, and there are a wide range of views about what the production, transport and use of

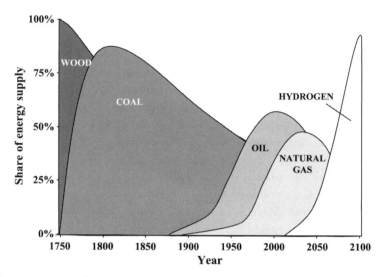

Figure 1.1. A misleading view of dominant energy forms.

this fuel might entail in terms of impacts and risks for people and the environment.

There are misperceptions about the role of hydrogen, with some commentators and even researchers describing it as if it were a primary source of energy (see the earlier quote of J. Rifkin in which he suggests that the hydrogen era will follow the fossil fuel era). Figure 1.1, a diagram that I have seen at more than one conference, depicts the evolution of human energy sources over time, and predicts a dominant role for hydrogen in future. The diagram shows how we have evolved from a global energy system dominated by wood and other forms of biomass to one in which coal, oil and then natural gas dominates. The diagram suggests that a hydrogen era will follow that of natural gas. However, there is a serious conceptual problem with this diagram; wood, coal, oil and natural gas are all primary sources of energy while hydrogen, like electricity, is not. A primary energy source is needed to produce the hydrogen. This source might well be wood, coal, oil, natural gas or some energy source not even in the diagram, such as nuclear or solar energy.

Many people now believe that hydrogen will become a dominant form of secondary energy in this century – and several recent books focus on this potential – but the hydrogen vision is still vague in many respects.[12] There is certainly no consensus on the source of primary energy from which hydrogen, electricity and other cleaner forms of secondary energy would be produced. During my career, I have reviewed sophisticated proposals for different electricity-hydrogen energy systems whose primary energy source ranged from nuclear to solar to hydropower to geothermal.[13]

Energy services

Energy services are associated with the familiar activities of our daily lives. In households, these include lighting, space conditioning (heating, cooling, ventilation), cooking, refrigeration, washing and drying of clothes, transport of people and goods, and the use of miscellaneous types of equipment – mostly electronic – that provide communication, entertainment, education and other domestic and commercial services. In the industrial sector, heat, applied directly from combustion or indirectly from steam produced on-site in a boiler, is used to reduce and transform materials, although in some industries mechanical power (grinding wood fiber into pulp) or electrolysis (aluminum production) are also important. Motive force from motors is used to drive conveyors, fans, blowers and pumps that provide ancillary services to the production process. Industries also need many of the same energy services as households – as do commercial and institutional buildings – such as lighting, space heating, cooling, drying, and electronic devices for services like communications and process control.

Defining energy system sustainability

Returning to our initial definition of an energy system, we see just how complicated it is to characterize any system as sustainable. We must account for all primary, secondary and tertiary forms of energy, and the many technologies involved in the production, transformation and use of energy. Even then, the concept of sustainability is elusive and contentious.

In this book, I apply a simple definition of energy system sustainability. To be sustainable, an energy system must meet two conditions.

- First, the energy system must have good prospects for enduring indefinitely in terms of the type and level of energy services it provides. Moreover, given the significant energy use that will be required to improve human well-being in much of the developing world, the size of the global energy system would ideally grow substantially over this century.
- Second, extraction, transformation, transport and consumption of energy must be benign to people and ecosystems. Flows of the energy system's material and energy byproducts must not exceed the ability of land, air and water to absorb and recycle them without significant negative disruption. In this sense, both the known, cumulative impacts of the energy system must be negligible and any extraordinary risks it poses must be extremely unlikely, and ones from which the system could recover within a reasonable period of time, perhaps aided by rehabilitation efforts.

Both of these conditions are inherent in most definitions of sustainability. If the system cannot endure, perhaps because some irreplaceable input is exhausted, it cannot be sustainable. If the system is ultimately toxic to humans and the environment, then it also will not endure, this time not because of resource exhaustion but because of disruption and destruction of natural systems and harm to humans.

Applying these two conditions, our current global energy system does not appear sustainable. First, the system is dominated by fossil fuels, a finite resource we are using up. In the 1970s and early 1980s, this concern was especially prevalent, triggered in part by the oil price shocks of that time. It has resurfaced in recent years with concerns that conventional oil production is at its physical limit, so causing the oil price increases seen in the first years of the twenty-first century. Second, in the process of exhausting this fossil fuel endowment, we cause human and ecological damage, some of it potentially irreparable. This concern has arisen with various pollutants in the past, and it is more recently associated with greenhouse gas emissions and the risk of climate change. Today, both concerns are at the forefront of people's minds. There is a widespread feeling that our fossil fuels-based energy system is a house of cards, one that when it collapses will bring down our economy and our environment along with it, as exemplified by several of the quotes earlier in this chapter. But is this damning characterization of our fossil fuel-based energy system a fair one?

1.2 What has been our experience with fossil fuels?

In terms of the first attribute of sustainability – endurance – fossil fuels are recognized to be non-renewable: their rate of creation by natural processes is measured in geological time while we consume oil and natural gas at a rate that most experts suggest will substantially deplete global stocks over the next century, perhaps resulting in a downturn in global oil production sometime within the next twenty-five years.

If we focus just on the supplies of oil – the fossil fuel that symbolizes our current energy system – the concept of resource exhaustion can be simply represented by dividing the fixed stock of the resource by its annual rate of production. This ratio indicates the number of years before the resource is completely consumed, assuming no change in the rate of consumption or the estimated resource stock.

But what can we learn from this ratio? Does it tell us that by knowing the magnitude of a finite resource like oil we can predict with some confidence the decade of its demise? Unfortunately – or perhaps fortunately – reality is much more complicated. The estimated stock of a non-renewable resource such as oil depends on a complex interplay between our incomplete knowledge of the physical magnitude of the resource, the state of our technological capacity to find, extract and process the resource, and its market value. A change in any one of these factors will change the estimated stock, even if the other factors stay constant.

Figure 1.2 portrays the interplay of these factors. It shows the relationship between the available quantity of oil (the horizontal axis) and the cost of producing these quantities (vertical axis), with available quantities arranged in ascending order of cost.* In some locations, the cost of production is extremely low, an example being some of the oil in the Middle East that can have a cost of production as low as $5 per barrel. Additional quantities are from less advantageous sites, which explains the rising cost curve.

When oil deposits are discovered they are added to the supply curve depending on where they fit with respect to cost of production. Over

---

* While economists typically draw supply curves like this to represent a flow of a commodity, the horizontal axis can be thought of here as the total quantity of the resource that is exploitable; in other words, it is the total stock of the resource.

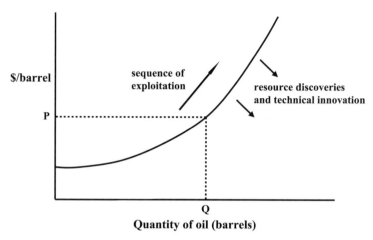

Figure 1.2. Global oil supply curve.

time, these new discoveries increase the quantity and reduce the price (shifting the supply curve down and to the right). Technological change that reduces the cost of finding and producing oil will also increase the supply of oil at a given price. At the same time, the market value of the resource indicates how much consumers are willing to climb up the oil supply curve as they consume mostly cheaper resources first and then shift to higher cost resources as these are used up. This dynamic of downward and upward price pressure makes it difficult to determine a fixed magnitude for the resource. As prices rise and technologies change, its estimated magnitude also changes. This information from the oil market may help us see if a finite resource like oil is becoming scarcer – if the price increases from resource depletion exceed the rate at which discovery and technological change lower production cost – but it does not tell us about the absolute magnitude of the resource.

In terms of my second attribute – the need for energy use to be benign or non-toxic for the earth's biosphere – humans have long been aware of the harmful byproducts of fossil fuel use. Historians have noted evidence of controls on fossil fuel combustion as early as 2,000 years ago in China. In Europe, concerns mounted in step with the industrial revolution from 1750 onwards, as soot and noxious gases from uncontrolled coal combustion clogged the air of burgeoning towns and cities, and the lungs of their inhabitants. Industrialization also brought increased wealth to these regions, in turn fostering rising expectations for improved quality of life as well as scientific know-how for taking corrective action.

Fossil fuels have a high energy density relative to the other carbon-aceous fuels such as wood, crop residues and animal waste, which means that from combustion they produce more heat and light per unit of mass. In units of megajoules per kilogram, rough estimates for energy density are: peat – 15 MJ/kg; wood – 18 MJ/kg; coal – 20–30 MJ/kg; natural gas – 45 MJ/kg; and oil – 50 MJ/kg. The continuous development of technologies that take advantage of this high energy density has intertwined increasing fossil fuel use with two centuries of economic expansion by industrialized countries.

But while economic output and energy use have both increased, they have not always done so at the same rate. The evolution of the ratio of energy use to economic output, called energy intensity, illustrates this divergence. This ratio is usually depicted as E/GDP, with E standing for energy, measured in physical units such as joules, and GDP standing for economic output, measured in constant monetary units such as dollars (with inflation effects removed). Figure 1.3 shows an estimate for global E/GDP over the past 150 years. For 100 years prior to 1950 it appears that energy intensity was roughly static. Since 1950, however, energy intensity has steadily declined; today we use less energy to produce a given amount of goods and services.

This trend of declining energy intensity over the last half century might offer some hope that fossil fuel related pollution would diminish, or at least grow more slowly. But the measure of total energy consumption tells a different story. Figure 1.4 shows total energy consumption over the past 200 years and the share of fossil fuels within that total. The era of industrialization is associated with a dramatic increase in the global use of energy, with fossil fuels playing a dominant role in the energy mix. Thus, while improvements in energy intensity do decrease energy consumption for a given level of economic output, the historical growth in economic output has been at a much faster pace than the rate of that energy intensity improvement. Per capita economic growth and rapid population growth have combined to outpace any downward influence from decreased energy intensity.

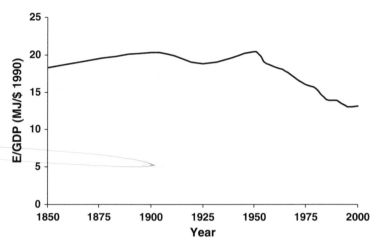

Figure 1.3. Global energy intensity: 1850–2000.
GDP is expressed in terms of International Geary-Khamis dollars. 'E'
represents primary energy consumption.

Sources: GDP data: A. Maddison, *The World Economy: A Millennial
Perspective* (Paris: OECD, 2001).

Energy data: N. Nakicenovic and A. Grubler, "Energy and the Protection of
the Atmosphere," *International Journal of Global Energy Issues* 13, 1–3
(2000): 4–56; and International Energy Agency, *Energy Balances of non-
OECD Countries 1998–1999* (Paris: OECD, 2000).

Humans have sought ways of reducing or preventing the emissions,
and other damages such as oil spills, associated with fossil fuel use.
While great strides have been made, this pursuit may at times appear
futile – we find a technological solution for one harmful byproduct of
fossil fuel use only then to become aware of yet another threat. Prior to
the industrial revolution, some European cities such as London already regulated the hours of the day for operating furnaces and the
months of the year for domestic burning of coal. With the advent of
the industrial revolution, more stringent laws were required, but problems with particulate emissions were still severe in London as late as
the 1950s, and are even more pronounced today in the cities of
developing countries – especially those relying on coal and charcoal
to meet domestic and industrial energy needs.

The rapidly expanding use of vehicles powered by internal combustion engines emerged in the 1950s as the next major environmental

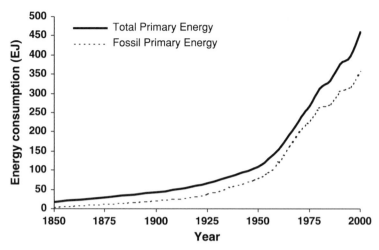

Figure 1.4. Global energy and fossil fuel consumption: 1850–2000.

Sources: Based on Nakicenovic and Grubler, "Energy and the Protection of the Atmosphere" (see figure 1.3).

Note: 1 EJ (exajoule) = 10^{18} joules.

challenge from fossil fuel use. Nitrogen oxides, particulates and other emissions from gasoline- and diesel-fueled engines are a major contributor to urban smog. While technological innovations have decreased these emissions significantly for each vehicle, the increase in the total number of vehicles threatens to offset these gains.

By the 1980s, policy makers began to acknowledge that acid gases from fossil fuel combustion concentrate in local and downwind regions as acid rain that damages ecosystems and corrodes human-built structures. Reducing sulphur dioxide emissions from coal combustion is achieved via sulphur scrubbers on smokestacks, more efficient coal combustion technologies, switching to low sulphur coal and switching from coal to oil, natural gas and other lower-emission energy sources.

In spite of these successful responses to the environmental challenges of fossil fuel use, scientists keep identifying new problems to worry about. The emerging concern is that CO_2 emissions from fossil fuel combustion are accumulating in the atmosphere and, along with other greenhouse gases from various activities, increasing the

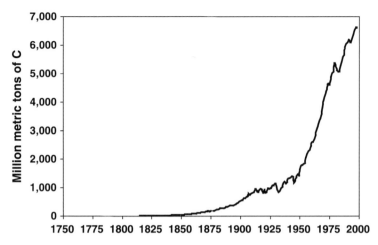

Figure 1.5. Global CO$_2$ emissions: 1750–2000.

Sources: CO$_2$ calculated from fossil fuel sources only.

Based on data in G. Marland, T. Boden and R. Andres, "Global, Regional, and National CO$_2$ Emissions," in *Trends: A Compendium of Data on Global Change* (Oak Ridge, Tenn.: Carbon Dioxide Information Analysis Center, Oak Ridge National Laboratory, 2001).

atmosphere's natural greenhouse effect such that the earth's climate could change significantly over this century. In effect, we are extracting a large quantity of carbon, for eons collected and stored beneath the earth's surface as fossil fuels, and in a short period releasing this back into the atmosphere where it is accumulating and perhaps changing how the earth captures and releases the sun's heat radiation. Figure 1.5 shows how human-generated CO$_2$ emissions have increased over the past 250 years.

As this brief history suggests, it can sometimes seem that with fossil fuels we identify and resolve one problem only to discover yet another damaging consequence from basing our economic system on them. One can't help seeing something more sinister in this relationship – perhaps an indication that industrial societies have made a Faustian pact that will require us to pay dearly one day for the ephemeral benefits of our current dependence. Do we need to take this risk? Do we need to base our energy and economic systems on fossil fuels?

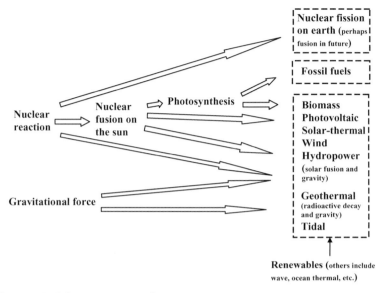

Figure 1.6. Primary sources of energy.

1.3 What are the alternatives to fossil fuels?

Although there are only the two fundamental energy sources – nuclear reactions that convert mass to energy and gravitational force – humans usually categorize their energy options according to the natural rate of regeneration (renewables vs. non-renewables) and the type of technology (nuclear vs. fuel combustion). Figure 1.6 shows the relationship between these two fundamental sources of energy – on the left side of the figure – and the primary energy sources that humans normally refer to – on the right side. Human-produced nuclear energy – fission and perhaps eventually fusion – is considered separately because of its requirement for sophisticated technical capabilities and its association with the particular risks of exposure to nuclear radiation and nuclear weapons proliferation. Fossil fuels are lumped together by virtue of being non-renewable hydrocarbons. Renewable energy includes all forms of energy that are available near the earth's surface in a continuous flow, such as geothermal, tidal and solar, even though these may differ in terms of their fundamental energy source.

Although it is not a source of energy, energy efficiency is sometimes depicted as an energy alternative because improvements in efficiency mean that primary energy use might grow more slowly or even decline. An energy system cannot be based on energy efficiency alone, but analysts nonetheless often distinguish three major alternatives to fossil fuels: energy efficiency, nuclear power and renewables.

Energy efficiency

While humans have continually improved the efficiency with which they convert primary energy into useful goods and services, calculations by physicists and engineers indicate a great potential for further improvement. Figure 1.3 provided a rough indication of energy efficiency improvement by setting energy input in a ratio with economic output (E/GDP), the latter measured in monetary units. But this ratio should really be thought of as *energy intensity* because it can change for reasons that do not relate to true physical changes in energy efficiency. For example, the monetary value of an output like shoes can change because of quality improvements, which increase GDP. For the E/GDP ratio to fall because of increased energy efficiency, this would be because of actual improvements in energy extraction, energy conversion, energy distribution and energy end-use devices and processes that reduced the difference between primary energy inputs and the energy services we receive.[14]

Promoters of energy efficiency point to the significant efficiency differences that exist between countries. Sweden and Canada, for example, have similar geography, climate, levels of urbanization and standard of living, yet their E/GDP ratios differ significantly. After allowing for differences in their industrial bases (Canada has a relatively larger share of GDP from resource extraction industries which are energy intensive), researchers found that Sweden was significantly more efficient in its use of energy than Canada. Buildings, appliances, industrial equipment and vehicles in Sweden are generally more efficient than their Canadian counterparts.[15]

While some researchers conduct intercountry energy comparisons like this as a way of estimating each country's potential for energy efficiency improvement, others focus instead on identifying the most energy efficient technologies available today and use these as a benchmark for estimating a country or industry's potential for energy efficiency improvement. Finally, in a third approach – this one more futuristic – some researchers use advanced engineering design to speculate on the potential improvements in energy efficiency over a longer timeframe which could result from a concerted program of research, development and commercialization. All three of these areas of research suggest that significant improvements in energy efficiency in industrialized countries could substantially reduce the need for energy supply expansion, even while energy services expanded.

It seems difficult to find a downside to energy efficiency. If all of our supply alternatives entail some negative effects, then using less can only improve things. But is it that simple?

Some energy experts argue that policies promoting profitable energy efficiency investments, through greater provision of information or via subsidies, will ultimately lead to higher energy use and greater environmental impacts. Energy efficiency is thus presented as a double-edged sword in that more efficient equipment costs less to operate, which will affect decisions about acquiring and operating such equipment. Rich people in the wealthy countries of the world certainly use more energy per capita than their poorer neighbors. Our cars and heating systems may be more efficient than forty years ago. But we also drive more, buy larger houses and acquire new innovations like air conditioners, water coolers, wine coolers, jacuzzis and a myriad other energy-using devices that did not exist back then.

A full assessment of energy efficiency's contribution must therefore examine not only the evolving efficiency of our equipment and buildings, but also the energy service wants of people in industrialized countries and the rising energy service demands of people in developing countries, all of which depends in turn on the full cost of providing energy services. We cannot fully assess energy efficiency's potential until we know what a cleaner, more benign energy system will cost, and for that we must review our energy supply alternatives.

Nuclear

For much of the thirty years following the Second World War, many energy experts assumed that nuclear power would eventually overtake fossil fuels as the dominant form of primary energy, and major industrialized countries subsidized the development and expansion of domestic nuclear power industries. A common phrase at the time was that nuclear would eventually be "too cheap to meter," just like the water supply systems in some North American cities.

The oil price shocks of the 1970s initially accelerated interest in nuclear power and contributed to decisions in France and Japan to expand dramatically their domestic nuclear industries. But almost every country developing nuclear power also had citizens with strong concerns about the risk of either nuclear accidents or ongoing radiation exposure from plant operation and waste handling. Anti-nuclear groups pointed to the possible link of nuclear power to the proliferation of nuclear weapons. Several smaller incidents and then the major accident at Chernobyl in the Soviet Union strengthened the growing anti-nuclear sentiment in the 1980s. Some jurisdictions with no nuclear power adopted moratoriums against development, while some jurisdictions with nuclear power passed laws to prohibit further expansion and eventually to phase out existing plants. It is difficult to gauge current public attitudes to nuclear power in industrialized countries because there have been few efforts to site and construct new plants in the past twenty years.

Renewables

Renewables advocates argue that renewable forms of energy are cleaner than fossil fuels and less risky than nuclear power. Renewable energy involves the capture of energy that is naturally and benignly flowing through our environment, a flow which will continue throughout the life of our sun. But assessing the character of renewable energy is not just about measuring benign energy flows. It is also about the technologies that capture and convert energy, and the land and water resources that are required in order to capture and use these diverse energy sources that are often of low energy density, intermittent, and inconveniently located. Again, we must look at the total energy system in order to make a complete assessment.

Hydropower is the result of solar power and gravitational forces. Humans first learned about 2,000 years ago how to capture hydropower potential by redirecting water through waterwheels and other devices. For the past 100 years, however, industrialized societies have mostly used hydropower's mechanical energy to spin electricity-generating turbines. This is associated with large and small dams that store water at higher elevations to increase the power potential of a site and enable a more even output of electricity through the seasonal variations in precipitation. Most hydro facilities are not environmentally benign; they alter stream flows, hinder or prevent the passage of migratory fish, and flood thousands of hectares of land that has high values for agriculture, forestry, transportation and human settlement. Because of these concerns, smaller-scale hydropower and run-of-the-river (no dam) hydropower are garnering increasing interest, especially in wealthier countries.

Biomass has been the most important energy source for humans since the discovery of fire, and today it is still the main source for almost half of the world's population. But the use of biomass can cause as much or more harm to humans and ecosystems than fossil fuels. Using wood for fuel is frequently associated with deforestation and even desertification. Combusting biomass in open fires for cooking and heating – still the norm for two billion people – is an enormous detriment to human health from poor indoor air quality. Indeed, the transition in the developing regions of the world from traditional cooking and heating with biomass to more efficient technologies using fossil fuels is associated with dramatic improvements in health and life expectancy. Instead of combusting it in open indoor fires, biomass must increasingly be used to generate electricity and to produce cleaner-burning liquid and gaseous fuels if it is to be a sustainable energy option.

Even windpower, sometimes touted as the most benign of the renewables, can have impacts. Some of these involve risks to biodiversity: proposed wind farms in California's mountain passes may interfere with the flight paths of the state's threatened California condors. Some of these simply involve human tastes: the concentrations of wind generators in parts of the Netherlands, Denmark and northern Germany are aesthetically offensive to some people.

While solar energy is responsible for renewables like wind, hydropower and biomass, we can also directly use the thermal and light energy radiating from the sun. But some of these uses of solar energy to provide useful heat and electricity can involve complex technologies with substantial land requirements or demands for rare metals.

Exploitable sources of geothermal energy are concentrated in relatively few locations. Geothermal energy can be used for space heating, as in Iceland, or for electricity generation, as in Iceland, Italy and the US. The environmental impacts from such facilities are minimal, but there is risk of aquifer disruption, increased release of sulphuric gases and perhaps localized seismic activity.

The exploitation of tidal power, if it includes a water barrier across a bay, disrupts intertidal habitat and the natural flushing mechanisms of environmentally sensitive bays and estuaries. Photos from my visit years ago to the world's largest tidal power site at La Rance in France were sufficient to convince my graduate students that tidal power is not necessarily benign. Smaller tidal power technologies that rely on tidal currents in narrow passages have negligible impact, but the low energy intensity of the water flow, the low rate of capacity utilization during slack and slow tide periods, and the distance of the best sites from the electricity grid render this option expensive in all but a few locations. Wave power can also be benign, but again faces the challenges of low energy density and inconvenient location, which increase development costs.

As these examples suggest, various forms of renewable energy can have environmental and human impacts depending on how they are developed and what technologies are involved. These types of challenges will intensify as modern renewable-based technologies are called upon to play a growing role in the global energy system.

1.4 Evaluating our energy alternatives: combining prediction and prescription

This initial survey of our global energy options anticipates the more detailed evaluation in later chapters. Humans have a great quantity and diversity of energy alternatives to meet their basic needs and emerging wants. But will they make wise energy choices when viewed in terms of the other things they value, especially in terms of environmental sustainability and economic cost? What energy forms will they favor? What technologies will they develop? Will they rein in their energy wants if the impacts from satisfying these are substantial?

In exploring these energy alternatives in this book, I begin by considering the physical and technical potential of each major option and its environmental impacts. I then proceed to a more holistic comparative evaluation, assessing the performance of each option against criteria that reflect competing goals and thus difficult trade-offs in the quest for a sustainable energy system. In this exercise, my exploration combines prediction and prescription. What do I mean by this?

While we cannot predict the future from the past, energy systems nonetheless possess inertial forces that constrain and shape our pursuit of a goal like energy system sustainability. One reason for energy system inertia is the slow rate of change, except following major destruction from war or natural disaster, of some components, particularly urban form, major infrastructure like transportation and electricity networks, major productive facilities like hydro dams, and long-lived buildings. Their slow rate of evolution fosters a certain degree of confidence to our predictive efforts, especially over timeframes in which major turnover is unlikely. This does not mean that we can predict precisely the character of an energy system 50 or 100 years hence. But it does mean that, with some degree of confidence, we can predict certain characteristics that are likely to endure over part of that timeframe.

Another source of inertia is the psychological attachment of key decision makers to the energy system they already know. This influences the focus of research and development, and the major investments in infrastructure and productive systems that ultimately determine the character of our future energy system. Even when the risk may be objectively comparable between two alternatives, risks can seem more manageable with the technologies and resources we already know.

Finally, basic human preferences are a source of inertia. In many respects, human preferences are malleable. Fads change quickly. Beliefs evolve at a more moderate pace, but can profoundly affect our behavior over long time periods. For an energy analyst, however, the basic human preferences with significant influence over energy use have considerable stability. Humans want comfort and convenience, which includes a sizeable living space and a comfortable indoor temperature. This factor alone has profound implications for the evolution of our energy system as populations grow and incomes rise over the next century. Humans have a strong desire to acquire things, whether for themselves or to offer as gifts. These require energy to produce and perhaps energy to use and dispose of. This acquisitiveness trait exists in traditional and modern societies and shows no sign of diminishing. Finally, humans enjoy mobility, which requires energy, and this desire for mobility increases in step with income.

Only through an understanding of these inertial forces can we identify the opportunities for shaping our future energy system and predict the likelihood of our policy efforts in this regard. It is in this sense that I describe this book as an exercise in prediction and pre-scription. First, we need to make predictions before we prescribe. If, at one extreme, we predict that a sustainable energy system will develop of its own accord, then the logical prescription is to do nothing – stay out of the way. If we predict that our system is on an unsustainable path, then we need to develop our prescription for shifting the system from this likely trajectory onto a different one. This prescription must be founded, however, on a realistic awareness of inertial forces, so that we can predict the likely effectiveness of our proposed policies.

We know that predictions are inevitably imbued with uncertainty because of the complex feedbacks in socio-economic systems. But uncertainty is not an excuse for inaction. Even so-called inaction is action; it is the deliberate choice to stay on the current path, allowing the forces that shape that path to operate without constraint. We must decide, therefore, where we are likely to be headed if we do nothing and then where we want to go. We cannot avoid prediction and prescription when it comes to determining our future energy system.[16]

In this book I apply this combination of prescription and prediction to the assessment of our major energy alternatives in the pursuit of a sustainable energy system. I describe and evaluate these alternatives in terms of what their attributes are now and are likely to be in the future. Then I compare them with each other, and test their appropri-ateness in terms of the diverse objectives society has when it comes to crafting a future energy system. While these major alternatives are not mutually exclusive – all are likely to be part of the future global energy system – experts and non-experts alike hold dramatically different visions about which of these might or should dominate. As I have noted, my exploration has led me to a hypothesis that I would have rejected out-of-hand five years ago. My goal in this book is to explain why and how my thinking has changed.

In making an assessment of sustainability, timeframe is obviously critical. Sustainability over 100 years differs from sustainability over 1,000 years. I focus frequently on the next 50–100 years. This period is long enough to allow for major transformation of the energy system, but not so long that it verges on fantasy. The technologies and behav-iors I discuss are familiar to experts and many non-experts today. But even 50–100 years is inappropriate when the issue is sustainability.

Human history is replete with examples of complex and apparently robust systems that appeared healthy for 50–100 years, and even centuries, only to collapse suddenly.[17] Thus, while I generally use 50–100 years for framing my analysis, I must address the very long term. I must explain why and how the energy system I describe has the capability to endure and evolve indefinitely.

The book has nine chapters. In chapter 2, I explore the path of our current energy system, making a projection of what it would look like 100 years from now were it to follow roughly the current trends. I only adjust trends where there is a widely held view of physical limitation, such as the limited availability of conventional oil and natural gas. Not surprisingly, the exercise suggests that our current path implies major impacts and risks for ecosystems and people.

In chapter 3, I focus on secondary energy. This is a critical component of energy system sustainability, but because it is not associated with the same degree of uncertainty and strong views as our primary energy choices, I use only this one chapter to produce an alternative to the current trends – a projection of how the secondary energy system might evolve in order to satisfy my definition of sustainability. This involves a growing role for hydrogen alongside electricity, and an increased use of biomass in the production of gaseous and liquid hydrocarbons for direct combustion.

While there is not complete agreement on our secondary energy choices in the drive to sustainability, our primary energy options are laden with controversy. In chapter 4, I examine the energy alternatives – the usual suspects – that have dominated much of the debate about what constitutes a sustainable energy system: efficiency, nuclear and renewables. Then, I devote the next two chapters to explaining my counter-intuitive hypothesis that fossil fuels are a legitimate contender. Chapter 5 focuses on endurance – the quantity of the resource and the way in which we can move between types of fossil fuels and eventually from fossil fuels toward other forms of energy. Chapter 6 focuses on cleanliness – how fossil fuels can meet our energy needs without significant impacts or risks to the biophysical system.

Given these options, what should humans do? What will they do? To respond to these questions, I conduct in chapter 7 a trade-off exercise in which I evaluate our major energy options based on environmental, economic and social performance, especially focused on the first two, but also recognizing the extent to which our choices in this domain are influenced by other social and political worries like nuclear weapons proliferation, terrorism and energy security. My general conclusion is that, in spite of what so many experts and laypeople are saying, we are not facing the imminent demise of the fossil fuel era, and we should not desire this demise even if we care greatly about environmental impacts and risks. This evaluation leads me to reflect on some commonly held views about our energy alternatives. People tend to feel passionate when it comes to energy; they often fit into camps that are dead against nuclear or fanatical about renewables or suspicious of energy efficiency or faithful to fossil fuels. My research for this book suggests to me that such passionate prejudgments about our energy options can dangerously distort our view of the evidence.

Although I end up concluding that a much more benign energy system is achievable from a technology, resource and economic perspective, changing course will not be easy. In chapter 8, I discuss the kinds of policies that are needed to influence the direction and pace of technological change. Here I have been influenced by my experiences as the head of an energy regulatory agency, as a member of international panels and as a policy advisor to governments at the local, regional and national levels. My own suggestions focus on how the insights of economists must be integrated with those of psychologists and policy advisors if we are to make any headway in pursuit of energy system sustainability.

In the conclusion, chapter 9, I reflect on the relationship between sustainable energy and a sustainable global economy. We may achieve the first and yet fail in pursuing the second. Ironically, cheap and clean energy could hasten the rate at which humans appropriate the earth's land and water, with obvious implications for biodiversity and perhaps ultimately the critical biogeophysical cycles of the earth.

Notes

1. Global Environment Facility, *Renewable Energy: GEF Partners with Business for a Better World* (Washington, D.C.: Global Environmental Facility, 2001), 3.
2. L. Brown, *Eco-Economy: Building an Economy for the Earth* (New York: Norton, 2001), 98.
3. P. Hoffman, *Tomorrow's Energy: Hydrogen, Fuel Cells and the Prospects for a Cleaner Planet* (Cambridge, Mass.: MIT Press, 2001), 83.

4. J. Leggett, *The Carbon War: Global Warming and the End of the Oil Era* (New York: Penguin Books, 2001), 332.

5. P. Raskin, T. Banuri, G. Gallopin, P. Gutman, A. Hammond, R. Kates and R. Swart, *Great Transition: The Promise and Lure of the Times Ahead* (Stockholm: Stockholm Environment Institute, 2002), 65.

6. H. Scheer, *The Solar Economy: Renewable Energy for a Sustainable Global Future* (London: Earthscan, 2002), xiv.

7. J. Rifkin, *The Hydrogen Economy: The Creation of the Worldwide Energy Web and the Redistribution of Power on Earth* (New York: Tarcher/Putnam, 2002), 8.

8. H. Geller, *Energy Revolution: Policies for a Sustainable Future* (Covelo, Calif.: Island Press, 2003), 16.

9. R. Heinberg, *The Party's Over: Oil, War and the Fate of Industrial Societies* (Gabriola Island, B.C.: New Society Publishers, 2003), 1.

10. P. Roberts, *The End of Oil: On the Edge of a Perilous New World* (New York: Houghton Mifflin, 2004), book jacket.

11. D. Goodstein, *Out of Gas: The End of the Age of Oil* (New York: Norton, 2004), 123.

12. See Hoffman, *Tomorrow's Energy*; Rifkin, *The Hydrogen Economy*; and V. Vaitheeswaran, *Power to the People* (New York: Farrar, Straus and Giroux, 2003).

13. For nuclear see C. Marchetti, "Hydrogen and Energy," *Chemical Economy and Engineering Review* 5, 1 (1973): 7–25; G. E. Besenbruch, L. C. Brown, J. F. Funk and S. K. Showalter, "High Efficiency Generation of Hydrogen Fuels Using Nuclear Power." Paper presented at the OECD/NEA Information Exchange Meeting on the Nuclear Production of Hydrogen, Paris, October 2–3, 2000. For solar see J. Ogden and R. Williams, *Solar Hydrogen: Moving Beyond Fossil Fuels* (Washington, D.C.: World Resources Institute, 1989); S. Dunn, *Hydrogen Futures: Toward a Sustainable Energy System* (Washington, D.C.: Worldwatch Institute, 2001). For hydropower, see B. Drolet, J. Gretz, D. Kluyskens, F. Sandmann and R. Wurster, "The Euro-Québec Hydro-Hydrogen Pilot Project [EQHHPP]: Demonstration Phase," *International Journal of Hydrogen Energy* 21, 4 (1996): 305–316. For geothermal, see W. Zittel, W. Weindorf, R. Wurster and W. Bussmann, "Geothermal Hydrogen – A Vision?" Paper presented at European Geothermal Energy Council's 2nd Business Seminar, European Geothermal Energy Council 2001, Altheim, Austria.

14. M. Patterson, "What is Energy Efficiency?" *Energy Policy* 24, 5 (1996): 377–390. Some of my own research effort in this area is reported in M. Nanduri, J. Nyboer and M. Jaccard, "Aggregating Physical Intensity Indicators: Results of Applying the Composite

Indicator Approach to the Canadian Industrial Sector," *Energy Policy* 30 (2002): 151–163.

15. See, for example, L. Schipper, S. Meyers and H. Kelly, *Coming in from the Cold: Energy-Wise Housing in Sweden* (Santa Ana, Calif.: Seven Locks Press, 1985).

16. See H. Simon, "Prediction and Prescription in Systems Modeling," *Operations Research* 38, 1 (1990): 7–14.

17. J. Tainter, *The Collapse of Complex Societies* (Cambridge: Cambridge University Press, 1988); J. Diamond, *Collapse : How Societies Choose to Fail or Succeed* (New York: Viking Penguin, 2005).

2 | *Is our current energy path sustainable?*

2.1 The art and science of energy system forecasting

To determine if our energy system is sustainable, we need to estimate where it is headed. Although the system currently works – which some might debate – this is no guarantee that it is not on the verge of exhaustion of a critical input or a catastrophic environmental collapse. To decide how, if at all, we should act upon our energy system today, we must decide if we are happy with where it is headed over the longer term. This means that we have to forecast the energy system's likely evolution in the absence of efforts to change course.

However, as one wag said, "forecasting is difficult – especially into the future." Indeed, exercises in forecasting and prediction are now recognized as so imbued with uncertainty and with the biases of forecasters that it has become fashionable for some energy analysts to pronounce their opposition to forecasting altogether. Certainly, it is true that hindsight analysis in recent years has revealed the abysmal predictive record of most energy forecasting exercises.[1] But does this mean that we should just throw up our hands and avoid forecasting?

Unfortunately, avoidance is not an option. Politicians, businesses and individuals are always making decisions that shape our future and these decisions are made with some implicit notion of how the world is likely to unfold. That implicit notion is a forecast. In the same vein, policy makers cannot abstain from making policy in areas where they have responsibility. Even a decision to do nothing is a policy.

If we estimate that current trends will continue, and they show that the energy system will of its own accord evolve to acceptable levels of impacts and risks, then the best policy for government may be to stay out of the way, aside from modest actions to increase the likelihood of this desirable outcome. If, however, we estimate that our current direction is unsustainable, then we must consider action to shift the energy system. But how do we decide how much confidence we can have in any forecast?

Energy forecasters, like other social scientists, debate the extent to which their profession is an art or a science. Sophisticated and rigorous analysis can identify inertial forces and reveal emerging trends that together may have a good chance of influencing future developments. Critics of forecasting have pointed out, however, that this does little to help us with the unforeseen events and revolutionary innovations that become increasingly likely as we extend our forecast time horizon. They contend that the sophisticated science of forecasting is much less sophisticated and much less scientific than it often appears. The famous economist J. K. Galbraith went so far as to say, "The only reason economists produce forecasts is to make astrology look respectable." But as someone else noted, economists also do it because this activity is in their job description, leading to the smug economist's observation that "To err is human, to get paid for it divine."

Once I was at an energy conference in which a presenter compared short-term oil price forecasts from the last several decades with actual price developments prior to and following each forecast. Most forecasts turned out to be simply a projection of the energy price trend of the previous six months. In other words, forecasters' views of the future were strongly biased by their most recent experiences. As it turned out, most of these forecasts were highly inaccurate; the immediate past was not a good predictor of the future. No wonder forecasting has been described as "driving a car blindfolded while guided by someone looking out the back window." Forecasting is certainly as much an art as a science.

I do not profess to be a great artist or a great scientist when it comes to energy forecasting, but I have studied enough forecasts (and produced a few myself I must confess) to offer some guidance to this esoteric world. I provide in this section a quick primer on energy system forecasting, and then discuss salient results from some of the extensive forecasting work that leading international organizations have recently conducted.

Our use of energy can be portrayed as the simple consequence of a few relationships between energy (E), global population (POP) and global gross domestic product (GDP). (This latter term is often referred to as gross world product [GWP], but I stick with GDP in order to keep the same term whether referring to countries or the planet.) At the most basic level, energy use depends on the energy intensity of the economy, E/GDP, the level of wealth per capita, GDP/POP, and the size of the population.

$$E = E/GDP \times GDP/POP \times POP$$

Growth in any of these individual terms will increase energy use. A growing population will increase energy use if each additional person has the same standard of living (GDP/POP) and the same energy requirements (E/GDP). Likewise, economic growth (increasing GDP/POP) will increase energy use for a given level of energy intensity (E/GDP) and population. We energy analysts look to demographers for population forecasts and to macroeconomists for GDP forecasts. Our job is to forecast the E/GDP term. This is where the fun begins.

In chapter 1, I showed the long-term historical development of global E/GDP. Staying with the driving-a-car-blindfolded analogy, one option is to look out the back window and assume that the general trend of the last fifty years will continue for the next fifty. This may be a good guess. However, if we look inside E/GDP, this cavalier approach creates some unease. The energy intensity term results from several different trends, some changing in unison, some offsetting. If we believe that the relative importance of any of these trends might change in future, we cannot assume that the evolution of global E/GDP will maintain its average, historic pattern.

The E/GDP trend could change for various reasons. Between 1975 and 1990, the rate of decrease of E/GDP accelerated in most industrialized countries because two energy price shocks, and fears of future price increases, triggered intensified energy efficiency efforts by businesses and consumers, in part spurred on by government policy.[2] Today, the views of energy experts about energy prices over the next twenty-five years vary significantly. Will the price of oil rise to $100 per barrel, settle at $50 or fall back to $20? In addition to price expectations, fundamental technological change could affect the E/GDP trend. A transformative technology with potential for widespread application may substantially improve energy efficiency. In industrialized countries this might be the development of the fuel cell. In developing countries it could be the rapid replacement of inefficient wood stoves by more efficient propane stoves – a form of fuel substitution with profound effects on energy intensity. As an aggregate indicator, E/GDP also masks the substantial differences in energy intensity from one sector of the economy to the other. Usually, the industrial sector is associated with high energy intensity relative to the service sector. Falling global E/GDP in the industrialized countries in this century is in part explained by the increasing importance of services in these economies. Lifestyle choice is another factor. Perhaps people in industrialized countries are on the verge of a major change in values – such as the shift to a conserver society – that would dramatically change people's acquisitiveness and demand for living space and mobility. This value shift could cause a new trend in E/GDP where it occurs.

The likely evolution of E/GDP in developing countries is difficult to discern, but is critical for determining the future E/GDP ratio at a global scale. Evolution of this ratio will depend on the relative importance of efficiency gains from technological advance versus the economic benefits from greater use of energy in industry and households. If more rapid industrial growth occurs in developing countries, this should create upward pressure on the global E/GDP ratio.

Energy analysts use historical reviews and visioning exercises to assess how the future might differ from the past. Statistical analyses of past responses to energy price changes try to distinguish price-driven changes in E/GDP from other factors. These studies usually require data from ten or more years because the full response to a change in price takes many years as households and firms gradually renew their stocks of energy-using equipment such as appliances, vehicles, industrial machinery and buildings. Not surprisingly, experts dispute the magnitude of price responses because the importance of price is difficult to detect over long time periods; fluctuations of other factors make it difficult to isolate the price effects, in part because energy price increases are often followed shortly by price decreases, masking the full long-run response to the original increase. Disaggregated analysis has also focused on individual forms of energy, calculating their specific E/GDP ratios and assessing their future prospects depending on various assumptions. Finally, energy analysts have disaggregated the economy into different sectors, each with its own ratio of E to the share of total GDP generated by that sector. This approach helps to understand and predict the role of structural change in how energy use might evolve.

Each of these refinements adds complexity to energy system forecasting and, as a consequence, energy analysts have built complicated computer models to keep track of all the elements and their potential feedback loops. I must confess to having contributed more than my share to this arcane world; the research group I direct is guilty of building models that try to keep track of all equipment stocks over time – "modelers-who-count-lightbulbs" is how one skeptic described us.

One feedback of particular concern for energy analysts is the interaction between energy supply and demand. Increases in energy demand require energy suppliers to turn to more expensive resources and technologies, resulting in higher energy prices, which in turn slow the growth of demand. Interactions between energy supply and demand can also cause indirect effects that show up at a macro-economic level. For example, higher energy prices would raise the prices of the products from energy-intensive industrial sectors, causing domestic and foreign purchasers to reduce their demand for these relative to less energy-intensive products and services. This structural change might also be accompanied by increases or decreases in overall economic output depending on the relative productivity of any new investments in the energy sector caused by the price change.

This economic view of energy is important, but it is sometimes criticized for abstracting from the critical physical and energy flows of the human energy system. While this is a concern in the energy field, it is equally a concern at a more general level in that economists and others are often guilty of portraying a human-focused system as if it were separate from the natural world rather than within it and highly dependent upon it. Figure 2.1 shows the energy-economy system portrayed in a manner consistent with a more holistic perspective in which its dependence on the biogeosphere is explicitly recognized.

The figure shows the flow of energy from the productive to the consumptive activities of the human economy. It also shows the flow of raw materials (metal ores, wood fiber, non-metallic minerals), including the currently modest portion that is recycled from consumers back to the productive sector to be reprocessed into new goods and services. The human-focused activity – the energy-economy system – is intimately linked to flows of energy and materials between itself and the surrounding environment, which is variously referred to as the biosphere, nature, earth's ecosystem or the biogeosphere. (This latter term is especially associated with all life-support systems, including all flows of energy and materials, associated with the biosphere, atmosphere and lithosphere.) Energy and materials are

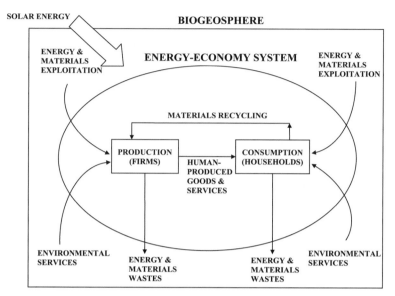

Figure 2.1. The energy-economy system within the biogeosphere.

the raw inputs to the energy-economy system. The productive sector
and final consumers also depend on environmental services – such as
clean air to breathe and clean water to drink or for industrial processes. The energy-economy system also depends on material inputs
from the earth's lithosphere such as high-grade mineral ores that we
refine into metals with the help of energy resources.

Energy and material wastes flow back into the biosphere usually in
the form of low temperature heat, such as the heat in gases rising from
industrial and residential chimneys, the heat dissipated from our house
walls and vehicle exhaust pipes, and the warm water entering a river
from a factory cooling system or urban sewage outlet. Material wastes
may be in the form of solids (industrial and household solid
wastes, particulates), liquids (urban sewage, industrial effluent) or
gases (emissions of acid gases, local air pollutants, greenhouse gases).

The figure also recognizes our sun's critical role in providing the
external energy source that drives the natural material and energy
cycles on earth. These cycles – in particular of carbon, nitrogen,
oxygen, water and heat – help provide the materials and energy
exploited by industry and the environmental services enjoyed directly
by individuals.

The two components of my preliminary definition of energy sustainability are readily apparent from figure 2.1. Our energy system is not sustainable if it exhausts irreplaceable energy inputs: for example if we use up oil stocks and have no ready substitute. It is also unsustainable if its material and energy wastes exceed the assimilative capacity of the biogeosphere, degrading some of the services it provides such as clean air, biodiversity and fresh water. If our energy system's CO_2 emissions exceed the earth's assimilative capacity – leading to rising atmospheric concentrations of GHGs (greenhouse gases), climate change and reduced biodiversity – again that system is unacceptable from an environmental sustainability perspective.

Figure 2.1 also has implications for how we should forecast the future of our energy system. First, we must forecast the consumption of energy supplies, and this forecast must be disaggregated to specific forms of energy given that some are exhaustible and all face constraints of some kind. This is the resource input side of the ledger. Second, we must forecast the waste streams, and this forecast must be disaggregated to specific types of energy forms and their wastes, given that each has its own particular threats for the integrity of the biosphere.* This is the waste output side of the ledger.

With all of these factors to consider, energy system forecasting is a complicated endeavor. No wonder that most energy experts focus on just one energy resource, such as oil or biomass, or just one energy system byproduct, such as air pollutants or GHGs. Indeed, comprehensive assessments of the future dynamics of the global energy system are usually only produced by integrated teams of specialists working under the auspices of an international agency or multilateral process of some kind. Fortunately, for my purposes, there have been several such efforts in recent years, and they have produced a wealth of data on these various components.

The one saving grace of forecasting is that by the time the future has proven you wrong, your forecast has been forgotten, and you may

---

* For example, if GHGs are measured in equivalents of carbon dioxide (CO_2e), these are found to differ significantly from one form of energy to another. Oil produces about 0.07t CO_2e/GJ, coal 0.09t CO_2e/GJ, and natural gas 0.05t CO_2e/GJ, while renewables and nuclear are considered to be essentially GHG free. See Intergovernmental Panel on Climate Change, *Revised 1996 IPCC Guidelines for National Greenhouse Gas Inventories*, Volume 3: *Reference Manual* (Paris: IPCC/OECD, 1997).

even have left the scene. This encourages long-term forecasts. Mine is for the next 100 years.

2.2 Generating a current trends projection of the global energy system

I have suggested that an assessment of energy system sustainability requires a timeframe of at least 50 to 100 years, and that we should be able to envision the basic characteristics and dynamic of a system that will continue indefinitely beyond that. In the past, only a few futurists looked this far into the future, but the oil supply concerns of the 1970s prompted a wave of long-range global energy forecasts such as that of W. Häfele in 1981.[3] More recently, concerns that anthropogenic GHG emissions are affecting earth's climate has motivated several organizations to produce long-term forecasts of energy demand in concert with comprehensive assessments of energy supply prospects.

In 1988, the United Nations Environment Programme and the World Meteorological Organization created the Intergovernmental Panel on Climate Change (IPCC) to assess the science, potential impacts, and options for mitigation and adaptation related to climate change. The IPCC assembles teams of researchers from around the world to focus on these specific components in order to produce multi-volume assessment reports every few years – 1992, 1996 and 2001. (I experienced the IPCC first-hand as a member during the production of the second assessment report, from 1993–1996, serving as a co-author in Working Group III which assessed the economic and social dimensions of climate change.) A key task is to forecast the possible evolution of the global energy system in order to anticipate how its contribution to GHGs might change over time, and thus to determine the magnitude of mitigation efforts required to stabilize atmospheric concentrations. In preparation for its third assessment report, the IPCC launched in 1996 a project to develop scenarios of the long-run evolution of anthropogenic GHG emissions, culminating in the Special Report on Emission Scenarios – which built upon earlier long-term scenario analysis by the International Institute of Applied Systems Analysis and the World Energy Council.[4]

Because the IPCC scenarios cover the period from the present to 2100, they are especially valuable for my focus on energy system sustainability. The International Energy Agency, Shell International Inc. and other agencies occasionally produce long-term outlooks, although these usually cover a shorter time period of thirty to fifty years.[5] The energy scenarios generated for the IPCC are described in its third assessment report and additional scenarios are in the world energy assessment of the United Nations Development Programme and the World Energy Council (in its 2000 report and its 2004 update).[6] I rely primarily on these sources for generating my outlook for the global energy system.

Traditionally, energy analysts generate a single, current trends forecast (also called reference case, baseline or business-as-usual) of energy demand and supply, and then examine how different policy strategies might divert the energy system from that path. (Whenever I use the term "business-as-usual" I am reminded of a conference in the early 1990s in which the Russian delegate – in lamenting the sorry state of his country's economy – insisted, with his thick accent, on using the term, "business-as-unusual.") In looking 100 years into the future, analysts are rightly nervous about using the term forecast, given the enormous uncertainties over such a long period. The IPCC instead developed scenarios: alternative visions of how the future might unfold. In its third assessment report, and the supporting special report on emission scenarios, the IPCC describes its multiple baseline approach in which it generated many different current trends of how the global energy system might evolve in the absence of policies expressly intended to reduce GHG emissions. Factors that might cause differences in the current trends outlook include population growth, economic growth, other efforts at environmental protection that might affect GHG emissions, the level of income equality, the pace and character of technological development and the extent of trade globalization. The resulting forty scenarios were organized into six subgroups and four families, each of the latter characterized by a single, illustrative scenario.

The forty scenarios present an extremely wide range of possible futures and as such convey great uncertainty about what might transpire over the next century. Figure 2.2 provides the range of energy demand and GHG emissions covered by the forty scenarios. According to the top graph in the figure, from a primary energy use level of 350 exajoules (EJ) in 1990, the scenarios show energy use in 2100 ranging from a high of 2226 EJ (scenario A1B) to a low of

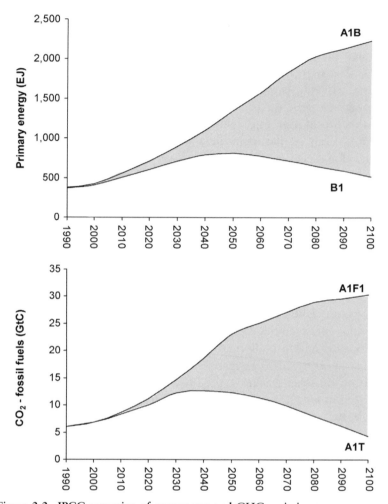

Figure 2.2. IPCC scenarios of energy use and GHG emissions.
Source: Intergovernmental Panel on Climate Change, *Special Report on Emissions Scenarios* (Cambridge: Cambridge University Press, 2000).

514 EJ (scenario B1), a four-fold difference. The bottom graph shows annual GHG emissions from energy use (counting only the carbon in carbon dioxide emissions, which is the major GHG) in 2100 ranging from a high of 30.3 GtC/yr (A1F1) to a low of 4.3 GtC/yr (A1T), a seven-fold difference. In other words, at least one of the scenarios

shows GHG emissions actually falling below 1990 levels even in the absence of any efforts to reduce these emissions.

The IPCC does not assign probabilities to any of these widely diverse visions of the future. This may be a reasonable strategy given that the IPCC functions as an information resource for policy makers, who can then apply their own judgment in considering which scenario or group of scenarios is most likely to occur. But the strategy is problematic. If energy analysts believe that one group of scenarios are more likely, should they not provide this view to policy makers? To suggest implicitly instead that every scenario depicts a future that is just as likely as any other hardly seems helpful to policy makers. A colleague who provides policy advice told me he once showed a similar graph to a politician who really didn't want to do anything. He noticed that in future speeches the politician kept mentioning that because emissions could decline of their own accord it would be imprudent to spend money on emission reduction for the time being. Perhaps the politician should have been told the consensus view, even though it might eventually be proven wrong, that there was a slim chance of the system evolving in this particular direction.

My interest differs from that of the IPCC in that I want to assess the implications of continuing on a path in which the general character of our energy system changes as little as possible. This is easier than the tasks facing the IPCC's scenario modelers in that I do not need to show how diverse the future can be; I simply need to show what the system might be like if current trends continue.

To frame my current trends projection, I reviewed, to the point of personal exhaustion, the many scenarios developed by the IPCC and other entities in recent years. I couldn't help wondering at times if I was the only person in the world – other than the authors and their hapless graduate students – to slog earnestly through this huge array of scenarios whose fundamental message seems to be, "when the time-frame is 100 years, conceivably anything could happen." From this review, I selected two mainstream scenarios to guide the construction of my own current trends projection. One is scenario IS92a. This is a scenario initially developed for the first assessment report of the IPCC in 1990, and then extended and updated in a 1992 supplementary report.[7] Many analysts have used this as the preferred current trends scenario for GHG mitigation studies. The other is scenario B from the recent world energy assessment of the United Nations Development

Programme and the World Energy Council. The assessment refers to scenario B as its "reference baseline because it was designed to represent a future characterized by incremental and gradual changes." It is a scenario that represents "a major improvement in the global energy system and its use, but it does fall short of fulfilling many indicators of sustainability . . ."[8]

Both of these scenarios share many assumptions, but they also differ in certain respects. Both assume similar trends for income growth: a global level of gross world product rising from $32 trillion ($US 2000) to above $200 trillion in 2100. Both assume similar trends for energy use: rising from 430 to about 1,500 EJ in 2100. Both assume a global population above 11 billion in 2100. They both show a stagnation of large hydropower as land-use conflicts intensify, a decline in conventional oil as supplies are exhausted, and a healthy growth rate for biomass (for electricity generation and production of biofuels) and other renewables such as solar, wind and small hydro. In meeting the huge increase in energy demand, however, the UNDP's scenario B relies on a dramatic expansion of nuclear and natural gas while the IPCC's IS92a suggests that coal will be more dominant. My current trends projection takes a median position between these contrasting views, as I explain below.

Table 2.1 shows my current trends projection of our global energy system's path to the year 2100. Relative to the two scenarios discussed above, I project a lower population in 2100. In recent reports, prominent population forecasters point to a significant slowing of growth rates in the past decades, implying a sigmoid-shaped (S) curve for global population over the 400 years from 1700 to 2100. (In contrast, global population nearly quadrupled over the past century, rising from 1.6 billion in 1900 to 6.1 billion in 2000.) Indeed, some recent studies suggest that the global population will peak at 9 billion. But in my current trends projection, I use 10.5 billion, a median value applied recently by the United Nations and other population forecasters.[9]

In a similar range to UNDP and IPCC scenarios, my current trends projection has global economic output increase from $32 trillion ($US 2000) in 2000 to $80 trillion in 2050 and $230 trillion in 2100. (For consistency with my earlier terms, I call global economic output GDP.) This implies an average global economic growth rate of 2% per year, similar to the average growth rates of recent decades,

Table 2.1. Current trends for the global energy system

	unit	2000	2050	2100
Population (POP)	billions	6.0	9.5	10.5
GDP	$US trill. 2000	32	80	230
GDP/POP	$US/capita	5,300	8,400	22,000
Energy (E)	EJ	429	770	1,390
Coal	EJ	100	220	650
Oil	EJ	163	160	110
Natural gas	EJ	95	200	160
Nuclear	EJ	9	20	90
Hydropower	EJ	9	20	30
Traditional biomass	EJ	45	70	90
Modern biomass	EJ	7	50	120
Wind	EJ	0	20	90
Other renewables	EJ	0	10	50
E/GDP	MJ/$US	13.6	9.6	6
E/POP	GJ/capita	71.4	81	132
Share fossil fuels		84%	75%	66%
Annual growth E/GDP			−0.69%	−0.93%

and results in global economic output that is seven times the current level.

Dividing global world product by the smaller population in my current trends means that average income is slightly higher in my projection than in these other two forecasts. Average per capita income (GDP/POP) grows from about $5,000 in 2000 to $8,500 in 2050 and $22,000 in 2100. The average income of $22,000 is comparable to current levels in industrialized countries. This is a global average, masking what would still be substantial differences in average incomes between some of the poorest and richest countries.

I assume that global primary energy intensity (E/GDP) will continue the downward trend of the past five decades, although its rate of decline will be slower in the first half of the century as developing countries expand their more energy intensive sectors, and then more rapid as these countries adopt more sophisticated technologies. Primary energy intensity falls from 13.6 megajoules per $US (2000) of gross world product to 9.6 in 2050 and 6 in 2100. This represents an annual rate of decrease of 0.69% from 2000 to 2050 and 0.93% from 2050 to 2100. The 0.93% is close to the rate of decrease that occurred during the fifteen years following the oil price shocks of the late 1970s and early 1980s.

As in the past, increases in population and especially economic output swamp declines in energy intensity so that total primary energy use grows from 429 exajoules in 2000 to 770 in 2050 and 1,390 in 2100, an increase of more than 200% over the next 100 years. On a per person basis, this translates into an evolution from 70 GJ/capita in 2000 to 80 in 2050 and 130 in 2100, a doubling of per capita energy use in 100 years.

Is this realistic? As a comparison, today's global average of 70 GJ/capita is about four times its 1900 level. Since that time, per capita energy use in industrialized countries has grown substantially while that of developing countries has stagnated. The US has grown in 100 years from about 100 GJ/capita to 340 and Japan from about 40 GJ/capita to 170. These are ratios of primary energy to economic output, which therefore includes domestic and industrial energy use. V. Smil points out that with improvements in energy conversion and end-use devices, the increase in energy services per capita is even more dramatic – an eight- to twelve-fold increase over the last century for many industrialized countries. This means that the typical American household potentially commands close to half a megawatt of power if it were to use all its devices at the same time (furnace, vehicles, appliances, etc.), an amount similar to the power available to a Roman landowner with 6,000 slaves or a nineteenth-century landlord employing 3,000 workers and 400 horses.[10]

If everyone in the world attained the US consumption of 340 GJ/capita, the global energy system would need to be almost three times my current trends projection for 2100, which would mean a ten-fold expansion. From our perspective today, a system of this magnitude seems unimaginable, just as the size of our current system would have been to people of 100 years ago. This has led some researchers to approach the issue from the bottom up: constructing a global projection by looking at the minimal level of energy services required to improve living standards to given levels in developing countries.

A. Reddy estimated the energy consumption that would provide a significant improvement in living conditions for poor rural inhabitants in the state of Karnataka in India.[11] If a rural household could convert from biomass to liquid petroleum gas (butane, propane) for cooking, it would use about 2.3 GJ/year. If the household were also electrified for minimal services of lighting, fans, refrigeration and entertainment, instead of being limited to just kerosene for lighting, it might require about 0.7 GJ/year, for a total of 3 GJ/year. For a household of four people, the demand would therefore be less than 1 GJ/capita, while achieving a significant improvement over having no electricity, collecting and burning biomass for cooking (and heating) and relying on kerosene for lighting. Once energy consumption in industry, transportation, institutions and energy production itself is included, however, the energy use per capita would be substantially higher, perhaps at 10 GJ/capita – still only one thirty-fourth of the current US level.

In another approach, J. Goldemberg and co-authors estimated the amount of energy required for everyone in the world to attain the energy services associated with the standard of living of the average European in the 1970s, if they were able to acquire the most efficient energy conversion and end-use technologies available in the 1980s.[12] The authors calculated that this required 30 GJ/capita (1 average kilowatt of power) – one-tenth the current US level. My current trends estimate for 2100 of 130 GJ/capita might therefore be seen as implying a minimum of 30–40 GJ/capita for the world's poorest members while those who are better off use anywhere from 150 to 400 GJ/capita, including energy consumed directly and energy required for producing goods and services.

It is important not to get too fixed on specific numbers. This only leads to disagreements, when what is important is the big picture. Even if an alternative estimate of current trends might not show as great a growth rate of energy per capita through this century, it should at least show that our global energy system is headed for dramatic expansion. Whether the exact size of the system is 860 EJ (a doubling) or 1,720 EJ (a quadrupling), most observers would agree that the system is likely to be significantly larger in 100 years. That information is sufficient for the rough assessment of system sustainability that I undertake at the end of this chapter.

In setting my current trends projection for the relative contribution of primary forms of energy, I struggled with several major uncertainties. While some experts believe that production of oil and gas use will decline significantly in the next few decades because of supply constraints, others believe that advancing technological capabilities will enable us to sustain output and perhaps expand it. I explore these issues in following chapters, but for now my current trends projection has oil and gas declining after 2050, albeit not as dramatically as some analysts predict.

There is also much uncertainty about the relative prospects for nuclear and coal in meeting the widening gap between expanding energy use and stagnant oil and gas output. My current trends projection has nuclear and coal both growing significantly although coal's share grows the most, reaching 47% of total primary energy by 2100. This is because coal is less expensive for making electricity (and projected to remain so) and for producing the liquid and gaseous fuels that might replace declining oil and natural gas stocks. Remember that my projection sustains the general character and trends of the current energy system, which means that there are no major policy initiatives to achieve environmental or security objectives.

My current trends projection for the major primary energy options are summarized in figure 2.3. In addition to my projections for fossil fuels, it shows hydropower growing to three times its current output. More significantly, it shows nuclear power growing to ten times its current production.* Some analysts argue that both of these sources of primary energy will grow little because of land-use conflicts with large hydro schemes and accidents and weapons-proliferation concerns with nuclear power. Nonetheless, an assumption of nuclear growth is a reasonable starting point for a current trends projection of our current energy path while an increasing amount of hydro growth could come

---

* My numbers for nuclear are lower than those in some agency reports because I convert the TWhs of electricity from a nuclear plant directly into their energy value of 1 kWh = 3.6 megajoules. Some agencies instead measure nuclear power by the fuel that a conventional thermal plant (say coal) would consume to generate an equivalent amount of electricity. Assuming a plant efficiency in the 33% range, the conventional conversion ratio becomes 1 kWh = 10.8 megajoules. Thus, while everyone agrees that nuclear power produced about 2,500 TWhs in 2000, some record this as 9 EJ of primary energy while others as 27 EJ. The nuclear power output of 90 EJ in 2100 in my current trends would be shown as 270 in some reports. Why do some agencies make this assumption that inflates nuclear power relative to other primary sources? Our energy statistics professor during my PhD studies in France claimed that the French nuclear industry insisted on this – both in France and internationally – so that nuclear would appear more crucial to the French energy system. I have no idea if this is true, but we students liked the conspiratorial sound of it.

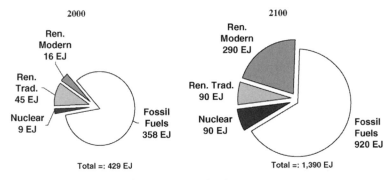

Figure 2.3. Current trends projection of primary energy use.

in the form of a large number of medium-sized hydro projects, especially in developing countries.

My assumptions for biomass and other renewables envision dramatic growth: four-fold for biomass, 820-fold for wind, and 110-fold for other renewables. Table 2.1 and figure 2.3 distinguish traditional uses of biomass (largely combustion of wood and crop residues for cooking and heating) from modern uses (conversion of biomass into gaseous and liquid fuels as well as electricity). Traditional uses continue to grow through more sustainable biomass production and more efficient wood-burning stoves and other equipment. The more dramatic growth occurs with modern biomass, which increases seventeen-fold from 7 to 120 exajoules by 2100. Even with this dramatic growth in total renewable energy, it only attains 27% of the global energy system by 2100, simply because the total system keeps growing through the century.

2.3 Sustainability indicators for the current trends projection

According to my definition in chapter 1, the sustainability of an energy system depends on its ability to be clean and enduring. For the 100-year current trends projection, I examine endurance briefly and then focus on cleanliness.

The current trends projection is inconclusive with respect to the endurance criterion, as this depends on one's assessment of the size and accessibility of the fossil fuel resource. As the quotes in chapter 1 showed, some energy experts and certainly many popular

commentators argue that current trends are leading to imminent exhaustion of oil and natural gas, extremely high energy prices, geopolitical conflicts over scarce energy resources, and even global economic
collapse. Yet other experts argue that the fossil fuel resource is plentiful. An additional question is whether or not it matters if fossil fuels
are soon exhausted, as long as their substitutes – nuclear, various
renewables, more energy efficiency – are capable individually or in
concert of replacing them without significant technological, social,
economic or environmental disruption. The assessment of endurance
must await chapters 4 and 5, where I review mainstream estimates of
our global energy resources.

It is possible, however, to make a preliminary assessment with
regard to the second sustainability criterion: environmental and
human impact. For simplicity, I focus on three indicators: indoor air
quality, urban air quality and atmospheric concentrations of GHGs.

Indoor air quality

As it has been since humans first discovered how to control fire, the
home cooking stove is still the most ubiquitous energy-using technology in the world. The rural poor in developing countries use about 45
EJ of biomass (and some solid coal) in mostly inefficient, poorly
ventilated stoves for cooking and some space heating. These stoves
emit into interior living space particulate matter (soot, ash and micro-
scopically small particulates) carbon monoxide, nitrogen dioxide and
dozens of health-threatening gases such as the hydrocarbons benzopyrene and butadiene. These contribute to respiratory infections,
asthma, bronchitis, pneumonia, heart disease, tuberculosis and lung
cancer. The World Health Organization estimates that these illnesses
from indoor air pollution cause as many as 1.6 million premature
deaths per year, almost entirely among women and children as they
have the highest exposure rates.[13]

If the traditional use of biomass continues to climb, from 45 EJ to
90, and global population increases to 10.5 billion, the annual premature deaths caused by poor indoor air quality could double by 2100.
This would be the outcome if biomass combustion in low efficiency,
poorly ventilated stoves remains dominant for that segment of the
global population whose numbers could increase to 6 billion of
the earth's 10.5 billion inhabitants by 2100. If, however, incomes

increase sufficiently for the very poorest to acquire efficient and cleaner stoves – which can reduce indoor particulates and noxious gases by 90% compared to traditional stoves – then premature deaths caused by indoor pollution would fall significantly. This would occur whether the technology involves the combustion of biomass in high efficiency, low emission stoves, or the conversion from biomass to gaseous and liquid fuels that are much cleaner burning even as an open flame on top of a stove. Research has typically shown that with modest increases in income, poor rural families in developing countries place a high priority on switching from solid fuels to propane or butane for cooking. If the global income assumed in my current trends projection is more evenly distributed in future, it is likely that a significant percentage of lower income people on the planet will shift to cleaner technologies for cooking, be these for the combustion of solid biomass, or the combustion of gaseous and liquid hydrocarbons.

Urban air quality

The continued dominance of fossil fuels in the current trends projection does not bode well for my second indicator of sustainability, urban air quality, but again this depends on assumptions about technological choices. During the nineteenth century, when coal was king, urban air quality in industrializing countries deteriorated badly because of the smoke and soot from chimneys and smokestacks. By the end of the century, government regulations and unfettered markets were combining to reduce this problem; regulations restricted coal use and required emission controls while cleaner-burning oil and natural gas outcompeted coal because of convenience and cost advantages. Air quality in major industrial cities improved.

The rapid emergence of the automobile in the twentieth century reversed this trend in urban air quality with emissions of nitrogen oxides and hydrocarbons reacting in sunlight to produce low-level ozone, the key component of smog. Particulates – smaller than those produced by coal combustion but perhaps more dangerous to human health – were also increasing with vehicle exhaust. Once again, however, government regulations in the latter half of the century appear to have reversed the trend. Emissions per vehicle have declined dramatically, and this has improved air quality even in cities in which the total number of vehicles has continued to increase.

In the cities of developing countries, however, the experience has been different: urban air quality has deteriorated markedly in almost every case, especially during the second half of the twentieth century, and this has coincided with a rapid increase in the uncontrolled combustion of fossil fuels. More and more inhabitants of cities in the developing world are extremely poor people who often rely on the most rudimentary technologies and fuels for cooking, and any vehicle ownership is limited to older, high-polluting models. These vehicles often sit idling in congested roadways. Municipal governments provide few services to the massive numbers of urban poor, and are ineffective in regulating their choice of technologies.

It is therefore highly likely that my current trends projection leads to a continued deterioration of urban air quality in the rapidly urbanizing areas of the developing world. In many of these cities, air quality is already at a crisis stage, responsible for many premature deaths each year. The World Health Organization estimated that urban air pollution killed about 800,000 people worldwide in 2000.[14] Even with significant reductions in the emissions from combustion, expanded vehicle use, industrial activity, greater heating and conditioning of air in buildings, and more thermal electricity generation could easily double the annual deaths as the global urban population increases from 3 billion in 2000 to a projected 7 billion in 2100.*

Greenhouse Gas (GHG) emissions

GHG emissions are convenient as a sustainability indicator because only the global level matters; one simply adds up the emissions no matter where they occur and compares these with the assimilative capacity of the environment. For my rough indicator of sustainability in this case, I compute only energy-related CO_2 emissions, which are estimated to account for 60% of the climate change effect – ignoring other GHG emissions such as nitrous oxides and methane.

---

* This would suggest that of a global population of 10.5 billion in 2100, developed countries (estimated in UN projections to make up 15% of the total in 2100), would have an urban population share of 85%, while developing countries would have an urban population share of 62%. Currently, 75% of the population in developed regions is urban, compared to 40% in developing regions. United Nations, *World Urbanization Prospects: the 2001 Revisions, Data Tables and Highlights* (New York: Population Division, Department of Economic and Social Affairs, United Nations Secretariat, 2002), 26.

In the absence of climate-focused policies, there is considerable uncertainty about the evolution of CO_2 emissions because these change depending on the rate of energy intensity improvement and the mix of primary energy forms. Since this is a current trends projection, I assume moderate reductions in energy intensity, a shift toward coal among the still-dominant fossil fuels, and the continued dominance of refined petroleum products among secondary energy forms. This means that virtually all of the carbon in fossil fuels ends up in the atmosphere after use. Figure 2.4 shows the resulting primary energy use and GHG emissions (BAU or business-as-usual in the figure indicates the main current trends projection). Energy-related GHG emissions are projected to triple from 6.4 gigatonnes of carbon (GtC) per year in 2000 to 19.6 GtC in 2100. This substantial increase is consistent with many of the scenarios generated by the IPCC and other organizations.

The figure also shows the effect of high and low assumptions reflecting my earlier discussions about the uncertainties for population growth, evolution of energy intensity, and the carbon intensity of the primary energy mix. The combinations of these assumptions that produce the highest and lowest path of CO_2 emissions are shown as the top and bottom lines in figure 2.4. The range is larger for CO_2 emissions because these are a function of three variables – population, energy intensity and share of fossil fuels in the primary energy mix – whereas energy use is a function of just the first two. Compared to the reference current trends projection, the low scenario emissions are about 33% lower while the high scenario emissions are about 40% higher. Emissions grow annually at 0.7% in the low scenario and at 1.4% in the high.

My current trends case would generate cumulative CO_2 emissions in the 100 years between 2000 and 2100 of about 1,200 GtC. For reference, the total anthropogenic CO_2 emissions from 1860 to 1995 are estimated at 360 GtC, of which 240 GtC were from fossil fuel combustion and 120 GtC from deforestation and other forms of land use change.[15] According to the current models of carbon cycling between the atmosphere and earth, the CO_2 emissions from my current trends case would result in a CO_2 concentration in the earth's atmosphere of over 650 parts per million by volume (ppmv) in 2100 compared to the pre-industrial concentration of about 280 ppmv, and this concentration would keep increasing rapidly into the following century. Climate scientists suggest that concentrations above 450 ppmv could substantially affect the earth's climate and make even

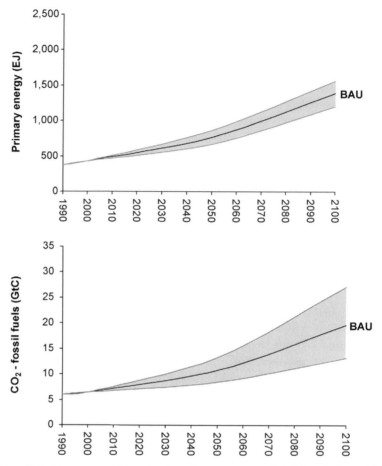

Figure 2.4. Current trends projection of energy use and GHG emissions: high and low values.

CO_2 calculated from fossil fuel combustion only.

stronger statements about concentrations above 550 ppmv. This CO_2 forecast is another reason that the current trends projection fails to satisfy my definition of energy system sustainability.

2.4 Unsustainability of the current energy path

Indoor air quality, urban air quality and GHG emissions provide an indication of the unsustainability of the current path of our energy system. In developing countries, the widespread use of biomass in domestic open fires causes significant death and illness every year. In many instances, biomass is harvested unsustainably, contributing to deforestation and even desertification. In both developing and industrialized countries, direct fossil fuel combustion to generate electricity and the combustion of refined petroleum products and natural gas to provide energy services in industry, commercial and institutional buildings, residences, and especially in vehicles, threatens air quality in urban centers as well as the global climate. Moreover, major research studies into the general health of the planet's biosphere indicates that the energy system is a leading culprit when it comes to causal factors in any deterioration of ecosystem services.[16]

Given the complexity of the energy system, it can be helpful to distinguish the endurance and cleanliness components of my sustainability definition at both the primary and secondary energy levels. At the secondary energy level, endurance is an issue only if our primary energy sources will not last because, as I noted in chapter 1, each form of primary energy can be called upon to produce the various forms of secondary energy.

Cleanliness, however, is as much an issue at the secondary level as it is at the primary level. Fortunately, there is more often agreement about our best options for secondary energy. The general assumption is that we need to accelerate electrification while also fostering hydrogen, heat and low-emission hydrocarbons like natural gas, methanol and dimethyl ether. Electrification is likely to continue rapidly through the century. A critical uncertainty is how far we might progress in realizing hydrogen's potential as the partner to electricity in what could become a secondary energy system with dramatic reductions of emissions and other negative impacts.

The choice of energy is especially problematic at the primary level. This is why I devote chapters 4, 5 and 6 to describing these major energy options and chapter 7 to a comparative evaluation of them in order to develop a sustainable energy projection. But our secondary energy choices are not without substantial challenges. I devote chapter 3 to a review of our options at this phase of the energy system, concluding with my own sustainable projection for our secondary energy system. This projection will be combined with the outcome of my assessment of our primary options to provide at the end of chapter 7 an indication of how the complete sustainable energy projection I produce would perform in aggregate in terms of indoor air quality, urban air quality, atmospheric GHG concentrations and other sustainability criteria.

Notes

1. Some sources include the chapter titled "Against Forecasting" in V. Smil, *Energy at the Crossroads* (Cambridge, Mass.: MIT Press, 2003); the chapter titled "The Forecasting Performance of Energy-Economic Models" in S. DeCanio, *Economic Models of Climate Change – A Critique* (New York: Palgrave Macmillan, 2003); E. Worrell, S. Ramesohl and G. Boyd, "Advances in Energy Forecasting Models Based on Engineering Economics," *Annual Review of Environment and Resources* 29 (2004): 345–381; and P. Craig, A. Gadgil and J. Koomey, "What Can History Teach Us? A Retrospective Examination of Long-Term Energy Forecasts for the United States," *Annual Review of Energy and the Environment* 27 (2002): 83–118.
2. International Energy Agency, *Oil Crises and Climate Challenges: 30 Years of Energy Use in IEA Countries* (Paris: International Energy Agency, 2004).
3. W. Häfele, *Energy in a Finite World: A Global Systems Analysis* (Cambridge, Mass.: Ballinger, 1981).
4. Intergovernmental Panel on Climate Change, *Special Report on Emissions Scenarios* (Cambridge: Cambridge University Press, 2000). N. Nakicenovic, A. Grubler and A. McDonald (eds.), *Global Energy Perspectives* (Cambridge: Cambridge University Press, 1998).
5. International Energy Agency, *World Energy Outlook* (Paris: OECD, 2002); Shell International Inc., *Exploring the Future: Energy Needs and Possibilities* (London: Shell International Inc., 2001).
6. Intergovernmental Panel on Climate Change, *Climate Change 2001, Third Assessment Report* (Cambridge: Cambridge University Press, 2001); J. Goldemberg (ed.), *World Energy Assessment: Energy and the Challenge of Sustainability* (New York: United Nations Development Programme, 2000); J. Goldemberg and T. Johansson (eds.), *World Energy Assessment: 2004 Update* (New York: United Nations Development Programme, 2004); N. Nakicenovic (ed.), "Energy Scenarios," chapter 9 in Goldemberg, *World Energy Assessment*.
7. J. Leggett, W. Pepper and R. Swart, "Emissions Scenarios for IPCC: An Update," in J. Houghton, B. Callander and S. Varney (eds.), *Climate Change 1992: The Supplementary Report to the IPCC Scientific Assessment* (Cambridge: Cambridge University Press, 1992).
8. Nakicenovic, "Energy Scenarios," 339.

9. B. O'Neill, F. L. MacKellar and W. Lutz, *Population and Climate Change* (Cambridge: Cambridge University Press; Laxenburg, Austria: IIASA, 2001).

10. V. Smil, "Energy in the Twentieth Century: Resources, Conversions, Costs, Uses, and Consequences," *Annual Review of Energy and the Environment* 25 (2000): 21–51. The energy values in Smil's tables are slightly lower than mine; I believe this is because his numbers exclude traditional biomass, he uses $US 1990 whereas mine are in $US 2000, and his data are for 1998 whereas mine are for 2000.

11. A. Reddy, "Energy Technologies and Policies for Rural Development," in T. Johansson and J. Goldemberg (eds.), *Energy for Sustainable Development: A Policy Agenda* (New York: United Nations Development Programme, 2002), 115–136.

12. J. Goldemberg, T. Johansson, A. Reddy and R. Williams, *Energy for a Sustainable World* (New Delhi: Wiley-Eastern Limited, 1988).

13. World Health Organization, *World Health Report 2002: Reducing Risks, Promoting Healthy Life* (Geneva: World Health Organization, 2002).

14. Ibid.

15. Intergovernmental Panel on Climate Change, *Climate Change 1995, Second Assessment Report* (Cambridge: Cambridge University Press, 1996), 11.

16. United Nations, *Millennium Ecosystem Assessment Synthesis Report* (New York: United Nations, 2005).

3 | *The prospects for clean secondary energy*

T HE growth depicted in the last chapter appears overwhelming in aggregate: global population almost doubling, economic output growing to seven times its current level and the energy system expanding more than three-fold. At this mammoth scale, how can any conceivable energy system satisfy my definition of sustainability? How can primary energy supplies meet this enormous need and, if they can, at what cost? How can the biogeophysical system absorb the waste products of our development and use of energy without suffering irreparable harm? What are the prospects for providing clean secondary energy for our daily needs?

While this book addresses all of these questions, this chapter focuses only on the last of them – the prospects for clean secondary energy. The chapter's brevity is not an indication of the unimportance of this issue, nor of a lack of controversy. Rather, it reflects the fact that the secondary energy issue is less complex; the options are fewer and the trade-offs more straightforward. Electricity is a clean form of secondary energy of which everybody wants more. Its use will expand through the century, dramatically so in developing countries. There are, however, end-uses for which electricity is less favorable relative to various forms of gaseous and liquid hydrocarbons, notably fuels for transport. While these end-uses have traditionally been met by combustion of refined petroleum products (gasoline, diesel, jet fuel, propane, butane) and natural gas, the resulting emissions are especially problematic for our sustainability concerns for urban air quality and atmospheric greenhouse gas concentrations.

There are three general options for addressing the environmental challenges of end-use combustion of hydrocarbons. We could develop combustion technologies that emit less, or even nothing if it becomes technically and economically feasible to attach emission capture devices directly to end-use technologies – such as a carbon capture device on an automobile. We could shift from higher emission to lower

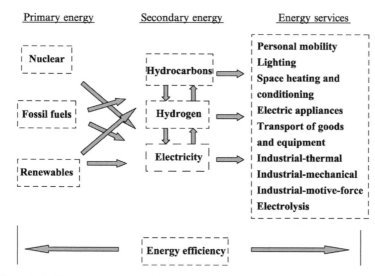

Figure 3.1. Energy system options.

emission hydrocarbons such as natural gas, and new synthetic fuels like methanol and dimethyl ether in the case of reducing emissions that affect urban air quality. We could switch completely away from hydrocarbon combustion toward zero-emission electricity and hydrogen, the latter used in fuel cells or combusted directly. I explain these options in this chapter and then conclude it with an assessment of the key factors determining the extent to which we are likely to favor any particular option as we pursue a sustainable energy system over this century.

I begin by extending the energy system presentation in figure 1.6 on page 19. That earlier figure showed that the commonly recognized primary forms of energy, fossil fuels and renewables, are the result of two fundamental energy sources: the gravitational forces of the earth and moon, and nuclear reactions in the form of fusion in the sun and fission in the center of the earth. Once the human ability to produce nuclear power is added to these (today fission, tomorrow perhaps fusion), we have the three primary energy sources that people commonly recognize – nuclear power, fossil fuels and renewables. Figure 3.1 links these three primary sources to our secondary energy options and the energy services (end-uses) I described in chapter 1.

The major energy services are on the right side of the figure. Growth in demand for these drives expansion of the energy system, especially with the rising incomes that enable people in developing countries to meet more of their basic energy needs.

At the secondary energy level, the three major options are hydrocarbons, hydrogen and electricity. While electricity is a homogeneous commodity, hydrocarbons as secondary energy can be categorized in various ways. They may be in gaseous, liquid or solid form, which affects their appropriateness for different end-uses. They may originate from fossil fuels or biomass, an important consideration in terms of greenhouse gas emissions. They may be associated with sophisticated, low-emission technologies or with open fireplaces for cooking and heating, a critical determinant for indoor air quality. Hydrocarbons include biomass, natural gas, coal and oil, the latter being normally divided into various refined petroleum products – particularly heating oil, kerosene (or jet fuel), gasoline, diesel, butane and propane. Hydrogen is included in the diagram even though its current contribution to energy services is negligible on a global scale. Its combustion or use in a fuel cell is virtually free of harmful emissions, which offers the promise of providing a partner alongside electricity in a clean secondary energy system. A fourth category of secondary energy, heat distributed in the form of hot water or steam in underground pipes, could be included in the figure. While its application is small on a global scale, limited primarily to low-temperature space heating and some industrial uses (like kiln drying of wood), it could become more significant depending on technological and economic developments. Finally, there are other small applications such as wind used directly to drive water pumps and the sun used directly to heat water.

Figure 3.2 shows the shares of secondary energy in the current energy system. Electricity is at 16% and biomass at 14% while processed and refined fossil fuels combine for 66%. This includes some final combustion of coal. The "other" category includes some direct heat, direct uses of wind for pumping and solar for direct heating. Hydrogen is not currently produced in significant quantities for energy end-uses.

Because of the potential to convert from one energy form to another, each of the three forms of secondary energy in figure 3.1 could be an input in the production of the other two, as indicated by the arrows

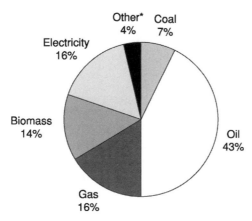

Figure 3.2. Global shares of secondary energy in 2002.

*Other equals heat, wind for direct pumping, direct solar, etc. International Energy Agency, *Key World Energy Statistics 2004* (Paris: International Energy Agency, 2004). Accessed on May 31, 2005 from http://www.iea.org/textbase/ nppdf/free/2004/keyworld2004.pdf.

between them. Electricity from a wind generator could be used to produce hydrogen via electrolysis of water. Hydrogen fuel cells in buildings might produce electricity for on-site consumption or provision to the electricity grid. Electricity or hydrogen could contribute to the processing of hydrocarbons. Hydrocarbons can be combusted to produce electricity or processed by steam reforming or gasification into hydrogen, as is explained in chapter 6.

The left side of figure 3.1 shows the multiple ways in which the three primary energy sources can produce hydrogen, electricity or processed hydrocarbons, although the efficacy of such conversions varies significantly from one combination to another. Nuclear power is used to generate only electricity at present, which in turn could produce hydrogen through electrolysis of water, but eventually nuclear power might be used to produce hydrocarbon chains and hydrogen through direct high-temperature processes. Fossil fuels can be converted into secondary hydrocarbons through refining and processing, into hydrogen through steam reforming or gasification, and into electricity through combustion in simple boiler-turbines or combined cycle turbines. Some renewables produce electricity directly (photovoltaics) while others first provide mechanical energy (wind, hydropower), chemical energy (biomass combustion in a boiler-turbine unit), or thermal energy (parabolic mirrors) to generate electricity. Biomass can be converted through gasification into hydrogen, and through various processes into gaseous and liquid hydrocarbons like ethanol and bio-diesel. Electricity from renewables can be used to generate hydrogen via electrolysis of water.

Effort at greater energy efficiency is depicted along the bottom of figure 3.1 to signify its potential application throughout the energy system. Energy efficiency can be increased in primary energy production, in the conversion of primary to secondary energy, in energy transport and delivery, and in the end-use devices that convert secondary energy into energy services.

In assessing our secondary energy options, I focus on electricity, hydrocarbons and hydrogen – the dominant options. The evolution of their relative shares over this century depends on several factors, including their own particular properties as sources of energy, technological developments, economic growth, and the trade-offs we are willing to make between our objective for clean secondary energy and the cost entailed in realizing it.

3.1 Electricity

Electricity is a flexible, zero-emission form of secondary energy that can be produced from any primary energy source. While we usually associate electricity with communications, lighting, electric motors, computers and various household devices, it can meet most energy needs. It can provide high-temperatures to transform metals (electric arc furnaces in steel production) or dry materials (electric kilns) in industry, moderate air temperature and flow in buildings (heating, ventilation and air conditioning), power vehicles of all sizes (cars, buses, trains), heat materials in households (domestic hot water, cooking, clothes drying), operate appliances requiring motive force (vacuum cleaners, lawn mowers, clothes washers, dish washers, fridges), provide motive force in industry (blowers, conveyors, fans, grinders, compressors), and furnish unique applications from inventions like microwaves, x-rays and electrolysis.

Electricity use is not without risks, notably from electrocution and sparks that start fires. Over the years, however, product engineers have designed safeguards that reduce these risks from the myriad of electricity-using technologies we come into contact with every day.

Electricity may also pose risks from exposure to the electromagnetic fields of high voltage transmission lines and from consumer products like televisions, radios, computers, cellular phones and microwave ovens. Researchers are working on understanding and reducing these risks, yet almost everyone accepts these as a reasonable trade-off for the enormous benefits we realize from electricity.

Given the objective of dramatically reducing indoor and urban emissions, one strategy is to promote the application of electricity to virtually all energy end-uses in urban areas. In the 1980s and 90s, France pursued such a nuclear-based electrification strategy – in this case in order to reduce dependence on foreign oil supplies – as it fostered electricity use for residential space heating and for many thermal applications in industry that are usually met by direct combustion of fuels. Other countries could follow this strategy, but several factors hinder electricity's ability to compete for certain end-uses, and many experts believe that such a profound transformation is neither necessary nor desirable.

First, there are the efficiency losses from electricity production. About 65% of global electricity is currently produced in fossil fuel thermal plants (the remainder being from nuclear, hydro and small amounts of biomass, wind, solar and geothermal). The average primary-to-secondary energy conversion efficiency of today's fossil fuel thermal plants is 35%, meaning that a great deal of primary energy is needed to produce electricity in this way (some types of newer thermal plants can achieve 60%). For some end-uses (furnaces, water heaters, stoves, industrial boilers) natural gas and refined petroleum products are as easy to handle as electricity, yet they can convert to end-use energy with 75–90% overall efficiency. Using thermal-generated electricity therefore requires more primary energy than simply using the fuels directly, and could lead to higher acid emissions and greenhouse gas emissions even while decreasing local air pollutants.

Second, relative to electricity, liquid and some gaseous fuels can be more easily stored. Engineers have not yet been able to solve the challenges of battery storage, weight, range and recharge time so that electric vehicles can provide a completely equivalent service to gasoline, diesel, propane, natural gas and other fuels for personal vehicles. Depending on the ability of these fuels to achieve lower emissions, the extra cost of switching to electricity for this end-use may not be worth it.

Given these constraints, electricity seems unlikely to penetrate all end-uses for the moment. However, it will continue to be favored in the many uses where it has unique capabilities, namely in the diverse and expanding applications related to its critical role in the information age. It will dominate communications, entertainment, computer applications and the rising demand for air conditioning in the developing world. But it will have difficulty competing against liquid and gaseous fuels for transportation and some thermal needs in industrial processes.

3.2 Hydrocarbons

We produce a wide array of hydrocarbon chains that we then combust at the point of end-use to provide energy services. Hydrocarbons usually come from fossil fuels, but they can equally be biomass that we combust directly as a solid or that we process into modern gases and liquids. As gases and liquids, hydrocarbons offer the convenience of high energy density, portability and ease of use in various end-use devices, and this has enabled them to dominate the global secondary energy market. The most common of these are gasoline, diesel, natural gas, kerosene, heating oil, propane and butane. Even these conventional products undergo continuous change, such as the development of unleaded and reformulated gasoline in recent decades. Increasingly, the energy industry is tailoring new synthetic variations of liquid and gaseous fuels to satisfy specific end-uses and environmental objectives. I discuss in chapter 6 developments in this direction with fossil fuels, and in chapter 4 I explain how liquid and gaseous hydrocarbons can be produced from biomass.

If hydrogen is to achieve importance in a sustainable global secondary energy system in which combustion of conventional gasoline and diesel has declined dramatically, it must compete with natural gas, propane and butane, which are already relatively clean-burning in mature technologies, and with the moving target of newer fuels such as methanol, ethanol, synthetic middle distillates, dimethyl ether and biodiesel.[1]

Methanol and ethanol are liquid alcohol fuels that can be produced from any carbonaceous feedstock by a number of processes. Methanol is currently produced from natural gas, especially at remote locations where the natural gas field is not connected to markets by pipeline.

While methanol is mostly used as feedstock in chemical production, it can be blended with gasoline. Ethanol is mostly produced from biomass, the notable example being the use of sugar cane residues in Brazil. It too can be blended with gasoline to reduce oil consumption. Use of natural gas and biomass as the primary energy feedstock reduces dependence on imports of oil or refined petroleum products, and in the case of biomass also reduces greenhouse gas emissions. Alcohol fuel blends do not significantly improve local air emissions relative to reformulated gasoline when used in internal combustion engines, but if used in more efficient fuel-cell vehicles emission benefits can be substantial. Vehicle manufacturers are experimenting with fuel-cell vehicles that would run on methanol. A potentially significant constraint is that methanol is associated with methyl tertiary butyl ether (MTBE), a gasoline additive derived from methanol to reduce emissions that is associated with potentially carcinogenic groundwater contamination from leaks. Methanol poses similar human and biosphere risks as MTBE, although not to the same degree.

Synthetic middle distillates and dimethyl ether are liquid synthetic fuels that can also be produced from any carbonaceous feedstock, notably through the initial production of synthetic gas by steam reforming of natural gas or gasification of coal (which I explain in chapter 6). These fuels can replace diesel in compression-ignition engines and have low emissions of particulates and nitrogen oxides. They can also be used as a transportable clean cooking fuel for remote rural areas. Biodiesel (from vegetable oils) can be mixed with these diesel substitutes if the goal is greenhouse gas reduction.

Even if none of these new fuels successfully challenges incumbents like gasoline and diesel, relatively clean-burning conventional fuels like natural gas, propane and butane could capture more of the secondary energy market. Refinements in the production, storage and transport of liquefied natural gas are enabling it to compete far beyond the range of natural gas pipeline systems, although demand is still limited to wealthier markets that can afford it.

Finally, the prospect for hydrocarbons depends not just on their combustion characteristics, but also on the efficiency of the end-use device. The hybrid gasoline-electric vehicle now on the market combusts gasoline in a regular vehicle engine, but captures energy from vehicle braking to run electric motors that also power the car. It achieves a significant efficiency gain over conventional internal combustion vehicles and therefore has lower emissions per distance traveled.

3.3 Hydrogen

Although hydrogen constitutes about 75% of the mass of the universe and accounts for more than 90% of its molecules, it is not found in isolation on the surface of the earth because pure hydrogen molecules are too light to be held by the earth's gravity. When isolated, its atoms bind together to form the molecule H_2. Hydrogen is a clear and odorless gas that can be oxidized into water, releasing energy and water vapor in the process. It is especially attractive as a secondary energy form in that, like electricity, it is effectively a zero-emission energy carrier. No matter how much secondary energy use grows, and no matter how concentrated in urban areas this growth is, local emissions will not increase if hydrogen replaces the combustion of hydrocarbons for secondary energy needs. Growth in energy demand would no longer offset technological refinements that reduce but do not eliminate emissions from the use of hydrocarbons. If the hydrogen were produced from primary energy sources with zero emissions, then it would also contribute to the reduction of acid emissions and greenhouse gas emissions. For these reasons, many hydrogen advocates and independent experts argue that a sustainable energy system requires dominance by a hydrogen-electricity tandem at the secondary energy level.[2]

Scientists have mused about the potential energy uses of hydrogen for several hundred years. Jules Verne had a character in his 1874 novel *The Mysterious Island* predict that hydrogen, separated from water by the use of electricity, would one day become the world's principal fuel.[3] In the twentieth century, interest grew in spurts with the development of niche applications for hydrogen after World War II, particularly as a feedstock for the production of ammonia fertilizer and in the production of lighter distillates in petroleum refineries. Concerns for energy system sustainability have become a motivator for hydrogen research in the last thirty years, initially portrayed in a 1975 book by J. Bockris.[4] Advocates predict a coming "hydrogen age," representing the pinnacle of a steady progression from humanity's early reliance on the hydrocarbons wood and coal, with their relatively low hydrogen-to-carbon ratios, then to oil followed by natural gas – each with a higher ratio – culminating in pure hydrogen as the cleanest possible fuel. Being mostly carbon, most coal has only a small amount of hydrogen. Oil products generally have a ratio of less than two hydrogen to one carbon, while natural gas's ratio is four to one, being mostly CH_4.

Hydrogen can be produced by using electricity to isolate the hydrogen in water (*electrolysis*), or by using the chemical energy in fossil fuels (and potentially biomass) to strip hydrogen from both the hydrocarbon fuel and steam (*steam hydrocarbon reforming*). Thermochemical splitting of water is a third approach that is currently seen as less promising, as it requires temperatures of 4,000°C. In electrolysis, two electrodes are immersed in water containing an electrolyte additive to improve conductivity. When a charge is applied, hydrogen is attracted to the negatively charged electrode and oxygen to the positively charged electrode. In steam reforming, steam reacts with the fossil fuel to produce a synthesis gas, which is cooled and then reacted with more steam in a water-gas shift reaction to produce pure hydrogen and a mixture of CO_2 and other gases. Steam reforming of natural gas is the principal means of producing hydrogen today for petroleum refineries and fertilizer plants. Another growing use of steam reforming is in the process of upgrading oil sands into synthetic oil, notably in the expanding oil sands production facilities in western Canada. I describe steam reforming in greater detail in chapter 6 when I survey the alternatives for producing hydrogen from fossil fuels.

Early advocates of hydrogen assumed that it would be combusted as a fuel in rockets, airplane jet engines and the internal combustion engines used in vehicles. While hydrogen has not yet been able to compete successfully with jet fuel, gasoline and diesel in their respective markets, rising environmental concerns combined with breakthroughs in fuel cell technologies have raised expectations for this form of secondary energy over the past two decades.

Fuel cells can combine hydrogen and oxygen to generate electricity, water and heat, at a higher conversion efficiency than direct combustion of hydrogen. Fuel cells are like an internal combustion engine in that they require a continuous flow of fuel, but like a battery in that they produce electricity from the flow of electrons between two electrodes. Although they were invented over 150 years ago, fuel cells only became a technology of interest with their application in the space exploration programs of the 1960s.

The most promising fuel cell design today is the *proton-exchange membrane* (other types include *alkaline, phosphoric acid, molten carbonate* and *solid oxide*). A polymer membrane (coated with a platinum catalyst) serves as an electrolyte between an anode and a cathode. Hydrogen molecules are fed in at the anode side of the cell and give up their electrons as they pass (as hydrogen ions) through the membrane to be reunited with their electrons and oxygen (from air) to form water at the cathode side. Electricity is produced by the passage of the electrons through a circuit on their way to the cathode. Thus, the inputs are hydrogen and air and the outputs are electricity, water and heat. Many fuel cells, each less than a fraction of an inch thick, must be stacked together to produce a significant amount of electricity.

Fuel cells may also become a key technology for the stationary production of electricity. In cogenerating electricity and useful heat, they operate silently without moving parts, which should reduce maintenance requirements. Their water output can even be used as a source of drinking water. Both water and heat outputs can be benignly dissipated if not needed.

Considerable attention has focused on the prospects for hydrogen fuel-cell vehicles. Over the next century, the rising global population is expected to coincide with continued urbanization on a massive scale. By 2100, the global total of 10.5 billion people could include an urban population higher than 7 billion – in towns and cities of 1,000 or more people. Personal mobility using private vehicles is projected to increase dramatically.[5] This means that the number of vehicles on the planet could increase from the current total of 600 million to 3–5 billion by 2100, with most of these located in cities. At this size of vehicle fleet, even the lower emission levels associated with natural gas and super-efficient vehicles are unlikely to improve local air quality above the levels that today account for about 800,000 deaths per year. At the same time, inhabitants of the wealthier cities of industrialized countries will continually push for further improvements in air quality.

These two drivers explain why some observers see hydrogen vehicles as almost inevitable. In essence, when it comes to the prospects for hydrogen, "necessity is the mother of invention"; if hydrogen fuel-cell vehicles are the best means of achieving zero emissions in cities, society will invent the required technologies and figure out a way to commercialize them. Skeptics caution, however, that energy history is replete with mistaken visions, as necessity confronted the real-world constraints related to thermodynamic limits, physical properties, economic costs, and even the preferences and concerns of users.

On the positive side, at 30% conversion efficiency (and still improving), fuel cells are significantly more efficient than internal combustion engines, and the energy content per unit mass of hydrogen is almost three times that of gasoline – 120 MJ/kg compared to 44 MJ/kg. On the negative side, hydrogen fuel cell vehicles must overcome several challenges related to hydrogen storage, refueling infrastructure, safety of compressed hydrogen, and the cost trajectory of fuel cells.[6]

In terms of storage, hydrogen has a very low energy content per unit volume compared to competing fuels. To store the same amount of energy in the form of liquid hydrogen as is contained in a tank of gasoline would require a tank three to four times larger. Hydrogen can be stored as a compressed gas, but this requires strong tanks (steel or composite materials) and these could still be vulnerable to explosion on impact. Current prototypes are not yet close to holding half the energy of a gasoline tank (to match the range once efficiency differences are included), and weight becomes a factor with pressure-reinforced tanks. Hydrogen can be stored in concentrated liquid form, but this requires maintaining its temperature below –253°C, which requires expensive, highly insulated tanks and significant use of energy for cooling. Researchers are also testing the storage of hydrogen by reaction with certain metal alloys to form metal hydrides. When required, the hydrogen is released by heating the hydride, but this too involves significant weight and expense. Finally, the storage problem can be addressed by reforming gasoline or methanol into hydrogen on board the vehicle. However, this approach requires each vehicle to have complex reforming equipment, and it does not prevent emissions of greenhouse gases, unless all carbon in the gasoline or methanol is captured and stored on the vehicle as part of the reforming process.

Skeptics also point out that the widespread use of hydrogen vehicles would require a refueling infrastructure comparable to that for gasoline. Viewed as a single lump-sum investment, this would indeed be massive. But niche markets for hydrogen vehicles could initially involve fleets like municipal vehicles and taxis that would require only a few refueling stations, and the system could grow incrementally from that, perhaps taking decades.[7] Also, a 15% blend of hydrogen introduced into natural gas would not affect natural gas pipelines or the appliances, furnaces and industrial equipment combusting the resulting mix of hydrogen and natural gas. This strategy would provide sufficient early demand to justify the construction of hydrogen production facilities that could eventually achieve economies-of-scale.

Compressed hydrogen gas currently offers the best option for on-vehicle storage of hydrogen, but it poses some risk to humans from an explosion. Hydrogen is ignited relatively easily, but the harm from a hydrogen explosion would be more localized than for many other fuels because hydrogen's lightness causes a quickly rising flame that emits little heat radiation; an object must be almost inside the flame to sustain burns. Also, because of its lightness hydrogen dissipates quickly upward from leaks. Progress in engineering design could soon lower explosion risks to levels that are comparable to what people readily accept today when using compressed fuels like natural gas, propane and butane. In assessing early concerns about these safety risks, it may be noteworthy to see the parallels with earlier concerns about gasoline, as in this quote from the US Congressional Record of 1875:

A new source of power . . . called gasoline has been produced by a Boston engineer. Instead of burning the fuel under a boiler, it is exploded inside the cylinder of an engine . . . The dangers are obvious. Stores of gasoline in the hands of people interested primarily in profit would constitute a fire and explosive hazard of the first rank. Horseless carriages propelled by gasoline might attain speeds of 14 or even 20 miles per hour . . . the cost of producing [gasoline] is far beyond the financial capacity of private industry . . . In addition, the development of this new power may displace the use of horses, which would wreck our agriculture.[8]

A final concern is the cost trajectory of fuel cells. With expanding commercialization, the costs of most technologies fall substantially at first and then more gradually. This is because of economies-of-scale from mass production and/or larger size units, and economies-of-learning as installers and operators learn through experience about beneficial changes to design and operating parameters. But not all new technologies follow the same cost declines from these two effects; this depends on thermodynamic limits and the costs of raw inputs among other factors. Fuel cells are currently produced with rare elements whose high costs may hinder the extent to which economies-of-scale and economies-of-learning can drive cost reductions.

It is too early to say which technology and fuel combination will dominate as fuel cell technology matures.* This depends on engineering developments, economics and the relative weighting of environmental concerns such as urban air quality and greenhouse gas emissions. If, like gasoline before it, hydrogen overcomes the initial hurdles related to production costs, safety concerns, fuel storage and infrastructure development, its future looks bright. It is not surprising that opinion leaders in industry, government and academia extol the virtues of an electricity-hydrogen future. But caution is prudent in the face of so much uncertainty.

3.4 Sustainable secondary energy projection for 2100

Electricity versus hydrogen versus hydrocarbons (of fossil fuel and biomass origins)

A sustainable energy system, as I defined it in chapter 1, requires low and in some cases zero emissions at the energy end-use level. Thus, most end-use devices would use either electricity or hydrogen, along with some combustion of natural gas, synthetic fuels and refined petroleum products, provided that GHG emission targets are met, and some combustion of gaseous and liquid biofuels, provided that local air emission targets are met. Competition between biofuels and fossil fuel-based hydrocarbons would be governed in part by the relative importance of reducing local air emissions versus GHG emissions, with biofuels favored when GHG emission control is paramount. Alternatively, we may develop devices that enable the cost-effective capture of local air emissions and GHG emissions at the point of end-use, and these might allow secondary energy hydrocarbons (of fossil fuel and biomass origin) to compete with electricity and hydrogen for various end-uses, perhaps especially with hydrogen for vehicles

---

* As noted, the fuel for fuel cells need not necessarily be hydrogen, although if hydrocarbons like methanol or gasoline are used instead there remains the challenge of on-board capture of carbon if greenhouse gas reduction remains a priority. See C. Thomas, B. James, F. Lomax and I. Kuhn, "Fuel Options for the Fuel Cell Vehicle: Hydrogen, Methanol or Gasoline?" *International Journal of Hydrogen Energy* 25 (2000): 551–567; J. Ogden, R. Williams and E. Larson, "Societal Lifecycle Costs of Cars with Alternative Fuels/Engines," *Energy Policy* 32 (2004): 7–27.

and other modes of transport. In developing a sustainable energy projection for secondary energy, I start with some inertial trends before turning to issues of greater uncertainty.

Several trends are likely to continue through much of the century. These include ongoing electrification, substantial substitution of hydrocarbon combustion by hydrogen use in fuel cells, conversion of fossil fuels into gaseous and liquid hydrocarbons with low local emissions from combustion, conversion of biomass into modern gaseous and liquid hydrocarbons, and expansion of network energy delivery systems for electricity, natural gas, hydrogen and in some cases heat.

Electricity will continue to be favored in the many end-uses where its advantages are unassailable, such as lighting and the diverse and expanding applications related to its role in the information age. It will also do well in air conditioning, a key energy service whose demand will increase along with incomes, especially in those regions of the developing world with hot climates. Electricity will have some difficulty competing against other fuels for transportation, industrial processing and space heating, although there will be niche opportunities (such as trains and urban mass transit) and regions where low-cost and low-emission electricity supply (such as in some hydropower-dominated systems) enables electricity to compete across a wide range of end-uses.

While electricity currently has a 16% share of global secondary energy, its worldwide production is expanding at a rapid pace. I project that its share will rise to about 30% by 2100, which means a six-fold increase in total production over the century. In the developing world, households with access to electricity will increase its use for basics like lighting, communications and domestic appliances, but the critical undertaking will be extension of access to those who lack any electricity service whatsoever – currently estimated at 1.6 billion people. The International Energy Agency estimates that a global investment of $10 trillion in the electricity sector over the period 2000–2030 will only succeed in reducing the number of people without electricity to 1.4 billion as half of the investment simply replaces aging facilities and as population growth swamps the considerable service expansion that is achieved.[9] Most of the people still without service in 2030 are expected to be in South Asia and Africa. China, in contrast, has achieved rapid electrification over the last fifteen years, a development I witnessed as an energy advisor. When I first visited China in 1990, I was told that almost 200 million people had no electricity. By the time of my visit in 2000, the estimate had fallen below 100 million, and by 2004 the International Energy Agency dropped the estimate to 20 million. As the century progresses and population growth abates, this pattern of service expansion will spread to other parts of Asia and eventually Africa.

Hydrogen's advance will be especially prominent in metropolitan areas of industrialized countries. This is where the demand for zero-emission secondary energy will be strongest and where the extra cost of developing hydrogen end-use technologies and hydrogen distribution systems can be more readily absorbed. California, with its relative affluence and sensitivities about air quality, has led the push for zero-emission vehicles and a hydrogen refueling network, but other US regions as well as Europe and Japan are not far behind. Nonetheless, the extent of hydrogen use in vehicles remains a great uncertainty as long as the challenge of hydrogen on-vehicle storage remains unresolved.

Hydrogen will make substantial inroads in developing countries too, but its ambit is likely to be restricted to metropolitan areas with their potential for economies-of-scale in distribution systems and where air quality conditions will be worse than those of industrialized countries. The dramatic growth in vehicle use in Chinese cities is already overtaking the traditional role of industry and space heating as the primary sources of local air pollution. If hydrogen vehicles and hydrogen distribution systems attain widespread use in industrialized countries, their dissemination to the cities of developing countries can happen within a few decades.

Non-metropolitan areas of developing countries are another story. This is where incomes will be lowest, air quality benefits smaller, and the costs of developing hydrogen distribution systems the highest given the lower density of potential demand. Because of this, I project that the hydrocarbon alternatives to electricity and hydrogen will retain almost a third of the global secondary energy market by 2100. This 30% is shared between biomass (solid or gasified), natural gas, and cleaner synthetic fuels. There will also be a small share for non-hydrocarbons in the form of steam and hot water used in industrial applications and commercial and residential space heating.

Biomass will still be used for basic space heating and cooking in many rural areas of developing and even industrialized countries. Sometimes the biomass will be combusted in its solid form, but increasingly it will be converted to gaseous and liquid fuels, first in smaller urban settings and eventually in outlying areas. Biodiesel will capture part of the transportation market especially by blending with conventional diesel in its traditional applications in trucks and heavier mobile equipment, a process that is already well underway in Europe.

A significant share of natural gas will still be combusted directly in industrialized countries, and increasingly in the urban areas of developing countries as distribution networks expand. The extent to which natural gas is combusted directly versus converted to hydrogen depends on the trade-off between this extra cost and the value of the environmental benefit, as well as the interplay between the rate of depletion of conventional natural gas reserves and the discovery and development of other natural gas sources, which will affect its supply price.

Hydrocarbons made from oil should remain competitive in the airline industry, and in rural areas of developing countries for cooking and light industry. These fuels have a portability that makes them advantageous for introducing modern commercial energy to poorer regions in developing countries that lack the networks for delivering hydrogen or even natural gas. Most importantly, these fuels are likely to be the least expensive means of quickly reducing the domestic combustion of solid fuels (biomass and some coal) for cooking and heating by the planet's poorest people, reducing the enormous health impacts caused by poor indoor air quality.

Hot water and steam may retain niche markets where modern district heating systems are already well established. In Scandinavian cities, notably, the substantial cost of developing district heat networks (central heat plants, right-of-ways, connections, proximity of buildings, meters, hot water distribution inside buildings) has already been incurred, an inertial force in district heating's favor. Small hot water distribution systems might also emerge in some locations to take advantage of waste heat recovery from electricity generation facilities. In future, central heat production may involve hydrogen combustion or hydrogen fuel cells.

This detailed look at secondary energy alternatives and their potential applications shows just how difficult it is to make a blanket assumption that we are entering a hydrogen-electric future. Even if hydrogen is promoted vigorously as a necessity for human health and the environment, there are many challenges to its comprehensive adoption. Hydrogen's prospects are best for specific uses in specific locations: in wealthier countries, in larger cities, in cities that have greater air quality problems, and in regions where the alternatives to hydrogen for certain end-uses are particularly expensive.

The greatest determinant of hydrogen's importance to the global energy system in 2100 is the evolution of automobile technologies. Although distaste for the automobile is common among environmentalists in wealthier countries, this animosity should not distract us from the large benefit that most people associate with this transportation device in both the industrialized and now developing regions of the world. To bring home this reality to my own energy modeling research team, I often insist that we refer to a private automobile not as a vehicle, but as a PMD – a personal mobility device. Many people love their personal mobility devices, and even in cities with excellent public transportation systems in Europe, North America and Japan, they stick to this device to the point of mind-numbing congestion. Indeed, from our recent detailed research into people's mobility preferences when comparing public transit and automobiles, we have considered again changing the name we use for a personal vehicle in order to more fully convey its perceived value, this time to PSED – personal status enhancing device.

What are the key determinants for the relative shares of secondary energy 100 years from now? Certainly the climate change concern looms large. If greenhouse gas emissions are to be dramatically reduced, humans need extremely low carbon emissions from secondary energy use. In this context, the choice of energy form and technology for road transportation becomes critical.[10] Given that they produce zero emissions from end-use, hydrogen fuel cell vehicles seem to be the obvious long-term solution. But this outcome is far from the certainty that hydrogen advocates suggest. Battery-electric vehicles could see a breakthrough in on-board energy storage and recharging time, with significant improvement to the attractiveness of this option. The recent development of hybrid gasoline-electric vehicles offers perhaps an even more significant long-run challenge because these vehicles can evolve in different directions depending on the relative importance of greenhouse gas emissions versus emissions affecting local air quality.

One possibility is the wide-scale commercialization of plug-in hybrids – hybrid vehicles whose batteries are recharged by plugging into the grid at home in the evening during off-peak hours. In this case, the internal combustion engine in the vehicle is rarely used for urban driving; the range of a fully charged battery with current technology is about 100 kilometers, which is more than the distance traveled by most urban commuters. The combustion engine would only be needed for providing supplementary power in urban driving and for long distance intercity travel. If extreme greenhouse gas concerns require that carbon emissions from transportation fall virtually to zero, biomass fuels (biodiesel, ethanol, methanol) or hydrogen could provide the energy for the rare times when the internal combustion engine is operating. The smaller contribution of hydrogen would also solve the on-board storage problem facing hydrogen fuel-cell vehicles, where much larger capacity for hydrogen storage is required because this is the only energy source for the vehicle. Whether the plug-in hybrid is using biofuels or hydrogen, this scenario requires that electricity production grow much more than I originally suggested, and this would need to be with zero-emission generation methods (presented in chapters 4 and 6).

Another possibility is the survival of the internal combustion engine by itself through various technological breakthroughs and energy substitutions. Biofuels, if they can be produced in sufficient quantity at reasonable cost (depending on competition for arable land), address the greenhouse gas concern in that carbon levels are kept constant in the cycle from biomass to fuel to atmosphere (as emissions) and back to biomass (through photosynthesis). But particulate and other emissions from continued reliance on hydrocarbon combustion for personal vehicles, as these grow to between 3 and 5 billion units worldwide, may still pose a major problem for local air quality. The best chance for survival of the internal combustion engine is either through joint development with batteries and electric motors in hybrid vehicles, or through the development of on-board devices that capture carbon from the vehicle exhaust system. This latter option has particular technological challenges.*

---

* Hydrogen could also be the fuel for internal combustion engines alone, but such vehicles would face the same storage challenges as hydrogen fuel-cell vehicles. If the storage problem is solved, the fuel cell is likely to dominate due to its greater efficiency.

Summary of sustainable projection

In summary, the transition toward a sustainable energy system at the secondary energy level requires a continuation and indeed an acceleration of the worldwide electrification trend, with a dramatic rate of expansion in developing countries. It also requires a shift toward reduced use of direct fuel combustion in the industrial sector and for home energy needs such as space heating and domestic water heating. But the key end-use where change is required is in transportation. Looking at personal transportation as a particularly important sub-segment, the path to zero emissions has significant uncertainties. Hydrogen fuel cell vehicles could become important by the middle of the century. Or, their development could be retarded or even halted by a greater use of electricity brought on either by developments in battery-electric vehicles or, more likely, by the widespread dissemination of plug-in gasoline-electric hybrid vehicles that use little gasoline.

In my own projection, I assume that by 2100 hydrogen will attain a 30–40% share of the secondary energy market – with expansion occurring especially during the second half of the century – while hydrocarbon fuels fall to 30–40%. These combusted hydrocarbons will increasingly be dominated by natural gas, although refined petroleum products and gaseous and liquid fuels from biomass will also be substantial. The open combustion of solid biomass in indoor areas must be negligible by 2100 or this cannot be called a sustainable energy system. But incomes in rural areas through almost all of the world should have risen enough for people to afford at least a low-emission solid fuel stove or heater, comparable to the transition that occurred in rural areas of North America in the early twentieth century. Evidence from throughout the world indicates that with rising incomes the acquisition of new technologies and alternative forms of domestic energy is a priority for most people. As long as commercial energy supplies are available, people with rising incomes make this energy transition without government policy intervention simply because of the resulting improvements to their lifestyle.

To reflect the considerable uncertainty, especially in the future shares of hydrogen and hydrocarbons, I show these in figure 3.3 as both ranging from 30–40% – as indicated by the 10% share that could be hydrogen or hydrocarbons. If greenhouse gas emissions remain a paramount concern for sustainability, hydrogen may achieve an even

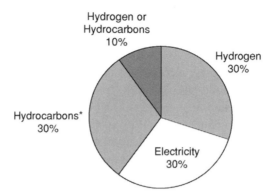

Figure 3.3. Sustainable projection for global shares of secondary energy in 2100.

*Hydrocarbons comprise substantial biofuels and natural gas, as well as lesser quantities of synthetic fuels and conventional refined petroleum products. Direct solar and heat from geothermal and cogeneration are excluded for simplicity, but would also exist in moderate quantities.

higher share than 40%, and of the remaining hydrocarbons a significant share will be produced from biomass to prevent a net increase in atmospheric concentrations of carbon. If greenhouse gas emissions are seen as less important, more combustion of hydrocarbons will occur as long as this is sufficiently controlled in urban areas to prevent adverse affects on local air quality.

From this projection for the secondary energy component of a sustainable energy system, I now turn to focus on primary energy. Given that we can make electricity, hydrogen and hydrocarbons from almost any primary energy source, and that we can use less of these if we achieve greater efficiency, we must decide if each of these options will make an equal contribution or if one or two options are likely to dominate. Many recent studies by international organizations present these options as if each had an equal chance of contributing to sustainable energy. But reality is rarely like that. While periods of major technological change can appear confusing, and even chaotic, in the early phases, this is usually followed by a shake-out period in which one or two technology paths emerge as leaders. How the major primary energy options compare to each other becomes a crucial question in the quest for a sustainable energy system.

In addressing this question, I distinguish fossil fuels from the other alternatives. Energy efficiency, nuclear and various forms of renewables have been frequently touted, individually or together, as the only options for sustainable energy. They are the "usual suspects" – which I review in chapter 4. As non-enduring and polluting as they are so often portrayed, fossil fuels are seen as the "unusual suspect" – which I turn to in some detail in chapters 5 and 6.

As in the case of our primary energy options, the preferred options for a secondary energy system will not be realized unless governments set the appropriate policies. I turn to this question in chapter 8.

Notes

1. J. Goldemberg (ed.), *World Energy Assessment: Energy and the Challenge of Sustainability* (New York: United Nations Development Programme, 2000).
2. S. Dunn, *Hydrogen Futures: Toward a Sustainable Energy System* (Washington, D.C.: Worldwatch Institute, 2001); H. Geller, *Energy Revolution: Policies for a Sustainable Future* (Covelo, Calif.: Island Press, 2002); P. Hoffman, *Tomorrow's Energy: Hydrogen, Fuel Cells, and the Prospects for a Cleaner Planet* (Cambridge, Mass.: MIT Press, 2001); J. Rifkin, *The Hydrogen Economy: The Creation of the Worldwide Energy Web and the Redistribution of Power on Earth* (New York: Tarcher/Putnam, 2002).
3. Hoffman, *Tomorrow's Energy*, 29.
4. J. Bockris, *Energy: The Solar-Hydrogen Alternative* (New York: Halstead Press, 1975).
5. A. Schafer and D. Victor, "The Future Mobility of the World Population," *Transportation Research Part A* 34 (2000): 171–205.
6. J. Romm, *The Hype About Hydrogen: Fact and Fiction in the Race to Save the Planet* (New York: Island Press, 2004).
7. See J. Ogden, "Prospects for Building a Hydrogen Energy Infrastructure," *Annual Review of Energy and the Environment* 24 (1999): 227–279.
8. US Congressional Record, 1875. I thank R. Williams for providing this quote.
9. International Energy Agency, *World Energy Investment Outlook* (Paris: International Energy Agency, 2003).

10. For an analysis of long-term vehicle technology options under severe constraints on greenhouse gas emissions, see C. Azar, K. Lindgren and B. Andersson, "Global Energy Scenarios Meeting Stringent CO_2 Constraints – Cost-Effective Fuel Choices in the Transportation Sector," *Energy Policy* 31 (2003): 961–976; and H. Turton and L. Barreto, "Automobile Technology, Hydrogen and Climate Change: A Long-Term Modeling Analysis," *International Journal of Energy Technology and Policy* (forthcoming, 2005).

4 | *The usual suspects: efficiency, nuclear and renewables*

THE oil crisis and fossil fuel price shocks in the 1970s boosted the prospects for energy efficiency, nuclear power and renewable forms of energy. Each of these alternatives experienced a surge of investment in R&D, demonstration projects and commercialization efforts. Each became the focus of government policy initiatives and public utility programs, sometimes attracting large subsidies. As the 1980s progressed, however, the prices of oil, natural gas and coal fell back to their historic levels. Unable to compete with fossil fuels except in special circumstances, each alternative experienced stagnating investment and declining policy interest.

The emerging concern for sustainable energy in the 1990s, especially the focus on climate change among wealthier countries, produced a new window of opportunity for efficiency, nuclear and renewables, as advocates extolled their environmental virtues. Dramatic improvements in energy efficiency might eliminate the need for primary energy expansion, and even enable its contraction. Nuclear power produces clean electricity while emitting no local air pollutants, no regional acid emissions and no greenhouse gases. All renewables emit zero greenhouse gases and even biomass can be converted to electricity and hydrogen so that it too has zero local emissions. When the focus is a sustainable energy system, these are the "usual suspects."

4.1 Energy efficiency

While energy efficiency is not a primary energy source, its potential contribution in the face of growing energy service needs was recognized three decades ago. In response to the oil supply crisis of the 1970s, energy efficiency analysts emphasized that the same level of energy service could require significantly different amounts of secondary and primary energy. If energy service demands grew by 20% over a twenty-year period while energy production, conversion and end-use technologies improved their efficiency by an average of 20%, primary energy requirements would not increase. For this time period at least, energy consumption and economic activity would be disconnected. When we look forward 50 and 100 years, concerted efforts to improve energy efficiency over such a long time period can have a profound effect on how much primary energy will be required by 2050 and 2100, with implications for the impacts and risks of the energy system.

The analysis of energy efficiency potential usually starts with some key concepts from thermodynamics, especially its first and second laws. In layman's terms, the *first law of thermodynamics* says "energy can neither be created nor destroyed" and the *second law of thermodynamics* says "energy quality always degrades during the use or transformation of energy in an isolated system." *First law efficiency* is measured as the "ratio of energy input to useful energy output of a device." Many modern devices have low first law efficiencies, indicating substantial room for improvement. However, energy analysts point to second law efficiency as the best way to understand just how much efficiency improvement may be possible. *Second law efficiency* is defined as the "ratio of energy input of a device to the minimum amount of energy theoretically needed to perform a task."[1]

(The first and second laws of thermodynamics are not to be confused with the first and second laws of economics, as once explained to me by an economics professor. The first law of economics states, "For every issue, two economists in the same room will hold diametrically opposing viewpoints." The second law states, "Both of these viewpoints will eventually be proven wrong.")

This distinction between the first and second law is illustrated by A. Lovins' memorable example of cutting butter with a chainsaw.[2] First law efficiency is the ratio of the motive force of the spinning chain to the gasoline consumption of the chainsaw. The energy actually required to do the task is immaterial as this approach focuses only on the inputs and outputs of the device itself. Second law efficiency is the minimum theoretical amount of energy necessary to cut the butter (the energy required to separate its molecules at a given temperature), divided by the gasoline consumption of the chainsaw. In this case, the choice of device to perform the task is a critical determinant of efficiency. While the first law efficiency in this example might be 30%, being the ratio of the motive energy of the spinning chain to the chemical energy of the burned gasoline, the second law efficiency would be extremely low – probably below 1% – because little of the chainsaw's motive force is applied to cleaving the butter, as opposed to spinning the chain and spraying butter around the room. The second law perspective is important because it awakens us to consider how well we match the energy device or energy source to the energy we actually need to perform a task.

The first and second law efficiency of our global energy system can only be crudely estimated. According to the World Energy Assessment, the roughly 400 exajoules (EJ) per year of primary energy deliver almost 300 EJ of secondary energy, which is converted into 150 EJ of output from the final energy conversion devices in industry and households.[3] (Because these numbers are based on what we can reliably measure, they exclude all human and animal power and some of the biomass used for traditional cooking and heating in developing countries.) This ratio of 400 to 150 yields a first law efficiency of 37.5%. But the 150 EJ represents the energy output from final energy conversion devices – the spinning chain of the chainsaw. The actual energy needed to perform the tasks provided by our energy system (heating, cooling, mobility, lighting) with today's best available technologies is estimated to be below 60 EJ, implying an efficiency level of less than 15% as we shift from first law toward second law analysis. True second law efficiency would be even lower than this, however, since its definition focuses on the theoretical minimum energy necessary to perform a task.

Basic engineering analysis demonstrates how to improve efficiency, especially if applied to both the upstream and downstream components of the energy system. The choice of technology for residential space heating provides an example. We can use electric resistance to heat the inside of a building. The efficiency of electric space heating is 100%, as virtually all of the electrical energy is converted into heat inside the room that is being heated. If the electricity is generated in a distant thermal plant, the ratio of the chemical energy of the plant's fuel (say natural gas) to the electricity it produces may be only 35% – the efficiency of the plant. Then, 10% of this electricity may be lost from the high voltage transmission lines (a transport efficiency of 90%). The use of electricity for space heating therefore has a total system first law efficiency of 35% × 90% × 100% = 31.5%.

If the natural gas were instead piped directly to the building and burned in a furnace to provide the same space heating service – internally distributed via forced air or hot water radiators – the first law efficiency improves significantly. The losses of natural gas pipelines are modest. The natural gas furnace may have an efficiency of 80% in that 20% of the heat it produces is lost up the chimney. The internal heat distribution system may also suffer losses depending on its design but these can be as low as 10% if the distribution system is mostly within the heated area of the building (an efficiency of 90%). Thus, the first law efficiency of using natural gas for space heating has a total system efficiency of 80% × 90% = 72%. Switching from electricity to natural gas space heating improves the first law efficiency of providing this service from 31.5% to 72%.

As this space heating example shows, we can estimate first law efficiency of an entire energy pathway, from primary energy to final energy services, by multiplying the efficiencies of each device on the path. This *full fuel cycle analysis* enables us to determine the most efficient of our current options. But how do we estimate how far we can get by focusing on energy efficiency over a long time period, such as fifty years or even a century? The answer hinges on our assessment of both the prospects for technological advances and the chances that people will adopt these new technologies in sufficient numbers and without significantly increasing their use behavior.

A common approach is to calculate secondary and primary energy demand under the assumption that the most energy efficient technologies currently available will achieve 100% market penetration by a certain time. Only the most energy efficient electric motors, boilers and machinery would be used in industry. Consumer durables like fridges, cars, furnaces and light bulbs would be at the highest commercially available level of efficiency. All thermally generated electricity would come from the most advanced combined cycle gas turbines.

A more futuristic approach involves exploring the implications of adopting efficient technologies and innovations that are not yet commercially available. Thus, special insulating materials, fuel cells (for vehicle mobility as well as combined heat and power in stationary applications) and other high efficiency pre-commercial technologies would be assessed in terms of their effect on total energy demand if widely disseminated.

A complementary approach is to select energy sources and devices that are appropriate from a second law efficiency perspective – focusing on the minimal amount of energy needed to perform a given task.

This approach can favor the application of devices that exploit lower quality but free energy sources such as thermal radiation from the sun and the waste heat from various industrial and energy conversion processes. For example, the flame temperature of a natural gas furnace is over 2,000°C, yet the energy task of space heating often requires increasing the internal temperature of a room by only 10 or 20°C relative to the external temperature. With proper design, lower temperature heat sources can provide the same space heating service of the natural gas furnace without requiring the production and transmission of a high quality form of energy like natural gas. Scandinavia and Eastern Europe are especially well known for the use of the waste heat from electricity generation to heat commercial and residential buildings. In the case of solar-thermal, dedicated heat collector systems or the building structure itself (passive systems) can capture low-density solar energy and provide all or some of the heating needs of a building, depending on the solar intensity and climate. On the flip side, using the building design principles applied in hotter climates – often borrowing from the traditional knowledge of cultures that have inhabited such regions for millennia – would minimize the need for secondary energy consumption for cooling.

Some analysts suggest that designing for energy efficiency should extend beyond energy using equipment and buildings to include integrated development of urban and industrial activity that captures the synergies between, for example, the thermal waste from some activities and the low-temperature heat requirements of others. *Community energy management* and *industrial ecology* are two overlapping concepts that exemplify this approach.

In community energy management, all land-use and infrastructure decisions that affect the evolution of urban form must include a careful consideration of how to improve the energy efficiency of the urban system. A district heating system would use the waste heat from a thermal electricity generation plant – a practice referred to as cogeneration or combined heat and power. Commercial and residential land-uses would be interspersed in order to reduce the need for mobility, and nodes of higher density development would be integrated with public transit networks.

Industrial ecology shares the concepts of community energy management, but focuses especially on situating industrial facilities in close enough proximity so that they can economically use each other's

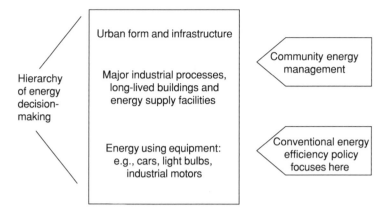

Figure 4.1. Hierarchy of energy-related decisions.

energy (and material) wastes. This is sometimes referred to as energy cascading because as the quality of energy declines after each use – the second law of thermodynamics – industrial facilities can be matched to energy needs of progressively lower quality. Again, this may involve the cogeneration of electricity and steam, with the latter distributed to adjacent plants, or it may simply involve the capture of waste heat from one plant by another even where electricity is not generated. If this approach also leads to the increased use of waste materials, there will be additional energy efficiency benefits, because recycling waste materials into products usually requires less energy than the production of such products from virgin ores.

Figure 4.1 presents energy-related decisions in a hierarchy that illustrates how community energy management reaches beyond the conventional focus of energy efficiency analysis on consumer durables, buildings and industrial equipment to the level of urban form and major infrastructure such as energy delivery networks and transportation systems.[4] The figure distinguishes three levels, with decisions at higher levels setting the context and constraints for decisions at lower levels. Urban form (density and mix of land-uses) and the siting of industrial activities determine the extent to which waste steam and hot water can be passed from one independent site to another, and the layout of public transit infrastructure determines transit's ability to provide an alternative for some uses of the private automobile. Like-wise, the coverage of different energy distribution networks – electricity, natural gas, perhaps hydrogen one day – determines the upper market potential for technologies that use these particular forms of energy; hydrogen-fueled vehicles are not an option where there is no hydrogen distribution system.

The hierarchy also depicts dimensions of energy-related decision-making that are of consequence for efforts to influence the evolution of the energy system. One dimension is time. Decisions at the top of the hierarchy, about urban form, major energy networks and transportation systems, have implications for decades and even centuries; some buildings built by the Romans are still in use today. This long timeframe means that profound changes to urban form and infrastructure can only occur slowly. Rome wasn't built in a day! Decisions at the bottom of the hierarchy, about individual equipment, are less constraining over time; if inefficient incandescent light bulbs last only one year on average, the decision to switch to a high efficiency light bulb can be revisited annually. Another dimension is the identity of the decision maker. Decisions at the top of the hierarchy are usually made by public agencies – regional and national governments, regional transit authorities, and municipal planners. Decisions at the middle of the hierarchy are usually made by large private and quasi-public entities – utilities, large energy corporations and major land developers. Decisions at the bottom of the hierarchy are usually made by private individuals – households, managers of commercial and institutional buildings, and managers and equipment suppliers at industrial plants.

Given this diversity of options and dimensions of energy efficiency, the estimation of its potential contribution to a sustainable energy system raises a number of questions. How broadly should we define actions to improve energy efficiency? Should we just look at equipment changes, or should we include transformations of urban form and infrastructure? Should we consider only available technologies, or should we also assess the potential for technological change? How do we compare efficiency actions to alternative, supply-side options like renewables and nuclear power? Should we stick to thermodynamic measures of energy efficiency, or do we need to include cost and consumer preferences in order to compare efficiency with supply-side alternatives?

The estimate of energy efficiency potential changes dramatically depending on how one responds to the above questions. While energy efficiency advocates argue that we can reduce our energy use by 75–90% without adversely affecting our standard of living, skeptics argue that even modest improvements in energy efficiency will come at a cost to the economy and our lifestyle.

If we could redesign our cities, transportation networks, energy grids, industrial processes, and all the technologies that operate within these in accordance with the second law of thermodynamics, we can conceive of a world in which we receive the same level of energy services (lighting, heating, mobility, consumer products) while using only 10% of our primary energy demand. Our energy system is far from its maximum technological potential for second law efficiency. While there has been little research to explore such a scenario in detail, F. Schmidt-Bleek and his co-researchers have presented this scenario as a desired objective not just for the global energy system, but for all material and energy flows on the planet – what they refer to as Factor 10, a ten-fold improvement in energy efficiency.[5] Using GHG emissions as a critical indicator, Schmidt-Bleek argues that if global GHG emissions must be cut in half, and if developing countries need to increase their material and energy flows five-fold in order to attain a decent standard of living, then the emissions from industrialized countries must fall by 90%. In this sense, the 90% reduction is more of a precautionary target based on ecological and social necessities than the outcome of a detailed analysis of technologies and thermodynamic potentials.

The prospect for energy efficiency is examined in more detail in the work of A. Lovins, whose research collaborations repeatedly suggest that about a 75% reduction in energy use for a given level of services – hence the label Factor 4 – is achievable in a relatively short timeframe (30–50 years) via a 100% adoption of technologies that are currently available.[6] Lovins claims, moreover, that this improvement in energy efficiency is cost-effective: it requires only the pursuit of profitable energy efficiency investment opportunities facing businesses and households. For example, the acquisition of the highest efficiency fridge available on the market might cost the householder an extra $100. If this cost were amortized over the life of the fridge using the standard bank lending rates for good customers, it would require extra annual payments of say $16 per year to the bank for the ten years of the fridge's lifespan. According to Lovins, however, this extra capital cost would be more than offset by the reduced annual electricity bills from the utility.

Energy system efficiency improvements of 90% or 75% may be possible, but these certainly represent the high end of estimates provided by most energy efficiency researchers, especially if these researchers are asked to limit their estimates to cost-effective energy efficiency improvement as defined by the fridge example above. The World Energy Assessment provides a survey of the research of the past decade in order to produce a best-guess estimate of the cost-effective energy efficiency potential for different regions of the world.[7] It suggests that industrialized countries could achieve cost-effective energy efficiency gains of 25–35% over the next twenty years. The prospects for transitional economies are as high as 40% given the low efficiencies of the energy conversion facilities (electricity plants, petroleum refineries) and the energy end-use equipment in the economies of the former Soviet Union and Eastern Europe. Estimates for developing countries vary considerably because just the slightest difference in the rate of energy service growth and technological diffusion can lead to dramatically different prospects for energy efficiency potential. Energy use in developing countries today, however, is often associated with older, less efficient technologies (used in steel plants, buses, electricity generation) while traditional household equipment like biomass stoves are notoriously inefficient.

If we could sustain this pace of energy efficiency improvement throughout the century, the downward evolution of E/GDP could be accelerated as shown in figure 4.2. Primary energy demand would thus be 904 EJ in 2100 instead of the 1,390 EJ shown in table 2.1 of chapter 2. If this were the only change, GHG emissions, to take one indicator of environmental sustainability, would likewise be lower by 35% (assuming a proportional reduction of each form of energy as energy demand falls).

This analysis is based on the estimates provided by the World Energy Assessment. These are the product of a comprehensive survey by some of the world's top energy efficiency experts, the culmination of an exhaustive review of the literature. This should be cause for confidence. The assessment even reports on earlier studies by my own research group, presumably cause for greater confidence for me personally in the estimates. Unfortunately – to my own

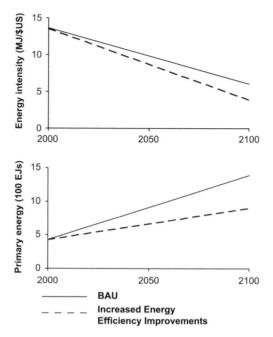

Figure 4.2. E/GDP and primary energy under a higher efficiency scenario.

embarrassment – the effect is the opposite. This is because my experiences of the past ten years have put a damper on my faith in these types of estimates of economic energy efficiency potential, even the estimates that I have been involved in producing. It is not that I am no longer in favor of energy efficiency as a key public policy goal in the quest for a more sustainable energy system. Rather, the issue for me is that my own research experiences, combined with a careful reading of the fascinating and sometimes aggressive debate between energy efficiency researchers and their critics, have led me to shift my views. I no longer believe that dramatic improvements in energy efficiency can be attained at such a low cost and as easily. What is particularly troubling to me is that while the World Energy Assessment's estimate is based on an apparently comprehensive survey of the energy efficiency literature – citing 250 references alone – I could not find in it a single reference to the works of the fifteen or so internationally recognized researchers who have raised serious questions about the methodology used by efficiency advocates for estimating cost-effective energy efficiency.

To understand why I am now troubled with some of these efficiency estimates, I must review briefly the history of our recognition of energy efficiency as a social goal and our experiences with trying to estimate its potential and then achieve it.

By the 1960s and 70s in industrialized countries, you didn't need to be a physicist or engineer specializing in thermodynamics to feel that we sometimes use energy wastefully (although even the word "wastefully" is not easy to define given that a greater use of energy resources is justified if they are the relatively cheaper productive input – compared to labor for example). This observation of wasteful use seemed especially pertinent in the US and Canada where relatively inexpensive energy resources had allowed these countries to develop energy-intensive industries and lifestyles compared to Europe and Japan. Environmentalists were concerned because they recognized the link between energy use and pollution. While there was occasional recognition by the public and politicians about the possible benefits of energy efficiency, many energy-related pollution problems were ultimately addressed by adding end-of-pipe technologies that cleaned up the emissions without improving energy efficiency. In some cases the emission control equipment (catalytic converters for cars) actually decreased energy efficiency.

Perceptions changed with the first oil price shock in 1973 when oil prices jumped from $3 to $13 a barrel overnight, and then in 1979 when they climbed to $40/barrel. Industrialized countries responded with an array of policies to reduce dependence on imported oil (especially from OPEC), including development of domestic oil resources (Alaska in the US), increased contracting with non-OPEC oil suppliers (Mexico, Norway, England, the Soviet Union), substituting from oil to alternatives like coal, nuclear, natural gas, and renewables, and pursuing greater energy efficiency.

With perfect timing, A. Lovins published a book called *Soft Energy Paths* in 1977 in which he proposed renewables as the alternative to fossil fuels and nuclear, and dramatic improvement in energy efficiency (what he called technical fixes) as the lucrative first step in any energy policy. According to Lovins, the most efficient technologies already available in the market might have a higher capital cost, but this higher cost would be more than offset by the money saved from lower energy bills. A more efficient fridge might cost more to buy, but its lower operating cost would more than compensate for the extra expense, especially as operating costs rose to pay for new supply investments. He saw opportunities for such profitable technical fix investments throughout the economy, claiming that it was as simple as walking down the street and picking up a $20 bill lying on the sidewalk. "So great is the scope for technical fixes now that the US could spend several hundred billion dollars on them initially plus several hundred million dollars per day – and still save money compared with increasing the supply!"[8]

In the early 1980s, a global recession, caused in part by the second oil price shock and intensified by US monetary policy, caused a downturn in US electricity demand just as many nuclear power plants were nearing completion – most of them at higher costs than originally estimated (in part because of shifting regulatory hurdles). State utility regulators tried to allow rate increases in order to protect utility revenues from the downturn in sales and to recover the higher construction costs, but as these increases were added to previous increases caused by higher oil prices the situation only worsened. Higher rates led to further demand decreases which in turn required yet more price increases in order to keep revenues constant – a negative feedback effect that some industry critics mischievously labeled "the utility death spiral." Several plants were halted in mid-construction while others were completed but not put into operation. Unable or unwilling to contemplate further price increases, utility regulators in many US states opted to break the "regulatory compact," the tradition by which utility shareholders and bondholders were ensured a full rate of return on investments that had received pre-approval – as had been the case with the nuclear plants. Without adequate revenue, utilities defaulted on billions of dollars in bonds and utility shareholders lost billions in equity as their shares were downgraded to reflect the true worth of the unutilized investments.

Suddenly, utility management, shareholders, bondholders, regulators and ratepayers in the US were made painfully aware of the substantial risks of new electricity generation investments, whether associated with fossil fuels like oil or with long payback investments like nuclear power. And Lovins was transformed almost overnight from a pariah of the electricity industry to the keynote speaker at utility conferences and the special guest in utility boardrooms around North America and beyond, preaching the virtue of investing in "negawatts instead of megawatts."[9] The 1980s became the energy efficiency decade as utilities and governments developed ambitious programs to foster energy efficiency, especially but not only in the electricity sector. In the period 1980–1995, US utilities spent about $20 billion to induce energy efficiency efforts by their customers.[10]

Energy efficiency programs – information campaigns and especially subsidies to encourage acquisition of the most efficient technologies – are referred to by utilities as *demand-side management*. Utilities compare these programs with investments in new generation in a process called *integrated resource planning*. While utilities and governments throughout the world have undertaken energy efficiency programs, the US experience provides the greatest opportunity for assessing their effects because of that country's well-developed tradition of requiring utilities to prove to their regulators in a quasi-judicial process that all expenditures are "used and useful." After some questionable programs in the early 1980s, many US states developed fairly rigorous processes for assessing the cost-effectiveness of demand-side management programs, using both cost–benefit analysis to decide on which programs to pursue – based on forecasts of future costs, efficiency gains and success rates – and eventually hindsight evaluations to determine if forecasted efficiency gains and economic benefits were actually realized.

Several prominent economists became involved in these reviews and in the subsequent public debate. With their natural suspicion of the presumed benefits from market intervention by government or regulated monopolies, economists asked, "If energy efficiency provides such real benefits, why haven't firms and households already taken the energy efficiency actions themselves?" Advocates of energy efficiency countered that blind faith in the theoretical efficiency of the market prevents economists from accepting real-world evidence to the contrary – prompting this often heard joke at energy efficiency conferences: "Why did the economist refuse to pick up the $20 bill lying on the sidewalk? Because if it were real, somebody would have already done so."

But can we ignore economists' concerns about energy efficiency? With at least two decades of energy efficiency efforts by utilities and government, what does the hindsight evidence show?

As is often the case, the hindsight evidence is not conclusive; analysts tend to find what they are predisposed to find, applying different cost accounting methods and different definitions of costs. S. Nadel reported in a 1990 survey that some efficiency programs were more costly than expected and some were less so, with an average cost for US industrial and commercial programs of 2 ¢/kWh.[11] P. Joskow and D. Marron found that when the utility costs of running a program were added to an accounting that focused only on the incremental effect of a program (excluding those who free-ride by accepting a subsidy to purchase equipment they would have acquired anyway), the costs were at least double this amount, increasing the cost of efficiency to that of new supply investments.[12] With an aggregate, back-of-the-envelope analysis, F. Wirl points out that the expenditure of $20 billion on demand-side management by electricity utilities did not result in a reduction in the electricity to GDP ratio of the US economy relative to those industrialized countries that made only negligible efforts at improving electricity efficiency.[13] Detailed studies have found that the anticipated energy efficiency gains of demand-side management programs tend to exceed the realized savings revealed by end-use hindsight analysis.[14]

There is, then, considerable controversy about the potential and the cost-effectiveness of increased efforts at energy efficiency. This is in part a technical issue, but it is especially a behavioral issue. Both my own research and my personal life experiences have caused me to look carefully at this controversy, sending me down a research path that I never expected to tread.

As a newly appointed academic in the late 1980s and early 1990s, I was keen to produce research like those of other efficiency advocates in order to convince policy makers of the magnitude and attractiveness of the efficiency potential. My research team took on a major efficiency estimation project for our local electricity monopoly, British Columbia Hydro, as part of a utility-stakeholder process. We produced volumes of sector- and technology-specific efficiency estimates and used an engineering-focused method of analysis that we thought would replicate the results of Lovins and others. Instead, our estimates of efficiency improvement were substantially lower than Lovins – closer to the current estimates of the World Energy Assessment at about 35%. In a subsequent journal article we described our efforts to understand why.[15] As far as we could make out, our lower estimates were primarily caused by the technological heterogeneity of industrial energy uses, which meant that isolated evidence of efficiency gains for motive force systems should not be extrapolated to the entire industry or even a specific industrial sector. For example, the addition of a variable-speed drive to an electric motor and pumping system would be appropriate in some pumping applications of the pulp and paper sector, but not in others where only a constant-speed drive system was appropriate – resulting in a much lower aggregate potential for efficiency improvement.

This technical issue was of concern, but at least our studies showed a substantial potential for cost-effective energy efficiency improvement, even if our estimate for the industrial sector might be 35% as compared to Lovins' 60% and greater.[16] Then, at a personal level, I became a homeowner in the late 1980s and got to experience first-hand the behavioral side of energy efficiency decision making, and to rethink the method we used for calculating costs. As an efficiency advocate, I was an early adopter of compact fluorescent light bulbs (a 15 watt compact fluorescent uses only 25% of the energy but should last eight times as long as a 60 watt incandescent bulb). I remember calculating for my students the financial returns I would achieve from the recent acquisition of ten to fifteen of these expensive but high efficiency lights for my home. Not wanting to disillusion them (or perhaps embarrass myself), I failed to mention that I had already broken one of these $30 bulbs in the store parking lot – by peering down into one end of the box to admire my new toy, having forgotten to close the other end. (If I included this extra cost, my calculations already would have showed a negative return – before even installing the first one!)

At home the real fun began. Several fixtures did not fit the elongated bulbs, forcing me to install some bulbs where their annual use rate would be quite low, further upsetting my economic calculations. I also went out and bought some new lampshades, and rebuilt some fixtures (continuing to conveniently overlook these costs in my calculation), but still the sites for installation were limited to about 40% of our house's lighting. I put one as a front porch light, but it quickly stopped working and the store clerk guessed that they could not be used outside – although no one was sure and there was no information on the package. Then my wife started to complain about the unpleasant hue (hospital-like), the apparently weaker intensity (even though the lumens were supposed to be the same) and the extra time to reach full intensity. Soon a few lights were discreetly transferred to the bottom of our kitchen cupboard during my absences. In the next two years, my kids destroyed one by crashing the standing lamp and four more quit of their own accord. The light bulb finally came on (the one inside my head) when at an energy conference one of my co-panelists asked our audience for a show of hands from those who had at least one compact fluorescent light in a drawer at home. Quite nervous, I raised my hand only to learn that my situation was universal.

What did all this mean? How do we calculate the return on energy efficiency investments? What is fair to include and exclude in the definition of cost? Should I ignore or include the broken lamp in the parking lot or my wife's dislike of the efficient bulbs? In the 1990s, the energy efficiency debate reached full intensity (unlike my efficient light bulbs), with the opposing approaches frequently referred to as engineering (or bottom-up) analysis versus economic (or top-down) analysis.

The bottom-up approach – usually associated with engineers, physicists and environmental advocates – focuses on the distinct characteristics of technologies. Equipment, buildings, industrial processes and even urban form and infrastructure are grouped in terms of the energy services they provide. Those that provide the same service (space heating, lighting, mobility) are assumed to be perfect substitutes except for differences in their financial costs (capital and operating). For each energy service, the financial costs in different time periods of the competing options are converted into equivalent annual payments in the same way that a bank amortizes mortgage payments, usually using the lowest possible interest rate (called the social discount rate). Just as Lovins showed in the 1970s, the higher capital costs associated with more efficient options are frequently offset by lower operating costs, meaning that society would make money by pursuing energy efficiency. Since energy efficiency in a fossil fuel-based energy system also reduces GHG emissions, the reduction of this and other pollutants is also considered to be a profitable activity. Recent studies, such as that of M. Brown and co-authors, show little evolution in this approach from the earlier work of Lovins.[17]

Many economists criticize the bottom-up approach for overlooking the fact that alternative equipment, buildings, industrial processes and urban forms are almost never perfect substitutes in the eyes of consumers and businesses. I use the mundane example of efficient light bulbs to illustrate several reasons for this.[18]

First, new technologies usually have a higher chance of premature failure than conventional technologies and therefore pose greater financial risk. New compact fluorescent light bulbs have exhibited higher rates of premature failure than conventional incandescent bulbs, requiring a higher-than-expected financial outlay because of early replacement in some cases. Accelerating the rate at which we force adoption of new, high efficiency technologies increases this expected cost of failure, just as I found out when several of my lamps quit long before the end of their expected ten-year lifespan.

Second, technologies with longer payback periods (relatively high up-front costs) are riskier if the cumulative probability of failure or accident, or undesired economic conditions, increases over time. Because of the higher purchase cost of compact fluorescent light bulbs, the chance of accidental breakage prior to paying back the initial investment is higher than for an incandescent light bulb. Each year there is a certain probability that my kids will knock over a lamp (hopefully declining with age – their age, not the light's) but the cost of replacement is dramatically higher with the compact fluorescent lights.

Third, two technologies may appear to provide the same service to the engineer but not to the consumer, who would pay more for one technology because of some perceived advantage. Many consumers, like my wife (and me, though I never admitted it to her), find compact fluorescent bulbs to be less than perfect substitutes for incandescent bulbs in terms of attractiveness of the bulb, compatibility with fixtures, quality of light and time to reach full intensity, and would pay more to maintain high levels of these non-financial attributes. Cost estimates that look only at financial costs are unlikely to provide a full accounting of the costs of switching to the energy-efficient alternative.

Fourth, not all firms and households face identical financial costs: acquisition installation and operating costs can vary by location and type of facility. This diversity means that a comparison of single-point estimates of financial costs may exaggerate the benefits of market domination by the highest efficiency technology available. The same technical limits to the application of efficient pump systems in the pulp and paper sector that we identified in our research applied equally to my efforts to find high usage lighting needs in my home in order to achieve the operating cost savings that would pay off the higher capital cost of the compact fluorescent lights.

The first two points relate to what economists call *option value*: the expected gain from delaying or avoiding an irreversible, risky investment.[19] The third point results from what economists call *consumers' surplus*: one technology may provide extra value to the consumer compared to a competing technology that nonetheless has the same financial cost.[20] The fourth point is simply a consequence of the diversity of technological opportunities in the real world, and thus the danger of assuming universal applicability and cost-effectiveness of a new technology.

When consumers and businesses are asked, induced or forced to switch away from a technology they would otherwise have chosen, most economists say that the full cost of this switch is the difference in financial costs plus or minus any intangible costs related to option value, consumers' surplus and heterogeneity. This perspective on decision-making explains why efficient technologies are not adopted more quickly and suggests that the full cost of societal adoption of energy efficient technologies is higher than presumed by bottom-up analysts.

My research and personal experience lead me to sympathize with this critique raised by economists. Ironically, with their portrayal of firms and households as one-dimensional financial cost minimizers, bottom-up analysts may be more susceptible than economists to the critique of having a simplistic, "rational-economic-man" view of the world. And the risks associated with energy efficiency investment suggest an alternative view of the $20 bill on the sidewalk. The response of the economist might be to say, "Yes, it looks like there is $20 in nickels and dimes scattered along the sidewalk and in the muck of the ditch. On closer inspection, however, some apparent coins are just pieces of worthless metal, some are difficult to find, some will take effort to clean, and in climbing into the ditch to gather coins I risk falling and injuring myself. I might profit from the effort to recover the $20, but I might not. I might even suffer substantial losses. I need to consider this carefully before deciding how much, if any, of the apparent $20 in coins I should try to recover because the costs of trying could exceed the benefits."

We should recognize that this reassessment of its full cost is not an outright rejection of energy efficiency as a worthwhile pursuit. The discussion thus far has focused on whether energy efficiency investments are as valuable to consumers and firms as a simple bottom-up analysis might indicate – with some evidence suggesting that they are not. But the environmental costs from energy-related pollution have not yet been incorporated in the analysis. Their inclusion might show that even expensive energy efficiency is worthwhile; its cost need only be less than the damages caused by the energy-related pollution that would otherwise occur, and less than alternatives for reducing that pollution – such as fuel-switching or installing end-of-pipe control equipment. If this is the case, then it is in society's interest to pursue energy efficiency for environmental objectives. The important lesson is to conduct a full accounting of our alternatives for achieving a more sustainable energy system so that policy makers can decide how much of each to pursue. In terms of our energy alternatives, we must assess the full impacts of energy efficiency, nuclear, renewables and even clean fossil fuels.

To determine how much energy efficiency is desirable in a holistic framework that includes environmental sustainability as a key consideration, we also need to know how to realize it. In a dictatorship government could strictly regulate all members of society by specifying the exact technologies for providing each energy service. In democratic market economies the issue is more complicated. Somehow, firms and households must be convinced that they should acquire energy efficient technologies. Perhaps they only need to be informed of the possible financial benefits. Perhaps they can be motivated by moral arguments. Perhaps they need additional financial inducements. Perhaps a political majority can be convinced to support more stringent policies that levy financial penalties (like energy taxes or GHG taxes) or even regulations that restrict to some degree their technology choices. Policy makers need help in understanding how firms and households will respond to these various policy options.

Growing awareness of this challenge has motivated me increasingly to focus my research on assisting those in and outside government to understand and estimate the likely response to environmental policy. As someone who builds energy-economy models, I have focused on combining the technological explicitness of bottom-up analysis with the more realistic portrayal of behavior that might be estimated from careful study of firm and household decision making, what we therefore refer to as hybrid modeling.[21] Perhaps because of the profound philosophical schism between bottom-up analysts and economists, very few researchers have taken this path. Instead, the two camps have sustained their battle with little signs of compromise.

Not surprisingly, technology analysts built bottom-up models that told policy makers that dramatic gains in energy efficiency could be easily attained. This encouraged the substantial expenditures on energy efficiency (mostly information and subsidy programs) over more than two decades by government and utilities, notably the $20 billion by the US electricity industry. Bottom-up analysts based this policy advice on the argument that market barriers were hindering the "socially optimal" level of energy efficiency investment. These barriers include being poorly informed about new efficient equipment, having inadequate access to capital for some borrowers who would benefit from efficiency investments, and a split incentive whereby the party who pays for the energy efficiency investment does not receive the benefit of lower energy bills (the landlord selects the appliances but the tenant pays the utility bills). In addition to the risk concerns about supply-side investments like nuclear and fossil fuels, and the bottom-up identification of possible economic benefits from energy efficiency investments, the existence of these so-called barriers provided the rationale for utility and government intervention in energy markets.[22]

Evidence on the effectiveness of energy efficiency programs began to emerge by the mid-1990s, after a decade of experience in numerous jurisdictions.[23] In the initial stages, most energy efficiency programs had focused on providing information: free audits of factories and homes, advertising, demonstration projects, product labeling, and educational programs. A relatively weak success rate convinced many utilities and their regulators to offer financial inducements such as grants and low interest loans. These increased the uptake of efficient technologies but have rarely achieved the promised transformation of the market.

For example, after twenty years compact fluorescent light bulbs have been unable to transform the residential lighting market. Sales have continually grown, but our best guess is that compact fluorescents still represent less than 10% of lighting services. In fact we know very little other than this sales data; I have been unable to find a detailed study of the percentage of lighting service actually provided by compact fluorescents. Such a study cannot rely on just sales data, but must include information on the percentage of these bulbs that have been installed (in light fixtures, not the bottom of drawers), and the hours of operation of installed bulbs relative to installed incandescents. As with many efficient technologies, a great deal of research is needed before we can fully gauge their impact on energy use and their cost-effectiveness.

By the 1990s, utilities shifted their efforts to programs that created incentives for producers rather than consumers, the idea being to provide financial inducements to producers to design and market more efficient equipment and phase-out the sale of least efficient equipment. There has been some success with this approach.

Economists also argue that even in cases where energy efficient technologies achieve substantial market penetration, the resulting lower cost of energy services elicits a *rebound effect* of increased energy service demand and thus greater energy consumption.[24] A recent study of personal vehicle use in the US estimated a 20% rebound, meaning that a 10% improvement in vehicle efficiency would result in a 2% increase in vehicle use, while a study of US manufacturing estimated a rebound of 24%.[25] A survey of rebound estimates for households in the US found ranges for space heating of 10–30%, space cooling of 0–50%, lighting of 5–12%, and automotive transport of 10–30%.[26] While these levels of rebound can lead to substantial downward revisions of energy efficiency gains, the magnitude is difficult to estimate and the values are contentious.[27]

These studies relate the cost of a service to the evolution of its demand. Economists also point to a more general phenomenon, which is that improvements in energy efficiency have always been associated with technological change and economic growth, and that these productivity gains encourage the use of more energy. This is why energy use in industrialized countries has grown along with economic output for the past 250 years. In this aggregate rebound effect, efficiency gains with individual technologies cannot offset the higher energy use caused by the explosion of new energy services and new energy-using technologies.[28]

There are two components to the aggregate rebound effect. First, improving the efficiency of individual devices is to no avail if the devices themselves are in a perpetual cycle of transformation into new devices providing augmented services. I am reminded of the Ancient Greek myth about Sisyphus' wasted efforts rolling a rock uphill each time I picture my colleagues in US and European energy laboratories working late nights to design a 15% efficiency improvement in this year's models of TVs and coffee makers only to find consumers next year adopting wall-size TVs and deluxe cappuccino machines that require three times the energy. (I hope that, unlike Sisyphus, my colleagues are able to take at least a short vacation before turning their attentions to next year's models.) Second, the use of energy is not simply the outcome of the degree of energy efficiency that can be achieved with today's technologies and energy end-uses, but rather the broad array of energy uses that humans invent as long as someone believes (or can be convinced) that the value of the service exceeds its full cost. There is considerable evidence that more efficient devices allow for the invention and commercialization of related devices. This spillover effect is in part responsible in today's industrialized countries for the explosion of new energy-using services, including outdoor patio heaters, spas, extra-large sport utility vehicles, decorative natural gas fireplaces, coffee mug heaters, desk-top water coolers, in-home entertainment systems, indoor and outdoor decorative lighting, and my favorite – the back massage chair – to name just a few. Furthermore, the overall level of services we demand is also affected by efficiency changes. More efficient vehicles may make people more willing to live further from where they work and to achieve lower density living, resulting in a different evolution of urban form and greater commuter distances than would otherwise have occurred.

Substantial improvements in energy efficiency will undoubtedly play a role in the shift to a more sustainable energy system. As this section has shown, the technical potential for energy efficiency improvement is substantial. This is a source of excitement and optimism for technology-focused researchers and environmentalists. However, it is also a source of frustration because the question of how much energy efficiency can be achieved and what that will mean for total energy consumption over time is complicated. The adoption of high efficiency technologies has costs that advocates and technologists usually ignore. Improvements in energy efficiency mean a reduction in the cost of using energy, which in turn can lead to a rebound of yet higher levels of aggregate energy consumption.

This challenge cannot be resolved by establishing an optimal target for energy efficiency. Rather, an awareness of its complexity can help us evaluate how different levels of energy efficiency improvement might compare to different levels of primary energy supply from alternatives like nuclear, renewables and fossil fuels.

4.2 Nuclear

Nuclear energy is the energy released during the fission of very heavy nuclei or the fusion of very light nuclei. Although substantial research into nuclear fusion continues, humans have thus far only produced usable energy from fission in nuclear reactors – in which a nuclear chain reaction is established and sustained in a controlled manner that produces large quantities of heat for the production of electricity in a conventional steam turbine. Electricity from nuclear plants can also produce hydrogen via the electrolysis of water. In this sense, nuclear is a stand-alone primary energy option for producing the two cleanest forms of secondary energy – electricity and hydrogen.

Nuclear technology has been used for over four decades to produce commercial electricity. There are several types of nuclear reactors, depending on the moderator that is used to control the speed of neutrons bombarding the nuclear fuel.[29] Light water reactors use natural water as the moderator but require a nuclear fuel enrichment process to increase the concentration of ^{235}U from its level in natural uranium. This is the most common nuclear power technology – about 80% of global capacity – dominating the systems in the US, France, Great Britain, Japan, Germany and Russia (355 units operating in thirty countries). This category includes both pressurized water reactors (PWR) and boiling water reactors (BWR). The remaining 20% of capacity is split between heavy water reactors, gas-cooled reactors and graphite-moderated boiling water reactors. Heavy water reactors use deuterium (heavy water) as the moderator and do not require enrichment of natural uranium. This technology was developed in Canada and has been exported to India, South Korea, Pakistan and Romania (forty-four units). Gas-cooled reactors have been confined to the United Kingdom (thirty units). Graphite-moderated boiling water reactors operate in Russia (thirteen units), the technology at the ill-fated Chernobyl plant in the Ukraine.

Fast breeder reactors are designed to use fast neutrons without a moderator to produce more fissile fuel (uranium dioxides and plutonium) than they consume. While such reactors dramatically increase the output (sixty-fold) from a given uranium resource, they introduce additional complexities for reprocessing spent fuel and recycling recovered plutonium. Experimental plants were developed in the 1980s,

but research and development of this higher cost technology has stagnated due to the growing awareness that global uranium supplies are
more abundant than originally believed.

Fusion reactors are a prospective technology that offers great promise but has been mired in the development stage for many decades. A
colleague recently told me that when he started his career in physics in
the 1960s he was told that commercial application of fusion was only
forty years away, and now when he is retiring after a forty-year career
he still hears experts say that fusion is only forty years away.

Installed nuclear capacity of about 350 GW in 2000 is 15% of
global electricity generation capacity; nuclear's share of electricity
generation, at 2,500 TWh, is a higher percentage of global production,
at 18%, because the world's 442 nuclear plants are used for baseload
(continuous) production rather than to meet fluctuating peak
demands. Industrialized countries account for about 80% of nuclear
capacity, but the role of nuclear varies significantly by country; it
represents about 20% of capacity in the US but has exceeded 80%
at times in France. After a period of rapid growth in the 1970s and
early 1980s, nuclear's market share has declined slightly over the past
fifteen years; few plants are being built (about twenty under construction in 2005) and forecasts assume a declining market share over the
next two decades as some existing plants are phased out and non-
nuclear capacity grows, especially in developing countries. But in a
dramatically growing global energy system, energy must come from
somewhere, so in the current trends projection in chapter 2 I show
nuclear output growing from 2% of total primary energy in 2000 to
6% in 2100. This requires a seven-fold increase in nuclear capacity
from 350 GW to 2,625 GW, meaning the siting, construction and
operation throughout the world of another 2,275 nuclear plants (if
the average size is 1,000 MW) over the next century in addition to the
renewal of all existing plants.

While this substantial expansion of nuclear presents many challenges, limitations of fissile materials is unlikely to be one of these. In
presenting the data on uranium resources and other fissile materials, I
need to explain first the distinction between resource and reserve. (I will
use these concepts again, especially when describing non-renewable
energy resources.) *Resource* is the estimated global natural occurrence of a particular form of matter or energy. Resource estimates are
highly uncertain and usually include deposits that are at much lower

concentration or of much lower quality than the deposits that are currently being exploited. *Reserve* is the subset of the resource that is available for exploitation today because of: relatively precise knowledge of its location and magnitude; technological capability to extract and process deposits at or above a threshold concentration level; and a projected cost of production that is below or not substantially above current market prices. These concepts of resource and reserve are commonly used in the mineral industry, including non-renewable energy resources.

The World Energy Assessment defines uranium reserves as uranium in deposits that are well known and that cost less than $80 per kilogram to recover.* Combining this with a cut-off for defining the total resource as $130 per kg, global uranium reserves are estimated at 1,890 EJ and global resources at 5,410 EJ.[30] If the resource cut-off is increased to $260 per kg, the resource base increases to 7,100 EJ. If uranium can be extracted from seawater, the resource estimate increases a further 700 times. There are also large resources of other fissile materials if needed – for example, thorium is comparable in global tonnage to uranium – but the surplus of uranium has foreclosed their current development after some initial experiments with thorium-fueled plants in the 1960s and 1970s.

Dividing reserves by current consumption produces the reserve: production ratio, an estimate of the endurance of supply if current consumption levels were maintained indefinitely. With a current consumption of uranium at 40 EJ, global reserves are forty-seven years and global resources are 180 (using the $80 and $130 definitions for reserves and resources). The increased output of my current trends projection would exhaust these reserves by the end of the century. However, as the market tightened, and uranium prices rose, the search for uranium resources would intensify, which would lead to upward revisions of the reserve and resource estimates. If uranium estimates do not increase significantly, reserve depletion would presumably drive up uranium prices until fast breeder reactors become economic, effectively extending the life of the uranium resource for thousands of years – even before including the uranium potential from seawater and

---

* The market price in 2004 was about $45/kilogram, but because the cost of uranium is such a small part of the cost of nuclear-generated electricity, a price of $80 is a reasonable threshold for establishing the reserves estimate.

the world's thorium resources. Resource scarcity does not appear to be a major constraint for nuclear power.

However, the industry faces other significant challenges.[31]

- The costs and investor risks of nuclear power have been higher than originally anticipated.
- Governments and the public are concerned that global dissemination of nuclear power technologies increases the risks of nuclear weapons proliferation.
- An emergent public and government concern is the potential vulnerability of nuclear plants to terrorist attack.
- There is widespread public concern about risks from the transport, treatment, storage and disposal of radioactive waste, which hinders the siting of nuclear-related facilities and increases costs.

I discuss each of these issues in turn.

The first issue is cost. One of the strongest arguments for nuclear power in the 1970s was that it was already, or would soon become, the cheapest means of generating electricity. It was commonly assumed that the costs of nuclear-generated electricity would continue to decline over the coming decades, while the oil price shocks of that era fostered the view that the cost of fossil fuel-generated electricity would continue to rise.

Several unanticipated developments in the 1980s shattered this view, especially with respect to the cost and investor risk of nuclear power. First, concerns about reactor safety and local resistance to the siting of nuclear plants – especially in the US – caused substantial increases in regulatory and security-related costs for nuclear plants. Second, some plants experienced unanticipated operational problems and premature malfunction of equipment and structures that led to substantial mid-life corrective investments and, in hindsight, higher capital and operating costs. This was especially a problem in the US, which lacked the technology standardization of countries such as Germany and France. Third, economies-of-scale have not materialized to the degree expected, and have certainly not surpassed the gains achieved by competing electricity sources, namely conventional coal plants, natural gas-fueled combined cycle gas turbines and some renewables such as wind power. Fourth, the economic downturn of the early 1980s revealed the substantial risk exposure to investors caused by the long period required for permitting and then constructing a nuclear plant under conditions of uncertain electricity demand. Many nuclear plants in the US were still under construction as demand turned down, leading to delays and sometimes a halt in construction, with the inevitable defaults on bond payments and dramatic investor losses. In Washington State, for example, the Washington Public Power Supply System (WPPSS) completed only one of its five intended nuclear power plants, with others halted in mid-stream, ultimately defaulting on $2.25 billion in bonds – the largest municipal bond default in US history. Pundits claim that WPPSS was doomed from the start, given that its acronym is pronounced, "whoops."

Financial risk may be especially important in future. Nuclear power developed at a time when the electricity industry was still dominated by large monopolies, state-owned in most countries. These monopolies tended to be less concerned with financial risk than might a private generating company in a competitive market. Even if the monopoly made a bad investment, its customers were captive – legally and physically prevented from migrating to lower cost producers. State-owned monopolies enjoyed the additional cushion of being able to lower their returns to government and even ask for subsidies if necessary. Indeed, in the case of nuclear power it is extremely difficult to determine the precise level of subsidy provided to the industry – whether publicly or privately owned – given the substantial government support for research and development, the implicit reliance on the state for insurance in the case of extreme accidents, and state absorption of various ancillary costs such as waste recycling and storage.*

Since the early 1990s, the industry has evolved, especially in industrialized countries, toward a model in which independent power producers play a dominant role in new capacity investment. While the California electricity restructuring fiasco of 2000 may slow the movement toward competitive electricity markets, it is unlikely to cause a return to the large monopoly model in generation.[†] Independent

---

* In the US, the Price-Anderson Act caps the liability of privately-owned nuclear plants in case of accidents, which has been estimated as a 0.5 ¢/kWh subsidy. D. Kammen and S. Pacca, "Assessing the Costs of Electricity," *Annual Review of Environment and Resources* 29 (2004): 301–344.

[†] The California electricity reform shifted virtually all of its wholesale supply provision and wholesale price determination to the short-term spot market, while retaining retail price controls, creating a serious potential for financial imbalances if wholesale prices were to increase dramatically. This occurred in 2000–2001 as the newly designed wholesale bidding procedure was unable to deal effectively with a combination of unscheduled plant outages and market manipulation.

power producers enjoy everywhere a growing market share and, as one would expect, these producers are much more sensitive to the financial risks of nuclear power relative to its competitors. Why pursue an investment in nuclear power – with its long lead time and high uncertainty of siting approval, construction cost, operating cost and demand forecasting – when you can build a small natural gas plant or a small wind farm which could begin operation in two or three years? Not one jurisdiction that has allowed a substantial role for independent power producers is today considering a serious proposal to construct a new nuclear power plant, and there is little likelihood of a reversal of this situation in the near term.[32]

Given the hidden subsidies at various levels, it is difficult to find complete agreement on the current cost of nuclear electricity, or on the likely cost of generation from a new nuclear plant. The estimated full cycle (capital and operating) costs of generating electricity from current nuclear power plants ranges from a low of 4–5 ¢/kWh ($US 2000) in France to a high of over 8 ¢/kWh in some US plants. Some of these high cost cases relate to the recovery of unforeseen capital expenditures caused by extended regulatory processes and additional safety concerns. The fuel cost of nuclear power is everywhere low, usually less than 0.5 ¢/kWh.[33] Total operating costs, however, tend to be substantially higher, at 1.4 ¢/kWh, because of the personnel requirements for full compliance with safety regulations (staff of 800–1,000 for a typical 1,000 MW plant). The estimated capital costs of new nuclear power plants range from $1,700 to $3,100 per kilowatt, a variation caused by differences between countries in terms of technology, regulatory requirements, and the cost of capital for government monopolies versus private investors in a competitive market.[34]

Several agencies and independent researchers rank nuclear as slightly higher cost relative to its major competitors.[35] But the ranking is sensitive to a few key assumptions. Mass production of standard-design nuclear plants could significantly reduce capital costs. Fossil fuel prices could continue their recent increases to the point where nuclear's lower operating costs offset its higher capital costs relative to

A frantic eight-month period of chronic supply shortfall and skyrocketing wholesale prices resulted in a utility financial crisis and involuntary power curtailments. The California government suspended the market reform and has reintroduced some elements of the monopoly electricity model. See J. Sweeney, *The California Electricity Crisis* (Stanford, Calif.: Hoover Institution Press, 2002).

coal or natural gas generation. Charges on greenhouse gas emissions could also raise the costs of electricity generated from fossil fuels. With a particular set of assumptions, the Nuclear Energy Agency claims that the costs of electricity from nuclear and conventional coal plants are both in the range of 3–6 ¢/kWh.[36]

One way to compare options is to assess a monetary value on the estimated environmental and social costs of nuclear and its competitors.[37] Depending on the assessment of environmental and social costs, this can result in different rankings. According to some research, nuclear ends up much worse off when all external costs are incorporated.[38]

The second of the four major challenges facing nuclear power is that the global dissemination of this technology increases the risk of nuclear weapons proliferation. If there is no breakthrough with fusion technologies, the fission-based nuclear industry must either find ways of extracting uranium from seawater or perhaps using thorium, or it may have to switch at some point during this century to fast breeder reactors.[39] The seven-fold increase in global nuclear capacity (from 350 GW to 2,625 GW) of my current trends scenario in chapter 2 should encounter rising uranium fuel costs that would rekindle interest in breeder technologies. If this occurs, each 1,000 MW fast breeder reactor would generate annually in its spent fuel about 10,000 kilograms of plutonium for reprocessing into new fuel.[40] When one considers that only 10 kilograms of plutonium can produce a nuclear weapon, it will be extremely difficult to prevent at least some plutonium from being diverted to that end, even given the limited share of the global energy system for nuclear – 90 EJ out of a primary energy total of 1,390 EJ in the year 2100.

There would need to be about five times this number of plants were nuclear to become the dominant energy source of the future, meeting much of the world's production of electricity and some of its hydrogen. Indeed, if nuclear plants last thirty-three years on average, my current trends scenario requires the completion of a nuclear plant every week over the next century, or five per week in the case where nuclear comes to dominate the world's primary energy supply.

Nuclear researchers are pursuing various avenues to reduce the risk that expanded nuclear power will proliferate nuclear weapons. One approach is to design fast breeder reactors so that the plutonium is never fully separated from the fission byproducts. This might reduce the chance of plutonium diversion to nuclear weapons, although it would still be difficult to prevent a government from doing this once it had the expertise and will. Another suggestion is to design large-scale, internationalized energy parks which contain all sensitive facilities and which are controlled by an international agency. Finally, if nuclear fusion technologies are ever developed to a commercial level, they offer significant advantages over fission technologies with respect to weapons proliferation and safety. While all of these proposals must be seriously considered, they nonetheless confront the general concern that widespread use of nuclear power increases the technical capability for any country to develop nuclear weapons, and this could include a country harboring grievances against a neighbor.

The third major challenge facing nuclear power – the threat of terrorist attack – gained notoriety following the terrorist destruction of New York's World Trade Center in 2001. While nuclear experts argue that nuclear plants are built to withstand extreme events like earthquakes and plane crashes, there is nonetheless a growing concern that inventive terrorists could find a way to severely damage a plant – perhaps causing widespread damage to people and the environment as occurred with the Chernobyl accident. The incentive would be especially strong if nuclear power were the dominant source of energy; such an attack would symbolize the vulnerability of an entire economy and could panic consumers and investors. In the eyes of many people, large, centralized power production units are inherently more vulnerable to terrorism than are small, decentralized units. This may not necessarily be true, but its perception is likely to remain a challenge for nuclear power as long as there is a concern about terrorist threats.

The fourth major challenge facing nuclear power is the widespread public concern about the risks of radiation exposure from operational accidents and leaks at nuclear plants or mishaps during the transport, treatment, storage and disposal of radioactive waste. A great frustration for nuclear advocates is the persistent unwillingness of the public in many countries to accept the industry's low estimates of risk from accidents. This controversy requires understanding of both the nature of radioactive risk and the calculation of that risk.

The fission chain reaction of a nuclear reactor produces radioactive byproducts (such as alpha, beta and gamma radiation) that can damage humans and the environment by altering the atoms and molecules of which they are constituted. While life on earth is always subject to flows of natural radiation, accidental releases of radiation from the nuclear industry could far exceed these levels. In humans, unnaturally high doses of radiation can quickly cause blood changes and skin damage, and eventually lead to physiological harms such as eye cataracts, leukemia, other cancers and genetic defects. The health and reproductive functions of other living things can similarly be disrupted by high radiation doses. The risk of radiation exposure means that the operation of nuclear reactors and the handling of their spent fuel and retired equipment must occur under carefully controlled conditions in secure containment structures. Risks from the operation of nuclear plants are certainly a concern, but the destination of spent fuel is equally problematic because this material must be stored for thousands of years before its radioactivity has declined to safe levels. While no country has come to complete agreement on the method for long-term storage of spent reactor fuel, the US is leading the way in pursuing a permanent storage facility at Yucca Mountain in Nevada.

According to the nuclear industry, many popular images of nuclear accidents do not reflect what type of calamity might actually befall a nuclear plant. Conventional plants in industrialized countries have been designed so that the most serious possible internally caused accident is a failure of both the primary and back-up cooling systems leading to a build-up of heat that melts or warps some of the structural elements and fuel core. Only in exceptional circumstances could this lead to significant radioactive releases into the atmosphere or water. The Three Mile Island accident in the US is an example of a substantial release, while smaller releases do sometimes occur, recent instances taking place in Japan.[41]

At Chernobyl, the nuclear reactor had an inherently unstable design, meaning that its risks were not reflective of other types of nuclear plants outside of Russia. Its moderator was graphite, but its water was used both as a coolant and as the steam source for heat transfer to the generating units. The infamous disaster of 1985 occurred when the coolant flow was reduced during a test, which caused greater reactivity. Rising temperatures in the core also caused the water to boil, a negative feedback that led to further temperature increase, further loss of water, and eventually the explosion. Unlike conventional plants outside of the Soviet Union at the time, the reactor also lacked a full containment vessel surrounding the reactor core.

Ideally, the nuclear industry would pose no risks to humans and the environment, but this is unrealistic and unfair when comparing it to other primary energy forms such as fossil fuels and renewables; each of these causes ongoing impacts and poses risks. The critical issue is to assess the extent of nuclear power's risks, a difficult calculation to agree on. The nuclear industry has a long experience in calculating the probability of accidents that might cause unnaturally high releases of radiation and the impact of those releases. This type of exercise is referred to as risk analysis.

Risk is defined by experts as an outcome (accident causing illness, death, environmental damage) multiplied by its probability of occurrence. Thus, if 1,000 nuclear plants operating over 100 years had a probability of having one accident causing 1 death during that time, the risk of human mortality would be 1/1000 × 1/100, or .00001 deaths per year of plant operation. According to the nuclear industry, the probability of accidental radiation releases is extremely low, and so too is the probability of human illness and death. One famous early assessment of nuclear plant risk suggested that the likelihood of an average citizen being killed by a reactor accident is comparable to being hit by a falling meteorite.[42] Historical evidence that has accumulated from decades of operating the many plants throughout the world supports the argument that the risk of serious accident is small, even when including the estimated impacts of the accidents at Three Mile Island and Chernobyl. Once the safety improvements that have been implemented since these accidents are incorporated in the analysis, the probability of significant damage to a nuclear reactor's core is estimated at less than .0001 per reactor per year of operation and the probability of significant radioactive releases is .00001.[43]

Much to the chagrin of the nuclear industry, the many technical studies demonstrating the low human and ecological risk from nuclear power have not allayed fears of the technology, even among some highly educated members of the public. Researchers have come up with various hypotheses to explain this. One argument is that people will, in certain circumstances, put a great deal of weight on the outcome rather than the outcome multiplied by its probability of occurrence. A potentially horrendous outcome – that evokes strong feelings of dread – will weigh heavily in people's minds even if it has a low probability of occurrence.[44] Unfortunately for nuclear power, the image of accidental radioactive releases induces dread through its association with horrible, unpredictable outcomes like cancers and birth deformities. The association of nuclear power with nuclear bombs does not help. Another argument is that people are less willing to accept risks that are outside their control, or outside the control of someone they trust.[45] They readily accept the risks of severe vehicle accidents, but the vehicles they travel in are normally under the control of themselves or someone they know well. They more willingly accept risks like radiation exposure from x-rays if counseled to by their doctors, again someone they know who belongs to a profession that cultivates an image of trustworthiness.

These factors help to explain the persistent mistrust of nuclear power even by those well informed of the extremely low probabilities of significant accidents. They also explain why it is increasingly difficult in democratic societies to site nuclear reactors, fuel reprocessing plants and waste storage facilities. Most people do not want to live next to nuclear facilities, and this is a major hurdle facing any effort to dramatically expand the role of nuclear in the global energy system.

This completes my review of the four major challenges facing the nuclear industry. If recent experience is a guide, these challenges are substantial. Yet nuclear advocates believe that the industry still can and should become the pre-eminent primary energy source for fueling a sustainable energy system. Nuclear power can last indefinitely depending on the technology, does not have the emissions problems of fossil fuels, and is making progress in addressing these four challenges. New designs should reduce capital and operating costs. There is hope that new modular nuclear plants will pose less financial risk and eventually rekindle the interest of private investors. The industry continues to explore technologies, processes and institutions that better safeguard against the diversion of nuclear energy to military ends. Further advances in this direction, and selected experiences, may ultimately reassure the public and political leaders that this risk has been reduced to an acceptable level. Concerns about terrorism may subside depending on international developments. If nuclear plants are not targeted – or even unsuccessfully targeted – this concern may too abate with time. Finally, public perceptions of the risks of nuclear power may change. Already, concern about the contribution of fossil fuels to climate change has changed the views of some toward nuclear power – as witnessed by the decision of Finland in 2003 to permit construction of a new nuclear plant.

4.3 Renewables

Except for the last 250 years, human civilization has been based on the renewable flows of energy through the earth's biosphere, and even today more than half of the planet's inhabitants still depend on biomass for their domestic cooking and heating needs. But the dramatic increase in energy use associated with industrialization, and the dominant role of fossil fuels within the energy mix of industrialized economies, has reduced the global contribution of renewables to about 14% of total primary energy in 2000 – 61 EJ out of a total of 429 EJ.[*] Although this percentage is relatively small, renewable energy use is nonetheless at its highest historic level.

When measured in crude physical terms, the earth's renewable energy resources far exceed our current and projected needs for primary energy. Solar power plants covering just 1% of the earth's deserts would meet total current electricity demand.[46] Thus, as a continuous energy flow that matches the 7-billion-year life expectancy of the sun, renewables satisfy the endurance dimension of my definition of energy system sustainability.

Renewables do not, however, perfectly match human needs in that these sources of energy are often intermittent, of relatively low energy density, and inconveniently located. Overcoming these three challenges can engender significant land use conflicts, environmental impacts, and high costs. By storing energy in the form of water, large hydropower reservoirs address the problem of intermittent water flows, but alienate valley bottoms from other valuable human or ecological uses. The low energy density of biomass and solar energy means that large areas of land may be required along with complex energy concentration processes and structures to meet the demands for high quality energy in the information age. The best tidal power and wind power sites are usually located far from demand centers, requiring land alienation and substantial capital outlays for energy transmission. The intermittency and hence unreliability of solar and wind energy mean that these two sources must be matched with large-scale

---

[*] This is based on a mix of data sources and on my conversion of nuclear electricity according to its energy value. The International Energy Agency estimates renewables at 16%. International Energy Agency, *Renewables in Global Energy Supply: an IEA Factsheet* (Paris: International Energy Agency, 2002).

energy storage, such as compressed air, or back-up capacity if they are to play more than a marginal role in the supply of energy. There are substantial technological, physical, social and economic challenges to renewables development at a large scale.

On the plus side, we have until recently ignored renewables in terms of our research and development efforts. Dramatic gains are now possible as we turn our attention to developing a slate of new technologies aimed at overcoming the intermittency, low energy density and location challenges.[47] In this section, I describe the major sources of renewable energy and present the prospects for technological advances and cost improvements that might one day allow renewables to dominate the growing global energy system, without requiring a dramatic reduction of the services provided by the economy. Table 4.1 provides an assessment of the renewable resource potential based largely on the World Energy Assessment and presents some of the detailed renewables assumptions behind the aggregate numbers in my current trends projection of chapter 2. It also shows the share of electricity generation by those renewables that also produce other forms of secondary energy like heat and liquid fuels.

Hydropower

Hydropower is the combined result of solar energy and gravitational force. Humans first learned 2,000 years ago how to harness hydropower by redirecting flowing water through waterwheels and other devices. By the Middle Ages in several parts of the world, controlled water flows were used to drive various kinds of grinders and hammers. Watermills for grinding grain were common in pre-industrial societies and are still used in some parts of the world. In the centuries-old hammermill I once visited in Denmark, a waterwheel turned a camshaft that in turn drove a large hammer up and down for shaping metal into guns and farm implements. For the past 100 years, however, industrialized societies have mostly used hydropower's mechanical energy to spin electricity-generating turbines. Hydroelectricity has spread worldwide and today accounts for one fifth of global electricity production. This energy form is associated with large and small dams that store water at higher elevations to increase the power potential of a site and enable a more even production of electricity through the seasonal variations in precipitation.

Table 4.1. Renewables resource estimates and current trends projection

Renewable Source (all values in EJ)	Estimates of Annual Potential Contribution		BAU Forecast		
	extreme resource	potentially economic	2000	2050	2100
Primary Energy					
Hydropower	150	29–50	9	20	30
Biomass	2,900	100–300	52	120	210
traditional biomass			(45	70	90)
modern biomass			(7	50	120)
Wind	6,000	250–600	0.11	20	90
Solar	3,900,000	1,500–50,000	0.16	8	30
Geothermal	600,000	500–5,000	0.3	2	20
Tidal/wave/current	145	1.5	0.002	0.01	0.1
Total	**4,500,000**	**2,300–56,000**	**62**	**170**	**380**
Electricity Generation					
Biomass	–	–	1	20	70
Solar	–	–	0.005	2	20
Geothermal	–	–	0.17	1	15

Like nuclear power, hydropower is conventionally viewed as an electricity generation option. This view is too narrow, for just like nuclear power the resulting electricity could one day in turn be used to produce hydrogen via the electrolysis of water.

Energy analysts distinguish between large hydropower – dams and reservoirs that significantly disrupt water flow regimes – and small hydropower – ranging from modest water retention facilities to benign, run-of-the-river systems. These latter may divert some water-flow to adjacent turbines but may simply involve the suspension of turbines in a river without any water diversion. Ten MW is sometimes used as a crude threshold to distinguish large from small facilities. In 2000, world hydroelectricity production was about 2,600 TWh (9 EJ), of which only about 4% was from small hydro plants (table 4.1). The total installed capacity of plants greater than 10 MW was close to 700 GW, while that of smaller plants was around 20 GW. The Three Gorges Project in China is the world's largest single hydropower complex with a projected capacity close to 20 GW. Although its installed capacity is almost double that of nuclear, hydropower produces just slightly more electricity because the average global capacity utilization for hydropower is only 40–45% depending on the year. This lower use rate reflects the tendency to size hydropower facilities in order to exploit periods of high water flow even though this results in underutilization of capacity during drier months and years of lower than average precipitation.

Because hydropower is a product of precipitation and terrain, its resource potential is unevenly distributed; many countries have little or no hydropower resources while a few are highly dependent on it. Hydropower dominates electricity production in New Zealand, Norway, Brazil, Switzerland and Canada, and plays a significant role in Russia, China, the US and several smaller countries. Large hydropower projects require substantial capital and long lead times before completion, and this has favored development in industrialized countries where about 65% of the economically feasible potential has been exploited. Much less of the economic potential in developing countries has been exploited, as low as 18% in regions such as Sub-Saharan Africa, centrally planned Asia and India.

If financial resources were available, developing countries especially could expand greatly their use of hydropower. In industrialized countries, in contrast, there is considerable public resistance to further large hydropower development, primarily because of the environmental impacts. In my current trends forecast of chapter 2, I show global hydropower output increasing to over three times its current level by 2100; current capacity would increase from about 700 GW to 2,300 GW and output from 9 to 30 EJ. The World Energy Assessment provides estimates for hydropower resource potential.[48] The total resource potential is about 150 EJ. The current economic potential (4–6 ¢/kWh in 2000 $US) is estimated at about 30 EJ. An additional 20 EJ are technically feasible, and may be economic, but their political acceptability depends on overcoming significant land-use conflicts.

The impacts of large hydro projects are well known, and have been the target of environmental concerns in industrialized countries for some time, concerns that are beginning to spread to developing countries. On the benefit side, large hydropower projects produce few emissions (there are, however, methane emissions for some decades after the flooding of a reservoir as dead plants decompose) and can conceivably last indefinitely if siltation is prevented or mechanically removed, and if the dam and other structures are refurbished as needed. Once the capital investment has been made, the operating costs are extremely low. Most hydropower facilities provide one or more additional benefits such as irrigation, recreation opportunities, flood control and open navigation through segments of a river system.

However, large hydropower projects are not environmentally benign. They alter stream flows (affecting chemical composition, temperature and silt loading of downstream water), impede or prevent the passage of migratory fish and mammals, and flood land that often has high value for agriculture, forestry, biodiversity, human settlements, communication networks and transportation corridors. The Three Gorges Project in China, which caused the displacement of over a million people, is only the most recent example of the many disruptive hydropower megaprojects. Some would argue that large hydro developments on silt-laden rivers should not be considered a renewable form of energy since the reservoir will eventually become clogged with silt. Large dams present potentially catastrophic risks of structural failure, whether caused by poor engineering design or by natural events such as earthquakes or landslides. Hydropower megaprojects pose economic risks, like nuclear facilities, because of the long lead time between the decision to build and the completion date, and some of the best sites are in isolated locations that are costly to connect to the grid. Most of China's best sites, for example, are far to the west of its densely populated areas, most of North America's are in the far north, and most of Russia's are in Siberia. Another risk for hydropower is if natural or human-induced changes in climate modify the timing or quantity of water flows.

While the technologies of hydropower electricity (dams, spillways, penstocks, turbines) are relatively mature, some technological advances in micro-turbine costs and environmentally sensitive design are improving the economic and political prospects for small-scale hydropower. This has fostered an expansion of micro-hydro in both industrialized and developing countries in recent years. However, even small hydropower developments, although not nearly as disruptive on an individual basis, can have significant cumulative and site-specific effects. It is not obvious, from an environmental and social perspective, that one hydropower project of 1,000 MW will be more harmful than 1,000 projects of 1 MW each – and those 1,000 small projects may be much less valuable if they are unable to store water and thus match output to the peak periods of electricity demand. In a comprehensive evaluation of small hydropower potential in the 1980s, the Northwest Power Planning Council in the US found that many of its best small hydro sites posed serious conflicts with competing land uses such as fishing, recreation, ecological preservation and ancestral sites of aboriginal peoples.[49]

The prospects for large hydropower are perhaps even more uncertain. This technology may still see significant development over the next century, but this will depend on the ability and willingness of project proponents to modify designs in ways that better mitigate the environmental and social impacts and risks listed above. Some recent developments in design and operation are encouraging. Some ways of reducing the impact of large hydropower include providing water ladders to enable fish to climb upstream of dams, constraining the timing and variation of water flows in order to maximize other values (water supply, recreation, wildlife), even at the expense of electricity benefits, and better management of reservoirs for water quality and biodiversity.[50]

Biomass

Biomass energy is a general term for all organic material that can be converted into energy, including residues from agriculture and forestry, organic material in municipal solid waste, and fuels from crops dedicated to energy production. In pre-industrial times, biomass provided energy for cooking, space heating, and lighting, while human and animal power (with some help from wind and water power) provided the mechanical energy for transportation, plowing, construction, drawing water and grinding grain. Much of this energy system configuration still exists today in the rural areas of developing countries.

The total use of biomass energy is inherently difficult to measure, especially because much of it does not involve commercial transactions. Globally, the primary energy use of biomass in 2000 was about 52 EJ. Of this total, roughly 45 EJ was consumed as traditional household fuel in developing countries, with some of this converted to charcoal for urban and industrial uses. This is why biomass is only a small percentage of primary energy in industrialized countries but is 42% of primary energy in India and up to 90% in the world's poorest countries in Africa and Asia. Modern uses of biomass comprise the remaining 7 EJ, mostly in the production of electricity and steam in industrialized and developing countries, such as in the pulp and paper industry, but also in some production of biofuels, as with ethanol in Brazil.

Combustion to produce thermal energy is the traditional way of using biomass, which is what humans have been doing since they discovered fire. The positive benefits of wood combustion to human well-being and longevity were undoubtedly enormous, but there were also costs. Archeologists tell us that the cave walls of our ancestors were coated with residues from the thick smoke that would have filled the air and clogged the lungs of cave dwellers. Smoke-filled interior spaces are still the norm for the one third of humanity that continues to rely on wood as its primary energy source, and the particulates and noxious fumes from cooking with open fires and inefficient and poorly ventilated stoves fueled by wood and crop residues have substantial health impacts, as I described in chapter 2. The transition in developing regions of the world from traditional technologies using biomass to more efficient technologies using fossil fuels (propane, butane) results in a dramatic improvement in indoor air quality and increased life expectancy.

Advanced technologies are now under development to convert biomass into various forms of secondary energy including electricity, gaseous and liquid biofuels, and even hydrogen. Figure 4.3, from the World Energy Assessment, shows the several options I describe below.

- Biomass combustion can produce heat for industry (combustion of wood residues to dry lumber and for thermochemical digestion of wood fiber in pulp and paper production), for agriculture (combustion of crop residues to dry grain and to produce sugar), and for domestic services (combustion of biomass for cooking and space heating). While this latter use of biomass is mostly limited to developing countries, some rural households in industrialized countries, notably Scandinavia, have automated biomass home heating systems that include emission control equipment. The lower energy density of biomass requires a greater throughput of material for a given level of heating, but the economics are especially favorable where there is an inexpensive biomass surplus. Biomass combustion can also heat water in a boiler for the generation of electricity in a steam turbine. Sources for combustion include wood residues in the pulp and paper industry, agricultural

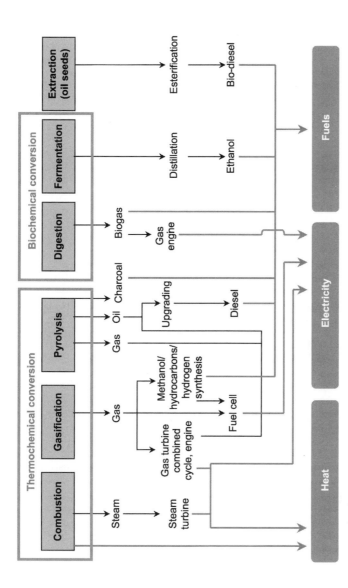

Figure 4.3. Options for biomass energy conversion.

Figure 7.1 in W. Turkenburg (ed.), "Advanced Energy Supply Technologies," chapter 7 in J. Goldemberg (ed.), *World Energy Assessment: Energy and the Challenge of Sustainability* (New York: United Nations Development Programme, 2000), 223.

residues (such as bagasse from sugar cane production), and peat in
Ireland. The process sometimes involves co-combustion with
natural gas, oil or coal in order to overcome the high moisture
content, low energy density, and variable supply of biomass
sources.

- Developments in thermal gasification processes offer the promise of
  converting biomass into fuel gases with various properties for
  combustion in gas turbines to generate electricity (integrated
  gasification combined cycle – IGCC) and perhaps eventually to
  produce methanol and hydrogen (using the Fischer-Tropsch
  synthesis gas conversion process I describe in chapter 6). The
  production of electricity or hydrogen could also be linked to carbon
  capture and storage technologies (which I also describe in chapter
  6). However, thermal gasification still has several challenges ahead
  of it, as tar and other residues need to be better controlled, and a
  steady flow of biomass is required if IGCC plants are to operate
  effectively – this is less of a challenge for conventional biomass
  steam combustion plants.

- Pyrolysis is a process that converts biomass to hydrocarbon gases,
  liquids (bio-oil) or solids (charcoal) by subjecting biomass to
  high temperatures in an oxygen-starved environment. While
  pyrolysis production of charcoal has been widely applied for a
  long time, and still is in developing countries, the production
  of liquid fuels is still in a pre-commercial phase as researchers
  try to overcome the corrosive and acidic properties of prototype
  bio-oils.

- In anaerobic digestion, bacteria break down organic matter to
  produce biogas (essentially methane) that can fuel a gas turbine. In
  rural areas the biomass source is crop residues or manure, as
  in China and India, while in urban areas the methane can be
  collected from landfills of municipal solid waste, if the waste has
  sufficient biomass content. This practice of anaerobic digestion has
  been applied for a long time in agricultural areas.

- In fermentation, bacteria and yeasts break down the sugars in plant
  material to produce ethanol (an alcohol), which can be concentrated via distillation for use as a motor fuel alone or blended with
  gasoline (called gasohol). While maize and grains are still
  somewhat disappointing in terms of the energy input to output
  ratio, the sugar cane used in Brazil is more productive and that
  country has an ambitious program in which gasoline for vehicle use
  contains a minimum of 23% ethanol.

- Bio-oil can be extracted from plants in processes that crush the seeds and remove solids. Thus, rapeseed oil produces rape methyl esters that are used as a diesel replacement (biodiesel) by some bus and taxi fleets in Europe and increasingly in personal vehicles.

These multiple options for converting biomass into secondary energy demonstrate how this primary energy source can provide the electricity, hydrogen and other gaseous and liquid fuels that could dominate an enduring energy system with low impacts and risks. In my current trends projection of chapter 2, total energy from biomass is projected to increase from today's 52 EJ to 210, a four-fold expansion (table 4.1). This increase is assumed to result from a much greater use of biomass residues from agriculture and forestry in developing countries, but also from the dedication of marginal forest and agricultural land throughout the world to biomass energy production. In aggregate, biomass' share of global primary energy increases slightly, from 12–15%. Traditional use of biomass, mostly for cooking in poor rural households in developing countries doubles from 45 EJ to 90 EJ – presumably much of this in improved stoves that have a much higher efficiency (currently below 15% on average) and much lower indoor and outdoor emissions. The latest design of solid fuel stoves for wood or coal can reduce indoor air emissions by more than 90% compared to traditional stoves. Modern uses of biomass increase seventeen-fold, from 7 to 120 EJ. More than half of this energy, 70 EJ, fuels electricity generation while the remaining 50 EJ is converted to ethanol and biodiesel for transport fuels or gasified for domestic and industrial consumption, depending on technological developments.

The World Energy Assessment provides estimates of the earth's biomass resource potential.[51] The annual global biomass production of 4,500 EJ (from 220 billion oven-dry tonnes of biomatter) generates a theoretically harvestable potential of 2,900 EJ. Estimating how much of this biomass could be sustainably dedicated to energy production depends on highly uncertain assumptions about the relative importance of competing uses for land and water supplies, possible degradation of soil and water, and the environmental impacts of biomass-to-energy conversion processes.

The first challenge involves competing uses for land and water. The substantial growth in the world's population over the next century will require significant increases in land dedicated to agriculture or in the

productivity of existing lands. Allocating productive land to biomass
energy could intensify land-use conflicts. Since water is also a constraining resource for agriculture, any of its allocation to biomass
energy will face similar challenges. If, however, the land used for
biomass energy would otherwise have remained forested, this relieves
the trade-off with food production, although monoculture forest plantations extinguish the biodiversity benefits of indigenous forests. Some
of the sugar plantations whose economic prospects are boosted by the
co-production of ethanol in Brazil are in areas that previously had a
vibrant tropical rainforest. Willow plantations in Sweden for electricity production and district heating may reduce that country's indigenous fir and deciduous forests. The most obvious way to avoid these
land-use conflicts is to acquire most biomass energy from the existing
flows of agriculture and forestry residues, retaining indigenous tree
species as much as possible. This may reduce significantly, however,
the amount of biomass available for energy production, hence the
trade-off between biomass energy output and other objectives such
as biodiversity and food production.

The second challenge involves the degradation of soil and water that
can occur from converting indigenous forests and grasslands to biomass energy production, the same problem that is associated with
agriculture (and in some cases forestry) as usually practiced. The
abundant use of fertilizers can cause nitrification of groundwater
and phosphate saturation of soils, the latter causing eutrophication
of lakes fed by runoff water. Heavy use of pesticides and herbicides
can impact water quality, with known and suspected risks to ecosystems and humans. Improper harvesting techniques can degrade soil
quality through increased erosion and nutrient leaching. Brazil's ethanol program, which expanded substantially in the 1980s, is associated,
according to some researchers, with decreased food production and
harmful effluents.[52] The means of addressing these problems are well
known, as witnessed by efforts in recent decades to significantly
improve the sustainability prospects of agriculture and forestry. These
same efforts must be applied to biomass energy, and would involve
crop selection and management practices that reduce the need for
these external inputs, on the one hand, and the replacement of these
inputs with more environmentally benign products on the other. This
would include a greater use of organic fertilizers, herbicides and
pesticides, retention of a minimum amount of crop residues for soil

replenishment, crop rotation and species selection to increase nitrogen fixing and nutrient uptake, and fallow periods for soil recovery.

The third challenge involves the air and water impacts from the processes that convert biomass into various forms of secondary energy, and then the use of that secondary energy. A major benefit of biomass is that its sustainable production creates a closed loop for CO_2 exchange between the atmosphere and the ecosphere, meaning that humans acquire energy without net increases in atmospheric concentrations of GHGs. If, eventually, biomass is used primarily for the production of electricity and/or hydrogen, other air emissions from final use are minimal. Otherwise, the combustion of gaseous, liquid and solid fuels produced from biomass causes many of the same emissions as combusting fossil fuels: nitrous oxides, carbon monoxide, particulates and other, potentially harmful organic compounds. The combustion of ethanol in Brazilian vehicles, for example, produces aldehydes, which react in the atmosphere to produce peroxyacetyl nitrate; this compound stunts plant growth and contributes to low-level ozone formation and thus urban smog. Finally, the various processes to produce hydrocarbon fuels from biomass – gasification, pyrolysis, digestion, fermentation, oil extraction – each involve their own complications in terms of ensuring that toxic byproducts do not enter land, water and air.

As these three broad challenges illustrate, the large theoretical potential for energy from biomass must be revised downward, perhaps significantly, once major trade-offs are accounted for. This will have cost repercussions as the value of alternative land uses and land degradation is properly accounted for, and as energy conversion processes are forced to meet environmental sustainability conditions. This explains the much lower estimate for potentially economic energy from biomass cited in the World Energy Assessment of 100–300 EJ.

When fossil fuel prices are low, energy from biomass is only economic in a few circumstances. This could change, however, as fossil fuel prices rise and as the cost of fossil fuel combustion is corrected to account for environmental risks from greenhouse gas emissions. Also, the new technologies for converting biomass into low emission fuels – especially but not exclusively electricity and hydrogen – are in their infancy, and their costs should fall with further efforts at research, development, demonstration and commercialization. While advances in biotechnology are difficult to predict, there is a significant probability that the next century will undergo a dramatic increase in environmentally benign agricultural productivity, freeing up significant tracts of land, at low cost, for biomass energy. In such a scenario, there could be a dramatic increase in the capacity for biomass energy to compete economically with other clean alternatives.

Wind

Wind is the movement of air caused by uneven heating of the earth's surface by solar energy. At a global scale, air that is more rapidly heated in the tropics flows towards the poles, influenced slightly by the earth's rotation. At a continental scale, air over land and sea heats at different rates, causing flows in various directions depending on the season. At a regional scale, the configuration of mountains, valleys, plains and smaller bodies of water can profoundly influence local air movement and speed. In pre-industrial times, humans used the mechanical energy of wind to power sailing ships and grind grain in windmills. Since the industrial revolution, fossil fuels have displaced most uses of wind, although wind is still used to pump water for livestock and agriculture in rural areas, especially in developing countries.

The fossil fuel price shocks of the 1970s and early 1980s sparked an interest in wind electricity turbines, and since the first installations in the 1980s this energy source has grown dramatically (25% annual growth rates in the 1990s) to a global capacity of 14 GW in 2000 and an estimated 40 GW in 2004. The electricity output from the 14 GW of capacity in 2000 was about 30 TWh (0.11 EJ). This low capacity utilization rate of 24% on average reflects wind's intermittency. At 1% of hydropower output, wind's contribution to the global energy system remains negligible. However, my current trends projection (table 4.1) shows wind electricity output increasing dramatically from 0.11 EJ in 2000 to 90 EJ in 2100, meaning an 820-fold increase in wind power output. This implies a 16% average annual rate of growth for the next fifty years, which slows to a 3% rate of growth in the second half of the century. If the average wind turbine size in 2100 is 4 MW (it could be much larger by then), there would be about 3 million wind generators on earth compared to about 45,000 in 2000.

Although various wind generator designs have been tested, horizontal-axis turbines dominate the market today. The turbine is supported high above the ground by a frame structure that can swivel so that the large rotor-blades always face into the wind. In the mid-1980s, average turbine size for new units was 100 kW, but this increased to 1.5 MW by 2000. Some new generators are 2 and 3 MW in size and manufacturers are testing 5 MW units. There is no physical barrier to sizes in the 20 MW range in a decade or so. While some wind turbines are sited in isolation, the norm today is to site many together in a wind farm, which maximizes the exploitation of favorable sites and reduces costs of grid connection, operation and maintenance.

While twenty-nine countries have active wind power programs, Europe has about 65% of global capacity, of which Denmark and Germany account for most, with Spain also becoming important. In some years Denmark meets 15% of its total electricity demand from wind. Other major players are the US with 21% and India with 10% of global capacity in 2000.

Estimation of gross wind power potential starts with an evaluation of wind maps, which class land (and some offshore) areas by quality of wind. The World Energy Assessment provides a theoretical resource estimate of 6,000 EJ. Recent experiences from individual countries – in assessing the percentage of favorable sites that are close to being economical and do not have major land-use conflicts – lead to the assumption that only 4% of land area might be realistically used for siting wind farms. This generates a much lower resource estimate of 250–600 EJ.

Wind power has obvious benefits in that it causes no air or water pollution, its small size and quick installation reduces the risks from market uncertainty, and its rapidly declining cost has been the great success story of renewable energy. Wind power cost has fallen from over 20 ¢/kWh ($US 2000) in 1980 to below 5 ¢/kWh at favorable sites in 2000, and there are prospects for further cost declines, evidence of the dramatic economies-of-learning effects that are possible with extensive diffusion of certain types of technologies. The success of wind has led advocates and skeptics to debate the potential for wind to grow from its role as a modest contributor to become perhaps the dominant electricity source in some regions.

The challenges for wind power are similar to many renewables: it has low energy density (low energy potential per unit of area), some of the best sites are inconveniently located relative to the grid or conflict with alternative land uses, and its output is intermittent (or variable).

While wind generators do not monopolize much land (other uses like ranching or farming can co-exist), they can dominate the viewscape of an area in a way that gives the impression of intensive land-use, becoming for some people an aesthetic affront. Examples are the conflicts over siting wind farms in the Lake District in the UK and offshore from Cape Cod in the US. Wind power may also experience specific conflicts with ecological values. To avoid such conflicts, future wind farms may be located further offshore or in isolated regions, but such sites require costly high-voltage transmission lines.

The intermittent nature of wind has generated a great deal of debate in terms of estimating its full cost; for comparison with the output from conventional nuclear, large hydro and thermal plants, wind cost estimates should include the cost of providing reliable power to meet peak demands. Since demand varies during the day and season, electricity supply technologies need to have "dispatchable capacity" (another term is "effective capacity") to ensure output to meet peak demand. All sides recognize that the capacity of wind generators is only utilized for 20–30% of the time because of the intermittent nature of wind. This is the rate of "capacity utilization." But when it comes to dispatchable capacity, some analysts argue that wind's capacity should be rated at 0%, while others say it may be as high as 30%. Those arguing for 0% note that there is always a chance of having no wind just at the peak time when electricity demand is highest. Those arguing for a positive value such as 30% point out that as the facilities providing wind power grow in number and diversify in location, the probability gets higher that at least some percentage of wind generators will be operating during times of peak demand, achieving a reliability comparable to that of conventional generators (which also have a possibility of failure at peak times). Disputes about this and other assumptions on the costs of intermittent supplies to the electricity grid have led to a vigorous debate about how the cost of wind power will evolve as its share of the electricity system climbs.[53]

Intermittent sources of renewable energy – namely wind, small hydro, solar and waves – will require connection either with stand-by thermal generation facilities (fossil fuel, nuclear or biomass) or with energy storage devices if they are to play a major role in electricity supply. Back-up thermal generation involves high capital costs, but also high costs of ensuring fuel supply during peak times and high costs of coordinating output with both variable renewable supply and variable demand. If conventional fossil fuel generation technologies are used as back-up, the renewable-dominated energy system would also generate some amount of emissions whenever the thermal generation is operating.

Energy storage is the other alternative for renewables. In the case of wind-generated electricity, energy storage involves the conversion of electricity produced during periods of surplus output (high winds when demand is low) into other forms of energy that can be stored, such as gravitational energy (pumping water up into a reservoir for later release), pneumatic energy (compressing air for later release to spin a turbine), kinetic energy (spinning a flywheel that can later be reconnected to a turbine) and chemical energy (producing hydrogen via electrolysis that can later be combusted to generate electricity; storing electricity in a battery).[54] These energy storage devices increase costs because of energy efficiency losses in converting energy back and forth to the storage medium and because of the capital and non-energy operating costs of the devices themselves. The efficiency of spinning flywheels is about 90–95%, compressed air about 75%, batteries about 70–80%, and hydrogen via electrolysis about 40–50%. A certain amount of energy storage is low cost because it exploits favorable geological features such as mountainous terrain for constructing dams to store water and underground geological formations that can store compressed air. But large amounts of storage will soon exhaust these opportunities, requiring more capital-intensive devices that increase costs. While the hope is that with R&D and economies-of-learning, energy storage will not add more than 1–2 ¢/kWh to the price of electricity from wind and other intermittent sources, the premium that storage adds to electricity costs is currently much higher in isolated systems where intermittent renewables are dominant (such as islands that rely heavily on wind or solar power, with back-up usually provided by diesel generators and batteries).

Solar

While solar radiation is the source for biomass, wind and hydropower, humans have also, since ancient times, designed buildings to absorb directly the sun's thermal energy (and in hotter climates to deflect this heat in order to maintain cooler indoor temperatures). These design characteristics are what analysts refer to as passive solar. More recently, humans have developed active solar technologies that capture the sun's thermal radiation and convert it into hot water or steam (to make electricity), and convert its light radiation directly into electricity. In future, electricity from solar energy could be used to produce hydrogen fuels via electrolysis of water.

Passive solar energy is exploited primarily through building and site design. Well-designed building shells in colder climates would ideally minimize heat loss and maximize absorption of solar thermal radiation. In hotter climates, they would deflect solar radiation. In continental climates, with hot summers and cold winters, the building shell should perform optimally according to the season. The ability to absorb or deflect solar thermal radiation is in part determined by site location and site design that exploits microclimate features such as vegetation, solar incidence, wind buffers and relationship to adjacent buildings. With this emphasis on buildings and sites, passive solar is normally analyzed as part of energy efficiency, as I noted in chapter 3 in my discussion of community energy management.

The earth intercepts an enormous amount of solar radiation. After subtracting the solar energy reflected back to space by the atmosphere, about 3,900,000 EJ are potentially available on the earth's surface, which is almost 10,000 times greater than the 429 EJ of the global energy system in 2000. Although solar radiation equates to about 1 kW per square meter, fluctuations due to time of day, season and weather mean that annual averages are more likely to be 100–300 watts per square meter at a given point. The World Energy Assessment incorporates these factors along with crude estimates of land availability to generate regional estimates for solar energy potential.[55] Their estimate ranges widely, from 1,500 EJ to 50,000 EJ, but even the low estimate suggests that available solar radiation alone exceeds my current trends projection for 2100 for the entire human energy system of 1,390 EJ.

As with wind, the fossil fuel price shocks of the 1970s and early 1980s sparked intensive interest in active solar energy systems. Many promising technologies have been developed and tested, but the results have not yet been as rewarding from an economic perspective; only in rare niche markets are solar energy technologies competitive today.

In describing active solar technologies, analysts usually distinguish between solar thermal and solar photovoltaic. Solar thermal technologies are further divided into devices for producing electricity and devices for space and water heating. The most common of these latter devices are flat-plate rooftop collectors that heat domestic and commercial hot water by passing it through a network of pipes exposed to the sun and returning it to a storage tank that usually has a supplementary heater based on conventional fuel or electricity. This well-known technology can be economic in areas that have intensive solar radiation and relatively high prices for alternative water heating fuels; by 1994 there were an estimated 7 million units and the market has continued to grow. A similar collector system can provide supplementary or primary space heating for buildings, but this technology has had less commercial success. With solar thermal production of electricity, a common configuration is comprised of: (1) a collector that captures and concentrates solar radiation, such as an array of parabolic mirrors; (2) a receiver that absorbs the concentrated sunlight and transfers it to a working fluid; (3) a transport and storage system that transports the fluid to the power conversion system; and (4) the power conversion system such as a steam turbine. Another interesting concept is the solar chimney, which funnels air heated by sunlight up a chimney, achieving enough force to turn a turbine. Yet another concept is ocean thermal energy conversion, in which the temperature differential between surface water heated by the sun and cold deep ocean water is exploited to drive a turbine. These and other approaches to solar thermal production of electricity are still at a developmental stage, with little interest in large-scale commercialization at this time.

In photovoltaic (PV) cells, solar radiation (as photons) striking a semi-conductor produces a difference in electrical potential (voltage) and the resulting electricity can be used immediately or stored in a battery. PVs convert solar radiation into electricity with an efficiency of about 10–15%. Since the average power density of solar radiation is about 100–300 watts per square meter, a considerable area would be required to produce the same output of a conventional fossil fuel, nuclear or hydropower plant. One estimate is that an area 750 kilometers by 750 kilometers would be covered with PV cells to meet current global electricity needs.[56] Although PV electricity is still not economically competitive for large-scale electricity production, it has experienced rapid expansion over the past decade because of its niche market advantages; PV systems are ideal for isolated applications requiring relatively small amounts of power, such as off-grid homes and farms, or communication signals. In these isolated applications, PV systems require a battery for storage to compensate for their unreliability as a power source. In the past decade, several countries have launched ambitious rooftop PV programs for grid-connected urban areas, which are sustaining a dramatic growth rate in PV production. At one point, in what appeared to be a game of one-upmanship, the Japanese launched a 10,000 roofs program, which the Germans topped with a 100,000 roofs program, and then the US with a 1 million roofs program. PV manufacturers must dream of a day when the Chinese respond with a 10 or 100 million roofs program.

In my current trends projection, solar electricity (thermal and PV) has difficulty competing with fossil fuels and nuclear given the generation costs for these technologies, as shown in table 4.1; active solar only attains 2 EJ by 2050 and 20 EJ by 2100. Since its output is estimated to be about 0.005 EJ in 2000, this represents a 13% average annual growth rate for the first fifty years (a 400-fold increase) followed by an average 5% growth rate in the second fifty years.* Most of this growth is expected to be in PV systems as opposed to thermal-electric because PV has the better ability to capture niche markets in sunny urban areas of wealthy countries (Japan, US) and in unelectrified, isolated locations in poorer countries where the alternatives for electricity production are costly.

Active solar thermal systems for producing domestic and commercial hot water are also expected to grow significantly, from 0.16 EJ in 2000 to 10 EJ by 2100, a sixty-three-fold increase. The combination of electricity and thermal production from active (as opposed to passive) solar systems would therefore increase in total from 0.16 EJ to 8 EJ in 2050 and 30 EJ in 2100.

Active solar energy technologies have many advantages. Smaller scale thermal-electric systems and PV cells can be located at the point of consumption, which can be ideal for isolated communities in poorer

---

* Estimating PV capacity and output is difficult due to rapid market growth and the technology's diffusion to remote rural areas. The International Energy Agency Photovoltaic Power Systems Programme estimated PV capacity to be 710 MW in 2000 for selected countries (including US, Japan and Germany, the largest markets). Assuming that global capacity was about 900 MW in 2000, generation would be equal to 1.46 TWh (0.005 EJ), based on an 18.5% capacity factor. International Energy Agency, *Photovoltaic Power Systems Programme, Trends in Photovoltaic Applications in selected IEA Countries between 1992 and 2001* (Paris: International Energy Agency, 2002), 6.

countries that face exorbitant costs of grid connection. Poorer countries are often located in sunny, equatorial regions with the maximum potential for solar energy. And solar electricity has virtually no environmental impact other than possibly from the manufacturing processes and disposal of retired equipment.

The major challenges facing PVs and solar thermal electricity technologies are cost, intermittency and land-use requirements. There is significant potential for cost reduction with increased production of all technologies and as ongoing research improves the efficiency of PV cells; 30% efficiency is technically possible but at a very high cost in the absence of further technological breakthroughs. While advocates point to the available desert that could be used for PV or solar thermal electricity generation, some environmentalists object to the presumption that desert land has no value in its natural state. A promising alternative, however, is the integration of PV cells into external wall and roofing material, which would avoid potential land-use conflicts. As with wind, solar's intermittency means that large-scale reliance requires the development of potentially costly energy storage so that power can be dependably dispatched to meet peak loads.

Geothermal

Geothermal energy is sub-surface heat that is a legacy of the earth's earlier molten state and the outward migrating heat from radioactive decay of uranium, thorium, radium and other unstable elements in its interior. The highest quality geothermal energy is found near the boundaries of tectonic plates where volcanism and other seismic activity produce high-temperature reservoirs near the earth's surface. These reservoirs, which are categorized as dry and wet steam, hot water, hot dry rock and magma, are non-renewable in the sense that exploitation would deplete the most favorable sites in say 30–50 years. But because the geothermal gradient of the earth's crust averages 30°C increase per kilometer of depth, humans can tap into the earth to capture lower quality geothermal energy at just about any location.

People have bathed in hot springs for thousands of years. Today, high-temperature geothermal resources can generate electricity while hot water resources can heat buildings and provide process heat for industry. The first geothermal electricity generation plant was built in

Italy in 1904 and the first geothermal municipal district heating system was constructed in Iceland in the 1930s. There are currently almost 10,000 MW of installed geothermal electricity capacity, half of which is located in the US and the Philippines. Italy, Mexico, Indonesia, and Japan each have just under 1,000 MW. Japan, Iceland and China are the leading users of geothermal for direct heat; almost all urban homes and offices in Iceland are heated by geothermal. The current electricity and heat uses of geothermal total 0.3 EJ, over 50% of the "other" category of renewables. Geothermal grows in my current trends from 0.3 EJ in 2000 to 20 EJ in 2100.

The full geothermal resource is difficult to estimate because it depends on how far into the earth humans are willing and able to probe. The World Energy Assessment provides an estimated annual flow of 140 million EJ that could be tapped within a depth of 5 kilometers, which reduces to 600,000 EJ using various criteria for accessibility, then 5,000 EJ based on becoming economical within forty to fifty years, and finally 500 EJ as almost economic today. Even this latter, much smaller estimate means that geothermal energy alone is potentially capable of providing all of the needs of the human energy system in 2000.

The development of geothermal is constrained largely because of its cost relative to current fossil fuel prices so that geothermal is economic in only the very best sites today. With all of its volcanic activity, it is not surprising that Iceland is the country that looks to become a model for the world in basing its energy system on geothermal energy, perhaps one day producing hydrogen from geothermal electricity. Geothermal is environmentally benign although extracting steam and hot water usually brings sulphur gases and carbon dioxide to the surface. This can be addressed by pumping these gases back into the reservoir with any wastewater. The Icelanders pump some of their geothermal wastewater into a lagoon that has since become an international destination because of the purported healing powers of its briny hot water.

Even in locations that do not have high temperature heat near the surface, the earth's heat can be a source for space heating with the installation of a ground-source heat pump. A heat pump is a device that uses mechanical energy in a compressing and condensing cycle to transfer heat from one environment to another at a higher temperature. The latent heat within any medium can be used, which is why there are ground-source, air-source and water-source heat pumps. A ground-source heat pump extracts heat from the ground by piping a fluid in a cycle from the surface to depths of about 100 meters and back again. The pump heats buildings in the winter, but can be reversed in summer to act as an air conditioner, transferring heat from the building to the ground. The main energy source is not geothermal energy, but rather whatever source is responsible for producing the mechanical energy of the pump – usually electricity. There is a large potential for heat pump energy around the world as long as the technology is matched with an electricity source to run the pump.

Tidal and wave

Tidal energy is caused by the gravitational force of the moon and sun on the earth which, depending on their alignment, distort somewhat the shape of the earth and shift the height of its ocean surface. The ebb and flow of tides creates a potential for energy-generating movement of water that might be controlled with the use of dams and sluice gates or simply exploited as currents passing through narrows. Larger, ocean currents are caused by the differential heating of oceans by solar energy, and these too can be exploited. The wind from solar energy causes waves, which can produce mechanical energy. The modern interest in tidal and wave power is a legacy of the oil price shocks of the late seventies and early eighties, but there were tidal-driven grain mills as early as the eleventh century in Europe. Long before that humans learned how to use slack tide and peak tidal flows to their advantage in the transport of goods and people.

Tidal power can be exploited by building a dam across a tidal basin or by suspending submerged turbines in a passage that has rapid currents. The dam delays the inflow and outflows of tides in order to create a difference in water level that will turn turbines located in sluice gates in the dam. Because the basin must have a significant tidal range to create much energy, there are only a few good sites in the world. Also, dams across tidal basins would have significant ecological impacts and the capital cost is high relative to the energy output, which only occurs when the sluice gates are open (capacity utilization in the range of 25%). The approach of submerging turbines in currents (tidal or solar driven ocean currents) is also limited in terms of the number and location of good sites. Wave energy technologies exploit the mechanical energy in waves to turn a turbine. This technology is still mainly in the pre-commercial phase.

The World Energy Assessment estimates a potential of 80 EJ for tidal energy and 65 EJ for wave energy.[57] Estimates of the economic potential over the next half century suggest that only one tenth of this is likely to be attractive. In my current trends scenario, I have kept this form of energy's contribution to a minimum. While advocates are convinced that technologies will eventually provide economical power from this huge resource, most experts believe that it will have trouble competing with the many other renewable options for producing energy.

Renewables overview

The underlying resource potential of almost every renewable form of energy is huge relative to the current human energy system. The potential of biomass, wind, solar and geothermal far exceed in their annual output the system in 2000 and the expanded system of my current trends projection for 2100. Even hydropower has this capacity if I include the potential energy from all surface flow of water on earth, and likewise ocean energy if I include the vast potential to produce mechanical energy from ocean temperature differentials.

Because renewables are generally associated with continuous flows of energy through the biogeophysical system, there is a tendency to think of them as homogeneous with respect to the concept of sustainability and in terms of their ability to compete with alternative forms of primary energy. They are, however, diverse in their physical and thermodynamic characteristics, and this leads to differences in terms of endurance as well as environmental and economic trade-offs.

Depending on how they are exploited, some renewables are not renewable. Siltation of the reservoir can reduce or eliminate a hydropower site's ability to generate electricity, even though total water flow has not changed. Soil degradation and erosion can hinder or destroy the production of biomass from a given land area, even though flows of solar energy and precipitation have not changed. While the geothermal energy available deep in the earth is renewable, the prime geothermal sites near the earth's surface are not; intensive exploitation would limit the lifespan of many locations to less than a century.

Depending on how they are affected by their three main challenges – intermittency, low energy density and inconvenient location – many renewables must overcome substantial environmental impacts and will incur significant costs in providing dependable energy. Energy-dedicated biomass plantations and large hydropower projects must vie with other highly valued land uses. Even seemingly innocuous wind generators face land-use constraints. PVs have a low efficiency for converting solar energy into electricity, yet some of the materials in PVs are expensive and toxic, requiring further advances in generating efficiency and materials handling. Intermittent, unpredictable energy sources make it difficult to match energy supply with the daily and seasonal cycles of human energy demand. To ensure that peak demands are met, an energy system dominated by renewables would require large-scale energy storage, something that can be extremely challenging from physical, technological, social and economic perspectives.

In addition to these differences between renewable forms of energy, each renewable resource covers a range of qualities and opportunities, which leads to a diversity of cost estimates. Large hydropower has been competitive for a long time, but new developments are getting more expensive as we increasingly recognize the social and ecological cost of flooding valleys. Wind turbines in the best sites may be competitive with other methods of generating electricity, but future developments may be forced to more isolated locations, which will add costs for long-distance transmission, and critical storage issues will emerge as wind comes to represent a larger share of the total electricity system in a region. While the timing of electricity generation from PV panels in sunny mid-latitude locations (such as Sacramento, California) almost perfectly matches the timing of the air conditioning load, PV is still far from competitive. Biomass energy from agriculture and forest residues takes advantage of a free input that does not require additional land, and is therefore substantially cheaper than biomass energy from dedicated energy plantations which must compete with other land uses. Biomass combustion is already competitive in some situations, but gasification of biomass presents substantial technical and environmental challenges.

Because of these factors, individual renewables resources, or the aggregate of all renewables, can be presented with the same type of upward sloping cost curve I used in chapter 1 to describe the supply of oil. (In this case, however, think of the units of supply on the horizontal axis as annual output instead of a fixed stock, given that the resource is renewable.) The issue for the renewables cost curve is whether the technology and land needed to overcome the various challenges in an environmentally acceptable way will result in renewables being more or less desirable than efficiency, nuclear or cleaner fossil fuels. In some respects, the cost curve will be upward sloping, because a greater annual output of renewables will require adding higher-cost renewable production. But the slope of the curve is also likely to decline as R&D and greater production induce economies-of-learning which in turn lead to cost decreases during the course of the century – especially if we make an effort for renewables to achieve minimum market penetration thresholds early enough. I return to this prospect in the discussion of policy in chapter 8.

4.4 Overview of the usual suspects: their potential and their challenges

Many advocates of nuclear power argue that we should pursue this option while advancing our efforts with renewables and energy efficiency. Many advocates of renewables argue that we should rapidly shift our energy system toward renewables in concert with a much greater effort in energy efficiency; in contrast, they tend to be less than enamored with nuclear power.

As this survey of energy efficiency, nuclear power and renewable energy has shown, each of these major options can legitimately contribute to the goal of a more sustainable energy path. It is not a physical or technological impossibility for nuclear power or renewable energy to become the dominant form of primary energy for the global energy system during this century. It is also thermodynamically possible for dramatic energy efficiency gains to stabilize and perhaps decrease primary energy demand while energy services expand threefold over the next 100 years. The evidence of this chapter is that a combination of all three of these options, or perhaps just a pairing of renewables with greater efficiency or nuclear with greater efficiency, could replace fossil fuels in the human energy system during the course of this century. If we want to stop using fossil fuels, we can. But should we want to?

Presumably, before launching such a major transformation, we would examine carefully the full implications of rapidly expanding one, two, or all three of these other options. What will the world be like when nuclear power is ubiquitous? What are the impacts and costs when renewables are rapidly scaled-up from their current marginal role to that of system dominance? How do we get households and firms to aggressively adopt only the most energy-efficient devices and a conserver lifestyle, while spurring innovators to extend the efficiency envelope?

In the past, most information about these three options has been provided by their promoters – who are keen to emphasize the positive. Researchers, analysts and politicians have rarely scrutinized these claims, given that these options have not posed a substantial threat to the reign of fossil fuels. But this is changing. As we now assess nuclear expansion, increase our energy efficiency efforts and propagate modern technologies that use renewables, independent researchers are examining more closely the accumulated experience of recent decades with each of these options. We have been siting, constructing and operating nuclear plants for three decades. We have been pursuing energy efficiency for the same length of time. A few of the modern renewables-based technologies, like wind turbines and photovoltaic cells, have penetrated niche markets and with policy support from government attained production thresholds that lower costs. We know a lot more about these alternatives than we did thirty years ago in the aftermath of the first oil crisis.

In this chapter, I have tried to give a flavor of what these decades of experience and more recent research can reveal about the performance of these three options if the intention were to dramatically expand their contributions. It reveals that, when carefully examined, the development of each energy option faces complications, impacts and limitations. We can identify significant energy efficiency potential; researchers have done that for decades. But the efforts at achieving this potential by energy utilities and government agencies have been only marginally successful, with most of this success coming during times when almost everyone thought that energy prices would continue to rise uncontrollably. We can mass-produce nuclear power plants, whether as large complexes or as a vast number of smaller, modular units. But siting nuclear facilities is unlikely to get easier in terms of local approvals and world powers may not agree to dissemination of this technology to certain regions of the world under even the most carefully monitored conditions. We can scale-up our use of renewables, emphasizing different renewables in different parts of the world. But there are significant land-use conflicts and costs entailed in the scale-up of an energy supply option that is often characterized by low energy density, intermittent output and inconvenient location – especially if the intention is that renewables completely replace fossil fuels over the course of this century in an expanding global energy system.

While the challenges facing these energy options are not sufficient justification for sticking with fossil fuels, they suggest that this option at least merits a careful review before we make the rash decision suggested by some of the quotes I provided in chapter 1. I offer this review in the following chapters by assessing fossil fuels in terms of endurance (chapter 5) and cleanliness (chapter 6) – my two key sustainability components. I then return in chapter 7 to compare the usual suspects in this chapter with fossil fuels in the development of a sustainable energy system for this century and beyond.

Notes

1. For a clear explanation of thermodynamic principles see K. Pitzer, *Thermodynamics* (New York: McGraw-Hill, 1995), or J. Kraushaar and R. Ristinen, *Energy and the Problems of a Technical Society* (New York: Wiley, 1993).
2. A. Lovins, *Soft Energy Paths: Toward a Durable Peace* (San Francisco: Friends of the Earth International; Cambridge, Mass.: Ballinger Publishing, 1977).
3. E. Jochem (ed.), "Energy End-Use Efficiency," chapter 6 in J. Goldemberg (ed.), *World Energy Assessment: Energy and the Challenge of Sustainability* (New York: United Nations Development Programme, 2000), 175.
4. M. Jaccard, L. Failing and T. Berry, "From Equipment to Infrastructure: Community Energy Management and Greenhouse Gas Emission Reduction," *Energy Policy* 25, 11 (1997): 1065–1074; and W. Anderson, S. Kanaroglou and E. Miller, "Urban Form, Energy, and the Environment," *Urban Studies* 33, 1 (1996): 7–35.
5. F. Schmidt-Bleek, *MIPS and Factor 10 for a Sustainable and Profitable Economy* (Wuppertal: Wuppertal Institute, 1997). Factor 10 means a ten-fold improvement or 90% reduction in material intensity per unit of service (MIPS) in the use of energy and materials.
6. A. Lovins, L. Lovins, F. Krause and W. Bach, *Least-Cost Energy: Solving the CO_2 Problem* (Andover, Mass.: Brick House Publishing,

1981); A. Fickett, C. Gellings and A. Lovins, "Efficient Use of Electricity," *Scientific American* 263, 3 (1990): 64–75; E. Von Weiszacker, A. Lovins and L. Lovins, *The Factor Four – Doubling Wealth, Halving Resource Use* (London: Earthscan, 1997).

7. Jochem, "Energy End-Use Efficiency," 174–217. For a detailed review of electricity efficiency potentials for industrial equipment, consumer durables and electricity supply technologies, see T. Johansson, B. Bodlund and R. Williams (eds.), *Electricity: Efficient End-Use and New Generation Technologies, and Their Planning Implications* (Lund: Lund University Press, 1989).

8. Lovins, *Soft Energy Paths*, 35.

9. A. Lovins, "Saving Gigabucks with Negawatts," *Public Utilities Fortnightly* 115, 6 (1985): 19–26; "Energy Savings Resulting from the Adoption of More Efficient Appliances: Another View," *Energy Journal* 9, 2 (1988): 155–162; and "Negawatts: Twelve Transitions, Eight Improvements, and One Distraction," *Energy Policy* 24, 4 (1996): 331–343.

10. F. Wirl, *The Economics of Conservation Programs* (Boston: Kluwer Academic, 1997).

11. S. Nadel, *Lessons Learned: A Review of Utility Experience with Conservation and Load Management Programs for Commercial and Industrial Customers,* report no. 1064–EEED-AEP-88 (New York: American Council for an Energy-Efficient Economy, 1990).

12. P. Joskow and D. Marron, "What Does a Negawatt Really Cost? Evidence from Utility Conservation Programs," *The Energy Journal* 13, 4 (1992): 41–74; P. Joskow, "Utility-Subsidized Energy-Efficiency Programs," *Annual Review of Energy and the Environment* 20 (1995): 526–534.

13. F. Wirl, "Lessons from Utility Conservation Programs," *The Energy Journal* 21, 1 (2000): 87–108.

14. F. Sebold and E. Fox, "Realized Savings from Residential Conservation Activity," *The Energy Journal* 6, 2 (1985): 73–88; E. Hirst, "Actual Energy Savings after Retrofit: Electrically Heated Homes in the Pacific Northwest," *Energy* 11 (1986): 299–308; G. Metcalf and K. Hassett, "Measuring the Energy Savings from Home Improvement Investments: Evidence from Monthly Billing Data," *Review of Economics and Statistics* 81, 3 (1999): 516–528; D. Loughran and J. Kulick, "Demand Side Management and Energy Efficiency in the United States," *The Energy Journal* 25, 1 (2004): 19–43.

15. M. Jaccard, J. Nyboer and A. Fogwill, "How Big is the Electricity Conservation Potential in Industry?" *The Energy Journal* 14, 2 (1993): 139–156.

16. A. Lovins, J. Neymark, T. Flanigan, P. Kiernan, B. Bancroft and M. Sheppard, *The State of the Art: Drivepower* (Snowmass, Colo.: Rocky Mountain Institute, 1989).

17. M. Brown, M. Levine, J. Romm, A. Rosenfeld and J. Koomey, "Engineering-Economic Studies of Energy Technologies to Reduce Greenhouse Gas Emissions: Opportunities and Challenges," *Annual Review of Energy and the Environment* 23 (1998): 287–385.

18. From the huge literature on this question, particularly clear expositions are provided by the following three articles: A. Jaffe and R. Stavins, "The Energy-Efficiency Gap: What Does it Mean?" *Energy Policy* 22, 10 (1994): 804–810; J. Scheraga, "Energy and the Environment: Something New under the Sun?" *Energy Policy* 22, 10 (1994): 811–818; R. Sutherland, "The Economics of Energy Conservation Policy," *Energy Policy* 24, 4 (1996): 361–370.

19. R. Pindyck, "Irreversibility, Uncertainty and Investment," *Journal of Economic Literature* 29, 3 (1991): 1110–1152.

20. A. Nichols, "Demand-Side Management: Overcoming Market Barriers or Obscuring Real Costs?" *Energy Policy* 22, 10 (1994): 840–847.

21. M. Jaccard, A. Bailie and J. Nyboer, "CO_2 Emission Reduction Costs in the Residential Sector: Behavioral Parameters in a Bottom-Up Simulation Model," *The Energy Journal* 17, 4 (1996): 107–134; M. Jaccard, J. Nyboer, C. Bataille and B. Sadownik, "Modeling the Cost of Climate Policy: Distinguishing between Alternative Cost Definitions and Long-Run Cost Dynamics," *The Energy Journal* 24, 1 (2003): 49–73.

22. A. Sanstad and R. Howarth, "Normal Markets, Market Imperfections, and Energy Efficiency," *Energy Policy* 22, 10 (1994): 811–818; M. Levine, E. Hirst, J. Koomey, J. McMahon and A. Sanstad, *Energy Efficiency, Market Failures, and Government Policy* (Berkeley, Calif.: Lawrence Berkeley Laboratory, 1994).

23. Two helpful overviews are: L. Berry, "A Review of the Market Penetration of US Residential and Commercial Demand-Side Management Programmes," *Energy Policy* 21, 1 (1993): 53–67; and D. Violette, *Evaluating Greenhouse Gas Mitigation through DSM Projects: Lessons Learned from DSM Evaluation in the United States* (Boulder: Hagler Bailly Consulting, 1998).

24. D. Khazzoom, "Energy Savings Resulting from the Adoption of More Efficient Appliances," *The Energy Journal* 8, 4 (1987): 85–89.

25. D. Greene, J. Kahn and R. Gibson, "Fuel Economy Rebound Effect for US Household Vehicles," *The Energy Journal* 20, 3 (1999): 1–31; and J. Bentzen, "Estimating the Rebound Effect in US Manufacturing Energy Consumption," *Energy Economics* 26 (2004): 123–134.

26. L. Greening, D. Greene and C. Difiglio, "Energy Efficiency and Consumption – the Rebound Effect – a Survey," *Energy Policy* 28 (2000): 389–401.

27. In 2000, an entire issue of *Energy Policy* was devoted to research on the rebound effect; for an overview, see L. Schipper (ed.), "On the Rebound: The Interaction of Energy Efficiency, Energy Use and Economic Activity," *Energy Policy* 28, 6–7 (2000): 351–354.

28. L. Brookes, "The Greenhouse Effect: The Fallacies in the Energy Efficiency Solution," *Energy Policy* 18, 2 (1990): 199–201. In response, see M. Grubb, "Energy Efficiency and Economic Fallacies," *Energy Policy* 18, 8 (1990): 783–785.

29. See World Nuclear Association, *Nuclear Power Reactors*, 2004, http://www.world-nuclear.org.

30. H.-H. Rogner (ed.), "Energy Resources," chapter 5 in J. Goldemberg (ed.), *World Energy Assessment: Energy and the Challenge of Sustainability* (New York: United Nations Development Programme, 2000), 166. Rogner's estimates assume that 1 tonne of natural uranium = 589 terajoules.

31. For recent overviews of the challenges facing the nuclear industry see, R. Garwin and G. Charpak, *Megawatts and Megatons: A Turning Point in the Nuclear Age?* (New York: Knopf, 2001); J. Deutch and E. Moniz (co-chairs), *The Future of Nuclear Power: An Interdisciplinary MIT Study* (Cambridge, Mass.: MIT Press, 2004).

32. M. Grimston and P. Beck, *Double or Quits: The Global Future of Civil Nuclear Energy* (London: Earthscan, 2002).

33. M. Ryan, "Fuel Costs Taking More of O&M Budget: Even as Costs Drop, Efficiency Rises," *Nuclear Fuel* 24, 14 (1999): 1–10.

34. J. Paffenbarger, G. Lammers and C. Ocaña, *Electricity Reform: Power Generation Costs and Investment* (Paris: International Energy Agency, 1999).

35. T. Drennen, A. Baker and W. Kamery, *Electricity Generation Cost Simulation Model*, report SAND 2002-3376 (Albuquerque: Sandia National Laboratories, 2002).

36. Nuclear Energy Agency, *Projected Costs of Generating Electricity* (Paris: Nuclear Energy Agency, 1998).

37. See, for example, A. Rabl and J. Spadaro, "Public Health Impact of Air Pollution and Implications for the Energy System," *Annual Review of Energy and the Environment* 25 (2000): 601–627; M. Radetzki, "Coal or Nuclear in New Power Stations: Political Economy of an Undesirable but Necessary Choice," *The Energy Journal* 21, 1 (2000): 135–147.

38. See O. Hohmeyer, R. Ottinger and K. Rennings (eds.), *Social Costs and Sustainability: Valuation and Implementation in the Energy and Transport Sector* (Heidelberg: Springer, 1997).

39. B. Van der Zwaan, "Nuclear Energy: Tenfold Expansion or Phase-Out?" *Technological Forecasting and Social Change* 69 (2002): 287–307.

40. See R. Williams, "Nuclear and Alternative Energy Supply Options for an Environmentally Constrained World: A Long-Term Perspective," in P. Leventhal, S. Dolley and S. Tanzer (eds.), *Nuclear Power and the Spread of Nuclear Weapons: Can We Have One Without the Other?* (Washington, D.C.: Brassey's Inc., 2002).

41. E. Lyman and S. Dolley, "Accident Prone," *Bulletin of the Atomic Scientists* 56, 2 (2000): 42–46.

42. N. Rasmussen (ed.), *Reactor Safety Study: An Assessment of Accident Risks in US Commercial Nuclear Power Plants* (Washington, D.C.: Nuclear Regulatory Commission, 1975).

43. S. Fetter, *Climate Change and the Transformation of World Energy Supply* (Palo Alto, Calif.: Center for International Security and Cooperation, Stanford University, 1999).

44. B. Fischoff, A. Bostrom and M. Quadrel, "Risk Perception and Communication," *Annual Review of Public Health* 14 (1993): 183–203.

45. P. Slovic, "Perceived Risk, Trust and Democracy," *Risk Analysis* 13 (1993): 675–682.

46. W. Turkenburg (ed.), "Advanced Energy Supply Technologies," chapter 7 in J. Goldemberg (ed.), *World Energy Assessment: Energy and the Challenge of Sustainability* (New York: United Nations Development Programme, 2000), 221.

47. For a detailed survey see T. Johansson, H. Kelly, A. Reddy and R. Williams (eds.), *Renewable Energy: Sources for Fuels and Electricity* (Washington, D.C.: Island Press, 1993).

48. Turkenburg, "Advanced Energy Supply Technologies," 253.

49. Northwest Power Planning Council, *Columbia River Basin Fish and Wildlife Program: A Multi-Species Approach for Decision Making*, Appendix B – Hydroelectric Development Conditions (Portland, Ore.: Northwest Power Planning Council, 2000).

50. R. Goodland, "Environmental Sustainability in the Hydro Industry: Disaggregating the Debate," in T. Dorcey (ed.), *Proceedings of the Workshop on 'Large Dams: Learning from the Past, Looking in the Future'* (Washington, D.C.: IUCN, World Conservation Union, and World Bank Group, 1997).

51. Rogner, "Energy Resources," 156.

52. O. Brilhante, "Brazil's Alcohol Programme: From an Attempt to Reduce Oil," *Journal of Environmental Planning and Management* 40, 4 (1997): 435–450.

53. J. DeCarolis and D. Keith, "The Cost of Wind's Variability: Is There a Threshold?" *The Electricity Journal*, January/February 2005: 69–77.

54. G. Berry, "Present and Future Electricity Storage for Intermittent Renewables," *Proceedings of the Pew Center Workshop 'The 10–50 Solution: Technologies and Policies for a Low-Carbon Future'* (Washington, D.C.: Pew Center on Global Climate Change, 2004).

55. Rogner, "Energy Resources," 163.

56. Turkenburg, "Advanced Energy Supply Technologies," 237.

57. Rogner, "Energy Resources," 166.

5 | *The unusual suspect: how long can fossil fuels last – and does it matter?*

As a non-renewable resource, fossil fuels appear to fail the endurance criterion by definition, and on this basis alone there are people who believe we should start now a deliberate and rapid transition to alternative forms of energy. Why sustain our dependence on oil, coal and natural gas only to leave future generations the unenviable burden of a crumbling economic system built like a house of cards? When we discuss candidates for sustainable energy, fossil fuels are indeed the "unusual suspect."

But how much oil, natural gas or coal is there? How long might these resources endure? How fixed is the relationship between each of these individual forms of fossil fuels and the secondary energy products consumed by businesses and households? What will happen as we exhaust our fossil fuel resources? Might we ever consider reliance on a depletable resource like fossil fuels to be a legitimate component of a sustainable energy system?

5.1 Fossil fuel use and economic growth

The dramatic growth in material wealth in industrializing countries over the last two centuries is associated with increasing exploitation of the high energy density of fossil fuels. This historical relationship is, however, the outcome of a complex interplay of technological innovations, shifts in economic activities, and the market dynamics of the three competing fossil fuels – which makes any projection into the future a perilous exercise. Technological innovations, changing economic conditions, and unforeseen political developments could influence the relationship in profoundly different ways. In chapter 1, I noted that energy intensity differs significantly from one industrialized country to another. This is equally the case for fossil fuel intensity. France produces most of its electricity from nuclear power and it has become an electricity-intensive economy with electricity providing thermal industrial applications and much of the residential space heating that are normally met by fossil fuels in other countries. China is rich in easily accessible coal and therefore relies heavily on this energy source for electricity generation, industrial processing, space heating in commercial, institutional and apartment buildings, and even for household cooking.

A few technological developments played a key role in forging the link between fossil fuel use and industrialization. Since the 1830s, the accelerating application of the coal-fired, high-pressure *steam engine* (steam driving a piston, as in a train locomotive) triggered a revolution in industrial production techniques and railway transport, increasing the productivity of labor and capital and driving rapid industrialization in Western Europe and North America. Coal consumption increased dramatically throughout the century and by 1900 had caught up with biomass, each then accounting for 50% of the world's primary energy.

Around 1900, three key innovations strengthened the bond between fossil fuels and industrial societies and set the pattern for developments throughout the twentieth century. The introduction of the *steam turbine* (steam spinning a turbine to directly drive machinery, pumps and compressors, or to generate electricity) launched another phase of factory redesign by combining with the second innovation, the *electric motor*, to launch the electrification revolution, with further dramatic effects on productivity. The third innovation, the *internal combustion engine*, revolutionized transportation so that cars, buses and trucks supplanted horses, trolleys and trains for the movement of people and goods.

From 1900 to 2000, the efficiency of simple steam turbines for electricity generation increased from 5% to about 35% while their typical size increased from 1 MW to 800 MW, with some units reaching 1,500 MW.[1] Just 2% of fossil fuel consumption was for electricity generation in 1900, but this reached 30% by 2000. The internal combustion engine underwent similarly dramatic refinements: from an engine mass/power ratio of 30g/W in 1900 to 1g/W in 2000, with the power output of vehicles increasing from 16 kW in 1920 to as high as 100 kW in 2000. In the middle of the century, the *gas turbine* (exhaust gases spinning a turbine) drove the development of jet aviation and later in the century became the premier technology for new investments in electricity generation, fueled primarily by natural gas.

From 1900 to 2000, the use of fossil fuels increased from 20 EJ to 358 EJ, and their share of primary energy rose from 50% to 84%.

Within the fossil fuel aggregate, significant shifts occurred; coal lost its dominant position as first oil and then natural gas gained prominence. Over the century, coal's share of primary energy fell from 50% to 23% while oil's rose from 1% to 38% and that of natural gas from 0% to 22%. Advances in crude oil refining enabled the production of liquid fuels to meet the needs of the internal combustion engine for the rapidly expanding automobile industry. Oil drilling successes in Texas at the turn of the century were followed by major discoveries in the Middle East in the 1940s and then quickly in other parts of the world. Offshore oil wells have developed since the first prototypes in the 1940s to take an increasingly important role in the industry, with huge platforms operating in waters deeper than 2,000 meters since the 1980s. As a liquid, oil is ideal for long-distance transport overland by pipeline or across oceans by deep-sea tankers, helping it to lead international energy trade in terms of the total value traded.

Some early uses of natural gas occurred in the US and parts of Europe, where deposits were located close to industrial activity. Given the primary value of oil, natural gas found mixed with oil in remote fields (called associated gas) was often flared because it was too expensive to construct gas-dedicated transport systems. But after the oil price shocks in the 1970s, natural gas use expanded dramatically, especially in industrialized countries that could afford the substantial investments to link major consuming areas with distant gas fields. Eventually, the development of long-distance pipelines and tanker transport of liquefied natural gas (initially for markets in Japan) expanded global trade and the fuel's growth rate was twice that of oil in the last two decades of the twentieth century.

Where these trends will lead is difficult to discern. Coal has maintained its market niche in electricity generation and oil in liquid transportation fuels. But natural gas is challenging coal in electricity generation while also capitalizing on its inherent advantages for domestic space heating and cooking, for many industrial thermal applications, and as a feedstock for petrochemicals. Natural gas advocates promote it as the plentiful and flexible "transitional fuel" that could supplant coal to reduce pollution and replace oil as it is depleted.*

---

* For example, the US President's Committee of Advisors on Science and
  Technology stressed the importance of natural gas as a transition fuel in its
  1997 report to the president. J. Holdren (chairperson), *Report to the President*

Ultimately, the future evolution of fossil fuel use depends on the relative supply cost of each fuel for the different energy-using technologies and end-use services in conjunction with its performance for achieving environmental and social objectives. A key consideration when the issue is endurance is the magnitude and distribution of each resource.

5.2 Fossil fuel resource estimates

I introduced the concepts of reserves and resources in chapter 4 when discussing the long-term supply potential of uranium and other fissile materials. Resource is the estimated natural occurrence of a particular form of energy or matter, while reserve is the subset of the resource that is "available" for current exploitation. Its magnitude depends on our state of knowledge of the resource's location and our technological capability to extract and process it at reasonable cost. The definitions of resource and reserve for fossil fuels differ from agency to agency, with some using distinguishing terms like proven reserves and probable reserves.* To further complicate matters, different agencies use different ratios to convert physical quantities (tonnes, barrels, m^3) into energy values. Since many of my numbers are from chapter 5 of the World Energy Assessment, I use its energy conversion ratios.[†]

Coal

Coal is categorized into four major types depending on carbon content, heating value and hardness. *Anthracite* ranks the highest in terms

---

on *Federal Energy Research and Development for the Challenges of the Twenty-first Century* (Washington, D.C.: President's Committee of Advisors on Science and Technology, Panel on Energy Research and Development, 1997).

* British Petroleum defines proven reserves as ". . . those quantities that geological and engineering information indicates with reasonable certainty can be recovered in the future from reservoirs under existing economic and operating conditions." British Petroleum, *BP Statistical Review* (London: British Petroleum, 2004), 4.

[†] One tonne of oil equivalent equals 42 GJ; 1,000 m^3 of natural gas equals 38 GJ; and one tonne of coal equivalent equals 29 GJ on a thermal basis. See H.-H. Rogner (ed.), "Energy Resources," chapter 5 in J. Goldemberg (ed.), *World Energy Assessment: Energy and the Challenge of Sustainability* (New York: United Nations Development Programme, 2000), 139.

of these attributes with the other three, in descending order of rank, being *bituminous*, *sub-bituminous* and *lignite*. The highest ranked coal (called *metallurgical coal*) is best for steel production while lower ranked coals are used for combustion in steam turbines to generate electricity. Estimates of world coal resources often only distinguish between hard coal (anthracite, bituminous and higher quality sub-bituminous) and soft coal (lower quality sub-bituminous and lignite).

World coal reserves are estimated at 1 trillion tonnes or 21,000 EJ, of which 80% is hard coal.* These are concentrated in North America, the former Soviet Union, China, India, Australia and Sub-Saharan Africa.

The world coal resource is estimated at over 7 trillion tonnes or 200,000 EJ, of which 80% is hard coal. Over half of this is concentrated in the countries of the former Soviet Union, especially Russia. North America, Western Europe and China also have significant resources.

Coal reserves are substantial compared to our current use rate. If coal consumption continued at its current rate of 100 EJ per year, reserves might last 210 years and the estimated resource 2,000 years. These long timeframes would decline of course if the exploitation rate were to increase or if not all of the resource were ever to become technologically or economically accessible. In my current trends scenario (table 2.1 in chapter 2), annual coal production increases six-fold from 100 EJ to 650 EJ by 2100, becoming 47% of the primary energy system. If coal's share then grew annually at 0.5% thereafter, the estimated coal resource would last about 400 years.

Oil

Statistics of oil reserves and resources make a distinction between conventional oil and unconventional oil. Conventional oil is generally defined as crude oil located in subterranean reservoirs from which it can flow or be pumped to the surface without substantial changes to its viscosity (lower viscosity oil has greater fluidity). The cost of

---

* The different ratios of billion tonnes of coal to EJ from resources to reserves (7 trillion tonnes = 200,000 EJ while 1 trillion tonnes = only 21,000 EJ) is presumably due to different concentrations of anthracite, bituminous and sub-bituminous within the hard coal category.

recovering crude oil varies with the location and characteristics of the reservoir. Some conventional oil is pooled in shallow large reservoirs and flows easily to the surface. But some conventional oil is more difficult to exploit because of low pressure, the depth of the reservoir, the heaviness of the oil, or the remoteness of the location – hence terms like deep oil, heavy oil, offshore oil, deep offshore oil and frontier oil. Technological developments have improved the ability to exploit these sources of conventional oil and have also increased the percentage that can be extracted from a given reservoir. *Enhanced oil recovery* injects a gas or liquid into an oil reservoir to raise its pressure and lower the oil's viscosity in order to improve the recovery factor; traditional recovery factors of 35% have been increased to 65% in some cases.

Unconventional oil encompasses various substances from which crude oil or a synthetic variant of it can be produced. *Oil sands* (also called *natural bitumen*) are loose-grained rock material bonded with bitumen, a molasses-like heavy oil. Synthetic oil is produced from oil sands by heating processes that can be applied *in situ* or after physical removal of material by strip mining. The choice of process depends on oil sand characteristics, depth of the deposit, costs and environmental impacts. Western Canada has a significant portion of the world's resource, and has recently seen major expansion of production. *Ultra-heavy oil* is a tar-like substance requiring steam injection for recovery as synthetic crude oil. Venezuela has about half of the world's resources and is currently developing some of these (called *orimulsion*). *Oil shale* is a fine-grained sedimentary rock that contains a waxy hydrocarbon material called *kerogen*. Large volumes of rock must be mined and then subjected to heat processes in order to yield petroleum products. The US has large deposits of oil shale but has only conducted pilot projects. Estonia has exploited its oil shale for electricity generation for decades.

Since oil is so critical to the global economy, many agencies assess its reserve and resource potential. But the inevitable uncertainties and differences in definitions mean that estimates, especially resource estimates, vary significantly. The World Energy Assessment summarizes major recent estimates of oil reserves and resources, and then provides its own estimates in separate accounts for conventional and unconventional oil.[2]

For remaining conventional oil reserves, several studies put these in the range of 6,000 EJ (150 gigatonnes). Estimates of the conventional

oil resource base range from 10,000 to 16,000 EJ (240 to 380 gigatonnes), with 12,000 EJ as a reasonable expected value.

Estimates of unconventional oil resources have even greater variability given the uncertainties about magnitude, future technological
developments, and ultimate exploitation costs. The World Energy
Assessment provides an estimate of unconventional oil reserves as
5,000 EJ and the total unconventional resource as 20,000 EJ.*

Together, the estimated conventional and unconventional oil resources are 11,000 GJ for reserves within a total resource base of
32,000 EJ. If global oil consumption continued at its current annual
rate of 163 GJ, currently estimated reserves would last sixty-seven
years and the estimated resource 200 years. In my current trends
projection of chapter 2, oil production declines during this century.
If, instead, oil production were to grow from 2000 onward at 0.5%
per year, the estimated resource would last less than 150 years.

Natural gas

As with oil, analysts distinguish between conventional and unconventional natural gas. Conventional gas is natural gas in pressurized
sedimentary structures in association with oil or by itself. Even non-
associated gas is never found in a pure state; it is usually mixed with
other gases, hydrocarbon liquids and water, thereby requiring processing prior to its long distance transport to market by pipeline.

Unconventional gas is gas that cannot be exploited by conventional
recovery techniques. Most analysts distinguish four types of unconventional gas. *Coalbed methane* is gas that can be extracted from hard

---

* It is unclear how the region-specific reserve and resource estimates provided in
  table 5.2 on p. 140 of the World Energy Assessment translate into the aggregate
  estimates of table 25 on p. 166. I use these latter estimates which are in the range
  of the aggregate estimates for unconventional oil provided by other agencies.
  The estimates of reserve / production ratios in table 5.1 (p. 6) do not always
  agree with data elsewhere in the document. For example, the 11,110 EJ of oil
  reserves in table 5.25, when divided by 1998 annual oil consumption of 142 EJ
  in table 11, yield a static reserve / production ratio of 78 years, not the 45 years
  reported in table 11. For other sources see World Energy Council, *Survey of
  Energy Resources 2001* (London: World Energy Council, 2001); M. Lynch,
  Facing the Elephant: Oil Market Evaluation and Future Oil Crises (Boulder:
  International Research Center for Energy and Economic Development, 1998);
  and H.-H. Rogner, "An Assessment of World Hydrocarbon Resources," *Annual
  Review of Energy and the Environment* 22 (1997): 217–262.

coal deposits, usually requiring fracturing of the coal. *Tight formation gas* is gas trapped in low permeability rocks that requires fracturing to be released. *Geopressurized gas* (also called *ultra-deep gas*) is gas dissolved in deep aquifers. *Gas hydrates* are deposits of frozen gas and ice located in polar permafrost and below sediments on the ocean floor.*

Estimates of conventional natural gas reserves depend on assumptions about the economic potential for enhanced gas recovery: raising reservoir pressure to increase recovery from 60% to 70%. Assuming that some enhanced recovery is economic, the World Energy Assessment estimates global reserves of conventional natural gas at 5,500 EJ and the entire conventional resource at 16,500 EJ – of which perhaps 5,000 EJ could be added to the conventional gas resource from enhanced recovery methods.[3]

Estimates of unconventional gas reserves and resources, as with oil, vary widely depending on some key assumptions, such as whether to include the huge but highly uncertain estimates of gas hydrates and geopressurized gas. The World Energy Assessment sets unconventional gas reserves at 9,500 EJ and the unconventional resource at 33,000 EJ. These totals exclude the enormous quantities of gas hydrates, estimated at 350,000 EJ, and geopressurized gas, estimated at 600,000 EJ. The exclusion of these latter two is problematic. While we have not developed the capability to exploit these resources, some analysts believe that the technological means could be quickly developed at reasonable costs. I exclude these from my resource estimates because of the high uncertainty, yet I feel there is a good chance they can eventually be exploited.

Combining conventional and unconventional gas yields total gas reserves of 15,000 EJ and a total gas resource of 49,500 EJ. If global natural gas consumption continued at its current annual rate of 95 EJ, reserves would last 160 years and the resource 520. In my current trends projection of chapter 2, natural gas use increased to 200 EJ in 2050 and then declined to 160 EJ by 2100. If natural gas use grew annually at 0.5% after that, the resource would last less than 300

---

* Not everyone believes that all fossil fuels were produced in the way we commonly presume. There are scientists who speculate that much natural gas originates from deep in the earth's crust. See T. Gold, *The Deep Hot Biosphere* (New York: Copernicus Books, 1999).

years. If gas hydrates and geopressurized gas were included in the resource total, and if consumption remained at the 2000 rate of 95 EJ, the resource could conceivably last 10,000 years.

Fossil fuel resource totals

Table 5.1 summarizes the estimates of fossil fuel reserves and resources. If current consumption levels and fossil fuel reserves both remained static, oil reserves would not be exhausted until the latter half of this century, natural gas reserves would last into the next century, and coal reserves would last 200 years. When the focus shifts to resources, at static consumption levels oil would last 200 years, natural gas 500 and coal 2,000. If consumption of each fossil fuel grew to the level in 2100 that I had depicted in my current trends scenario of chapter 2, and then if oil and natural gas use continued to grow at 0.5% per year after that, then the oil resource would last under 150 years, natural gas under 300, and coal under 400.

Since all three forms of fossil fuels can be converted into liquid and gaseous hydrocarbon forms of secondary energy as well as electricity and hydrogen, table 5.1 combines the reserve and resource estimates into one fossil fuel aggregate. Total fossil fuel reserves are 47,000 EJ and the total resource is 280,000 EJ. As an aggregate, fossil fuel reserves would last 130 years at current use rates and the resource almost 800 years. I have not projected an indefinite growth rate for fossil fuel consumption in aggregate, but from the individual resource projections in table 5.1 it is apparent that the total resource could support an annual growth rate of 0.5% for about 300 years – again excluding the huge potential from gas hydrates and geopressurized gas.

5.3 Controversies in estimating fossil fuel endurance

The single value estimates of resources and reserves in table 5.1 should not imply precise knowledge. Estimates will vary with assumptions about the potential for future discoveries, the evolution of technologies to extract and exploit reserves, and future economic conditions. Indeed, fundamental differences in these assumptions help explain the gap between those who do and those who do not believe that fossil fuel penury is imminent. Part of the dispute appears to result from the different ways that professions define resources and reserves.

Table 5.1. *Summary of fossil fuel resource estimates*

Fossil Fuel	Production in 2000 (EJ)	Total Reserves (EJ)	Total Resource (EJ)	Reserve/ Production in 2000 (years)	Resource/ Production in 2000 (years)	Resource/ Production with growth (years)
Coal	100	21,000	200,000	210	2,000	<400
Oil	163	11,000	32,000	67	196	<150
Conventional		6,000	12,000			
Unconventional		5,000	20,000			
Natural Gas	95	15,000	49,500	158	521	<300
Conventional		5,500	16,500			
Unconventional		9,500	33,000			
Total Fossil Fuels	358	47,000	281,500	131	786	

Note:
- Unconventional natural gas does not include geopressurized gas and gas hydrates.
- My assumptions for the last column are: coal grows to its BAU level of 650 EJ in 2100 (1.9% annual rate) and at 0.5% thereafter; oil grows from 2000 at 0.5% annual rate; and natural gas grows to its BAU level of 160 EJ in 2100 and continues at 0.5%.

Geologists tend to focus on the distinguishing physical properties of a resource, and use these to estimate fixed global magnitudes for its reserves. These reserves are thus a fixed stock that is depleted through consumption. Economists, in contrast, comprehend an energy resource like oil as an economic commodity whose available quantity is determined by the profitability prospects for its producers when competing with other sources to provide secondary energy to businesses and consumers. From this perspective, the reserves are on-shelf inventory that producers replenish from the resource base through exploration and development to offset consumption. Their goal is to keep the size of the reserves relatively stable over time since small reserves could lead to unsatisfied demand and loss of market to competitors, while large reserves imply excess inventory with the attendant decline in net returns to investors. Economists claim that this explains why reserve-production ratios have remained relatively constant over the last 100 years for a commodity like conventional oil; the global R/P ratio has not exceeded forty years nor been less than twenty years.[4] When it has risen to the upper levels, companies stop looking for oil, and when it falls to the lower levels they have an incentive to explore more vigorously and to innovate ways to enhance recovery from existing reserves.

The geologist's approach is associated with a model developed in the 1950s by M. Hubbert.[5] He postulated that discoveries of oil reserves in a given oil-bearing basin would trace a bell-shaped curve over time, with discoveries first increasing in step with exploration, then hitting a peak after which they would slow as efforts in the same basin confronted diminishing returns. Oil production would have the same bell shape, but would lag the discoveries by about ten years, given the time it takes to incorporate new reserves into production. The right tail of the production curve signifies depletion of the reserve and eventually the cessation of production.

From the available exploration data, Hubbert determined in 1965 that the peak of oil discoveries in the lower forty-eight US states had occurred in 1957 and from this he predicted that peak production would occur ten years later. As it turned out, his prediction was quite accurate, with peak production occurring in 1970.

Some experts have extended Hubbert's model to the global scale. C. Campbell, J. Laherrere, R. Bentley, K. Deffeyes and other researchers have predicted that global oil discoveries have peaked and that global oil production will hit Hubbert's peak within a decade or two at most.[6] Similarly, some researchers predict that natural gas production will peak after 2020, and then follow a similar pattern of decline. These advocates of a global application of Hubbert's model base their analysis on a detailed review of the discovery and production rates in the world's currently active oil and gas fields, plus an assessment of the potential from less intensively explored sedimentary basins. While they acknowledge the back-up potential for unconventional oil and gas, they suggest that these cannot be brought into production fast enough to offset the growing gap between declining production and increasing demand. As a result, they portend a crisis in oil and gas markets reflected by fuel scarcity, sustained high prices and global economic recession. Populist writers, some of whom I quoted in chapter 1, have focused on the resulting image of crisis, with ominous book titles including such phrases as "peak oil," "the end of oil," "carbon war," "out of gas," and "the party's over."

Another group of researchers, notably M. Adelman, C. Watkins, M. Lynch, J. Ryan and P. Odell, offer an alternative view.[7] They argue that the depiction by Hubbert and his followers of ultimate oil reserves overlooks the role of price and technological change in determining the magnitude of these reserves at any given time. Technological change improves our ability to find oil and to exploit what we find less expensively, thus increasing estimated reserves. Price increases shift more of the resource into the reserve category, signifying that this portion of the resource has become economically attractive to exploit. These two factors may shift peak production further into the future. Even if peak production has actually been reached, they will shift out the right side of Hubbert's bell curve so it is no longer symmetrical. Because future outward shifts of the curve are unknowable – depending on unknown future changes in price and technology – the ultimate magnitude of the reserve is also unknowable.

Advocates of Hubbert's curve make much ado about the critical time when society passes peak production, suggesting that this signals the start of rapidly rising prices, political troubles and economic crises.* But the critics of this view argue that reaching peak production for a given non-renewable resource will be imperceptible to the

---

* There is now even a society called Association for the Study of Peak Oil, http://www.peakoil.net.

average person, unless it happens to coincide with some short-term supply crisis and price spike caused by a war, misguided policy or a major technical failure in the energy system – all of which happen from time to time. In this situation, media commentators may be able to convince a significant number of people that the price increase is caused by the peaking of oil production. Imminent catastrophe has its attractions.

The belief that we will soon run out of a key non-renewable resource is not unique to our time. Historians have found statements far back in history warning of impending exhaustion of one resource or another, and indeed humans have exploited some renewable resources to the point where the resource's regenerative capacity was diminished or destroyed. Attentiveness to the possibility of resource destruction or depletion seems prudent. But what are the facts when it comes to the recent history of oil?

Political events caused a dramatic jump of oil prices in 1973 with an oil embargo during the Arab–Israeli war and another jump in 1980 with the closure of supply facilities during the Iranian revolution, but these price increases were widely interpreted as evidence of the imminent exhaustion of world oil reserves. The media and even government reports were full of claims that oil prices would continue to rise for decades while oil supplies dwindled and economies contracted. Instead, however, the economy responded to the higher oil prices in multiple ways whose combined effect was to bring oil prices back down by the mid-1980s where they mostly stayed for more than a decade (figure 5.1).

The oil price increases triggered demand and supply responses. On the demand side, the higher oil prices reduced economic growth for a year or so, encouraged lifestyle changes that conserved energy, motivated investments in more energy efficient equipment, accelerated structural change away from energy-intensive goods and services, and prompted some consumers and businesses to switch from petroleum products to electricity and natural gas. Some of the response to higher prices was instantaneous: the immediate fall in airline and long-distance vehicle travel. Some of the response took several years to materialize: the acquisition of more efficient technologies and the switch to alternative fuels as consumers and businesses replaced their furnaces, vehicles, boilers, equipment and buildings.

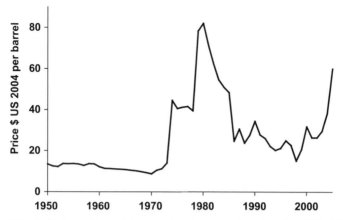

Figure 5.1. Inflation-adjusted international price of crude oil: 1950–2005.

Based on data in British Petroleum, *Energy in Focus: Statistical Review of World Energy 2004* (London: British Petroleum, 2004). Updated to 2005 from media sources.

On the supply side, the higher oil prices intensified exploration for conventional oil, stimulated improvements in enhanced oil recovery, drove research and development of unconventional oil, and encouraged investment in natural gas, coal, nuclear and renewables like wind, solar and biomass. Many of these investments took time to materialize, but eventually they produced competitive pressures that helped lower the international price of oil. From the late 1970s to 1990, for example, the production cost of North Sea oil fell from $35 per barrel to $15. Only efforts by the OPEC cartel of oil exporting countries prevented the price of oil from settling at an even lower level during the period 1986–2002. Its price mostly remained above production cost – in the $20–$25 per barrel range instead of the $10–$15 range – because of the willingness of OPEC to restrain its output and thereby yield market share to higher cost non-OPEC producers in Russia, the North Sea, Mexico, the US, Canada and elsewhere.

While the low oil price since 1986 diminished concerns about impending resource exhaustion, the recent return to high oil prices from 2002 through 2005 has had the opposite effect. Hubbert's curve is again in vogue and people talk of the prospect of long-term supply shortages and sustained oil prices at $100 per barrel and higher. Again, political events have played a significant role. It is no accident that the high oil prices coincided with the invasion of Iraq by a coalition led by the US and the UK, as well as with political unrest in Venezuela that has disrupted oil supply from that country. But there is evidence that a fundamental market imbalance is also at play, as the surging oil demand from China and other high-growth developing countries seems to have outstripped the capacity of the global oil supply system. What will happen next? Are we finally entering that prophesied phase of rising oil prices and economic disruption as ultimate oil reserves run out? This time, is the party really over?

While the full market response to recent high oil prices is difficult to discern, there is already evidence of the same equilibrating feedbacks that occurred during the high oil prices of the late 1970s and early 1980s. On the oil demand side, the rate of growth appears to have slowed in response to higher prices, in part because of efficiency, in part because of fuel switching. On the supply side, investment is increasing along some of the same technological paths that were initiated thirty years ago. With conventional oil, there are expanding efforts at enhanced oil recovery, deep-sea oil, and frontier oil. Unconventional oil sources, like the Canadian oil sands, are undergoing expansion, and investors are again exploring opportunities to produce petroleum products or synthetic substitutes from natural gas (in Qatar and elsewhere), coal and biomass.

In projecting into the future, the cost of these plentiful alternative sources should provide an upper bound for the long-run average price of oil. Recent research indicates that substantial additions to conventional oil can be brought on stream at a full production cost (which includes exploration, development and extraction) of less than $20 per barrel while unconventional oil from oil sands has a full production cost of about $25. Synthetic substitutes for refined petroleum products produced from natural gas and biomass also are economic when oil prices are in the $25 per barrel range. Finally, new investments in coal plants that produce refined petroleum products are profitable once oil is above $35 per barrel. If these sources expand in response to the profits offered by oil prices above $50 per barrel, the long-run effect could drive the price of oil back down to $35 and perhaps lower.[8]

This potential for supply expansion in response to higher prices provides an insight into the debate between geologists and economists about oil and gas resource limits. To some extent both are correct.

Geologists who claim that we are exhausting conventional oil reserves much sooner than the public realizes may be correct. But economists who claim that this is not the catastrophe that popular doomsayers proclaim may also be correct. A declining supply of conventional oil will put upward pressure on crude oil prices and this will translate into rising prices for refined petroleum products like gasoline. If these higher prices fail to stimulate more output of conventional oil, they will stimulate increased production of synthetic oil from unconventional sources and, if high enough, synthetic gasoline from natural gas, coal and biomass. The cost of these alternatives creates an upward ceiling on the long-run price of conventional oil and of the refined petroleum products made from it.* Humans slow and eventually halt their search for conventional oil when the returns from this activity are likely to be lower than the returns from pursuing conventional oil's substitutes. When this happens, the reserves of conventional oil are exhausted in the economic sense that none of the remaining resource can be profitably exploited.†

What will this mean for consumers? If the cost of production of gasoline from the alternatives to conventional oil is not substantially higher in the long-run, consumers will be unconcerned and probably unaware that substitution is occurring. All they may experience is a gradual increase in the market price for what appears to be the same product – gasoline to fuel their vehicles. This upward trend will likely be imperceptible in the face of the usual short-run price fluctuations

---

* R. Heinberg suggests that this transition cannot be smooth because the unconventional alternatives require much more energy for processing into synthetic petroleum products – as measured by "energy return on energy invested." See R. Heinberg, *The Party's Over: Oil, War and the Fate of Industrial Societies* (Gabriola Island, B.C.: New Society Publishers, 2003). Economists would not see the significance of this concept because the energy source (oil sands, coal, the sun) is essentially a free good if it has no alternative use. Just as we would not reject photovoltaics because of the low efficiency of solar cells we would not reject oil sands as an energy source. What matters is cost, although for an enduring energy system, as I have defined it, that cost should include minimal impacts to land and people. I address this issue in the next chapter on fossil fuel cleanliness.

† "The total mineral in the earth is a non-binding constraint. If expected finding-development costs exceed the expected net revenues, investment dries up and the industry disappears. Whatever is left in the ground is unknown, probably unknowable, but surely unimportant: a geological fact of no economic interest." (p. 2) M. Adelman, "Mineral Depletion with Special Reference to Petroleum," *Review of Economics and Statistics* 72, 1 (1990): 1–10.

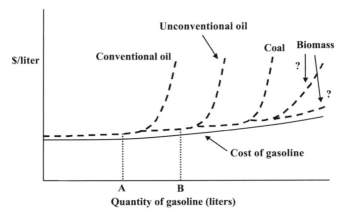

Figure 5.2. Global gasoline supply curve.

inherent in any commodity, a normal consequence of the difficulty for
markets to perfectly balance supply and demand at any given time.

Figure 5.2 is an adaptation of the oil supply curve in figure 1.2 of
chapter 1. The graph again depicts the long-run relationship between
price per unit and cumulative production, but in this case the commodity is gasoline instead of crude oil – crude oil being just one of
several primary energy feedstocks for the production of gasoline. The
dotted lines depict the full underlying costs of producing and
marketing gasoline first from conventional crude oil, then from unconventional oil, then coal, and then perhaps a non-fossil fuel source
such as biomass. If quantity A on the horizontal axis indicates cumulative demand at the corresponding price on the vertical axis, conventional oil supplies are sufficient. Over time, as consumption drives
cumulative demand to quantity B, gasoline suppliers must shift to
unconventional crude oil. If unconventional crude oil is more expensive to extract and then refine into gasoline, consumers must pay
more. If it costs about the same, the gasoline cost line is essentially
flat and prices would be unaffected by the need to acquire supplies
from this alternative. A similar logic applies to the supply and cost of
gasoline from coal. Because of high uncertainty about future land use
conflicts, the graph shows two possible curves for the cost of gasoline
from biofuel: the cost could be relatively flat or rise steeply depending
on the value of alternative uses of land for agriculture or the preservation of biodiversity.

Figure 5.2 explains why we might use up an apparently valuable resource and yet experience little or no long-term price increase – even though prices may fluctuate wildly on a short-run basis. It implies a sequential transition of gasoline markets from 100% reliance on conventional oil to the addition of unconventional oil, then coal, and so on. The real world is, however, more complicated. Each alternative for producing gasoline actually comprises a heterogeneous mix of high and low cost resources. While most gasoline today is produced from conventional oil, there is also supply from oil sands (Canada), coal (South Africa) and biomass (Brazil). The graph also does not depict the time effects of technological innovation. Looking forward, it appears that the alternatives to conventional oil are relatively more expensive. But once these are developed, economies-of-scale and economies-of-learning could result in lower costs, even lower than the current production cost of gasoline from conventional oil. Ironically, the cost of gasoline might actually trend downward over the next fifty years even as we exhaust our highly valued supplies of conventional oil. The capability to continue producing gasoline from fossil fuels is enormous, as the resource assessment in this chapter shows.

It is in this sense that some economists argue that depletion of conventional oil is of little consequence if substitution by alternatives will not affect production costs and consumer prices of secondary energy. All that matters is whether or not humans have substitutes they can readily develop or innovate. For any given resource, this could be correct. It could also be incorrect. It could be that there is no possible substitute for a particular highly valued non-renewable resource, and that economists are guilty of letting abstract models get in the way of seeing reality. (As I once heard, "What is the difference between used car salesmen and economists? At least used car salesmen know they are lying.") But those who portend an imminent global energy crisis as conventional oil passes Hubbert's peak may be even more guilty of deluding themselves and others, as they close their eyes to the vast resources available to produce the secondary energy products that conventional crude oil currently provides.

5.4 Does individual resource endurance matter?

The first part of my definition of energy system sustainability stated, "the energy system must have good prospects for enduring indefinitely in terms of the type and level of energy services it provides." With the benefit of the resource assessment of the past few chapters, I can now explain more precisely my meaning.

First, my definition refers to the "energy system," not individual primary energy resources. Individual components of that system need not endure as long as the system as a whole does. Some people might argue for a definition in which each component must be capable of lasting forever. But I have to ask why. Why would we set a restriction that did not allow us to use non-renewable forms of energy just because they were non-enduring over a very long timespan? What if exploitation of these forms of energy allowed us to better pursue other objectives such as better health for the rural poor because of improved indoor air quality? What if the resulting lower cost of providing energy services allowed the dedication of more resources to provision of clean water, soil conservation and protection of biodiversity? What if fossil fuel exploitation generated wealth that accelerated progress toward health, education and equity? Why make an advance judgment to forgo such benefits without fully evaluating the pros and cons? Why rule out the use of a resource simply by virtue of its non-renewable character?

Second, my definition refers to "good prospects of enduring indefinitely." We are not certain about the everlasting endurance of anything – including the sun.* But we can conduct a careful analysis of the forms of energy and technologies that constitute or could constitute our energy system, and then assess their individual and collective ability to endure indefinitely. The analysis so far suggests that not a great deal of human ingenuity – beyond that which has already been forthcoming over the last few centuries – is required for us to say with considerable confidence that several energy forms and technologies have excellent prospects of enduring indefinitely. Nuclear power and almost each form of renewable energy are capable of collectively meeting the needs of a significantly expanded human energy system on a continuous basis. Even fossil fuels may last from half to a full

---

* There is the story about a professor who noted that life on earth would be terminated in seven billion years when the sun burned out. A distressed student approached the professor after his lecture and asked him to repeat the statement. After hearing it, with a great sigh of relief, the student said, "Thank goodness, I thought you said seven *million* years!"

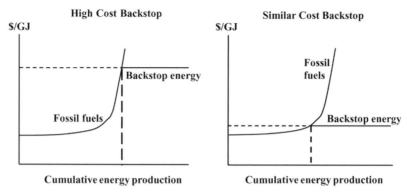

Figure 5.3. Scenarios of fossil fuel scarcity.

millennium, and that is based just on our imprecise knowledge of this resource and our current technological capabilities.

Finally, my definition focuses on the type and level of services provided, including the expanded services that are needed to improve dramatically the lives of the less-well-off people on the planet, requiring an energy system perhaps three times the size of today's by 2100. This is the trickiest part of the definition because it injects economics into the analysis. The physical analysis has shown that we have considerable resources. But what would they cost? If we stick to the path of consuming non-renewable resources such as fossil fuels, what will the transition from these to their replacements look like? Will the transition be relatively smooth and seamless, as depicted by the flat cost curve for gasoline? Or, will it be abrupt, entraining a traumatic withdrawal of human society from an energy-intensive lifestyle it can no longer support?

These alternative scenarios are shown in figure 5.3. Again, cost per unit is on the vertical axis and cumulative production on the horizontal axis. If we agree that fossil fuels are finite, we depict them with a cumulative production curve that eventually slopes steeply upwards. This implies that beyond some point it becomes increasingly costly to find and develop the remnants of a non-renewable resource like fossil fuels. If enduring, higher cost substitutes are available, such as renewables and perhaps nuclear, we depict these with a horizontal curve that continues indefinitely to the right, implying continuous output at an unchanging cost. Economists refer to this continuous, constant cost substitute as a *backstop technology.*[9]

The key issue for the stability of our energy future is whether the backstop costs a lot more than fossil fuels. With a relatively high cost backstop, as shown on the left side of the figure, the transition causes a dramatic and permanent rise in energy prices. This could be traumatic if the transition must happen quickly. An example would be a relatively quick and permanent increase in the price of electricity – from say 4 ¢/kWh to 20 ¢/kWh – caused by a forced switch from thermal electricity generation with rapidly depleting fossil fuels to photovoltaic generated electricity. Depending on the importance of electricity's role in the economy, this energy transition could result in much higher total costs of production throughout the economy, a much lower level of economic output, and consequently a decline in living standards.*

If, however, the cost of the backstop is only slightly higher than that of the non-renewable it replaces, as on the right side of the figure, then the transition is unlikely to be disruptive. The switch to the backstop would be imperceptible to consumers – much like the primary energy switching along the gasoline cost curve in figure 5.2. In this case, the fact that fossil fuels are non-enduring is inconsequential; they are a component of the energy system that is phased out as the system transitions to one or more backstop alternatives, while maintaining the same level of energy services at about the same cost.

Which scenario provides a more realistic depiction of the prospects for our fossil fuel-dependent, global energy system? This has been the subject of much debate.

In the seventies, N. Georgescu-Roegen warned that the accelerating development by humans of detachable organs (vehicles, buildings, toys) depends on a reliable flow of low cost, high quality energy that may expire with the exhaustion of fossil fuels. At the time of his writing, potential saviors like solar photovoltaics and windpower (what he calls "Prometheus III") appeared to be much higher cost

---

* Economists argue, however, that prices would edge higher than production costs (even the cost of the highest cost producer operating in the market) as producers earned *scarcity rents*: an extra return reflecting future values forgone by consuming a non-renewable resource today instead of waiting to consume it in the future when its price is higher due to increasing scarcity. Prices for the exhaustible resource will rise earlier toward the cost of the backstop as impending scarcity is recognized. This ensures a relatively smooth transition in terms of the evolution of price, even when the backstop has a much higher production cost. See R. Solow, "The Economics of Resources or the Resources of Economics," *American Economic Review* 64 (1974): 1–14.

and perhaps "unviable" (unable to become net energy producers). He concluded that, "The only reasonable strategy . . . is conservation, so as to gain as great a time lead as possible to wait for the uncertain Prometheus III, or, alternatively, to change without great convulsions from the present high level of industrial activity to one probably analogous but not identical to that of the past wood age."[10] In other words, we should consciously curb now our energy intensive tendencies in order to reduce the probability of future crises due to sudden, unforeseen resource scarcity.

An eclectic mix of physicists and economists offered the counter argument that the huge availability of other sources of energy combined with human ingenuity would ultimately provide a ready replacement for fossil fuels as needed. Physicists A. Goeller and A. Weinberg spoke of an "age of substitutability" in which low cost energy would allow humans to continue their energy-dependent ways provided they directed their ingenuity to the development of alternatives to fossil fuels. The optimistic economist J. Simon presented the outcome of this human endeavor as virtually inevitable – humans would innovate low cost energy substitutes to fossil fuels as needed. "Necessity is the mother of invention." More recently, R. Ayres, hardly an optimist about humanity's ability to live sustainably, acknowledged that innovation since the time of Georgescu-Roegen's analysis has shown the potential for humans to develop alternatives to fossil fuels at what may be a comparable cost over the long run.[11]

While many economists tend to see a great potential for humans to find substitutes for any material or energy input, many non-economists tend to be less optimistic. Sometimes I feel caught between these two world-views. Certainly, energy markets are not immune to cataclysmic events. I cannot ignore, however, evidence of how quickly costs have declined for alternatives to fossil fuels that at the time of Georgescu-Roegen's writing seemed high cost and perhaps unviable. In my student days, it was commonly assumed that the oil price shocks of the 1970s and early 1980s signaled impending exhaustion of global fossil fuel supplies – and this was associated with continuously rising energy prices. But those high prices triggered significant responses from both the demand and the supply sides, and eventually oil prices fell back to their original levels.

Now, at the beginning of the twenty-first century, we are in a period of relatively high oil prices. Once again, prophets foretell of cataclysmic events, of the desperate need for a quick transition away from fossil fuels. I am puzzled that these prophets seem so unaware or uninterested in exploring the dynamic that sustained high oil prices would trigger. By how much will energy demand fall? Attracted by the high oil prices, where will investment concentrate? Will it be on finding yet more conventional oil? Will it be the production of refined petroleum products from coal or biomass? When enough time has passed for this technological and resource transformation, will the average price of energy be much higher than it is today?

The evidence of this chapter suggests that sustained higher energy prices would unleash a substantial response from the many alternatives to conventional crude oil. A key issue, however, is the extent to which these can be developed with minimal impacts and risks to the biosphere, and what that might cost. I now turn to this issue.

Notes

1. Efficiency and power estimates in this paragraph are from V. Smil, "Energy in the Twentieth Century: Resources, Conversions, Costs, Uses, and Consequences," *Annual Review of Energy and the Environment* 25 (2000): 21–51.
2. J. Goldemberg (ed.), *World Energy Assessment: Energy and the Challenge of Sustainability* (New York: United Nations Development Programme, 2000), 139.
3. Ibid., 144.
4. For 1980–2003: British Petroleum, *Energy in Focus: Statistical Review of World Energy 2004* (London: British Petroleum, 2004). For 1900–1980: British Petroleum, *Statistical Review of World Energy 1998* (London: British Petroleum, 2004).
5. M. Hubbert, "National Academy of Sciences Report on Energy Resources: Reply," *Bulletin of the American Association of Petroleum Geologists* 49, 10 (1965): 1720–1727.
6. C. Campbell and J. Laherrere, "The End of Cheap Oil," *Scientific American* 278, 3 (1998): 78–84; R. Bentley, "Global Oil and Gas Depletion: An Overview," *Energy Policy* 30, 3 (2002): 189–205; and K. Deffeyes, *Hubbert's Peak: The Impending World Oil Shortage* (Princeton, N.J.: Princeton University Press, 2001).
7. M. Adelman and M. Lynch, "Fixed View of Resources Limits Creates Undue Pessimism," *Oil and Gas Journal* 95, 14 (1997): 56–60; M. Adelman, "Comment on: R. W. Bentley, 'Global Oil and Gas Depletion,'" *Energy Policy* 31, 4 (2003): 389–390; C. Watkins, "Oil

Scarcity: What Have the Past Three Decades Revealed?" *Energy Policy* (forthcoming, 2005); J. Ryan, "Hubbert's Peak: Déjà Vu All Over Again," *International Association of Energy Economics Newsletter,* 2nd Quarter, 2003; P. Odell, "Dynamics of Energy Technologies and Global Change," *Energy Policy* 27, 13 (1999): 737–742, *Oil and Gas: Crises and Controversies 1961–2000* (Brentwood, UK: Multi-Science, 2001) and *Why Carbon Fuels will Dominate the 21st Century's Global Energy Economy* (Brentwood, UK: Multi-Science, 2004). The argument is expanded to all resource industries by J. Krautkraemer, "Non-Renewable Resource Scarcity," *Journal of Economic Literature* 36, 4 (1998): 2065–2107.

8. For cost estimates, see M. Adelman and C. Watkins, "Oil and Natural Gas Reserve Prices 1982–2002: Implications for Depletion and Investment Cost," Working Paper 03–016, MIT Center for Energy and Environmental Policy, 2003; R. Skinner and R. Arnott, *The Oil Supply and Demand Context for Security of Oil Supply to the EU from the GCC Countries* (Oxford: Oxford Institute for Energy Studies, 2005); Odell, *Why Carbon Fuels Will Dominate*; R. Dunbar, M. Stogran, P. Chan and S. Chan, *Oil Sands Outlook: Potential Supply and Costs of Crude Bitumen and Synthetic Crude Oil in Canada 2003–2017* (Calgary: Canadian Energy Research Institute 2004).

9. P. Dasgupta and G. Heal, "The Optimal Depletion of Exhaustible Resources," *Review of Economic Studies* 41 (1974): 3–28; W. Nordhaus, "The Allocation of Energy Resources," *Brookings Papers on Economic Activity* (1973/74): 529–570.

10. N. Georgescu-Roegen, "The Crisis of Resources: Its Nature and Its Unfolding," in G. Daneke (ed.), *Energy, Economics and the Environment* (Lexington, Mass.: Lexington Books, 1982), 22. See also N. Georgescu-Roegen, *The Entropy Law and the Economic Process* (Cambridge, Mass.: Harvard University Press, 1971).

11. H. Goeller and A. Weinberg, "The Age of Substitutability," *American Economic Review* 61 (1978): 1–11; J. Simon, *The Ultimate Resource* (Princeton, N.J.: Princeton University Press, 1981); R. Ayres, "The Second Law, the Fourth Law, Recycling and Limits to Growth," *Ecological Economics* 29 (1999): 473–483.

6 | *Can we use fossil fuels cleanly – and what might it cost?*

THE planet appears to have sufficient fossil fuel resources for these to play a significant role in the global energy system far beyond this century, and to enable a smooth transition to alternatives as needed. As fossil fuel use continues, however, the associated environmental threats – degradation of soil and water, alienation of land, smog, acid rain, and climate change – may intensify to the point where cleanliness concerns far outweigh endurance concerns. Many argue that this is already the case. But is it inevitable that fossil fuel use harms humans and their environment? What have we done in the past to mitigate the negative consequences of fossil fuel use? How cleanly could we use fossil fuels in future if we made a sincere effort?

6.1 Environmental and human impacts from fossil fuel use

While the high energy density of fossil fuels has been exploited with increasing effectiveness first in the steam engine, and then in the steam turbine and internal combustion engine, the harm from fossil fuels is manifest in air, water and land, ranging in scope from local to global. These effects are associated with all stages in the fossil fuel chain, from exploration and extraction to processing, transport and final use. Humans have tried to reduce the impacts from fossil fuel use, and have met with some successes, although these incremental improvements are under continuous pressure from the relentless growth in total consumption.

Ongoing impacts and extreme event risks

As I noted in the discussion of nuclear power in chapter 4, the "risk" of a negative environmental or human impact is the magnitude of the impact multiplied by its probability of occurrence.[1] If a coal mining accident that kills ten people has a 10% probability over 100 years,

168

the risk is one person's death by coal mining accident in that time-frame. The concept of risk gets more challenging to apply, however, when the impacts we are assessing get more complex. Is it instructive to conclude that an oil spill with a 50% chance of reaching shore and destroying six bird species represents a risk of three extinct bird species? What about events with extremely high impacts but extremely low probabilities, such as a catastrophic nuclear accident? Does probability multiplied by impact provide a helpful way of portraying this type of risk?

In my survey of the environmental and human impacts from the use of fossil fuels, I find it helpful to split these impacts into two groups according to their risk profile: on the one hand, *extreme event risks*, and, on the other, what I call *ongoing impacts and risks*. Extreme event risk refers to events that have an extremely low probability of occurrence but could have an extremely severe impact. Examples include a large oil spill from an ocean going tanker, a massive offshore oil well blowout in an ecologically sensitive area, a major refinery explosion, a serious coal mining accident, or severe radiation exposure to a large natural area or human population from a nuclear accident. Some risk analysts support this separate consideration of extreme events.[2] I believe it is particularly important for comparing our major energy options, as I explain when comparing fossil fuels to other options in chapter 7.

Extreme event risks are contrasted in table 6.1 with ongoing impacts and risks. With ongoing (or operating) impacts, we know certain occurrences with a high degree of confidence. We now understand the relationship between industrial acid emissions and the acidity levels in downwind lakes. We know precisely the amount of natural habitat that is alienated by an open pit coal mine. By the term risks, I mean uncertain but non-extreme impacts. While we know that CO_2 is a greenhouse gas, there is considerable uncertainty in our understanding of the relationship between changes to its atmospheric concentration and changes to the climate. While we know that nitrous oxide emissions affect human health, our understanding of all of the risks involved is far from precise.

Ongoing impacts and risks to land are especially associated with the production and processing stages of fossil fuels. For anybody traveling past an open pit coal mine, oil sands operation, or the well-dotted landscape of an oil and gas producing region, it is hard to overlook the

Table 6.1. *Ongoing impacts and extreme event risks from fossil fuels*

	Ongoing Impacts and Risks			Extreme Event Risks
	Air	Water	Land	
Production exploration extraction	combustion and fugitive emissions (GHG and other)	groundwater / ocean contamination, water diversion/depletion	hazardous waste, ecological disruption, erosion	subsidence, well-head blowouts, mine accidents, landslides
Processing purification manufacturing	combustion and fugitive emissions (GHG and other)	water diversion/depletion, contamination	hazardous waste	refinery fires
Transportation (pipelines, tankers, trucks)	combustion and fugitive emissions (GHG and other)	water contamination (spills)	ecological disruption	pipeline breaks, pipeline explosions, tanker oil spills
Use consumer use waste disposal	combustion emissions (GHG and other); urban smog, health-damaging pollutants	acid rain (coal), water contamination (road runoff; spills)	site contamination (spills)	explosions, poisoning

physical disruption to the land from fossil fuel extraction. The presence of industry structures, roads, drilling activity and seismic testing during exploration (from explosives or other methods) can disturb existing flora and fauna by displacing animal migrations and altering species behavior. Site impacts may continue long after a well has ceased producing or a site has been mined; the area may remain barren if not properly reclaimed, or land may be contaminated from waste – debris, process chemicals, sand, shale, heavy hydrocarbon residues, spent solvents, drilling waste fluid.* Extreme event risks such as subsidence (land caving in over wells), well-head blowouts, coal mine explosions and collapses, and various accidents all heighten the potential for land-related impacts to the environment and people. End-uses of fossil fuel products can also impact the land, as with seepage from leaking fuel storage tanks (including small tanks adjacent to residences) and the uncontrolled disposal of used lubricants such as used motor vehicle oil. While these latter effects are individually smaller and localized, the cumulative impacts and risks can be significant.

Ongoing impacts and risks for water are less immediately apparent, but can also be substantial. The waste streams noted above have the potential to contaminate groundwater. Contamination can also occur in abandoned wells if deep brine-water reservoirs are allowed to enter shallow freshwater aquifers. A significant amount of wastewater – often briny and high in metal elements, oil and grease – is generated during field processing to separate water from the extracted crude oil. Disposal of this water traditionally occurred in open pits, creeks, and roads, but today disposal regulations are stricter and the water may be reinjected into the well, enhancing oil and gas recovery by increasing reservoir pressure. Other freshwater impacts include the disruption of surface and groundwater from large scale surface mining, acid mine drainage formed when dissolved pyrite from coal mines forms a dilute acid, and water diversion for uses such as coal washing and steam generation. Marine water faces extreme event risks, such as major oil spills from tanker accidents and blowouts at offshore platforms, but

---

* About one million tons of hazardous waste is produced each year in American oil fields. R. Bryce, "More Precious than Oil," *Texas Monthly* (February 1991): 109.

also ongoing impacts from activities such as the routine dumping of fuel-tainted ballast water by freighters and persistent leaks from offshore wells, platforms and undersea pipelines. These can result in loss of marine plant and animal life, and may leave shorelines uninhabitable for some time.

Ongoing impacts and risks to air are usually associated with fossil fuel combustion, although production and processing activities can be significant contributors through the escape of evaporated gases from wells, processing facilities, refineries, pipelines, storage tanks and vehicle refueling. In addition to the risks of injury from mine accidents, underground coal mining remains a dangerous occupation because of the difficulty of shielding miners from toxic dust and gases that cause a variety of lung ailments. Coal mines in some developing countries are especially notorious for high rates of miner illness and premature death because of exposure to these gases. It is emissions from fossil fuel combustion, however, that garner the most attention, and for good reason as their harmful effects cover a wide range that includes indoor air quality, urban air quality, regional acid precipitation and possibly the global climate. In the following paragraphs I review each of these in turn.

As I noted in chapter 2, the use of solid fuels for cooking in open indoor fires and inefficient, poorly ventilated stoves is responsible for perhaps 1.6 million premature deaths per year in developing countries. While the fuel is usually biomass (sometimes after processing into charcoal), some coal is used in countries where it is plentiful and cheaper than biomass, mainly in China. Burnt in this way, coal emits the same harmful byproducts as biomass, namely particulates and carbon monoxide. Depending on the type of coal, it may also emit sulphur oxides and trace elements of arsenic, lead, fluorine and mercury. Substantial improvements to indoor air quality are possible by the widespread adoption of efficient, well-ventilated stoves. However, it is difficult with solid fuel stoves, whether using biomass or coal, to pre-mix the fuel and air sufficiently to achieve good combustion without expensive and sophisticated equipment. The easier way to achieve cleaner indoor air is to switch to kerosene and the liquid petroleum gases propane and butane.

This transition away from solid cooking fuels is closely associated with income. Once past a certain income threshold, households switch away from solid fuels for convenience if not for health reasons, of which they may be unaware.* The first step is to gaseous and liquid fuels because distribution is easier; small trucks and carts can deliver household-size tanks holding kerosene, propane or butane. The electricity and natural gas used at the higher income levels in most major cities of developing countries require capital-intensive distribution networks, a service not available in urban slums, smaller towns and the rural areas where most of the world's poor live. At least with respect to indoor air quality, energy-focused policy may not be required, as increases in income for the earth's poorest inhabitants drive this energy transition.

Because kerosene, propane and butane are produced from fossil fuels, improvement in indoor air quality is largely the result of substituting fossil fuels for renewable energy (in the form of solid biomass). This may seem ironic given the common association, by people in wealthy countries, of fossil fuel use with negative human health impacts and risks. Yet if all poor households in developing countries could switch tomorrow away from solid biomass combustion to gaseous and liquid forms of fossil fuels for cooking and space heating, over a million lives per year would be saved. Of course, improvement to indoor air quality is also possible by the adoption of low-emission biomass stoves or by the conversion of biomass into gaseous hydrocarbons. Biogas digesters in India, China and other developing countries convert animal and crop wastes into gas that is used domestically for cooking and heating and by light industry for various thermal applications. There are hopes to greatly expand the penetration of low-emission biomass-based technologies and fuels, but several decades of effort have met with only limited success.[3]

The association of the industrial revolution with greater fossil fuel combustion coincided with a process of rapid urbanization in industrializing countries that is now spreading to the rest of the world. Fossil fuel combustion became concentrated in urban areas, as did its emissions and their air quality effects. These effects depend on the fuel type, combustion technology and ambient meteorological conditions. Even prior to the industrial revolution, Londoners relied on coal

---

* Acquiring, storing, handling and residue disposal with solid fuels is time consuming and unpleasant work; and solid fuel stoves may heat interior space during the summer when it is not desired. See World Bank, *Energy Services for the World's Poor* (Washington, D.C.: World Bank, 2000).

for domestic use and so its air quality problems predated industrialization by several centuries.* Incomplete combustion of coal generates large and small particulates, uncombusted hydrocarbons, carbon monoxide, nitrogen oxides and sulphur dioxide. With industrialization, emissions increased by orders of magnitude and high emission levels spread from large cities to mid-sized cities and even to small industrial towns. Prior to 1900, coal-fired steam engines were the predominant source of emissions, but in the twentieth century these partnered with and were eventually replaced by coal-fired electricity generation plants and automobiles as major urban emission sources.

Air quality in coal-based cities, like London and Pittsburgh, was especially affected by smoke (particulates) and sulphur dioxide. Particulates are associated with lung ailments like asthma and tuberculosis, and the risk of cancer because of trace metals and carcinogenic hydrocarbons that enter the lungs attached to small particles. While industrialized countries have reduced coal combustion as a cause of poor urban air quality, it is still important in many cities in Eastern Europe and in developing countries, China being especially noteworthy.

With the exception of a few cities, gasoline combustion in automobiles has largely replaced coal combustion as the primary threat to urban air quality, first in the major cities of industrialized countries and now increasingly in the metropolises of developing countries. The number of automobiles has grown exponentially from 10 million in 1910 to 100 million in 1955 to over 700 million in 2000.[4] The growth rate shows signs of abating in industrialized countries but not in developing countries. When combusted, gasoline, diesel and other hydrocarbon vehicle fuels emit nitrogen oxides, carbon monoxide, particulates, and pure and partially oxidized hydrocarbons. These latter gases (like benzopyrene) are emitted from vehicle tailpipes because of incomplete combustion, but also escape as pre-combustion evaporation from the fuel system components (fuel tank, fuel lines, carburetor) and during refueling. Nitrogen oxide and hydrocarbon emissions from vehicles play a key role in the production of urban

---

* Although London's pre-industrial experiences with coal are well documented, J. McNeill suggests that Kaifeng, China, was the first city in the world to convert from wood to coal, which it did for about 100 years in the eleventh century. See J. McNeill, *An Environmental History of the Twentieth-Century World* (New York: Norton, 2000).

smog as they react in sunlight to produce low-level (tropospheric) ozone (O_3). Human impacts and risks are mostly lung-related, but smog can also affect animal health, inhibit plant growth, reduce visibility and, depending on acidity levels, corrode human-built structures. Gasoline combustion can be controlled to produce much smaller particulates than coal combustion, but research now suggests that tiny particulates, less than 2.5 micrograms instead of 10 micrograms, may pose even more severe human health risks.

The second major category of fossil fuel-related air emissions concerns their regional effect on ecosystems. Sulphur dioxide (SO_2) and nitrogen oxide (NO_x) emissions from the combustion of coal, gasoline, diesel, heating fuel, natural gas and other fuel products mix in the atmosphere with water vapour, particulates, hydrocarbons and other pollutants (ammonia from non-energy sources) to form acid compounds such as sulphuric acid (H_2SO_4) and nitric acid (HNO_3) that precipitate to earth in snow or rain – hence the term *acid rain*. Acid deposition also occurs in a dry form, with SO_2, sulphur particulates and nitrogen compounds settling to earth. Fossil fuel combustion accounts for 80% of human emissions of sulphur dioxide and 70% of nitrogen oxides.[5] Acid precipitation can occur hundreds of kilometers downwind, which is why acid rain is a regional and sometimes international challenge. It came into prominence as an issue in North America and Europe, but is now a concern in eastern Asia and elsewhere as fossil fuel energy use increases around the globe. By changing the acidity of water, acid rain can affect plant life and harm some species of fish. By changing the acidity of soils, it causes damage to trees and crops. The mountainous border area of the former East Germany and the Czech Republic was particularly notorious for *waldsterben* (forest death) from its long-standing reliance on high-sulphur coal in industry and electricity generation. I retain a lasting memory of mountainsides of tree skeletons from my visit to the region in 1991. Acid rain can also corrode natural and human-made surfaces, a threat to renowned archeological structures around the world as alkaline materials like limestone and marble are more rapidly eroded.

The third major category of fossil fuel-related air emissions concerns their global contribution to anthropogenic greenhouse gases in the atmosphere. Naturally occurring greenhouse gases, such as CO_2, in the earth's atmosphere slow the loss of heat into space, keeping the earth's surface warmer than it otherwise would be. For 1,000 years before 1800, CO_2 concentrations were stable around 280 parts per million (ppm). Because much of the carbon in fossil fuels ends up as CO_2 after combustion, the increasing emissions accompanying the industrial revolution have corresponded with a growing concentration of CO_2, which stood at 370 ppm by 2000. Fossil fuel combustion accounts for 75% of anthropogenic emissions of CO_2 with deforestation contributing much of the rest. Other anthropogenic GHG emissions are also on the rise, some of which are energy-related. Atmospheric concentrations of methane, which has twenty-one times the GHG effect of CO_2, have increased, in part because of fugitive leaks from the fossil fuel industry, although agriculture is a much more important source. Nitrous oxide (N_2O), a less important GHG, has also seen its atmospheric concentration increase, in part because of fossil fuel combustion.

Many scientists suspect that rising atmospheric concentrations of GHGs will increase the earth's temperature and affect climate in difficult-to-predict ways, perhaps increasing the frequency of extreme weather events. A general warming may also melt part of the polar icecaps, causing sea level rise that threatens vulnerable, low lying countries like Bangladesh. Efforts to measure the earth's average temperature (a difficult task in itself) appear to indicate gradual temperature increases, showing that near-surface air temperatures and ocean surface water temperatures around the globe have increased by 0.3– 0.6°C since the late nineteenth century. The eleven hottest years since 1860 have all occurred since 1983 and mountain glaciers have generally been in retreat all over the world. From some of its scenarios that are similar to my current trends scenario in terms of GHG emissions, the IPCC forecasts that the average global temperature over the next 100 years will increase by between 1.4 and 5.8°C.[6]

Historical efforts at cleaner fossil fuel use

My discussion of the cleanliness challenges of fossil fuels has been heavily weighted toward emissions-related issues as these have rightly garnered the most attention over the past forty years – and still do given the current international focus on GHGs and the air quality crisis in the large cities of industrialized and especially developing countries. The water and land use challenges from fossil fuel use should not, however, be overlooked.

The requirements for land protection and rehabilitation from fossil fuel activities in industrialized countries are much more stringent now than forty years ago. Over the past decade, comparable standards have been spreading to countries of the former Soviet Union, and some of the newly industrializing countries in eastern Asia are also starting to tighten their standards. Increasingly, there is pressure on multinational corporations to apply voluntarily the same standards for environmental protection in their operations in developing countries that they must adhere to in industrialized countries. This is not to suggest that fossil fuel extraction is currently associated with pristine natural environments. Some especially damaging practices, such as coal mining that involves mountain top removal, in the US and elsewhere, have yet to be phased out. It remains to be seen if the land rehabilitation requirements for oil sands development in western Canada will be adhered to. The land impacts of many types of fossil fuel developments, however, are much reduced from several decades ago, and requirements are expected to become even more stringent.

All of the human sources of oil contamination of seawater have been in decline over the past forty years, with the incidence of major accidents falling to such an extent that deliberate, illegal dumping of oily ballast by freighters has now surpassed accidental oil spills.[7] Even in the case of deliberate dumping, more sophisticated air reconnaissance is now progressing in tracking down the remaining perpetrators. There is still much controversy about offshore oil exploration and extraction, in part because it is so difficult to assess the full impact of activities on marine and coastal ecosystems. Opponents point to the despoliation associated with petroleum extraction in the deltas of the Niger in Africa, and the Tigris and Euphrates in Iraq. They argue that underwater detonations for seismic mapping in some coastal areas causes harm to whales because of their sensitivity to sonic shock waves. Advocates, in contrast, point out that by augmenting ocean floor irregularity, the underwater structures of offshore oil rigs have been shown to increase marine biodiversity in the Gulf of Mexico and the North Sea. They also note that natural systems have recovered from oil spills faster than many environmentalists predicted, although this is certainly a disputed claim.*

* A recent article notes that some effects on animal populations and some oil residues in beach sediments were still found up to eleven years after the *Exxon Valdez* oil spill in Alaska in 1989, but does not suggest the "permanent ecosystem

The extreme cases of freshwater despoliation by the fossil fuel industry have also been curbed by regulatory initiatives over the past forty years, but at the same time more complex, larger processes and the sheer growth of the industry have offset some of these gains. Refineries are cleaner per unit of output, but the quantity of crude oil they process is much greater. Coal mines and oil sands plants have expanded too, and the copious amounts of water they process affects outflow water quality and temperature. In urban areas, regulations and even financial incentives have had some success in reducing accidental and deliberate flows of liquid hydrocarbons (lubricants, fuels, solvents, other petroleum-based chemicals) into runoff water into adjacent lakes, rivers and oceans. Nonetheless, some flows are still at potentially toxic levels, especially in those developing countries where regulatory controls are more lax or less effectively policed.

Combustion emissions still represent the major environmental and human challenge from our reliance on fossil fuels. The dominant concerns for policy have been urban smoke and soot, urban smog, regional acid rain and global climate change.

Prior to the industrial revolution, London – which had mostly shifted to coal for domestic cooking, heating and artisan production in the sixteenth century – already regulated the hours of the day for operating furnaces and the months of the year for domestic use of coal.[8] As the industrial revolution progressed, the smoke and soot contribution from industrial smoke stacks surpassed that of domestic chimneys in major industrial cities in Europe, North America and soon Japan. With perhaps the worst problems, industrial Britain led the regulatory response. The Railway Clauses Consolidated Act of 1845 required railway engines to reduce smoke by improved combustion; the Improvement Clauses Act of 1847 required lower factory emissions; and the Sanitary Act of 1866 empowered authorities to take action against smoke nuisances.[9] In spite of these measures, local air conditions in London continued to deteriorate with greater industrialization until an estimated 4,000 people died in the great London smog of 1952, leading to the UK Clean Air Acts of 1956 and 1968 which sharply regulated coal combustion in cities and required tall

destruction" claim that I remember hearing frequently at the time. C. Peterson, S. Rice, J. Short, D. Esler, J. Bodkin, B. Ballachey and D. Irons, "Long-Term Ecosystem Response to the *Exxon Valdez* Oil Spill," *Science* 302 (2003): 2082–2086.

chimneys for some industries in order to disperse their emissions.[10] Where necessary, other cities emulated London's regulatory response and local air quality problems related to coal use were largely resolved in industrialized countries by the 1960s. In developing countries, however, technological and regulatory advances are continually under siege from the overwhelming effects of economic and population growth. Calcutta and Beijing stand out as coal-based metropolises whose occasional successes with regulating coal have been overtaken in terms of air quality by the relentless growth in total fuel use as the cities expand.[11]

Unfortunately, the progress in reducing smoke in most coal-based cities coincided with the emergence of vehicle exhaust as a new threat. This challenge appeared first in North America with its much higher rates of automobile use. Los Angeles experienced the worst smog conditions having a sunny climate (sunlight triggers the conversion of nitrogen oxides and other precursors into ozone), coastal breezes and surrounding mountains that keep the same air mass trapped for days, and the highest rate of automobile ownership with 4 million cars in 1960. By the late 1940s, Los Angeles already had special agencies to regulate emission sources, and in 1970 the California Air Resources Board, an independent regulatory commission under the California Environmental Protection Agency, passed regulations requiring catalytic converters and other devices to reduce vehicle emissions. A new vehicle in 1996 produced about a sixteenth of the nitrogen oxide emissions of a new vehicle in 1970.* Small particulates from vehicles have also been reduced. Smog in the Los Angeles basin has decreased relative to the 1970s, but growth in the vehicle stock has partly offset technological gains. The number of vehicles in the Los Angeles basin had grown to 10 million by 2000 and, more importantly, because individual vehicles are driven more per year, total vehicle travel increased almost three-fold between 1970 and 1990.[12] Evidence is also mounting that a focus on personal vehicles should not overlook the increasingly important role of larger mobile sources such as planes,

---

* The exhaust emission rate of light-duty gasoline vehicle in 1979 was 3.44 grams of nitrogen oxides per mile (assuming industry average fuel, zero mileage, at high altitude), but only 0.21 grams per mile in 1996; US Environmental Protection Agency, *AP-42: Compilation of Air Pollutant Emission Factors*, Volume II: *Mobile Sources*, 5th edition (Research Triangle Park, N.C: US Environmental Protection Agency, 2001), Appendix G, Table 1.1b.1.

ships and trains. Collectively, these can account for a significant share of urban air emissions, yet regulations tend to be less stringent.

In most metropolises of developing countries, rapidly rising vehicle ownership, more lax regulations and longer survival rates for older vintage vehicles overwhelm technological advances so that vehicles continue to play a key role in deteriorating urban air quality. Mexico City and São Paulo are developing country examples of this phenomenon; both are cities of almost 20 million people in which it is difficult to imagine how air quality can be much worse than it is today even though emissions per vehicle have decreased in the last twenty years. Recent data from Asian cities paint the same dark picture. In the Mumbai-Bombay airshed, nitrogen oxide levels quadrupled between 1981 and 1991.[13] In Hong Kong, ground level ozone increased by 50% between 1990 and 2000.[14] In Delhi, a composite indicator of air pollution nearly doubled between 1991 and 1996.[15] This pattern appears to be the same for any large urban concentration in the developing world, but in many cases either the data are not collected or collection has only recently begun.

Smog is notorious, but it is by no means the only threat to urban air quality of recent decades. At the same time that cities grappled with smog, lead emissions from gasoline were identified as another threat. As an additive to gasoline, lead improves engine performance, but as a post-combustion emission it accumulates in the bloodstream of animals and humans, one of its risks being harm to children's mental development. The Soviet Union actually led the world in banning lead from gasoline in urban areas in 1967. The US, European countries and Japan soon followed by launching phase-out programs in the 1970s, such that between 1977 and 1994 lead concentrations in the air of US cities declined by 95%, with corresponding decreases in the lead concentrations in children's bloodstreams. Although the concern is not as severe, lead substitutes in gasoline are unfortunately now themselves suspected of posing risks.* Emissions of other trace metals,

* As noted in chapter 3, Methyl Tertiary Butyl Ether (MTBE), which was introduced as a substitute for lead as an octane booster in fuels, has been linked to groundwater contamination at sites where even small quantities of the chemical have leaked from gasoline storage tanks. See US Environmental Protection Agency, *Achieving Clean Air and Clean Water: The Report of the Blue Ribbon Panel on Oxygenates in Gasoline*, EPA420-R-99-021 (Washington,

caused by fossil fuels along with other sources, have also been of concern.

Acid rain affects urban areas, but it is especially seen as a regional threat because its range of dispersion can extend hundreds of kilometers from the source. As with smog, considerable regulatory and technological progress has led to improvements in industrialized countries over the last two decades, but these developments have not translated into reductions in acid rain in developing countries because of weaker regulations, lack of compliance in any case, and the offsetting effect of rapid growth in total fuel consumption. Reducing sulphur dioxide emissions from coal combustion provides the greatest reduction of acid rain, which is achieved via flue gas desulphurization, more efficient coal combustion technologies, switching to low sulphur coal, and switching from coal to oil, natural gas or other energy sources. With a progression of more stringent policies, coal-fired electricity generating plants in the US produced in 1995 one third of the sulphur emissions they produced in 1970, and the amount has fallen substantially since then.* Europe has made similar progress, accelerated by the mass closure of coal-fired, high-emission industrial and electricity generation plants in eastern Europe after the collapse of the Iron Curtain in 1990. In the eastern US, deposition of sulphur decreased by 26% from 1989 to 1998, while deposition of nitrogen increased by 2%.[16] Again, this especially is a threat for many developing countries, such as China, with their rapidly growing automobile ownership and negligible success in controlling sulphur emissions. An estimated 34 million metric tons of SO_2 were emitted in the Asia region in 1990, over 40% more than in North America, and modeling simulations indicate that these emissions will triple by 2020 if no action is taken beyond current levels of control.[17]

D.C.: Environmental Protection Agency, 1999). California banned the use of MTBE in reformulated gasoline in 2003.
* The average SO_2 emission rate in electricity production in 1970 was 204 grams per kWh of coal-based electricity generated. This declined to 63 grams per kWh in 1995. Calculated based on net generation at electric utilities emission data from US Energy Information Administration, *International Energy Annual 2001* (Washington, D.C.: US Department of Energy, 2002) (on-line database: www. eia.doe.gov/iea/, accessed August 23, 2002), table 8.3; and annual electric utility SO_2 emissions from electric utilities from US Environmental Protection Agency, *National Air Pollutant Emission Trends Report, 1900–1995* (Research Triangle Park, N.C.: US Environmental Protection Agency, 1996), table A-4.

Efforts to reduce greenhouse gas (GHG) emissions are still in their infancy as the possible connection between human activities, such as fossil fuel combustion, and climate change has only recently seen a rising tide of public and political support. In 1988, the United Nations created the Intergovernmental Panel on Climate Change (IPCC), which produced its first assessment report in 1990. At the 1992 Rio de Janeiro Earth Summit, the United Nations Framework Convention on Climate Change was signed by 165 states, which set a voluntary goal to halt the rise in their CO_2 emissions by returning to their 1990 GHG emission levels by 2000. The second assessment report of the IPCC (1995) further supported the position that humans are influencing the climate and that efforts should be undertaken to reduce emissions. In the Kyoto Accord of 1997 industrialized countries (and countries formerly part of or under the influence of the Soviet Union) committed to specific GHG targets for 2010, equating to 5.2% below 1990 emission levels for the signatory countries.[18] The US and Australia later withdrew from the accord, but with Russia's ratification in 2004, the protocol achieved the critical threshold of ratification by 55 countries that collectively accounted for 55% of emissions from the industrialized signatories that had committed to reductions (called Annex I countries) – thus the protocol became a binding international agreement in 2005.

As of 2005, most countries with significant GHG abatement commitments are not on a path that will see them achieve their Kyoto targets through domestic actions alone, but there are provisions in the protocol for them to get credit for reductions they cause by purchasing emission permits from other signatories and by making abatement investments in developing countries that do not have specified targets. However, with countries like China and India not having abatement commitments under the protocol, and with the US having withdrawn from it, Kyoto compliance will not deflect the upward trajectory of human-produced GHG emissions and the resulting increase in atmospheric concentrations. The negotiators and signatories of Kyoto were well aware of this in 1997, but knowing that they could not hope to achieve a comprehensive solution at once, they saw value in reaching an initial international agreement that would provide experience and a starting point for future negotiations aimed at more substantial reductions over a longer timeframe. Negotiations for the post-Kyoto period began in 2005 and will grow in importance and profile in the years leading up to 2010.

In summary, while the impacts and risks to land and water from fossil fuel extraction may be manageable with adequate regulatory constraints, the multiple dimensions of combustion-related air emissions are more problematic. Technological and regulatory progress that reduces but does not eliminate emissions linked to poor local air quality and regional acid rain can be offset by overall growth in population, urbanization, and the material acquisition associated with rising incomes, especially in the developing regions of the world. Furthermore, we now suspect that GHG emissions present a global climate threat that has implications for energy system decisions everywhere in the world. In the remainder of this chapter I assess the prospects for reducing and even eliminating the various emissions from fossil fuel use. In a global energy system that might be more than three times its current size in 100 years, much hinges on this.

6.2 Technologies and processes for lowering fossil fuel emissions

While humans have found various ways to reduce emissions, they have not, until recently, focused on the goal of zero emissions. But the suspicion that climate change is driven especially by GHG emissions from fossil fuel use has changed this. The holy grail of zero emissions from fossil fuels has become an obsession of a large and rapidly growing body of researchers. The explosion of ideas and literature in this field makes a broader perspective difficult to attain.

In an effort to get this perspective, I categorize in figure 6.1 the major technologies and processes for reducing or eliminating emissions from fossil fuel use into four options. The first three options involve choices about technologies and fuels that reduce but do not eliminate emissions. As these are generally well known, I present all of them briefly in this section. Then I devote all of section 6.3 to the emerging technologies and processes for achieving zero emission use of fossil fuels – the path down the right side of figure 6.1.

Fuel switching

Substitution of one fossil fuel by another is one way to reduce emissions. In the case of GHG emissions, natural gas has a ratio of one

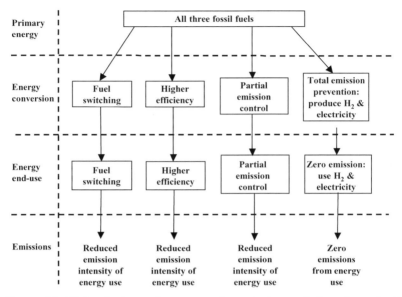

Figure 6.1. Technologies and processes for reducing emissions from fossil fuels.

carbon to four hydrogen atoms, petroleum products have about one carbon to two hydrogen atoms and most forms of coal are made up of a lot of carbon with very little hydrogen. Natural gas is generally cleaner burning with respect to other air pollutants too, so switching from coal or oil to natural gas is how fuel-switching can reduce most emissions. An example of fuel switching at the energy conversion level would be to shift from coal to natural gas in the thermal generation of electricity. An example at the end-use level would be to shift from gasoline to compressed natural gas in vehicles or from an oil furnace to a natural gas furnace in a house.

Historically, market forces have driven environmental improvements from fuel substitution almost as much as pollution-focused policy. The higher energy density and handling convenience of oil motivated its replacement of coal during the twentieth century as the dominant energy source for industrialization, and this substitution improved urban air quality.[19] The replacement of high sulphur by low sulphur coal in the US over the past fifteen years was driven in part by environmental policies but facilitated by railway deregulation that decreased the cost of shipping low sulphur coal from Wyoming and other western states to eastern coal-burning plants. Efforts to develop private, competitive electricity markets in England and Scotland over the past fifteen years enabled new natural gas-fired generators to outcompete existing coal-fired plants, with a consequent reduction in SO_2, NO_x, particulate and CO_2 emissions from electricity generation. Natural gas-fired electricity generation and space heating is growing rapidly throughout industrialized countries at the expense of coal and oil, with significant urban and regional air quality benefits, and slower growth in GHG emissions. Coal use for domestic cooking is also in decline as incomes rise in countries like China, where the dissemination of kerosene, propane and butane results in substantial improvements in indoor and outdoor emissions.

Fuel switching has also been driven by public policy, although an overview suggests that results have been mixed. Cities in different parts of the world (industrialized and developing) have achieved modest vehicle emission reductions by promoting switching from gasoline to alternatives such as natural gas and propane. However, many of these policies have not resulted in significant market transformation, and fuel switching can involve difficult trade-offs; the greater use of diesel relative to gasoline in European cars reduces some emissions at the expense of higher particulates (although advances in lower particulate diesel are now significant).

Increased energy conversion efficiency

The second path in figure 6.1 to reduce emissions from fossil fuel use is to increase energy efficiency. I discussed the technical and achievable potential for increased end-use energy efficiency in chapter 4. On the energy supply side, however, there is also considerable potential for efficiency gains in the conversion processes that produce secondary energy. The following two possibilities in the production of electricity and heat are particularly promising.

Combined cycle gas turbines (CCGT) are gas turbines (like jet engines) that spin an electricity generating turbine with their exhaust, which is then used to produce steam for a steam turbine that also generates electricity. Because the double use of the exhaust gases exploits more of the energy released by combustion in the gas turbine, the efficiency of a natural gas CCGT can approach 60% whereas that of a stand-alone steam turbine is about 35%. Natural gas is the preferred fuel for CCGTs, but the use of coal in integrated gasification-combined cycle (IGCCs) plants is now a distinct possibility, as I explain later in this chapter. CCGTs fired by natural gas were the fastest growing electricity generation technology in industrialized countries in the 1990s.

Cogeneration is the combined production of electricity and useful heat. In this case, the heat from thermal electricity generation also provides steam or hot water for nearby industrial processes or even domestic space heating and cooling. Because useful energy is captured from the heat twice, the first law efficiency of cogeneration plants can exceed 80% (ratio of fuel input to electricity and useful heat output). Cogeneration is already common in several industries like pulp and paper, steel, petrochemicals and oil refining, but there is substantial low-cost potential for its expansion in these and other industries, and for space heating and cooling in residential, commercial and institutional buildings. District space heating is widespread in northern and eastern Europe, Russia and China.

The combined effect of fuel switching and these more advanced conversion technologies can substantially reduce emissions even while fossil fuels retain a dominant role in the global energy system, and even without a major regulatory thrust. On this basis, advocates like R. Bradley argue that fossil fuels can continue indefinitely as the driver of the global energy system, becoming progressively cleaner as their use expands and human expectations evolve.[20] But in many cases, the reduction of emissions from fossil fuel use has been the result of regulatory requirements for emission controls.

Partial emission control

With partial emission control, the intent is to achieve cleaner flue gas either by controlling the parameters of combustion itself (combustion temperature, fuel characteristics, burner technology, recycling of emission gases) or by extracting from the flue gas the most harmful emissions by using various types of filters, mechanical scrubbers and chemical scrubbers. Humans have been making efforts and achieving progress on this path for at least a century.

The parameters of combustion can be modified by changing the constituents of processed hydrocarbons and the combustion technology.

- Ongoing developments over the past century in burner tip technologies, ventilation systems, and exhaust control have dramatically reduced the particulates and noxious gases from domestic and industrial combustion (stoves, furnaces, boilers) that would otherwise compromise indoor air quality in homes, offices and factories.
- Hydrogen sulphide (H_2S), CO_2 and other gases and liquids are routinely removed from natural gas, resulting in cleaner combustion emissions.
- The development of lead-free, reformulated gasoline over the past twenty-five years has decreased lead and other harmful constituents of vehicle emissions.
- Recent efforts to change the properties of diesel fuel are expected to substantially improve this fuel's notorious particulate emissions.

Another approach is to capture most harmful emissions from flue gases in order either to recycle them back into the combustion phase or to divert them to safe storage or a separate end-use.

- Catalytic converters, introduced on vehicles in the 1970s, process exhaust fumes in order to reduce carbon monoxide, hydrocarbon, and nitrous oxide emissions.
- Selective catalytic reduction equipment on large combustors, such as natural gas-fired turbines, reduces nitrous oxide and other emissions.
- Industry and thermal electricity plants use electrostatic precipitators and baghouse filters to capture particulate matter from flue gases. The precipitators use the static charge acquired by moving smoke and dust to attract particulates to an electrically charged rod, which then settle into a catchment vessel. This is now common in coal-fired electricity generation plants and some dirtier industries.
- Most (97%) of the sulphur dioxide (SO_2) from combusting fossil fuels, especially coal, can be removed by desulphurization scrubbers that spray a mixture of water and lime through the flue gas to precipitate calcium sulphite ($CaSO_3$). Sulphur emission scrubbing from coal-based combustion is now conventional practice, especially in industrialized countries.

Ongoing technological developments continue to reduce emissions of particulate matter, sulphur dioxide, nitrogen oxides, carbon monoxide, and other compounds from the combustion of fossil fuels. This explains why total emissions of some of these have trended downward in industrialized countries in recent years in spite of growth in overall fuel consumption. But if the global energy system grows over this century as I suggest in my current trends projection of chapter 2, the reduced emissions resulting from fuel switching, higher efficiency in energy conversion, and partial emission control are unlikely to prevent deterioration of air quality in major urban centers, especially in developing countries. Even relatively clean running vehicles in Mexico City will result in poor air quality if 5 to 10 million vehicles operate in its airshed alongside all of the other fuel combustion sources in this huge and growing megalopolis. Moreover, these three options for emission reduction will not prevent continued increases in GHG emissions if the energy system grows as I project. Indeed, if fossil fuels are still to play a role in the global energy system, preventing emissions from fossil fuel use becomes an objective that is increasingly relevant. While the focus of much new research is especially on the prevention of CO_2 release to the atmosphere, the technologies and processes under consideration address all potentially harmful emissions from the use of fossil fuels.

6.3 Technologies and processes for total emission prevention

The literature on preventing carbon emissions from fossil fuel use seems to double every year, making it precarious to say anything definitive about which paths are more likely to emerge when the inevitable technological shake-out occurs.[21] In this section, I provide an overview of the major technological options that are likely to remain relevant in the years to come – the right side path of figure 6.1. Because coal is considered to be the most plentiful fossil fuel, but also the least desirable in terms of cleanliness of use, I focus below on options that can use coal as the primary energy source.

Although these options are generally categorized as zero-emission, this is not entirely accurate. Virtually every emission prevention technique designed thus far allows at least some escape of CO_2 into the atmosphere. A more precise term, therefore, would be near-zero-emission processes. I stick with the term zero emission for simplicity and to signify that if any of these processes were to become the global norm for converting fossil fuels into clean secondary energy, the effect would be a profound reduction in CO_2 emissions, which could be pursued to the point of stabilizing atmospheric concentrations.

Capturing carbon is one thing. Disposing of it is quite another. In this section, I focus on processes for capturing carbon and then turn in section 6.4 to the storage question. Consistent with most current views, I focus on processes involved in capturing and storing carbon in the form of CO_2.

Post-combustion CO_2 capture in electricity generation plants

Some commentators have suggested that the challenge of preventing CO_2 emissions from fossil fuel combustion is fundamentally different from the previous emission reduction challenges that the industry has dealt with – by virtue of the fact that CO_2 is an inescapable byproduct of fossil fuel combustion. But academic and industry researchers seem unimpressed with this apparently daunting task, and have tackled this new challenge no differently than their predecessors solved earlier problems in reducing SO_2, particulates, NO_x and other emissions. Indeed, one of the approaches being considered is to install yet another apparatus for purging an unwanted emission from the post-combustion flue gases of fossil fuel electricity generation plants.

Figure 6.2 presents the major elements of this process for a coal-fired power plant, in this case using pulverized coal or fluidized bed technology, but the general approach can apply to plants fired by natural gas, oil, refinery residues, and even biomass. To reduce complexity, this power plant has only a simple steam turbine. As the figure shows, coal and air are fed into a boiler and the combustion produces steam to spin an electricity generating turbine. The flue gases from combustion are subject to the conventional technologies that are currently applied for reducing other emissions, namely selective catalytic reduction (SCR) to reduce NO_x emissions, flue gas desulphurization (FGD) to reduce SO_2 emissions, and electro-static precipitators (ESP) or baghouse to reduce particulates.

Capturing CO_2 from a power plant's flue gases does not require the development of new technologies; some industries have a long history of extracting the gas for various production requirements. One possible approach is to install a membrane in the flue gas stream that

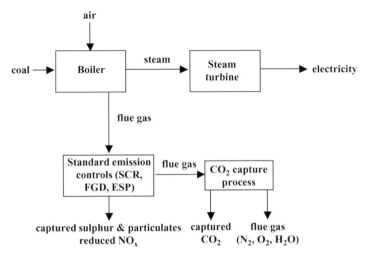

Figure 6.2. Post-combustion CO_2 capture from a coal-fired electricity generation plant.

Note: SCR = selective catalytic reduction to reduce NO_x; FGD = flue gas desulphurization to reduce SO_2; ESP = electro-static precipitation to reduce particulates.

diverts the flow of CO_2 while allowing the passage of other gases. The likely practice, however, is to react the flue gas with a solvent that binds to the CO_2. The solvent is then heated to release a stream of pure CO_2 in a separate stage, and finally is recycled back into the flue gas to repeat the process. The residual flue gas (mostly N_2, O_2 and H_2O) is vented to the atmosphere. Some CO_2 escapes along with this gas; most CO_2 capture technologies currently under serious consideration prevent 85–90% of the carbon in the fuel from reaching the atmosphere.

This "CO_2 scrubbing" technique can be integrated into new coal-fired power plants, and even retrofitted on to some existing plants. The energy required to run the capture process, however, would decrease the efficiency of a typical plant by 8–9%. To reduce this energy penalty, researchers are exploring new solvents and improved ways of integrating them with the rest of the power plant. An alternative for these plants is *oxyfuel combustion*. Pure oxygen, produced in an air separation unit, would be fed into the combustion chamber, resulting in a flue gas rich in CO_2 and water vapor. The water vapor would then be condensed in order to isolate the CO_2-rich gas stream.

Because of the energy requirements of the air separation unit, this approach would decrease the efficiency of the coal plant by a similar 8–9% with current air separation technologies, although this may be reduced in future as novel membranes for separating oxygen from air become commercialized.

Thermal power stations and some types of large industrial plants are stationary sources of CO_2 emissions for which this post-combustion capture approach would be relatively easy to implement. When it comes to smaller-scale fossil fuel combustion, however, the technological challenge is daunting. Carbon capture implies that equipment like home furnaces and personal vehicles would be fitted with miniature versions of the elaborate processes involved in CO_2 extraction, concentration and disposal in a coal power plant. This seems unlikely, although technological surprises can never be completely discounted.

The more likely scenario for total emission prevention, as presented in chapter 3, is a substantial increase in the end-use role of electricity and hydrogen and a commensurate reduction in the end-use combustion of hydrocarbons. Recognition of this has generated considerable interest in the technologies and processes that produce from fossil fuels these two key forms of secondary energy while capturing CO_2 and other emissions.

Gasification with CO_2 capture in producing electricity and hydrogen

As I noted in chapter 4, pure hydrogen (H_2) has long been produced for use in industry, especially as a feedstock for ammonia production in fertilizer plants but also for production of higher fraction fuels in oil refineries and, more recently, for the production of synthetic oil at oil sands plants in western Canada. Although hydrogen can be produced using any form of energy, most current production is based on the catalytic reaction of natural gas (mostly methane – CH_4) with steam – called steam methane reforming. Steam and methane are combined in a reactor at temperatures between 750 and 900°C where they react to form a synthesis gas (*syngas*) comprising mostly carbon monoxide (CO) and H_2. The syngas is cooled and then combined with steam before being passed through a catalyst to provoke a water-gas shift reaction that splits the water to make even more H_2 while the oxygen

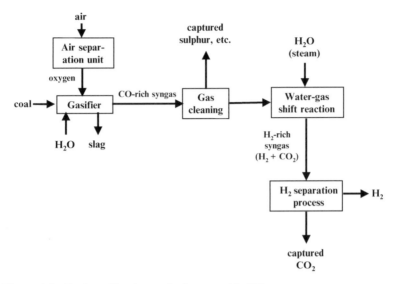

Figure 6.3. Coal gasification to hydrogen with CO_2 capture.

atoms in the steam combine with the CO to produce CO_2. The mixture of CO_2 and H_2 is then split into separate gas streams using a chemical solvent. Because there has been little concern in the past for capturing pure CO_2, the practice thus far has been to separate the H_2 but leave the CO_2 with other fuel gases for combustion, which means that all of the carbon in the natural gas eventually ends up as emissions of CO_2 and CO to the atmosphere.

If coal is the energy source instead of natural gas, and if the CO_2 is to be captured, some extra steps are required, but again these involve conventional technologies. Since coal contains relatively little hydrogen, water is the major source of hydrogen in coal-based processes; coal provides the necessary energy for separating the hydrogen in water from oxygen. Figure 6.3 outlines the major steps in using coal to produce hydrogen with CO_2 capture.

The first step is coal gasification – subjecting the coal to oxygen and steam under pressure. This relies on a process developed in Germany in the 1920s and used today in South Africa as a preparatory stage for the *Fischer-Tropsch process* that produces synthetic liquid fuels from coal. The figure shows that an air separation unit produces oxygen, which is fed into the coal gasifier along with steam. Gasification produces a CO-rich syngas comprising mainly CO and H_2. The gas then enters a gas cleaning unit that extracts sulphur, mercury and other potentially toxic compounds (depending on the properties of the source coal) using solvents and other processes. An alternative config-uration involves delaying some gas cleaning until after the next stage. The gas is then reacted with steam in the same water-gas shift reaction described for steam methane reforming, producing an H_2-rich syngas of hydrogen and CO_2. A solvent can then capture the CO_2 from the syngas, leaving pure H_2 as the output. Researchers are trying to develop membranes that filter the CO_2, ideally during the shift pro-cess, instead of capturing it with solvents, an innovation that could reduce the energy and material costs of separation.

Producing hydrogen from coal requires considerable energy, espe-cially for generating the pure oxygen needed to reach high tempera-tures in the gasifier and for the steam used in the coal gasification and the water-gas shift reaction. The energy ratio of the coal input to the hydrogen output is about 65%. Production of hydrogen from natural gas using steam methane reforming can achieve efficiencies above 80%, but this must be traded off against the higher cost of natural gas as both a hydrogen feedstock and energy source. Coal and water are cheaper than natural gas as energy and hydrogen sources respect-ively, and with rising natural gas prices, industry increasingly looks to coal gasification as the less risky investment for hydrogen production.

This coal gasification process can capture as much as 99% of sulphur and other pollutants, some of which can be processed into commercial chemicals. The slag residue from the gasifier can be used as a harmless material feedstock in road construction and other civil works.

While hydrogen has an important role as an industrial feedstock, it is rarely called upon to provide energy. Indeed, the development of hydrogen as a major source of secondary energy is hindered by the chicken and egg problem that faces all revolutionary changes in tech-nology – hydrogen using technologies need major expansion of hydro-gen production and distribution facilities to justify their widespread dissemination, and vice versa. For this reason, most industry observers expect that coal gasification with carbon capture will first establish a market in electricity generation, a form of secondary energy that already has an established end-use market and delivery system.

Figure 6.4 shows another coal gasification process, but this time with the resulting syngas generating electricity in a combined cycle

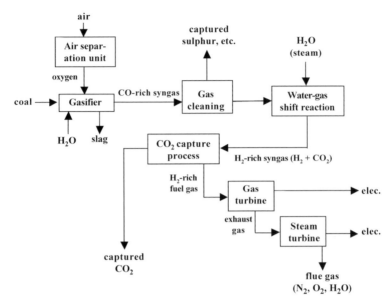

Figure 6.4. Coal gasification to electricity (IGCC) with CO_2 capture.

turbine – what is called *integrated gasification combined cycle* (IGCC). The only difference with the previous diagram is that the H_2-rich fuel gas after carbon capture need not be pure hydrogen because it is to be combusted in a combined cycle turbine (gas turbine and steam turbine) rather than exported from the plant.

While its key technological components have all been in commercial operation for different applications, no commercial-scale IGCC plant has yet been constructed. This is because, without the requirement for carbon capture, IGCC plants are typically 10–20% more expensive than conventional coal combustion plants. The situation would change if penalties were charged for CO_2 emissions. In anticipation of this, the US government launched in 2003 its FutureGen initiative: a $1 billion IGCC plant that would generate electricity (275 MW) but also serve as a laboratory for producing hydrogen from coal and for carbon capture and storage technologies. Since then, several governments have launched initiatives to build demonstration IGCC plants with carbon capture in mind and major electricity companies have announced plans to build commercial-scale IGCC plants.

In presenting these major technology options in figures 6.2–6.4, I have deliberately kept things simple. In each case only one form of secondary energy is produced: either electricity or hydrogen. The gasification literature, however, is full of increasingly complex configurations in which a fossil fuel input (and biomass in some cases) is gasified into syngas, which is then converted into not just electricity and hydrogen, but an array of synthetic fuels such as methanol, Fischer-Tropsch liquids (synthetic gasoline and diesel) and dimethyl ether, and perhaps even into various synthetic chemicals such as acetic acid, methyl acetate, ethylene and propylene. These so-called *polygeneration plants* (or *energyplexes*) could be financially attractive because of their ability to generate value from so many of the process byproducts and to achieve higher energy efficiency from using available waste heat.[22] They are also exciting for engineers to design. (One label I've heard for these synthetic fuel and chemical complexes is "SynCity – an engineer's dream of a place for a good time.")

But producing synthetic fuels from polygeneration plants can serve more than just the fantasies of engineers. These fuels can be designed ("designer fuels" one engineer told me excitedly) to combust with extremely low emissions of local pollutants, perhaps replacing conventional refined petroleum products in certain situations.

Even without the production of synthetic fuels from gasification, there is a great deal of excitement about the prospects for coal-fired IGCC to become the premier process for producing electricity with carbon capture. At the same time, some researchers and industry experts believe that we should not dismiss prematurely post-combustion capture in conventional coal-fired power plants. These have an advantage in that the electricity generation technology is simple and has been in commercial operation for a long time. Moreover, carbon capture equipment can be retrofitted to existing coal power plants, which are the dominant electricity generating technology in the world today. Once a few existing coal plants have been converted, widespread adoption could be achieved over several decades as plants are refurbished or replaced on existing sites.

In terms of fuel choice, the processes for zero-emission production of hydrogen and electricity could equally use natural gas or oil as the energy input instead of coal. Given their higher hydrogen content and greater energy density, these fuels can be more efficiently converted into hydrogen and electricity, but they are more expensive inputs than coal. Capital costs will also be different from one form of energy to another, including the equipment for controlling other pollutants. The choice of fuel will depend, therefore, on the interplay of these various factors, and will vary from one locale to another.

Biomass is also a potential fuel for energy conversion plants with carbon capture. Biomass gasification plants have not yet been demonstrated commercially, but there is considerable optimism among researchers. In any case, post-combustion carbon capture is already a technologically viable option for biomass combustion plants, or for combustion plants that co-combust biomass alongside coal. In concert with carbon capture and storage, the use of biomass as input fuel creates a process with negative GHG emissions – operating like a carbon vacuum cleaner that sucks CO_2 out of the sky in producing biomass via photosynthesis, then generates electricity and hydrogen in biomass-fueled IGCC plants that capture the carbon as CO_2, and then stores it.[23] For some people this sounds too much like science fiction – a way for humans in future to manage the climate of the planet by increasing and decreasing the concentration of CO_2 in the atmosphere. But technologically, this is not a big step from our current capabilities.

Regardless of the input fuel or technology for carbon capture, this vision of zero-emission use of fossil fuels depends on whether the captured carbon can be permanently and safely prevented from reaching the atmosphere. Carbon storage is another field whose literature seems to double every year.

6.4 Carbon storage

For the last several decades, some industries have been required to safely store or convert into marketable products various solid and gaseous wastes. Particulates that are removed by electro-static precipitators and other collection systems (fly ash) find uses as material in structural fill, as dewatering and bulking agents, as road base materials, and as a feedstock in cement and concrete. Because most nitrogen generated by combustion comes from the air rather than fossil fuels, changes in combustion technologies are the main mechanism for reducing nitrogen oxide emissions. Capture and storage is normally not necessary, but with gasification technologies nitrogen in coal can be converted into fertilizer. In the case of sulphur, the conventional practice involves de-sulphurization processes that recover sulphur in solid form (surface solids storage), which can have a market value for various processes and products. Declining prices in sulphur markets, however, have led to the development of acid gas injection deep into geological formations – these acid gases are hydrogen sulphide (H_2S), CO_2 and other compounds that are mixed with natural gas in its reservoir and must be separated in order to produce marketable natural gas.

If our energy system is to continue to rely on fossil fuels while evolving into a zero emission system, almost all carbon from fossil fuel use must be captured and stored. This means that we could conceivably require permanent storage capacity for the over 6,000 gigatonnes of carbon (GtC) in the estimated fossil fuel resource base. A *carbon sink* is the term used for a medium in which carbon is currently stored or potentially can be stored. The three major sinks that have been identified for carbon storage (or *sequestration*) are surface storage, ocean storage, and geological storage.

Surface storage of carbon can be achieved with natural and industrial processes. Living and dead biomass on the planet is already a major carbon sink. Forestry and agricultural carbon management can increase carbon storage in plants and soil by increasing or modifying vegetative cover and by altering tilling practices, and most signatories of the Kyoto Protocol are now exploring these avenues. By itself, however, this form of sequestration cannot prevent the build-up of GHGs in the atmosphere because the mining of fossil fuels continually introduces to the earth's surface and atmosphere carbon that had been stored for millennia in sedimentary layers. While forestry and agricultural practices in parts of the world may for a time achieve net sequestration of carbon, at some point this approach is likely to run up against diminishing returns if it tries to sequester all carbon from the current trends expansion in fossil fuel combustion.* It is also

---

* It has been suggested, however, that at fairly low cost humans could spend the next decades and even centuries reforesting the substantial areas of the earth's surface that were deforested over the last 5,000 years (without substantial loss of agricultural land) as well as huge areas that, with the help of human ingenuity, could be converted from desert and semi-desert to forest and grassland for the first time since the last ice age. Over 2 billion hectares of deforested land worldwide have been estimated to be technically suitable for land-management techniques that produce intensive vegetative cover. For a description of some of the analysis, see, R. Dixon, J. Winjum, K. Andrasko, J. Lee and P. Schroeder,

uncertain that future land-use decisions will adhere to sequestration commitments made decades earlier.

Another possibility for surface storage is for humans to extract elemental carbon from oil and natural gas directly and store it as solid carbon bonded with other elements to produce carbonate rocks. This may ultimately turn out to be the solution, but considerable R&D is required before we know if this can be achieved at a reasonable cost on a large enough scale.

Ocean storage was initially seen as the most promising means of storing carbon. The oceans are already a major carbon sink, but their capacity to hold carbon can be augmented by pumping CO_2 into ocean depths from where it would not resurface because of its physical properties relative to seawater. At ocean depths below 800 meters, CO_2 changes from gas to liquid and below 3,000 meters it would have negative buoyancy relative to seawater, meaning that it would sink to the ocean floor. The potential storage capacity of this option far exceeds the carbon in the earth's estimated fossil fuel resources. However, the option raises environmental concerns about how acidity changes caused by increased CO_2 might affect deep ocean lifeforms. It is also expected that increased concentrations of CO_2 in the atmosphere will naturally increase the rate of CO_2 uptake in aquatic biomass, but an endeavor to manage this process is likely to be more difficult to control than land-based strategies.

Geological storage has garnered the most attention in recent years. For several decades, the fossil fuel industry has had experience transporting CO_2 and injecting it in underground geological structures. In more than seventy sites worldwide, CO_2 is injected into oil reservoirs to increase pressure as part of enhanced oil recovery (about 20–30 million tonnes annually). CO_2 injection is also a means for enhanced natural gas recovery and for dislodging methane from deep coal deposits as part of coal-bed methane production.

"Integrated Systems: Assessment of Promising Agroforests and Alternative Land Use Practices to Enhance Carbon Conservation and Sequestration," *Climatic Change* 30, 1 (1994): 1–23. In contrast, some research suggests that converting agricultural land to forests may be more costly than frequently assumed by studies that ignore the economic opportunities and preferences of landowners. See, R. Stavins, "The Costs of Carbon Sequestration: A Revealed Preference Approach," *American Economic Review* 89, 4 (1999): 994–1009.

A highly relevant demonstration is provided by the recent development of a major enhanced oil recovery project in western Canada. Since 2000, a plant in North Dakota has been shipping CO_2 to Saskatchewan for injection into an aging oil field to increase its yield by 30%. The North Dakota plant is a coal gasification facility that produces a hydrogen-rich gas for industrial uses and a stream of CO_2 as a byproduct. Instead of being vented to the atmosphere, 20 million tonnes of the CO_2 will be shipped over the next thirty years to the Canadian field in a 320 kilometer pressurized pipeline. Industry, governments and researchers are closely monitoring the project as it integrates all of the essential components of a zero-emission fossil fuel system – coal gasification, production of a hydrogen-rich fuel, capture of pure CO_2 in the gasification process, a long CO_2 pipeline, and geological storage of the CO_2.

This and other economically attractive projects indicate the feasibility of a concerted effort to sequester CO_2 in depleted oil and gas reservoirs. However, current and future depleted reservoirs have a combined carbon storage capacity of only 300–600 GtC, not nearly enough to contain all carbon from fossil fuels if these were to continue to dominate the global energy system through this century and beyond. Other research has widened the search for suitable geological storage sites to include the much more plentiful deep saline aquifers which underlie sedimentary basins at depths greater than 800 meters – far deeper than typical freshwater aquifers, which are found at 300 meters and less. Figure 6.5 shows the relationship between saline aquifers and the other two geological storage opportunities.

Contrary to the common understanding of the word aquifer, saline aquifers are not underground bodies of water, but rather porous rock infiltrated with highly saline water (oil and gas reservoirs are also usually in aquifers). Depending on pressure, porosity and other conditions, the pores of deep saline aquifers are capable of absorbing large quantities of CO_2, which would have a liquid-like density at these pressures. Researchers note the serendipitous association between fossil fuel deposits and deep saline aquifers, as they are co-located in sedimentary basins around the globe.[24] While aquifers that are capped by an impermeable sedimentary layer are ideal, this is not essential for long-term storage. If injected far enough from the reservoir boundary, the CO_2 may eventually either dissolve into the aquifer water (hydrodynamic trapping) or precipitate as a solid carbonate mineral by

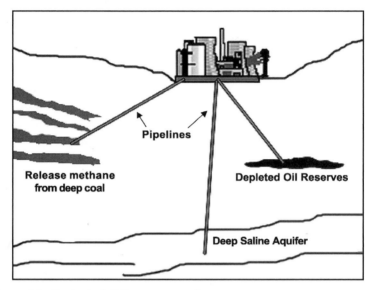

Figure 6.5. Geological CO_2 storage options.

reacting with the surrounding rock (mineral trapping). If dissolved into the aquifer water, the flow rates are such that in a million years most CO_2 would not have traveled more than 10–20 kilometers from the injection site. Efforts to estimate the total CO_2 storage capacity of deep saline aquifers are still crude, but the capacity is known to be huge. While initial estimates ranged from 3,000 to 10,000 GtC, of which two thirds are onshore and one third offshore, more recent analyses is converging around the middle of the range. Conveniently, this matches the planet's estimated carbon endowment in fossil fuels.

From its experience in enhanced oil and gas recovery, the petroleum industry is familiar with the properties of hydrocarbon saline aquifers, and with the dynamic properties of injected CO_2. But prior to the recent concern about climate change, there had been little interest in CO_2 sequestration in saline aquifers. This changed with Norway's implementation of a \$55 per tonne CO_2 tax in the early 1990s, which motivated the Sleipner project in 1996, which injects CO_2 into a deep saline aquifer below the North Sea, not for enhanced oil or gas recovery, but simply to avoid the carbon tax. In this case, the carbon source is a reservoir of natural gas about 300 meters below the sea floor whose high CO_2 content must be reduced to meet market specifications. A process on the offshore platform uses a chemical solvent to separate CO_2 from the natural gas and then inject it into a saline aquifer 1,000 meters below the sea floor.[25] The solvent is continually recycled in the process, and the cleaned natural gas is shipped by pipeline on the sea floor to northern Europe.

The practice of acid gas injection also provides information on geological disposal of CO_2. Natural gas reservoirs can contain significant quantities of hydrogen sulphide (H_2S) and CO_2 along with water and other compounds. In natural gas processing, sulphur recovery for commercial sales and gas flaring have been the standard method of acid gas disposal. However, in some jurisdictions in the 1990s, notably Canada and the US, regulators no longer allowed flaring in certain areas and a depressed sulphur market ruled out sulphur recovery. As a consequence, in western Canada alone the period 1990–2005 saw the establishment of forty-five acid gas injection sites.[26] About half of these are in depleted oil and gas reservoirs, but the rest are in deep saline aquifers that have no hydrocarbons. The average CO_2 content of the acid gas is about 60%, but the content ranges by site from 15% to as high as 98%.

Researchers, industry staff and government officials now closely monitor the existing projects in which CO_2 is being geologically sequestered. Several new projects are in the planning stages or under development in Norway, Algeria, Australia, the UK and the US.

Geological sequestration also requires the transport of CO_2, but there is extensive commercial experience since 1970 with long-distance CO_2 pipelines, some of which extend more than 300 kilometers. The US and Canada now have over 3,000 kilometers of pipelines carrying CO_2 from various sources for injection as part of enhanced oil recovery projects, resulting in the sequestration of about 50 million tonnes annually. These have operated without major concerns or incidents.

Nonetheless, while transport and geological sequestration of CO_2 may be fairly well understood by industry experts, most of the public is ignorant of the practice. Geological sequestration of CO_2 is an approach to environmental mitigation that will strike some people as a stopgap measure that transports rather than eliminates a risk to the environment and people. If this practice were to become widespread as part of a strategy to use fossil fuels cleanly, the impacts and risks need to be better understood.[27]

One risk is that CO_2 will leak back to the atmosphere, defeating the whole purpose of the exercise. Experts are confident, however, that while isolated incidents might occur – such as failure of the cap on an old oil well that holds pressurized CO_2, or leakage at the exposed edge of an aquifer – their impact on the global balance would be minor. Most geologically sequestered CO_2 will not return to the atmosphere in millions of years. If it finally does escape, the biomass gasification vacuum cleaner idea may become relevant, but who knows what humans will be capable of by then.

Another risk is a leak from a pipeline or storage site that results in temporary pooling of CO_2 in a local airshed. High concentrations of CO_2 can cause human fatalities; these have occurred in the past following natural releases related to seismic and volcanic activity in Indonesia and Cameroon, which killed 500 and 1,700 people, respectively.[28] Most experts suggest, however, that if similar location restrictions and safety procedures were applied to CO_2 transport and storage as are currently applied to natural gas, the risks to the public would be at the same acceptable level.

Other possible risks that are less well known include contamination of drinking water, mobilization of sub-surface contaminants, ground shifting and induced seismic activity. So far, the indication is that none of these are likely to be of major concern, but there is still a considerable degree of uncertainty.

This generally positive view of earth scientists and other experts is important, but policy advisors know that no matter how low the risks of a particular technology, public perception is critical. Advocates of the zero-emission use of fossil fuels need to educate the public about the types of risks and their potential magnitude as well as engaging them in the planning and siting process.

Future public attitudes are difficult to anticipate at this point, although the experience in siting and attaining regulatory approval for acid gas injection in North America suggests that broad-based public acceptance is attainable. Thus far, however, there is virtually no public awareness of the possibility of carbon capture and geological storage, and researchers have only just begun to test how members of the public might react when presented with information about CO_2 sequestration.[29]

I have encouraged my own research team to explore the potential dynamics of public opinion. One of our recent studies presented members of the public with different representations of this technology to test for future stability of public views.[30] In part, this involved exploring the extent to which geological storage of CO_2 would be perceived of as similar to siting a nuclear waste repository or an urban waste landfill. Preliminary survey results suggest that a significant segment of the public will see the risks of carbon dioxide storage as much closer to those of a new landfill, suggesting good prospects for public acceptance as long as the local concerns are addressed through consultation and appropriate management and monitoring plans.

6.5 What would zero-emission fossil fuel use cost?

With carbon capture and storage, fossil fuels can become a zero-emission primary energy source. But the legitimacy of this vision depends on our confidence in the technologies involved and the public's acceptance of them. A critical factor is cost.

In the last decade, a great deal has been written on the projected costs of fossil fuel-derived energy with carbon capture and storage. While initial estimates covered a substantial range, the estimates have narrowed in the last few years as experts compare assumptions and share new information in conferences and international processes.[31] A key document reflecting this work is the IPCC report on carbon capture and storage, which synthesizes the extensive literature of recent years.[32]

Carbon capture and storage cost estimates are constructed from individual estimates for the three separate components: capture, transport and storage. Capture represents about 90% of the costs in most estimates.

- Estimates have been generated for carbon capture in conventional coal combustion plants, coal IGCC plants, and natural gas combined cycle plants as well as for prospective coal and biomass polygeneration plants producing electricity, hydrogen and synthetic fuels. These estimates cover a wide range because they are sensitive to different assumptions about fuel input costs (natural gas and coal), technology costs, regulatory costs, and the value of energy outputs (electricity, hydrogen, synthetic fuels and process heat) – ranging

from \$75 to \$125 per tonne of carbon (tC), or about \$21 to
\$34/tCO$_2$.*
- Because of the years of industry experience, there is little range in
  the estimates for the costs of CO_2 transport. Assuming a pipeline
  distance of 100–200 kilometers, the cost would be \$14 to \$18/tC,
  or about \$4 to \$5/tCO$_2$.
- Sequestration costs can be negative or positive depending on
  whether the CO_2 has value for enhanced oil and gas recovery. The
  sequestration cost estimates therefore range from −\$20 to +\$20/tC,
  or about −\$6 to +\$6/tCO$_2$.

When all three components are combined, the total estimated cost
ranges from \$70–\$165/tC abated (\$20–\$45/tCO$_2$). One way of inter-
preting these numbers is to convert them into estimates of their effect
on the cost of production of electricity and hydrogen. In the case of
electricity generation, carbon capture and storage would add 2–3
¢/kWh to the cost of electricity from an advanced coal plant (combustion or IGCC), increasing its total production cost to 6–7.5 ¢/kWh
(assuming that sulphur, fine particulates and other emissions are also
captured). In the case of hydrogen production, carbon capture and
storage would add about \$2–4/GJ over the current cost of producing
hydrogen from natural gas reforming.

When the objective is to shift to a clean energy system over a long time
period, these costs do not present an overwhelming barrier. Electricity
prices currently vary by at least 3 ¢/kWh from one jurisdiction to the
next as a result of regional resource endowments and historical investment choices (hydropower, nuclear, coal, natural gas, renewables).
Indeed, the move toward market prices in some jurisdictions has been
associated with short-run price fluctuations far exceeding 3 ¢/kWh.

But whether or not our current preference for fossil fuels should be
sustained as we shift toward a cleaner energy system depends on how
this primary energy option compares to others. I now turn to this task by
conducting an evaluation that includes cost information in conjunction
with the other real-world considerations that might influence our choice
of energy option, such as international politics, differences between
industrialized and developing countries, regional and local politics,
public perceptions of risk, and institutional and industrial momentum.
From this process, I develop a sustainable energy projection to provide

---

* A molecule of CO_2 weighs 3.66 times more than a molecule of C. My numbers
  do not convert exactly because of rounding.

the clean and enduring primary energy supply that will provision my sustainable secondary energy projection of chapter 3.

Notes

1. For definitions and the general methodology of risk analysis, see M. Morgan and M. Henrion, *Uncertainty: A Guide to Dealing with Uncertainty in Quantitative Risk and Policy Analysis* (Cambridge: Cambridge University Press, 1990); and D. Kammen and D. Hassenzahl, *Should We Risk It? Exploring Environmental, Health, and Technological Problem Solving* (Princeton, N.J.: Princeton University Press, 1999).
2. See V. Bier, Y. Haimes, J. Lambert, N. Matalas and R. Zimmerman, "A Survey of Approaches for Assessing and Managing the Risk of Extremes," *Risk Analysis* 19, 1 (1999): 83–94.
3. A. Reddy, "Energy Technologies and Policies for Rural Development," in T. Johansson and J. Goldemberg (eds.), *Energy for Sustainable Development: A Policy Agenda* (New York: United Nations Development Programme, 2002), 115–136.
4. M. Walsh, "Global Trends in Motor Vehicle Use and Emissions," *Annual Review of Energy and the Environment* 15 (1990): 217–243; Organization for Economic Co-operation and Development, *Outlook 2000 – Perspectives 2000* (Paris: OECD, 2000).
5. S. Smith, H. Pitcher and T. Wigley, "Global and Regional Anthropogenic Sulphur Dioxide Emissions," *Global and Planetary Change* 29, 1–2 (2001): 99–119; J. Olivier, A. Bouwman, K. Van der Hoek and J. Berdowski, "Global Air Emission Inventories for Anthropogenic Sources of NO_x, NH_3 and N_2O in 1990," *Environmental Pollution* 102 (1998): 135–143.
6. The discussion of GHGs is based primarily on Intergovernmental Panel on Climate Change, *Summary for Policy Makers, Synthesis Report, Climate Change 2001: Third Assessment Report* (Cambridge: Cambridge University Press, 2001). Already, in its earlier 1995 report, the IPCC concluded, "the balance of evidence suggests a discernible human influence on global climate." See Intergovernmental Panel on Climate Change, *Climate Change 1995, Second Assessment Report* (Cambridge: Cambridge University Press, 1996), 22.
7. J. McNeill, *An Environmental History of the Twentieth-Century World* (New York: Norton, 2000), 305.
8. S. Dewey, *Don't Breathe the Air* (Texas: Texas A&M University Press, 2000), 25.
9. Atmosphere, Climate & Environment Information Programme, "History of Air Pollution," *Encyclopedia of the Atmospheric Environment* (Manchester: Manchester Metropolitan University, 2002).

10. Dewey, *Don't Breathe the Air*, 26.

11. McNeill, *Environmental History*, 80.

12. California Air Resources Board, *On Road Activity*, Emissions Inventory Series (Sacramento: California Air Resources Board, 2002); M. Wachs and D. Beal, "Taxing our Highways," *Westways*, November/December 2000.

13. G. Haq, W. Han, C. Kim and H. Vallack, *Benchmarking Urban Air Quality Management and Practice in Major and Megacities of Asia* (Seoul: Korea Environment Institute, 2002), 34.

14. C. Fung, "Clean Air for Hong Kong," in G. Haq, W. Han and C. Kim (eds.), *Urban Air Pollution Management and Practice in Major and Megacities of Asia*, Proceedings of Workshop, Air Pollution in the Megacities of Asia Project, Seoul, Korea (Seoul: Korea Environment Institute, 2002), 98.

15. T. Panwar, "Air Pollution Management in India," in Haq, Han and Kim, *Urban Air Pollution Management and Practice*, 62.

16. US General Accounting Office, *Acid Rain: Emissions Trends and Effects in the Eastern United States* (Washington, D.C.: General Accounting Office, 2000), 4.

17. R. Downing, R. Ramankutty and J. Shah, *RAINS-ASIA: An Assessment Model for Acid Deposition in Asia* (Washington, D.C.: The World Bank, 1997), 1–3, 11.

18. Kyoto Protocol to the United Nations Framework Convention on Climate Change; Conference of the Parties, Kyoto, 10 December 1997, United Nations Framework Convention on Climate Change, FCCC/CP/1997/L.7/Add.1, Article 3.

19. For an overview of historical developments, see McNeill, *Environmental History.*

20. R. Bradley, *The Increasing Sustainability of Conventional Energy*, No. 341 (Washington, D.C.: Cato Institute, 1999).

21. For an overview of the options, see Intergovernmental Panel on Climate Change, *IPCC Special Report on Carbon Dioxide Capture and Storage* (Cambridge: Cambridge University Press, 2005); S. Anderson and R. Newell, "Prospects for Carbon Capture and Storage Technologies," *Annual Review of Environment and Resources* 29 (2004): 109–142; International Energy Agency, *The Prospects for CO_2 Capture and Storage* (Paris: International Energy Agency, 2004); and http://www/fossil.energy.gov.html.

22. K. Yamashita and L. Barreto, "Energyplexes for the 21st Century: Coal Gasification for Co-producing Hydrogen, Electricity and Liquid Fuels," *Energy* 30 (2005): 2453–2473.

23. J. Rhodes and D. Keith, "Biomass Energy with Geological Sequestration of CO_2: Two for the Price of One," in J. Gale and Y. Kaya (eds.), *Greenhouse Gas Control Technologies*, Proceedings of the Sixth International Conference on Greenhouse Gas Control Technologies (Oxford: Elsevier Science, 2003), 1371–1377.

24. B. Hitchon, W. Gunter, T. Gentzis and R. Bailey, "Sedimentary Basins and Greenhouse Gases: A Serendipitous Association," *Energy Conversion and Management* 40 (1999): 825–843.

25. J. Gale, N. Christensen, A. Cutler and T. Torp, "Demonstrating the Potential for Geological Storage of CO_2: The Sleipner and GESTCO Projects," *Environmental Geosciences* 8, 3 (2001): 160–166.

26. S. Bachu and W. Gunter, *Characteristics of Acid Gas Injection Operations in Western Canada*, Report PH4/18 to the Greenhouse Gas R&D Programme (Paris: International Energy Agency, 2003).

27. For an overview of safety issues, see S. Holloway, "Safety of Underground Disposal of Carbon Dioxide," *Energy Conversion and Management* 38 (1997): S241–245.

28. See P. Allard, D. Djlevic and C. Delarue, "Origin of Carbon Dioxide Emanation from the 1979 Deng Eruption, Indonesia: Implications for the Origin of the 1986 Nyos Catastrophe," *Journal of Volcanology and Geothermal Research* 39 (1989): 195–206.

29. See S. Shackley, C. McLachlan and C. Gough, *The Public Perceptions of Carbon Capture and Storage* (Manchester: Tyndall Centre for Climate Change Research, 2004); C. Palmgren, M. Morgan, W. Bruine de Bruin and D. Keith, "Initial Public Perceptions of Deep Geological and Oceanic Disposal of Carbon Dioxide," *Environmental Science and Technology* 38, 24 (2004): 6441–6450.

30. J. Sharp, M. Jaccard and D. Keith, *Public Attitudes Toward Geological Disposal of Carbon Dioxide in Canada*, Report to Environment Canada and the Alberta Ministry of Environment (Vancouver: Simon Fraser University, 2005).

31. My own involvement has been in producing estimates for zero-emission fossil fuel use in China as a member of the China Council for International Cooperation on the Environment and Development. This vision is presented for China in N. Weidou, T. Johansson, J. Wang, Z. Wu, Y. Mao, Q. Zhu, F. Zhou, Z. Li, B. Anderson, U. Farinelli, M. Jaccard and R. Williams, "Transforming Coal for Sustainability: A Strategy for China," *Energy for Sustainable Development* 7, 4 (2003): 21–30.

32. Intergovernmental Panel on Climate Change, *Special Report on Carbon Dioxide Capture and Storage*.

7 | *Sustainable energy choices: comparing the options*

OVER the next century and beyond humans will try to meet the growing demand for energy services resulting from population growth and the hoped-for improvement in the living standards of the planet's poorest people, whose needs seem so great today and whose children and grandchildren represent a growing percentage of humanity. We have four major options for addressing these growing service demands, each of which has its attractions. Energy efficiency reduces the need for primary energy while simultaneously addressing environmental objectives and is consistent with an ethical distaste for resource waste. Nuclear power emits no air pollutants or greenhouse gases and reflects the human passion for increasing technological sophistication. Renewables involve interception and use of the ubiquitous and continuous flow of energy in nature around us. Fossil fuels are not renewable, but the resource can endure for centuries and is a high quality form of energy that can be converted at modest cost and low environmental impact into electricity and hydrogen – the cleanest forms of secondary energy.

What should humanity do? What will humanity do? Should we pursue all four options equally? Should we focus just on one? Is there an optimal combination? How would we make this decision? To what extent is our decision constrained by inertial forces of technology and society?

In this chapter I address these questions. I start by developing criteria to reflect the major objectives and constraints that would influence our choice of primary energy options. I then assess how each option performs against these criteria individually, followed by a multi-criteria comparison in which I assess their relative strengths and weaknesses. From this assessment, I develop a sustainable energy projection for this century for our primary energy needs.

For a complete picture of the global energy system, however, the sustainable energy projection for primary energy in this chapter must be combined with the sustainable projection I produced for secondary energy in chapter 3. Decisions at the secondary energy level to use more electricity, develop an extensive hydrogen production and distribution system and allow some continued combustion of cleaner-burning hydrocarbons (especially natural gas and biofuels) work in concert with decisions at the primary energy level to ensure that the conversion of secondary energy has almost zero emissions, negligible land and water impacts and low risks of more extreme events.

As I noted in chapter 1, this exercise has prescriptive and predictive elements. I am prescribing a global energy system in which impacts and risks are substantially reduced from today's levels. This is what must happen if our energy system is to be considered sustainable. Energy-emissions' contributions to poor indoor air quality, polluted urban air, acid precipitation and rising greenhouse gas concentrations must be reduced to negligible levels. Land and water impacts from energy-related activities must be prevented from causing permanent destruction of habitat or accumulation of toxins.

As a basis for this prescription, however, I make several predictions about our major energy choices. In chapter 3, I predict that hydrogen will become a partner alongside electricity in a low emission secondary energy system, although I note that cleaner-burning natural gas and synthetic fuels (including biofuels) will remain significant, the latter especially in rural areas of developing countries. In chapters 4 to 6, I project the future performance of each of the four energy options in terms of physical magnitude, technical potential, costs, and environmental and human impacts. In this chapter, I bring these elements together to generate a sustainable energy projection that achieves my prescriptive goals but that also satisfies my effort to predict how the human energy system is most likely to evolve in the quest for clean and enduring energy.

In this exercise, I am interested in assessing how the major energy options will fare when humans focus on the goal of a sustainable energy system even if that means that one option might dominate the others. Much of the recent analysis on transforming our energy system – especially climate focused analysis conducted by large international bodies of experts – tends to produce compromise paths in which each of the major options might play an equal role in the future. But real world evidence suggests that in most cases of technological change, some technologies, processes and resources do much better than others. With the global energy system, this could be the case in the future, just as it was in the past when coal replaced wood and then oil replaced coal. Undoubtedly, every option will continue to make some contribution. But in my comparison of options for a sustainable energy system, I am not constrained in the role I attribute to each.

7.1 Criteria for comparing energy options

One way of deciding between energy options is simply to compare current costs and pick the cheapest. If this were the universally accepted method, the lives of energy analysts would certainly be easier. Politicians would be happier too. Unfortunately, there are complications.

First, current costs might be a poor indicator of future costs. How rapidly will fossil fuel extraction costs rise as we exhaust today's easily accessible conventional reserves and switch to unconventional supplies? Will renewables cost a lot more as the scale of their application increases? Will a technological breakthrough lower substantially the cost of nuclear?

Analysts have developed techniques to aid decision-making in the face of this uncertainty. A basic approach is to forecast cost trajectories for each option based on our understanding of its magnitude and probable technological development. Whether implicitly or explicitly, decision makers always do something like this when comparing options with uncertain future costs. A more complex treatment could involve sensitivity analysis, in which uncertain parameters that affect future costs are adjusted over a plausible range in order to find out which option is more robust – performs better under a wide range of future outcomes – or which option is more stable – limits cost variability within the tightest range.

Further sophistication can be added by incorporating information on the attitudes of decision makers to risk. A risk-averse decision maker might want to compare the worst outcomes that could occur with each alternative under future possible developments. Variations on this approach might look at regret, the difference between outcomes under different futures rather than just under the worst outcome, or might try to expand the representation of a single decision maker to reflect in some way the diversity of attitudes to risk that might exist in a given society.[1]

The second reason why options cannot be compared just in terms of current costs is that key decision factors may be overlooked if these are not easily reduced to monetary values – examples being some environmental impacts and risks, and vulnerability to geopolitical conflict. Prices may reflect these factors in part – high prices for crude oil may reflect a risk premium related to geopolitics – but rarely are we satisfied that these factors are reflected sufficiently for major societal choices to be based solely on the response of individuals and businesses to current market prices.

Economists refer to social benefits and costs that are not reflected in prices as *externalities*. These are usually negative impacts associated with the uncompensated use of a common property resource like air or water.

One response to externalities, often advocated by economists, is to estimate monetary values for these negative impacts and adjust the cost of each option accordingly – in effect internalizing the externalities. Monetization of all external costs could be combined with one or several of the techniques described above for addressing uncertainty, but there would only be a single cost account for each option. This approach is sometimes referred to as conventional cost–benefit analysis.

However, trying to combine all decision factors into a single monetary value is difficult and controversial.[2] Some impacts, like lost income from respiratory illness or crop damage, may be readily convertible into monetary units because wages and crops already have market values. But what about the diminished view from smog, or the harm air pollution causes to wild animals and natural vegetation? Monetary estimates by independent researchers for such values can vary by a factor of ten.[3] Monetization also faces the challenge of converting impacts and benefits in different time periods into present value equivalents. Finally, some risks are especially difficult to assess in monetary terms. What is the monetary value of oil supply disruption or the interruption of electricity supply for several hours? While one can estimate roughly the cost of reduced economic activity in these cases, it is virtually impossible to estimate the monetary value of all the intangible inconveniences to society brought on by such a disruption.

Frustrations with efforts at full monetization have led analysts to propose decision-making techniques that keep separate accounts for attributes that are not easily monetized. Each account – corresponding to a criterion for decision making – can be measured in different units, which can be quantitative or qualitative. There would be a financial cost account, measured in monetary units. But for non-monetized costs and benefits of importance to the decision maker there would be one or more other accounts. An environmental account might be measured in detailed quantitative units, or in a few qualitative comments such as better, average and worse. A social account might indicate effects on income distribution or other indicators of equity, measured in numerical or qualitative units. There may be other accounts depending on factors that are especially important to the decision maker.

Many variations of this general approach have been developed and applied over the last several decades. Common terms are *goals achievement matrix*, *multi-attribute utility analysis* and *multi-attribute trade-off analysis*, but a generic name is *multi-criteria decision making*.[4] I need not delve into the intricacies of these variations; each has its own perspective on how to solicit the objectives of decision-makers, how to structure the options, how to measure attributes, and how to compare the options in a trade-off evaluation process.

For comparing our primary energy options, I apply a simple multi-criteria approach comprising the following steps: the identification of key decision criteria; an assessment of the individual performance of each option against these criteria; and then a trade-off comparison of how each option performs relative to the others in order to project a likely sustainable energy trajectory. While some analysts generate long lists of decision criteria, I believe that I can most effectively represent the key decision factors and achieve my transparency objective if I limit my trade-off comparison to the following four.

Projected cost means the likely evolution of each energy option's monetized cost in producing my forecasted mix of clean secondary energy, which is dominated by electricity and hydrogen. There are many studies estimating the projected financial costs for efficiency, nuclear, renewables and fossil fuels over the next twenty or thirty years, but few extend beyond that. While my horizon encompasses the entire century, I base my estimates initially on these studies that project into the next few decades, especially ones produced by large teams of interdisciplinary experts rather than by advocates of one particular option. To project further into the future, I make assumptions about the upper and lower limits for the costs of each option based on estimates of its resource magnitude and evolving cost of production, and on the prospects for future technological change. This analysis results from my review of expert opinions on the long-term evolution of energy options' costs. For example, relatively new technologies, or technologies currently at a low market share, are likely to see more dramatic cost declines with market dissemination and with the passage of time, an example being PV cells. A finite resource like conventional natural gas may see its cost of production rise but its upper level is constrained in the long-run by the likely production cost of substitutes like coalbed methane and unconventional gas.

The cost estimates should not be distorted by subsidies and should include costs of ensuring minimal ongoing impacts and risks to land, air and water. My estimated cost for nuclear power should be increased by any subsidies the industry receives for treating and storing radioactive waste and for decommissioning retired facilities. My estimated cost for fossil fuels should include the costs of bringing international oil tanker design up to the highest standards among industrialized countries (which have profoundly reduced accident risk) and for rehabilitating land disturbed by petroleum and coal exploitation. My estimated cost for renewables should include the costs of overcoming intermittency in the production of reliable electricity.

Extreme event risk to the environment and humans is a criterion to reflect the importance of extreme events (extremely low or unknown probability of occurrence, severe outcome) to the public and politicians when considering energy options. Under financial costs, I assume that each energy option has incurred costs – sometimes substantial – to significantly minimize ongoing impacts and risks to humans and the environment. In spite of these efforts to reduce impacts and risks, energy options differ with respect to the extreme event risks they pose. Since the 1970s, risk analysts have acknowledged conditions under which risk averse decision makers might justifiably focus on extreme events when comparing options.[5] This may occur under conditions of pure uncertainty or where the probability of an extreme event is very small. The nature of the extreme event can also be important to the decision maker, with some extreme event risks seen as more of a concern than others.

Geopolitical risk is a criterion that focuses on how international politics affects the relative attractiveness of energy options. A stable and safe supply of commercial energy is essential to modern economies, yet energy options differ in terms of their vulnerability to the pursuits of political movements, individual countries, or groups of countries. The geopolitical history of the international crude oil market and the civil uses of nuclear power are the most noteworthy illustrations of this criterion's importance, but it may also apply to other options. Concerned for decades that oil import dependence might constrain its foreign policy options, China only recently relaxed its constraints on oil imports but now is acquiring foreign oil companies. During its apartheid racial regime in the 1950s–80s, South Africa produced synthetic oil from domestic coal in order to shield itself from oil import sanctions. France responded to the oil import disruptions and risks in the 1970s by converting its electricity system to nuclear power based on domestic technologies and expertise. Brazil responded to the same crisis by developing domestic production of ethanol from sugarcane. The energy choices of most countries are influenced to some extent by considerations of geopolitical risk.

There have been attempts to monetize geopolitical risk. The most noteworthy examples involve using the cost to the US of its ongoing military presence in the Middle East, including wars in 1991 and 2003, to indicate the monetary value of crude oil's geopolitical risk.[6] However, this approach has never been particularly credible, given that international politics involves so much more than considerations of access to resources. For comparing energy options, it would be necessary to decide which military expenditures to include when calculating the full cost of oil. Attempts to monetize geopolitical risks would obscure rather than clarify trade-off analysis, but this is not a reason to ignore this key factor in evaluating energy options.

Path dependence is the final criterion I use for comparing energy options. Evolutionary and institutional economics are two terms for analysis that focuses on the extent to which the existing complex of institutions and industry constrains or otherwise influences the future options for economic growth and technological evolution.[7] In general, policy efforts to shift this complex on to a dramatically different technological path are difficult and thus more costly compared with less ambitious adjustments to the current path. These extra costs are difficult to monetize, however, as they involve not just the higher initial financial costs of new technological paths but also the intangible costs of changing institutional norms and modes of decision-making.

This inability to reflect all of these factors in monetary terms is why I apply this as a separate criterion.

In explaining the inertial or lock-in forces of path dependence, analysts point to several factors.[8] Dominant, mature technologies benefit from compatibility with each other and economies-of-scale. For new technologies to compete, their chances are better if they are evolutionary, meaning that they mesh easily with the existing complex of technologies and institutions by reinforcing that path or by exploiting existing niche opportunities within it. A hybrid gasoline-electric vehicle is evolutionary in that it uses an internal combustion engine and the existing gasoline refueling infrastructure. It can capture market share by targeting high-use niche markets like couriers and taxis, where its better energy efficiency provides economic benefits. A hydrogen fuel-cell vehicle is more revolutionary in that it has a different engine platform and requires new technologies and major investment for a hydrogen production, delivery and refueling infrastructure. This is why some automobile manufacturers are investigating the concept of fuel-cell vehicles that store gasoline or methanol and reform it into hydrogen onboard the vehicle, or even fuel cells that directly use methanol. This inertia in favor of dominant technologies is further reinforced by existing institutions, legal frameworks, government policies and industry standards.[9] Social values, as expressed through consumer preferences and political expectations, also contribute to path dependence.

In terms of my prescriptive and predictive dichotomy, this fourth criterion is different from the other three in that its role is primarily predictive. We do not choose an energy option because it has inertia in its favor. We choose it because it performs best in terms of our relative preferences for low energy costs, low environmental impacts and extreme event risks, and low geopolitical risks. However, when we wish to incorporate an element of prediction into our prescriptive analysis, a major advantage like path dependence cannot be ignored. Thus, in my trade-off comparison of the options, I use this fourth criterion for the purposes of prediction rather than as a decision factor. This helps ground the analysis in the real world. Some technological and social visionaries concoct images of an entirely transformed global energy system, sometimes achieved within just fifty years. In such visions, these inertial forces are often ignored.

7.2 Individual performance of each option against the criteria

All of the usual suspects – efficiency, nuclear and renewables – as well as the unusual suspect – fossil fuels – offer the possibility of playing a major or even dominant role in the shift toward a more sustainable energy system. But they perform differently against the evaluative criteria. For the projected financial cost criterion, this individual performance is evaluated quantitatively whereas for the other three the evaluation is qualitative.

Projected cost

The cost of energy efficiency is controversial, with some advocates arguing that reducing energy use by 30–75% in industrialized countries is profitable at current prices. However, a substantial body of research suggests that this analysis overestimates technically achievable efficiency gains, underestimates risks associated with new efficient technologies with lengthy payback periods, underestimates intangible costs to consumers of adopting technologies that are not perfect substitutes for current equipment, overlooks cost decreases to energy supply technologies that make efficiency investments less profitable, and overlooks new profit seeking practices and consumer preferences that by increasing energy demands partially offset efficiency gains. As I explained in chapter 4, only a fraction of the so-called profitable energy efficiency actions are likely to be economically beneficial on the basis of cost alone (excluding externalities). Beyond this, some additional energy efficiency will cost only a modest amount, so effort to achieve this may become financially justified depending on how the treatment of externalities changes the costs of options on the supply side – nuclear, renewables and clean use of fossil fuels. But only if the development of clean secondary energy leads to significantly higher energy prices will a substantial increase in the rate of energy efficiency improvement occur. Is this likely to happen?

The energy and environment literature is rife with estimates for future energy supply costs, much of it driven by the intense focus on reducing CO_2 emissions. I have reviewed several studies in the process of developing my own set of numbers for the costs of producing electricity, hydrogen, low-emission synthetic fuels and biofuels.[10] My cost estimates are based on these studies, but also incorporate my

Table 7.1. Projected electricity cost (¢/kWh in $US 2000)

Coal–PC post-combustion	Coal– IGCC	NatGas– CCGT	Nuclear	Hydro	Wind	Biomass	Solar– PV
6–7.5	5.5–7	5.5–7	6–10	6–8	6–8	6–8	15–20

Note: PC = pulverized coal; IGCC = integrated gasification combined cycle; CCGT = combined cycle gas turbine; PV = photovoltaic.
Assumed input prices are coal $1.5–3/GJ, natural gas $5–7/GJ, biomass $2–5/GJ.

reading of the particular constraints and opportunities facing each option over the course of this century – resource constraints, land-use constraints, regulatory constraints, infrastructure costs and potential cost reductions due to economies-of-learning. Adjustments such as these are necessary because most cost estimates are focused on the technologies and resources that are seen to be most plausible for energy supply investments over the next ten to thirty years. To produce an estimate for the century, additional assumptions about these long-term constraints and opportunities are required. I explain the key assumptions behind each of my numbers in the discussion below.

Table 7.1 presents my estimates for the cost of generating electricity from alternative supply sources over the coming century. The values are in cents per kWh in $US (2000). Confidence in the values is obviously higher for the earlier decades of the century. The range for each estimate indicates both the increase in uncertainty further into the future and the likelihood of movement as various constraints and opportunities come into play over time. These costs are assumed to reflect the costs for each option were it to experience large-scale development – which requires consideration of both cost reducing and cost increasing aspects.

All three fossil fuel technologies include the full cost of carbon capture and storage – reducing carbon emissions from each source by about 90%, as indicated in chapter 6. They also include desulphurization, low nitrous oxide emissions and capture of particulates in the case of coal combustion. The two coal options – the same two described in chapter 6 – are combustion of coal in a standard steam turbine with post-combustion capture of CO_2 and other emissions, and integrated gasification with a combined cycle gas turbine (IGCC), with CO_2 capture from the syngas. Conventional coal combustion is usually shown with a slightly higher cost, as I have here. Some studies show natural gas as the cheapest fossil fuel option for generating zero-emission electricity, but my cost estimate reflects the transition over the course of the century from conventional natural gas toward higher cost unconventional sources as well as the effect of the recent trend for international trade in liquefied natural gas to bring natural gas prices into line with oil prices on a per unit of energy basis. I assume that the price of raw coal does not increase appreciably in real terms over the course of the century, given the plentiful supplies listed in chapter 5, but a dramatic increase in coal use would see some price rise as the industry shifts toward less easily accessed deposits.

The wider cost estimate for nuclear power of 6–10 ¢/kWh reflects the diversity in how countries develop this technology, disputes about its full costs, and uncertainty about its future costs. Some countries like France have been able to develop apparently low-cost nuclear power. Developing countries like China might be able to follow this model. But most cost estimates based on currently operating plants do not include the full costs of siting new facilities, treating and permanently storing all nuclear waste, and operation of international institutions and monitoring mechanisms to ensure a safe worldwide expansion of the technology. These can push the estimated cost into the higher end of my range.

The table presents four renewable alternatives for electricity generation – hydro, wind, biomass and solar PV. These four are most promising in terms of projected cost and resource magnitude, although geothermal and other renewables also have significant prospects. The range in the cost estimate for each renewable reflects the uncertainty as to how large-scale development will affect the countervailing factors causing cost reductions and cost increases. Renewables advocates focus on the economies-of-scale and economies-of-learning that will lower costs as renewables achieve a growing share of the global energy system. Skeptics caution, however, that there would also be upward cost pressures if renewables were to become the dominant source of energy.[11] For hydropower, windpower and geothermal, among others, development occurs first at the most favorable sites and then proceeds to less favorable, higher cost sites. The low energy density of most renewables means that wide-scale expansion will increasingly confront competition for land with non-energy uses, as in the case with biomass. Because many renewables provide only intermittent energy, the additional costs of energy storage must be included as renewables provide a larger share of energy supply. This can lead to substantially higher costs unless research and development realizes significant gains in reducing the costs of non-hydro energy storage.

Thus, the range of 6–8 ¢/kWh for hydropower indicates that some low cost sites are still available in developing countries, but that over the century the industry must shift to higher cost sites and to a greater reliance on small hydro in both developing and developed countries. Much of the small hydro will not include storage reservoirs and therefore will incur additional costs for alternative storage. The range of 6–8 ¢/kWh for wind generation stands in contrast to claims that new wind generators cost only 4 ¢/kWh and that costs are still falling with larger turbines and economies-of-learning. But the intermittency of wind means that some form of energy storage or back-up will be required to ensure that electricity dispatch is matched to fluctuating demand at all times. There is considerable uncertainty about long-term energy storage costs on a massive scale, but storage with reliable dispatch is likely to add 2 ¢/kWh, and perhaps more depending on the energy storage or back-up generation that is eventually required. Windpower will also progress from better sites to less favorable sites over the course of the century, with rising siting, development and transmission costs as an additional consequence. The estimated cost for electricity from biomass of 6–8 ¢/kWh applies to both conventional biomass combustion for a steam turbine and biomass IGCC if that technology proves to be more attractive. When waste biomass is the main source of supply, the costs are at the low end of the range but if energy uses of biomass are to expand dramatically this resource must compete for land with agriculture, preservation of wilderness and other uses, pushing up the cost of biomass electricity. At a very large scale, the cost of biomass could be well above the upper limit in the estimated cost range. The wide cost range for solar PV reflects the great uncertainty about where costs, which have been falling rapidly, are likely to asymptote over the century. Some experts feel that costs will fall well below the lower bound of 15 ¢/kWh in the table, but this value is meant to include the amount of storage that would often be required to ensure that solar power can be dispatched to match load fluctuations.

Table 7.2. Projected hydrogen cost ($/GJ in $US 2000)

Coal gasification	Natural gas steam-methane reforming	Nuclear electrolysis of H_2O	Wind/Hydro electrolysis of H_2O	Biomass gasification
8–10	8–10	18–25	18–25	10–15

Note: Assumed input prices are coal $1.5–3/GJ, natural gas $5–7/GJ, and biomass $2–5/GJ. For electrolysis, see table 7.1 for assumed electricity prices from each source. GJ of hydrogen based on "higher heating value."

To the extent that any alternative can be located close to the point of use, it can reduce transmission and distribution costs as well as line losses of 7–10% on average. This improves the prospects for solar PV and other renewable alternatives in some circumstances. However, the best renewable energy sites for wind, hydropower and other renewables like ocean and geothermal are often far from the demand, meaning that substantial development of renewables would encounter rising costs.

With the exception of solar PV, the estimated costs are not substantially higher than current electricity generation costs in most regions of the world. Generation costs for zero-emission fossil fuels and some renewables are in the range of 6–8 ¢/kWh. Adding transmission costs yields a final price to large industrial customers of 8–10 ¢/kWh. When the extra distribution costs for small customers are also added, this produces residential rates of 10–14 ¢/kWh. For much of the world, these final prices are not more than 25–50% higher than current prices for residential and industrial customers. The prospects for profitable electricity efficiency are diminished if electricity supply costs rise by only this amount as we shift toward a cleaner energy supply system.

Table 7.2 presents my estimates for the cost of producing hydrogen from alternative supply sources over the coming century. The values are in dollars per gigajoule (GJ) in 2000 $US. As with electricity, these cost estimates reflect the cost of an option were it to experience large-scale development – which requires consideration of both cost reducing and cost increasing aspects. The range for each estimate indicates both the increase in uncertainty further into the future and the likelihood of upward or downward change as various constraints and opportunities come into play over time. The wider range of the cost estimates for each option compared to those for electricity reflects the lack of experience with large-scale hydrogen production.

Unlike electricity, there are also significant cost differences between options. Producing hydrogen via gasification or steam reforming is substantially less expensive than via electrolysis of water. Unless there is a major breakthrough in electrolysis processes, the gasification of coal and the steam methane reforming of natural gas, both with carbon capture and storage, offer the least costly means of producing hydrogen. Biomass gasification offers the lowest cost method of producing hydrogen from renewables, but it still has higher costs than coal gasification because of capital cost differences and land competition were this option to become the dominant means of producing hydrogen. Other candidate processes for hydrogen production, such as the thermal splitting of water, are excluded from the table because their costs will not be competitive without a major technological breakthrough.

If hydrogen is to play a significant role in the global energy system, it is likely to be especially important as a transportation fuel, initially in large urban areas. Given all of the uncertainties about long-term hydrogen transport and storage capabilities, the estimated cost of shifting to hydrogen for the services provided by personal vehicles is highly uncertain. This requires a set of cost estimates for fuel production, fuel delivery, vehicle engine platforms, fuel storage and the efficiencies at each link in the chain. Some analysts suggest that even in the long run the costs of fueling personal vehicles with hydrogen will result in double the energy service cost – on a person-kilometer-traveled basis – compared to gasoline and diesel. Others suggest that within a few decades these costs could be quite comparable.[12] Again, if this latter case is true, the prospects for reduced energy use due to efficiency and mode switching away from personal vehicles will be diminished accordingly.

In chapter 3, I included various forms of cleaner-burning hydrocarbons as the third category of secondary energy in a sustainable energy future. This is because the cost of a wholesale switch to electricity and hydrogen would be exorbitant and, in any case, unnecessary as long as hydrocarbon combustion had fallen to levels where it was not having a significant negative impact on urban air quality or atmospheric concentrations of greenhouse gases. Another factor is the extent to which the hydrocarbons are produced from biomass, which offers another means of preventing increased atmospheric concentrations of GHGs. Therefore, the combustible hydrocarbons I include when estimating the costs of the energy system are natural gas, synthetic fuels (methanol, dimethyl ether) and biofuels (biodiesel, ethanol). Their projected costs over the century are \$5–7/GJ for natural gas, \$5–10/GJ for synthetic fuels, and \$7–15/GJ for biofuels.

I have already explained the rationale for the natural gas price – a gradual shift toward unconventional gas during the course of the century and a stronger linking of natural gas and oil prices. The wide range for synthetic fuels reflects the different ways in which they might be produced. The lower part of the range might reflect synthetic fuels produced in coal polygeneration plants, where they would benefit from the overall efficiency of the facility. Biofuels range from the relatively lower costs realized in some of the production of biodiesel to the higher costs of ethanol production, and the potential land-use constraints were biomass to become a dominant source of fuel production with plantations dedicated to energy.

Neither of my two energy cost tables includes oil as an energy input. Given the reserves of conventional and unconventional oil I listed in chapter 5, this exclusion perhaps appears surprising. Indeed, the coal gasification processes for producing electricity or hydrogen (or both) with carbon capture and storage could use oil as an input. I have omitted oil because it has the shortest projected lifespan among fossil fuels and because it is so valuable today for producing the refined petroleum products that are critical to the global energy system. As we shift toward zero-emission production of electricity and hydrogen, the energy inputs in tables 7.1 and 7.2 are likely to receive the most attention. In the development of fuels for niche markets, however, conventional oil and then unconventional oil will continue to play a critical role. None of the major ways of producing oil and its refined petroleum products (from conventional oil, unconventional oil, coal or natural gas) had a cost of production in excess of \$40/barrel in my survey of chapter 5, which is equivalent to \$7/GJ. This suggests that consumption of refined petroleum products must be constrained by policy; it is not resource depletion and the resulting high prices that will save the world from oil-related pollution.

Given the large current supplies, the cost of coal is unlikely to increase significantly over the course of the century, although it will experience short-term fluctuations whenever price instability affects a key substitute such as oil or natural gas. Natural gas should see a gradual increase in price with the shift from conventional to unconventional resources.

It is possible that expanded production of secondary energy products from coal and unconventional oil sources, like oil sands, will cause much greater impacts to land and water, and restrictions on these impacts will drive up supply costs over the century. One of the surface mining oil sands facilities in western Canada has disrupted the landscape over a 40,000 hectare area with exposed overburden, slag heaps and tailings ponds. Open pit coal mines are notorious for disrupting great swathes of land. Large coal energy conversion plants, like the coal to synthetic gasoline plants in South Africa, use a great deal of land and water.

According to my sustainable energy definition, the impacts on land and water of these activities must be negligible over the long run. This means that water quality and temperature must be returned to levels that do not disrupt biodiversity, and that disturbed land must be returned to its natural state without toxic residues affecting long-term ecosystem viability. Research suggests that much still needs to be done, but expectations and practices have improved dramatically in many areas and research is helping to focus on what is required for effective site rehabilitation.[13] The costs of doing so are unlikely to increase the production costs of energy from coal and unconventional oil by more than 5–15% from their current levels. In the case of oil sands at least, future developments in western Canada will have less impact, as most deposits are too deep for surface mining, requiring the application of less intrusive in-situ extraction techniques.

Several factors will affect the evolution of the cost of nuclear energy. While the cost of fissile material is unlikely to increase, continued public concerns will keep security, operating, regulatory, waste treatment, waste disposal, and insurance costs of nuclear plants at substantial levels. Siting new plants will be especially onerous in industrialized countries, adding significantly to up-front costs and investor risk, and in some cases becoming an absolute barrier. The long lead time before a given nuclear plant is operational is another cost factor, one that grows in importance as electricity markets shift toward greater market liberalization and private investment – even if, after California's electricity reform fiasco in 2001, competition is limited to the wholesale level in most jurisdictions. Competitive electricity markets expose nuclear plant investors more fully to the financial risks of such long lead-time investments.

Although wind, hydro and biomass appear to be cost competitive for electricity generation, this depends on assumptions about location, quantity and the cost of storage. In industrialized countries, most of the best large hydropower sites have been exploited and remaining sites often conflict with high-value alternative uses. In developing countries, conflict with other land uses is also becoming important, especially as rural inhabitants assert their political rights. The Chinese displaced about a million people for the Three Gorges Project, but they and other governments in developing countries are gradually losing the authority to impose projects of similar magnitude and impact. The cost of micro-hydro is usually higher because of the intermittency of water flows. Many developing countries have climates with extreme seasonal variations in precipitation, which reduces the capacity utilization of micro-hydro facilities and increases the need for storage. The apparent low cost for biomass is associated primarily with the use of crop residues. Beyond this, the supply cost for biomass energy may rise steeply if biomass-to-energy plantations must compete for land with agriculture and other uses. On the other hand, dramatic advances in biotechnology over the century could reduce the value of agricultural land and accordingly the cost of biomass energy.

PVs provide the best means of generating electricity from solar energy and the technology has already penetrated niche markets for off-grid applications. Its cost is high, but as a new technology this should fall substantially as cumulative production grows. The structural integration of PV panels into roofing and building sidings offers hope for a significant cost reduction. A special challenge for almost all renewables is that although their operating costs are low (renewable flows of energy are mostly free), their up-front investment costs are high. This is especially a problem for PV. Its installed capital cost is about five times higher than that of most competing electricity generation technologies, and this is a substantial barrier for poorer regions. If intermittent renewables are to grow significantly they also need to be coupled with energy storage systems, and the costs of these are likely to be substantial.

Stepping back to compare all of the energy supply costs, there are some situations in which the competing sources of supply are similar in cost. This suggests that other criteria will play a role in our choice of energy option.

Extreme event risk

Both energy efficiency and renewables appear to fare well when it comes to extreme event risk. Even the risks of failure of large hydro dams are well understood by experts and there is considerable public confidence in this expertise.

As noted in chapter 4, nuclear power is especially vulnerable to the tendency for the public to emphasize catastrophic outcomes even though these have extremely low probabilities of occurrence. This can seem irrational to nuclear advocates, but it is consistent with a rational risk averse strategy for decision making. Some analysts suggest, moreover, that nuclear power faces an additional burden in that the type of extreme event it is associated with is particularly frightening to many people. The unseen radiation exposure associated with a nuclear accident signifies potential damage to the human genetic code and possible mutations in future generations. Dread of this type of extreme event is profound, even among well-informed and well-educated people, and this represents a serious handicap for nuclear relative to its competitors, especially for the siting of new plants. In the US, for example, even if the federal government strongly supports the establishment of nuclear power facilities at new locations, local authorities have control over site permitting and opposition groups have numerous legal and public relations means at their disposal.

Because of the potentially devastating consequences of a nuclear catastrophe, there is also a fear that nuclear facilities are ideal targets for terrorist attack. This possibility can appear to increase the probability of occurrence for what is otherwise an extremely unlikely event.

Fossil fuel use can be associated with various types of extreme events, although none of these appear to be at the same level of significance for the public and decision makers as the risks of a major nuclear accident. There have been marine oil spills, refinery explosions, pipeline explosions, and coal mining accidents (slides, mine collapse or explosion). However, the risks are mostly local and well understood, and can be diminished by efforts to tighten safety standards and to mitigate impacts in the aftermath of an accident. While an emerging risk from fossil fuel combustion is the possibility of climate change from accumulated greenhouse gases, this risk does not apply to the zero-emission fossil fuel option.

As noted in chapter 6, more aggressive geological storage of CO_2 is in its early stages, so forecasting how the risks of large-scale development might be perceived by the public one or two decades hence is challenging. However, CO_2 has been injected underground for decades as part of enhanced oil recovery and more recently in acid gas injection programs. Localized risks from a significant leak do not appear to be of a different magnitude from the kind of risk the public faces every day from oil and gas pipelines, petroleum refineries, gas processing plants, enhanced oil and gas recovery, transport by truck, rail and ship, and even the use of oil and gas inside public and private buildings. The industry has a good safety record, but major accidents occur from time to time, and these do not lead to shifts in opinion against the use of fossil fuels. Slow leaks of CO_2 could affect the achievement of greenhouse gas reduction objectives, but experts suggest that these slow leaks can be offset by a modest quantity of biomass gasification with carbon capture and storage.

Geopolitical risk

It is often assumed that renewables are like efficiency in that, as domestic energy alternatives, neither poses geopolitical risk. While this is true for efficiency, the apparent immunity of renewables from geopolitical risk might simply reflect their small share of the global energy system. Would that change if renewables were to dominate? In a renewables energy future, would each country become autarkic, meeting virtually all of its energy needs from indigenous renewable resources in a small-is-beautiful future? Or, would some countries have substantial advantages that enabled them to profit by exporting renewables-based electricity, hydrogen and synthetic fuels to countries less favorably endowed?

Although some advocates claim that the development of renewables would result in uniform energy costs between countries and the end of significant energy trade, the evidence suggests otherwise. Renewable resource endowments on the planet are as geographically heterogeneous as fossil fuel resources. Perhaps Mongolia would export wind-based electricity to China. Perhaps Middle-East countries, their conventional petroleum resources declining, would cover large areas of desert with PV arrays, exporting electricity directly or using it to produce hydrogen for export via pipeline and tanker. Perhaps biomass-rich countries would produce electricity and hydrogen and synthetic fuels for export. Under such heterogeneity of resource endowments and likely trade interdependence, it seems plausible that renewable energy could be vulnerable to exploitation as a pawn of geopolitics just as water, another vital renewable resource, is today.

Nuclear power is a different story. Several times over the past decades, the dissemination of nuclear technology, ostensibly for domestic power production, has been associated with diversion to nuclear weapons development. Israel, India and Pakistan cached weapons production under their domestic nuclear power programs. Iraq tried to do this in the 1980s until Israeli fighter jets destroyed its main facility. North Korea and Iran are contemporary threats. Dominant powers in the world are wary that disgruntled, threatened, or ambitious governments in unstable regions may try to develop nuclear weapons in order to improve their bargaining power, and that even terrorist organizations might try this.

This risk presents a substantial barrier to the global dissemination of nuclear power, perhaps especially to the poorer regions of the planet where electricity demands should grow the fastest. Use of nuclear power will only increase significantly in OECD countries if there is sufficient demand, if it can outcompete other energy sources (in competitive markets) and if local populations permit the siting of new plants. It may grow in countries like Russia, India and China, although the US and other global powers are likely to be concerned about safeguarding measures if the nuclear industry grows to dominant levels in these energy systems. But its development in the Middle East, Africa and much of Asia is less likely to be acceptable to the US and the other major powers for some time yet.

Some would argue, however, that the geopolitical risk of global dissemination of nuclear energy is small compared to the risk of reliance on petroleum imports – meaning that the geopolitical criterion actually works in favor of nuclear power. This was the rationale behind the French and Japanese nuclear programs in the 1980s. Sudden restrictions of oil exports from the Middle East will quickly disrupt the global energy market and indeed the global economy. The region also dominates the membership of the Organization of

Petroleum Exporting Countries (OPEC), a cartel that tries to boost oil prices or at least prevent their collapse by agreeing to member production quotas.* Periods of political instability in the region are correlated with oil price instability and downturns in economic growth: the Arab–Israeli war and oil embargo in 1973, the Iranian revolution in 1979, the Iraqi invasion of Kuwait and subsequent expulsion by NATO in 1991, and the Anglo-American invasion of Iraq in 2003.

With its extensive petroleum resources, Russia is less exposed to international oil market turbulence. There is, however, considerable concern in the US, Europe, Japan and increasingly China and India that the geopolitical risks of oil will intensify, perhaps rapidly, over the coming decades as global dependence on OPEC and especially Middle East oil increases. Oil resources in the US, China and Europe (North Sea) are being depleted while oil imports by industrialized countries and many developing countries like China are increasing rapidly. The two charts of figure 7.1 show how both the US and China are projected to experience a substantial growth in oil import dependence over the next decades if current trends continue. The US dependence on imports rose to 50% of total consumption by the late 1970s, fell in the 1980s in response to higher oil prices and development of Alaskan oil, but increased back to 50% in the late 1990s and is expected to reach 70% within two decades. China's situation is even more dramatic as it has scant prospects for domestic oil development, yet its automobile stock is growing at a tremendous rate.

For some analysts, this worsening trend is reason enough for a rapid transition away from oil. The argument is that because conventional oil will not endure and its rate of consumption is increasing, oil import dependence will increase the power of exporting countries who would control the oil market in order to extort wealth from and influence the politics of industrialized countries. This argument has been made in many articles and books since 1973, but the concern has intensified again in recent years in concert with growing US oil import dependence and the US-led military interventions in Kuwait, Afghanistan and Iraq.[14] The beneficiary of an off-oil policy could be one of several alternatives depending on the perspective of the author or interest

* The members of OPEC are Algeria, Gabon, Indonesia, Iran, Iraq, Kuwait, Libya, Nigeria, Qatar, Saudi Arabia, the United Arab Emirates and Venezuela.

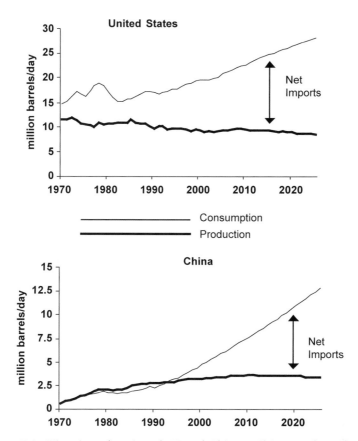

Figure 7.1. Historic and projected US and Chinese oil import dependence

Data Sources: Future Projection: US Energy Information Administration, *International Energy Outlook 2004* (Washington, D.C.: US Department of Energy, 2004), table D4: World Oil Production by Region and Country, Reference Case, 1990–2025, table A4: World Oil Consumption by Region, Reference Case, 1990–2025.

Historical Data: US Energy Information Administration, Department of Energy, *Annual Energy Review 2002* (Washington, D.C.: US Department of Energy, 2003), table 11.5: World Crude Oil Production, 1960–2002; table 11.10: World Petroleum Consumption, 1960–2001.

group. Some authors lump all fossil fuels together with oil when discussing geopolitical risk. Others see a sharp difference.

As it grows in significance, natural gas has achieved comparable status to oil in some respects. When natural gas trade was limited to pipeline transport, its geopolitical significance was more regional than global. The North American natural gas market involves US trade with Canada and Mexico, neighbors with a history of stable political relations. The US has been concerned in the past about European dependence on natural gas imports by pipeline from the Soviet Union and potentially antagonistic North African countries like Libya and Algeria, but these concerns have diminished with the collapse of the Soviet Union, improved relations with Libya and stability in Algeria. As tankers carrying liquefied natural gas grow in importance, the resource's geopolitical importance may increase.

Coal seems to pose virtually no geopolitical risks, either currently or in the foreseeable future. This fossil fuel is distributed widely around the planet, with key countries like the US, Russia and China being particularly well endowed, and India also owning substantial resources.

The evaluation of the geopolitical risks of fossil fuels must be understood in its full dynamic. While conventional oil provides the quintessential example of geopolitical risk, switching away from all fossil fuels makes little sense if the goal is to reduce this risk. Coal and natural gas are plentiful in many regions of the world. Major deposits of unconventional oil, namely oil sands, ultra heavy oil and oil shale, are located far from the Middle East. If we have indeed passed Hubbert's peak for global conventional oil resources, then rising costs of conventional oil will trigger development of unconventional oil, conventional and unconventional natural gas, and coal, and these could reduce geopolitical risk by dispersing energy production to different regions of the world. Although few acknowledge the possibility, the passage of Hubbert's peak could mark the end of an era for oil-related geopolitical risk, but ironically without ending our reliance on fossil fuels.

Path dependence

Since the 1970s, countries throughout the world have made significant inroads in increasing energy efficiency and this has enriched the expertise in government, industry and to some extent among the general public in wealthy countries. Yet this has not resulted in a significant shift away from the historic relationship between energy use and economic output.[15] Energy intensity of economic activity has declined, but it has been swamped by increases in total activity such that total energy use keeps rising. Moreover, energy efficiency can be a double-edged sword in that it reduces operating costs, which can lead to greater use of equipment for the original energy service and the extended application of such improvements to related energy services. Improved efficiency of fridges can foster the development of small water coolers in offices. Improved efficiency of light bulbs can foster the greater use of lighting for safety and security. At the same time, completely new energy-using technologies appear every day in all sectors of the economy, especially among final consumers. The net effect is that gains in energy productivity are strongly correlated with economic growth, that in turn leads to dramatic increases in total energy consumption. The expectation that additional energy efficiency can offset a large portion of the growth in energy service demands presents a significant challenge from a path dependence perspective.

Nuclear energy has lost its momentum of two decades ago. The global rate of new plant construction has plummeted – no new nuclear plants have been built in the US in twenty years and several European countries prohibit new plant construction. R&D funding has fallen to the point where countries such as the US are in jeopardy of losing the capability to relaunch the industry; federal US funding declined from $1,796 million to $282 million between 1985 and 2000. While France, Finland and China are still in a good position to expand their nuclear programs, other countries would have greater difficulty. These include the US, Canada, South Korea, India, Pakistan, Belgium and some of the countries formerly within or under the influence of the Soviet Union.

With renewables, the path dependency criterion depends on the form of energy. Large hydro is stagnant in most industrialized countries, but China and several other developing countries still have a substantial potential for large hydro projects, and are continuing to develop their resources – although lack of investment funds is often a constraint. Biomass is readily available in the form of crop residues, so biomass energy is likely to gain attractiveness. Brazil's experience with ethanol and Europe's development of biodiesel provide testing grounds for countries to learn about successes and obstacles. Wind-power and PV have considerable momentum because of the strong push for windpower in industrialized countries and the opportunity that windpower and PV offer rural areas to access electricity without major investments for grid connection.

Because of their perceived environmental benefits, renewables are enthusiastically touted as the successor to fossil fuels in the global energy system, but in terms of path dependence, they must overcome the complex of industrial structures and institutions favoring fossil fuels. Even as recently as 1996, after years of professed support for renewables by governments and private interests, US R&D expenditure for fossil fuels was approximately double that for energy efficiency and renewables combined; about 75% of R&D was from private sources for fossil fuels, but only 25% for renewables.[16] Moreover, since the private sector usually dominates R&D funding rather than governments, the dominant oil, natural gas, coal and thermal electricity generation companies set the priorities for R&D support. These industries tend to invest in what they know best – fossil fuels and their associated technologies.[17]

As the objective shifts to zero-emission fossil fuels, their path dependence advantage is diminished but still substantial. The incorporation of carbon capture at fossil fuel thermal plants should be fairly straightforward, but will involve wide-scale application of new technologies and processes, such as post-combustion capture of CO_2 in steam plants and coal-fired IGCC plants with CO_2 capture. Likewise, while the development of more CO_2 pipelines is a reasonable extension of existing know-how and infrastructure, the large-scale geological sequestration of this gas implies a major new industrial and institutional endeavor, requiring decades for development. As each of the coal plants (that collectively generate 40% of the planet's electricity) reaches retirement age, its site could be redeveloped as a new coal gasification plant for IGCC production of electricity, perhaps including production of hydrogen and other synthetic fuels. Such plants would rely largely on technologies and engineering expertise that are familiar to industry experts operating today's coal-fired generators, coal plants that produce synthetic fuels, petroleum refineries, petrochemical plants, plants producing hydrogen from steam reforming of natural gas, and fertilizer plants. New plants could be gradually added at the most favorable coalfields as the cost of CO_2 transport is a small component of total carbon capture and storage costs. Current owners of coal resources, coal thermal plants and the transmission grids connected to these would have an economic interest in promoting and investing in such a strategy.

7.3 Trade-off comparison for a sustainable energy projection

If these four criteria are dependable indicators of the key factors to consider when evaluating our primary energy options, they show that no option is superior on all counts. The choice is not obvious. One might conclude that we can and should pursue all four options with equal vigor. But if history is any guide, this is rarely a dependable approach – and the world rarely unfolds this way anyway. There are usually winners and losers, or at least options that fare better even though all are pursued to some extent. In this section, I compare the options in terms of these criteria in order to generate my own assessment of the path that humanity is likely to follow if its goal is to achieve a clean and enduring energy system.

From this trade-off assessment I construct a sustainable energy projection to the year 2100. In building this scenario, the magnitude of energy demand is determined by the interplay of energy service growth with plausible and even forceful efforts at energy efficiency. The shares of primary energy options resulting from the multi-criteria analysis then produce the shares of secondary energy in my sustainability projection in chapter 3.

I try to be transparent in this analysis by summarizing in table 7.3 my assessment of each energy option's performance against the evaluative criteria. Energy efficiency and renewables are generally free of extreme event risk and geopolitical risk. Some efficiency and renewables are economic relative to zero-emission fossil fuels and nuclear, but their costs rise if more ambitious growth is pursued in too short a timeframe. Greater use of renewables, especially if rushed during the next few decades, will entail higher costs because renewables are particularly associated with new technologies that need more R&D and that have not yet benefited from the economies-of-scale and economies-of-learning that result from greater production. As technologies diffuse, the competitive position of renewables could improve, but this depends on whether exhaustion of the most favorable sites occurs faster than innovation and expanded production can

Table 7.3. Multi-criteria comparison of energy options

	Projected cost	Extreme event risk to environment and humans	Geopolitical risk	Path dependence
Efficiency	Some competitive. Costs rise steeply for dramatic reductions.	No risk.	No risk.	Disadvantaged.
Nuclear	Slightly higher cost.	High perceived risk.	High risk.	Disadvantaged.
Renewables	Some competitive, some higher cost. High costs if dramatic expansion in short time period.	No risk.	No risk yet. Moderate risk possible with larger scale.	Disadvantaged.
Fossil fuels	Competitive. Slightly higher cost with carbon capture and storage.	Moderate to low risk.	Oil perceived high risk. Coal – opposite.	Strongest position.

lower costs. The eventual cost of large-scale energy storage is a big uncertainty for the intermittent renewables like wind and solar, which could lead to much higher costs as their market share grows. In terms of path dependence, a greater push for efficiency and renewables must overcome the dominance of fossil fuels.

Nuclear power is slightly higher cost than the best alternatives for electricity generation, and substantially higher cost for hydrogen production via electrolysis. Nuclear has a high perceived risk with respect to extreme event risk and geopolitical risk. Two decades ago, nuclear power had an advantage in terms of path dependence, but it has lost this momentum in all but a few countries.

Zero-emission fossil fuels have the strongest position in terms of path dependence. They should remain economically competitive, especially given the plentiful resource base, the opportunity to substitute between fossil fuels with only modest increases in production costs, and the moderate cost of producing hydrogen, electricity and synthetic fuels in zero-emission processes from natural gas, coal and eventually unconventional natural gas. Conventional and unconventional oil may also play a role in the zero-emission production of electricity and hydrogen depending on the growth of these reserves as energy prices rise. With a growing role for coal, unconventional oil and unconventional natural gas, the geopolitical risk associated currently with conventional crude oil should diminish for fossil fuels as a whole. Extreme event risk should not be great, although there is still some uncertainty about the local risks of carbon storage in geological formations.

The challenge for nuclear

Because nuclear power has lost its momentum in all but a few countries, it needs a compelling argument to get back on track over the next decades if it is to achieve a larger share of primary energy in the second half of the century. Nuclear advocates believe that depletion of conventional oil and natural gas, greenhouse gas emissions from fossil fuel combustion, the carbon-intensive character of coal, the high current cost of most renewables when storage is included, and the dramatic expansion of the global energy system together provide the impetus for a nuclear renaissance.

While there is some basis for this argument, it depends on a fairly static view of the technologies associated with its three competitors.

Zero-emission coal gasification is likely to produce electricity at a comparable or lower cost and hydrogen at a much lower cost. Some wind and hydro sites can produce electricity at a comparable cost already and crop residue biomass is likely to produce hydrogen and relatively clean-burning gaseous and liquid fuels at comparable or lower costs. Efforts to increase energy efficiency will be more politically palatable for governments and industry than the siting of a new nuclear plant, especially in wealthy countries.

Overall, nuclear scores equally or negatively against zero-emission fossil fuels, efficiency and renewables on all four criteria. Given its challenges in the areas of extreme event risk and geopolitical risk, nuclear probably needs to be substantially cheaper than the alternatives if it is to have a chance of playing a dominant role in the global energy system for the foreseeable future. It does not have this cost advantage today and appears unlikely to achieve it during the next fifty years unless fossil fuels are deliberately abandoned while efficiency and renewables are pursued too aggressively. The best hope for nuclear is if large, relatively stable countries like China and India make the industry the centerpiece of their national energy strategies, but even expansion in these two countries would be insufficient for nuclear to realize a dramatic increase in its share of the global energy system.

In my current trends projection in chapter 2 (table 2.1 and figure 2.3) nuclear grows ten-fold over this century, from 9 to 90 EJ. On the basis of this trade-off comparison, I now revise this downward to 40 EJ in my sustainable energy projection. This still represents a five-fold expansion, with 2,000 plants worldwide in comparison to the current total of 430. Most of this expansion would occur in the latter half of the century, keeping nuclear's share of total electricity generation not far below its current 17% market share. (I integrate this projection for nuclear into a single sustainability projection for the global energy system at the end of this section.)

The limits for efficiency's contribution

Regardless of whether one favors renewables, nuclear power or fossil fuels, most people agree in principle that energy efficiency has highly desirable attributes and should be pursued. There are, however, several challenges to the achievement of rapidly declining primary energy intensity (the ratio of primary energy to world economic output), which is the goal of our energy efficiency efforts. Since I explained these in chapter 4, I only summarize here.

First, a rapid decline in energy intensity is not always possible or desirable. In my current trends projection, energy intensity declines by 0.8% annually during the century and still the global energy system grows to more than three times its current size. Yet global energy intensity was constant between 1850 and 1950, and only declined at an average annual rate of 0.7% during the last several decades, a period with frequent expectations of rising energy prices and widespread government and utility energy efficiency efforts. Even if the rate of intensity decline could somehow be sustained through the century at the high rate of 1.2% annually, the global demand for primary energy would still grow to 920 EJ, more than double its current level.

Second, economic growth in developing countries will require a lot of energy for the steel, cement and other heavy industries whose output is required to construct buildings, factories and essential infrastructure. Growing energy demand from final consumers will cause strong upward pressure on energy intensity, again especially in developing countries where the increasing demand for heating and air conditioning of larger living spaces, all sorts of appliances, and greater personal mobility will strongly correlate with rising incomes. The energy demands associated with China's rapid economic growth of the past two decades illustrates this link.

Third, an energy system dominated by conventional oil and natural gas is able to take advantage of the high energy density and high conversion efficiency of these two primary forms of energy. As that system evolves toward unconventional oil, unconventional natural gas, coal, renewables with storage, and nuclear (depending on how its primary energy input is accounted), more energy will be required by the energy system itself. Oil sands extraction requires significant energy inputs. Zero-emission conversion of coal to electricity has a lower efficiency than conventional technologies. Offshore windfarms require long transmission lines that lose energy as a function of distance. The conversion processes required for providing energy storage alongside intermittent renewables will also use a lot of energy. Our exhaustion of the highest quality energy endowment and our demand for cleaner secondary energy will create, for global energy intensity indicators, an upward push to counter the normal downward push resulting from technological change.

Fourth, energy efficiency is usually more expensive than it is portrayed by advocates who ignore key intangible factors like the risks associated with new technologies and with technologies requiring longer payback periods, as well as the strong preferences of some consumers for less efficient technologies – like powerful, large personal vehicles. More efficiency would be economic if the final price of energy were to double. But the evidence suggests that energy prices in a sustainable energy system might be no more than 25% higher than today's. It appears that electricity, hydrogen and synthetic fuels can be produced with zero emissions and low impacts and risks to land and water at energy production costs about 25–50% higher. Since the cost of the commodity typically represents less than half of its final price, after transmission, distribution and taxes have been added, even a 50% increase in the commodity cost would only result in a 25% increase in the final price seen by consumers. This is within the range of oil and natural gas price increases in the period 2000–2005. Dramatic increases in energy efficiency trends will be difficult to achieve if final prices to businesses and consumers do not increase by more than 25–50% over most of the century.

Fifth, energy efficiency is a double-edged sword in that efficiency improvements lower the operating cost of energy services, which can result in a rebound in the demand for the service or some related service. Efficient light bulbs lower the cost of lighting, which may not increase the demand for interior lighting but may surface as increased demand for exterior decorative and security lighting. Rebound is more likely if efficiency improvements are not supported by substantial increases in energy prices.

These factors make it difficult for policies in favor of energy efficiency to make great gains in accelerating the normal tendency for energy intensity to decline gradually. Thus, under most scenarios of population and economic growth, the global energy system in 2100 is unlikely to be much below 1,200 EJ. In the absence of dramatically higher energy production costs, the only way to achieve this outcome would be via high energy taxes and forceful energy efficiency regulations. Governments have not been able to sustain these types of policies in the past, and this would be especially difficult to justify if relatively inexpensive energy supply were of low impact and low risk.

For my sustainable energy projection, therefore, I assume that the global energy system in 2100 will require 1,200 EJ of primary energy instead of the 1,390 of my current trends scenario in chapter 2. This will require an average decline in the energy intensity of the global economy of about 1% per year through the century. The primary energy system therefore increases almost three-fold, which is still a dramatic slowing of growth compared to the sixteen-fold expansion during the previous century.

Renewables versus clean fossil fuels

Renewables and zero-emission fossil fuels will compete for the dominant position in meeting the needs of a sustainable energy system over the coming century. Renewables may appear to many people to be more attractive in terms of both cleanliness and endurance, but zero-emission fossil fuels have a cost advantage and a substantial path dependence advantage. Even with rapid growth, renewables would be hard pressed to overtake fossil fuels by the end of the century given the small base they must start from in what will remain a rapidly growing global energy system. There would be a greater possibility if renewables were significantly lower cost than zero-emission fossil fuels, thereby motivating business and consumers to switch as soon as they had the chance. Instead, the evidence suggests that zero-emission fossil fuels will remain economically competitive with renewables because of the abundance of exploitable reserves of unconventional oil, unconventional natural gas, and especially coal – which will impede the ability of renewables to replace them quickly. Even if those who emphasize the global significance of Hubbert's curve are correct, and conventional oil production soon begins an inexorable decline, this should have no significance for the competitive position of fossil fuels relative to renewables in the early decades of this century. Conventional oil is but a small component of the aggregate fossil fuel resource, and its potential fossil fuel substitutes may be more expensive per unit of fuel delivered, but not greatly so. Also, a more rapid expansion of renewables will more quickly confront the problems of energy storage and land-use conflicts instead of allowing research and development the time to produce innovations that could address these challenges and reduce costs. In these circumstances, an effort to push the market share of renewables substantially beyond the already rapid growth in my current trends projection is likely to raise the total costs of the energy system with no appreciable benefit in terms of the key trade-off criteria for choosing among energy options. It is difficult to envision the political will for such an effort.

Since greenhouse gas emissions, especially carbon emissions, have a dominant place in current discussions about energy sustainability, I assess in greater detail how energy options and specific technology choices could affect the evolution of these emissions. Coal-fired electricity plants produced almost one third of anthropogenic carbon emissions in 2000, and this share grows dramatically in my current trends projection of chapter 2. In the next decade or so, efforts to increase the role of wind, hydropower and natural gas in electricity generation can only slow slightly the growth of carbon emissions relative to the current trends projection. However, on a ten-to-fifty year timeframe, carbon capture and storage technologies will pass from the demonstration stage to commercial dissemination, provided there are policies to motivate the installation of these higher cost technologies and processes. Most of the components of this option are already commercially proven. Once this overall process is demonstrated as a total package for zero-emission fossil fuels, it will become much easier for governments in the middle decades of the century to enact more forceful policies that lead to universal compliance with carbon capture and storage requirements at coal-fired and natural gas-fired electricity generators. With these policies raising the cost of electricity from fossil fuels, renewables will find opportunities to compete. But even the high growth rate I envision for renewables will not erase fossil fuel dependency over the course of the century.

For the transport of people and goods – the other great source of carbon emissions – the picture is more complicated, as I noted in my discussion of clean secondary energy in chapter 3. It is important to assess not just the end-use emissions of the transport mode itself (personal vehicle, public transport, ships, trains and planes) but also the life-cycle emissions. What emissions occur upstream in the production of the electricity, hydrogen or hydrocarbon fuels used in the mode of transport? Some analysts argue that gasoline combusted in efficient internal combustion engines will still be desirable in cases where the life-cycle emissions will be less than those of electric vehicles recharged from a fossil fuel-based electric grid, or fuel-cell vehicles using hydrogen produced from fossil fuels (if these processes lack carbon capture and storage). The case for efficient internal combustion engines is even stronger if some of the hydrocarbons they use are produced from biomass.

Thus, with perhaps the exception of air travel (which can use jet fuel or convert to biofuels if need be), the alternatives for clean transport of goods and people appear to be equally viable at this point. One alternative is super-efficient internal combustion engines fueled by gasoline, synthetic fuels, natural gas or biofuels. But if global mobility trends continue as I expect they will, this alternative cannot be dominant because it will not satisfy my sustainability requirements for greenhouse gas emissions and local air pollutants.

A second alternative is hydrogen fuel cells with the hydrogen mostly produced by gasification of fossil fuels with carbon capture and storage (the cheapest zero-emission way of producing hydrogen). A third alternative is the wide-scale adoption of efficient plug-in hybrid engines that substantially increase the use of electricity in transportation. This alternative could be superior to the second if hydrogen production costs, hydrogen storage problems, and/or high fuel cell costs offset the benefits of more efficient hydrogen production directly from fossil fuels (as opposed to producing electricity) and the efficient hydrogen fuel cell engines.* In this case, there is a chance for market dominance by high efficiency plug-in hybrid engines fueled primarily by expanded

---

* While the estimates vary from one study to another, an efficiency comparison of the two pathways looks like this. Hydrogen could in future be produced from natural gas at perhaps 60% efficiency and from coal at perhaps 50% efficiency (including in both cases the energy costs of carbon capture and storage), then there are energy losses in transport and storage, and the fuel cell and electric motor of the vehicle could have a combined efficiency of 45% – for a total pathway efficiency of about 18–23%. In contrast, electricity could be produced from natural gas (CCGT) at about 50% efficiency and from coal (IGCC) at about 40% (again including the energy costs of carbon capture and storage), then after relatively modest losses for electricity transmission, the hybrid car with electric plug-in and internal combustion engine (running mostly on electricity) could have an efficiency of 30% – for a total pathway efficiency of about 12–15%. While the hybrid pathway is less efficient than the hydrogen fuel-cell pathway, it might be lower cost depending on the costs of hydrogen production, hydrogen transport and storage, on-board vehicle storage of hydrogen, and fuel cell costs. For other efficiency estimates, see M. Hoffert, K. Caldeira, G. Benford, D. Criswell, C. Green, H. Herzog, A. Jain, H. Kheshgi, K. Lackner, J. Lewis, H. Lightfoot, W. Mannheimer, J. Mankins, M. Mavel, L. Perkins, M. Schlesinger, T. Volk and T. Wigley, "Advanced Technology Paths to Global

production of zero-emission electricity from fossil fuels and renewables. The small amount of fuel they combust could come from fossil fuels (gasoline, natural gas, synthetic fuels) or biomass (bio-diesel, ethanol) if required to meet greenhouse gas reduction targets.

What is important from a primary energy perspective, however, is that zero-emission fossil fuels have a good prospect for playing a significant role in all three of these technology-energy alternatives for transport of people and goods. If this assessment proves to be correct, fossil fuels would continue to dominate electricity generation (currently the domain of coal and natural gas) and play a significant role in transport (currently the domain of oil). This technology-energy evolution at the secondary energy level would occur in step with an evolution at the primary energy level from conventional oil, natural gas and coal in the current system to unconventional oil, unconventional natural gas and additional coal as the century progressed. If it turns out that potential fossil fuel reserves are more limited than current assessments indicate, then growing energy demand will lead to gradually rising fossil fuel prices and eventually open the door to a more rapid growth of renewables in the later decades of the century – as well as greater opportunities for energy efficiency and perhaps nuclear.

In spite of the competitive challenges for renewables, their potential contribution to transport and electricity generation leads me to increase their output in my sustainable energy projection from the current trends scenario of chapter 2 – even though this is a scenario in which they already experience extremely high growth rates through the century. While the current trends projection has renewables reaching 380 EJ by 2100, I project that with a strong push to a cleaner energy system they can reach 480 EJ by 2100. This means that in my sustainable energy projection the contribution in 2100 from renewables alone exceeds today's entire global energy system of 429 EJ in 2000.

Table 7.4 disaggregates my sustainable energy projection into individual forms of renewable energy and contrasts it with the current trends forecast of chapter 2. In the current trends projection, the traditional combustion use of biomass doubles from 45 to 90 EJ by 2100. If this were to happen, even more humans would perish each year from

Climate Stability: Energy for a Greenhouse Planet," *Science* 298 (2002): 981–987; and J. Ogden, R. Williams and E. Larson, "Societal Lifecycle Costs of Cars with Alternative Fuels/Engines," *Energy Policy* 32 (2004): 7–27.

Table 7.4. Renewables: current trends projection versus sustainability projection

	2000	Current trends projection 2100	Sustainability projection 2100
Total renewables	**61**	**380**	**480**
Total biomass	52	210	210
Traditional biomass	45	90	30
Modern biomass	7	120	180
Total hydro	9	30	50
Large hydropower	8.64	28	20
Small hydropower	0.36	2	30
Total W-S-G-O	0.57	140	220
Wind	0.11	90	120
Solar	0.16	30	60
Geothermal	0.3	20	30
Ocean (wave, tidal, current)	–	–	10

poor indoor air quality. However, in my sustainable energy projection, solid fuel combustion for local uses (household, agriculture) declines to 30 EJ by 2100. Of this 30 EJ, rising incomes and deliberate policies ensure that open combustion of this solid fuel is replaced almost entirely by combustion in efficient, low-emission stoves and furnaces. The rest of the biomass in the sustainable energy projection is used to produce electricity (sometimes involving co-combustion with coal and including carbon capture and storage) or converted into gaseous and liquid fuels for combustion in domestic, industrial and transportation uses. These uses of biomass with modern technologies increase from 7 EJ in 2000 to 180 EJ by 2100. Thus, modern biomass represents a significant share of the hydrocarbons that are part of the sustainable secondary energy projection in chapter 3.

In the current trends projection, large hydropower was assumed to comprise most of the expansion from 9 EJ in 2000 to 30 in 2100. However, in the sustainable energy trajectory, large hydro faces greater constraints because of environmental impacts so that it only grows to 20 EJ while small hydro (<10 MW) grows from 0.36 EJ in 2000 to 30 in 2100. Because much of this small hydro is in areas of intermittent water flows and has limited reservoir capacity, there are additional costs for energy storage.

In the sustainable energy projection, I show the other renewables growing even faster than in the current trends forecast. While they grow from 0.57 EJ in 2000 to 140 EJ in 2100 in the current trends forecast, they grow to 220 EJ in my sustainable energy projection. If renewables are to contribute more under a sustainable energy system, much of the growth must come from wind, solar, geothermal and ocean because biomass and hydropower already face substantial physical limits and environmental constraints in the current trends forecast. Thus, in the sustainable energy projection, wind grows from 0.11 EJ in 2000 to 120 in 2100 and solar, most of it PV, from 0.16 EJ in 2000 to 60 in 2100. Part of the PV growth results from integration of PV cells into roofing and building material, which lowers its cost and facilitates its widespread dissemination in industrialized countries initially and then in developing countries. Geothermal is limited in terms of economically favorable sites, so its annual growth rate is lower but still substantial, from 0.3 EJ in 2000 to 30 EJ in 2100. Some of this is due to the development of ground source heat pumps that use another energy input (electricity, gas) to exploit the temperature differential between the earth's surface and sub-surface at different times of year. The ocean-related renewables – tidal, wave and current – are assumed to remain at a modest level in all but a few regions, reaching 10 EJ by 2100. They are the most disadvantaged economically, and will be challenged to compete with all the other renewables and zero-emission fossil fuels for market share.

Total renewables in the sustainable energy trajectory are therefore at 480 EJ, of which all but the 30 EJ of domestic biomass consumption (in low-emission stoves and furnaces) is with modern technologies generating electricity from biomass, hydropower, wind, solar, geothermal and ocean renewables, and producing liquid and gaseous fuels from biomass.

7.4 The continued dominance of fossil fuels

In this multi-criteria comparison, I assess how the options for a more sustainable energy system are likely to fare in competition with each other, given the criteria I think are most important to human decision-making with respect to energy. Cost is critical, although cost should not be seen as a single point estimate; the costs of each energy option rise with a greater contribution or a more rapid development, some more than others. When the cost comparison is inconclusive, then other factors carry greater significance. These include attitudes to extreme event risk, concerns about geopolitical risk, and the speed with which society can adopt revolutionary technologies that require a dramatic change from the current path.

From this comparison, I construct a sustainable energy projection in which the contribution of each of the four options is determined by its performance against the criteria in comparison to its competitors. In this scenario, nuclear power grows substantially from its current output, but its role remains limited because it lacks the significant cost advantage needed to overcome its disadvantages with respect to extreme event risk and geopolitical risk. Its contribution is limited to electricity production, where it almost maintains its share of the global market in what is an expanding industry. Energy efficiency makes a much greater contribution than in the past and therefore energy intensity levels sustain a rate of decline of 1% annually throughout the century. Energy efficiency's contribution is constrained, however, because of the inherent energy intensity of some of the energy service demand growth in developing countries, the greater energy needed in the energy sector itself as we exhaust the highest quality energy sources, the moderate prices for energy, and the rebound of energy service demand as energy operating costs fall with more efficient devices. Energy efficiency does not stop the primary energy system from expanding almost three-fold. Renewables see a dramatic rate of growth and an increasing market share. However, because they start from such a small base, and because they will not have a substantial cost advantage over zero-emission fossil fuels for the production of clean secondary energy, they do not take over the dominant role in the energy system by the end of the century.

My sustainable energy projection is summarized in figure 7.2. At all levels of the energy system, intensified energy efficiency effort reduces the total primary energy demand to 1,200 EJ. Of this total, nuclear provides 40 EJ, renewables 480 and fossil fuels 680. Fossil fuels fall over the century from 84% of primary energy to 57% while modern renewables climb from 4% to 38%.

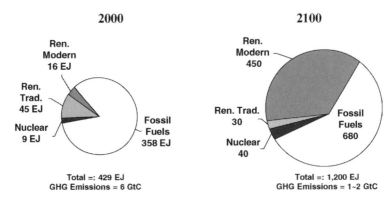

Figure 7.2. The sustainable fossil fuel future.

This figure provides the primary energy shares that accompany the
secondary energy shares I presented in my sustainable energy projection in chapter 3. At the secondary level, electricity accounts for
30%, hydrogen for 30–40% and hydrocarbons (of which a considerable amount are biofuels) for 30–40%. What is notable is that at
the primary energy level, the sustainable energy projection is not
that much different than the current trends forecast in terms of the
relative shares of each option. What is concealed in figure 7.2 are
the introduction of carbon capture and storage along with the greater
use of hydrogen at the secondary level. If the process of extracting
fossil fuels and converting them to clean forms of secondary energy
can be as low impact and low risk as the evidence suggests, and if fossil
fuels are understood to be plentiful when considered in aggregate
as they should be, they are likely to dominate the global energy
system through this century and continue in a significant role into
the future.

I provided in chapter 1 a sampling of quotes from the often-heard
argument that we must switch quickly away from fossil fuels if we are
to have a sustainable energy system. The result of my assessment of the
evidence and this multi-criteria comparison leads to a very different
outcome. Certainly, fossil fuels lose market share, but by 2100 their
output has almost doubled, from 358 EJ to 680. This contrasts with
the popular image of a resource and an industry forced by depletion,
environmental harm and rising costs into rapid decline. But can this be
called a sustainable energy future? Does it satisfy my original definition of energy system sustainability?

Four common indicators of the environmental and human sustainability of an energy system are indoor air quality, urban air quality, regional acid emissions and greenhouse gas emissions. The increase in incomes in developing countries in concert with the shift to low-emission gaseous and liquid fuels produced from fossil fuels and biomass dramatically improve indoor air quality, reducing human mortality and morbidity from this cause by 80–90% by the end of the century. While this is primarily a natural outcome from individual choices as incomes rise, the growing availability of low-emission, low-cost liquid and gaseous secondary energy from fossil fuels contributes significantly. In contrast, an accelerated effort to replace fossil fuels with higher cost renewables is likely to slow the improvement in indoor air quality, with a greater negative impact on human health than any other development in the global energy system.

Urban air quality improves significantly, not just in industrialized countries but also in developing countries. The rising concentration of wealth in the large cities of developing countries fosters increased local concern for urban air quality and improvements in governance capability that together enable the implementation of policies that phase out polluting technologies and secondary energy forms. Cities have the greatest incentive and the financial means to expand electricity and some natural gas use, develop hydrogen distribution and refueling networks, increase rapid transit infrastructure, capture waste heat for low temperature needs, and pursue new renewable options like PVs integrated into roofing and siding of buildings. With the predominance of clean secondary energy, conventional air pollutants are at only a fraction of their current levels in urban areas, leading to a significant reduction in human morbidity and mortality.

The declines in acid emissions achieved in industrialized countries in the last few decades spreads to developing countries with the shift toward a sustainable energy system. As coal plants are converted to zero-emission processes around the world, sulphur is captured and sequestered alongside CO_2 or separated for commercial use if there is a market.

While net CO_2 emissions do not fall to zero, because of the continued combustion of natural gas and clean burning synthetic fuels as well as the incompleteness of carbon capture processes (90% capture), they fall dramatically as the fossil fuel industry shifts to zero-emission processes for producing clean secondary energy. A greater use of biomass also reduces net CO_2 emissions, and some biomass gasification is even associated with the extraction and sequestering of CO_2. Figure 7.2 shows the results of my calculation of annual global CO_2 emissions by 2100 according to the mix and conversion processes for primary and secondary energy in the sustainable energy scenario. Human-produced carbon emissions fall from 6 Gt today to 1–2 Gt in 2100. This contrasts markedly with my current trends projection in chapter 2, which had carbon emissions rising to about 20 Gt by 2100. If a significant part of the shift to zero-emission fossil fuels is achieved during the middle decades of the century (2030–2070), the concentration of CO_2 in the atmosphere should remain below 550 parts per million, an important level for climatologists worried about climate disruption.*

In terms of other physical effects on land, oceans and fresh water, there is no doubt that a larger human population and a correspondingly larger global energy system will have impacts. Some of the current concerns with our energy system will intensify as exploration, development, exploitation and transportation pose continued risks of small and large disruptions to ecosystems and people. If we are serious about a more sustainable energy system, we must continue to pursue aggressively the progress of the last century in which we lowered many of these impacts from the energy industry without increasing its costs significantly. Given the rate of advance in science and technology, this is an achievable goal.

Concerns about land and water impacts also apply to renewables. As these grow in market share, we may see that their impacts can be just as significant given the scale-up challenges related to their intermittency, low energy density and inconvenient location. This will restrict the development of some renewables – such as large hydro reservoirs, tidal barriers, bio-energy plantations, and sensitive geothermal sites. We can foster innovations that minimize impacts and risks, develop major energy storage facilities such as underground storage of compressed air and thermal energy, integrate PV arrays into roofing and

---

* M. Hoffert and co-authors found that about 82% of energy supply would need to be non-carbon emitting to stabilize atmospheric concentrations of CO_2 at 550 parts per million in a global energy system that reached a size of 1,450 EJ in 2100. See M. Hoffert, K. Caldeira, E. Haites, L. Harvey, A. Jain, S. Putter, M. Schlesinger, S. Schneider, R. Watts, T. Wigley and D. Wuebbles, "Energy Implications of Future Stabilization of Atmospheric CO_2 Content," *Nature* 395, 29 (1988): 881–884.

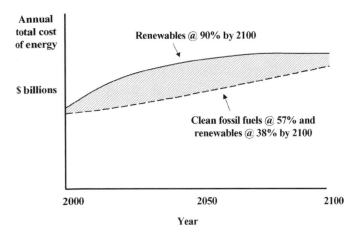

Figure 7.3. Projected annual energy system costs with and without clean
fossil fuels.

values, but the relative magnitudes are indicative.* The top line represents the annual total system costs (capital and operating) of a forced
switch to renewables so that they comprise 90% of the global energy
system by 2100. The bottom line represents my sustainable energy
projection. The vertical distance between the lines in any year represents the difference in annual total system costs. The whole shaded
area between the curves represents the cumulative difference in total
costs between the two paths.

In the near future, the curves are close together because the immediate expansion of some lower cost renewables like windpower is
economically competitive with the first phases of developing and
adopting zero-emission fossil fuels. But as the switch to renewables
accelerates in order to supplant all fossil fuels in an expanding energy
system, the costs rise faster than for the scenario that does not try to
force out fossil fuels quickly; some higher cost renewables are forced

---

* As an approximate indication, a recent report on energy cost estimated annual
 energy sector investment of $500 billion (US$ 2000) annually for the next thirty
 years, which equates to about 1% of gross world product. This figure includes
 neither energy supply operating costs nor investment costs in energy end-use
 technologies. See International Energy Agency, *World Energy Investment
 Outlook* (Paris: International Energy Agency, 2003).

building materials, exploit run-of-the-river hydro opportunities, a carefully exploit residual biomass from agriculture and forestry. 1 this will take time. Developing renewables too quickly will be cos and will present unnecessary risks of negative public reaction.

The need for time applies to social attitudes as well. A fello researcher once told me about the generation gap among Dani people in their attitudes to windpower. Many older Danes feel th wind generators are a blight on the bucolic landscape of their chil. hood, where the only vertical imposition on the rolling farmlar was the steeples of their beloved white churches. However, th younger generation, which has grown up with modern wind turbine always in view, and with an educational system that emphasize their environmentally benign character, tends to find the moder. viewscape acceptable and even heartwarming. This is not to sugges that Danish windpower advocates eagerly await the passing of th older generation!

In terms of extreme event risks and geopolitical risks, this sustain able energy projection differs dramatically from the current trends projection, but even its restrained level of nuclear expansion should only occur if the informed public in a given jurisdiction accepts that the risk of radiation exposure is negligible and if major political powers are satisfied that geopolitical risk has been minimized by strong international safeguards. If not, the contribution from nuclear should be decreased, with the difference offset by slight increases in the three other options. The geopolitical risks of crude oil dependence will also be minimized in this energy future as domestic energy resources such as coal and renewables vie with imported crude oil for market share, decreasing the vulnerability to disruptions in the latter's supply.

What about total costs of the energy system? The higher energy quality of fossil fuels in combination with their path dependence advantage makes this path lower cost than a rapid switch to renewables, nuclear, greater energy efficiency, or any combination of these in the span of one century. Figure 7.3 compares the total annual energy costs (investment and operating) for two energy futures that I calculated from the cost information earlier in this chapter and the market shares of each energy option in my sustainable energy projection (for primary and secondary energy). I have omitted numbers from the vertical axis to signify the uncertainty about this cost in absolute upon the market prematurely, before experience and economies-of-scale can lower their costs and reduce their performance risks, and before lower cost energy storage can result from sustained research and development. The costs for estimating this line were taken from the higher cost estimates in tables 7.1 and 7.2 for producing electricity and hydrogen from renewables only, plus some extra costs for a more rapid expansion of renewable energy transport and storage infrastructure. In contrast, my sustainable fossil fuel projection benefits from continued use of high quality oil and natural gas reserves (conventional and unconventional) and the path dependence advantages of using much of the existing fossil fuel infrastructure and developed sites. Toward the end of the century, however, the depletion of the lowest cost sources of fossil fuels, combined with the cost reductions realized by renewables as they achieve technological maturity and wider diffusion in step with capital stock turnover, brings the two cost trajectories close again.

One might interpret this annual cost convergence in 2100 to mean that future generations will be indifferent about the energy path we choose because energy service costs will be about the same 100 years from now no matter what. However, the gap between the paths over the course of the century implies a large difference in economic performance, and the loss in economic output associated with rapidly abandoning fossil fuels will carry over into future economic output. In a country like Bangladesh, richly endowed with natural gas as it is, the forgone economic benefits of a deliberate and early push for renewables would equate to funds that could instead be dedicated to the development of thousands of schools, hospitals and other services that would improve the lives of immediate generations, and pass on a greater capability to generate wealth and well-being for following generations. Developing countries, especially, cannot afford to be cavalier about what might seem to be modest annual differences in the cost of energy options.

What about endurance? Even if this cleaner fossil fuel future has low impacts and risks for humans and the environment, fossil fuels are still a finite resource that we will eventually exhaust. Yet consuming a non-renewable resource matters little if a ready substitute is available at a comparable cost. To substitute completely from fossil fuels to renewables in the span of a century is costly. At a measured pace, however, we can evolve toward a renewables-dominated global energy system that may not have substantially higher energy costs than today. This implies the relatively smooth transition from an exhaustible to a renewable backstop resource that I depicted earlier in figure 5.3. This transition could take half a century or it could take several centuries. Its pace will not matter to people living during the transition because the forms of secondary energy that they are familiar with – electricity, hydrogen and low-emission hydrocarbons – will evolve gradually at most. Although fossil fuels are still the dominant primary energy source, this energy projection satisfies my definition of sustainability in providing low-cost, clean and enduring energy services to an expanding global population. As we gradually shift from fossil fuels towards renewables, and perhaps eventually nuclear, the energy system can continue indefinitely to provide this level of services.

Ignoring a low cost option just because it will not last forever is strange to me. It seems to result from people using a definition of sustainability requiring that every component of the energy system must be guaranteed to last forever. For example, in arguing against carbon capture and storage, D. Goodstein says, "And in any case the coal will eventually run out, whereas we're trying to think long-term here."[18] Making a similar argument against the US converting coal to hydrogen for its hydrogen needs, J. Turner says, "the energy required for the necessary sequestration of CO_2 would increase the rate at which coal reserves are depleted . . . US 250-year coal reserves drop to 75 years or so, which is not at all sustainable."[19] But do we need such a rigid approach? Does this mean that humans shouldn't have started using fossil fuels in the eighteenth century if they had known at that time that this energy was non-renewable? Would humanity be better off today had they done that? Will our energy system really be more sustainable if we transition away from fossil fuels in the next three decades instead of the next three centuries?

The sustainable fossil fuel future is both likely and desirable in my view. But it is far from certain. Various surprises could change the outcome. Geological storage of CO_2 could prove technically unviable for some reason, or there could be a strong public reaction against it. The cost of integrated PV could fall more rapidly than originally assumed, changing the relative costs of renewables and zero-emission fossil fuels. Advances in biotechnology could improve agricultural and forestry productivity in ways that dramatically reduce the costs of biomass energy. A breakthrough in research to produce hydrogen directly from sunlight could have a similar effect, as would an innovation that somehow eliminated radiation leak as a risk from nuclear reactors and waste storage sites.

This vision of the future will not be attractive to everyone. Some will still argue that fossil fuels are inherently toxic and that humans cannot be trusted to use them cleanly. There is evidence to support this position, but much more to indicate that we have improved substantially our control of impacts and risks, and can quite easily make further advances.

Some will argue that we cannot smoothly transition from fossil fuels to renewables or nuclear in the distant future, that an energy system based on fossil fuels is a house of cards that will collapse catastrophically past some depletion threshold like Hubbert's peak. Viewed in the short term, markets do sometimes seem cataclysmic. From a long-term perspective, however, scarcity engenders a price increase, which in turn triggers technological and behavioral responses, and our plentiful global energy resources provide many avenues for response. There is much evidence in support of this.

Some will argue that we should husband fossil fuel resources because they may have a higher value in future. But what higher value is there than providing clean fuel to the over two billion poor people on earth whose health would improve dramatically from low-cost energy and technologies that improve indoor air quality, clean up urban air, reduce acid emissions and reduce the risks of climate disruption? Clean and cheap energy is but one of the conditions needed for economic and social development, but it is a critical one.

Some will argue that the sustainable fossil fuel strategy is the antithesis of "small-is-beautiful" – leading to massive coal-mines, coal polygeneration plants, and hydrogen networks.[20] Certainly, there will be economies-of-scale factors in favor of large plants when it comes to zero-emission processes for fossil fuels, so if size is an important criterion, this vision will be less attractive. Even renewables, however, already face pressures for larger-scale production as their importance to the global energy system increases and innovators seek ways to gain a competitive advantage in renewable energy production. In spite of decades of arguments for a small-is-beautiful technology commitment, few members of the public seem to be convinced that this is an important criterion. Small size units are valued when they are assumed to be cleaner or to ensure local control of investment decisions, but these objectives can also be pursued without a fixation on small-scale technologies. Denmark, the first country to push windpower to a significant role in its electricity system, started with individual wind turbines of 100 kW, but is now developing massive offshore wind farms of 200 MW – equal to a modest-sized coal plant with major transmission lines and related facilities. An outcome that may be satisfying to most people is one that mixes small and large scale along with local and centralized control. This outcome is equally possible under a renewables energy future and a sustainable fossil fuel future.

Finally, some might ask why I call this a "fossil fuel future" since it combines increased energy efficiency with a primary energy portfolio of nuclear, renewables and fossil fuels. Perhaps there is a mischievous motive in my choice of this phrase. But having heard and read so many calls for the rapid expulsion of fossil fuels from our energy system, and then having looked carefully at the evidence, I feel the need to proclaim bluntly the counter position – that this form of primary energy can and should be an integral part of our sustainable energy future, and can indeed dominate it for a long time to come provided we use it cleanly. There seems to be a compelling argument for delaying the complete transition away from fossil fuels until their declining energy quality and the increasing difficulty of accessing remaining reserves means that they no longer have an advantage over the other options.

Discussions of our energy options too often simplify the world into good guys and bad guys. Fossil fuels are bad because they do not endure forever and can be used in a toxic manner – so we should switch quickly away from them. But reality is more complex. Fossil fuels are a product of solar energy that like any other form of energy have more or less impacts and risks depending on how carefully we exploit them. We must not confuse means and ends. The end is to have a clean, low-cost and enduring energy system. With that in mind, let's carefully assess our means of getting there. When we do this, we may see the evidence differently.*

---

* Apparently it was the famous economist John Maynard Keynes who once said, "When convincing evidence refutes what I previously believed, I change my opinion. What do you do sir?"

The transition to a much cleaner and lower risk energy system is desirable, achievable and affordable over the course of this century. However, this will not happen on its own. I turn now to policy design: how we begin the transition to a sustainable energy system.

Notes

1. See A. Stirling, "Science and Precaution in the Appraisal of Electricity Supply Options," *Journal of Hazardous Materials* 86 (2001): 55–75; and M. Viklund, "Energy Policy Options – from the Perspective of Public Attitudes and Risk Perceptions," *Energy Policy* 32 (2004): 1159–1171.
2. For a recent description of the issues as they emerge in an analysis of the electricity sector, see P. Soderholm and T. Sundqvist, "Pricing Environmental Externalities in the Power Sector: Ethical Limits and Implications for Social Choice," *Ecological Economics* 46 (2003): 333–350.
3. Frequently cited estimates are European Commission, *ExternE: Externalities of Energy* (Luxembourg: Office for Official Publications of the European Communities, 1995), and *External Costs: Research Results on Socio-Environmental Damages Due to Electricity and Transport* (Brussels: Director-General for Research, European Commission, 2003); R. Ottinger, D. Wooley, N. Robinson, D. Hodas and S. Babb, *Environmental Costs of Electricity* (New York: Oceana, 1990); O. Hohmeyer, *Social Costs of Energy Consumption* (Berlin: Springer-Verlag, 1988).
4. For one of the classic presentations, see R. Keeney and H. Raiffa, *Decisions with Multiple Objectives: Preferences and Value Tradeoffs* (New York: Wiley, 1976). For recent overviews of the application of these techniques to energy-environment issues, see L. Greening and S. Bernow, "Design of Coordinated Energy and Environmental Policies: Use of Multi-Criteria Decision-Making," *Energy Policy* 32 (2004): 721–735; M. Bell, B. Hobbs and H. Ellis, "The Use of Multi-Criteria Decision-Making Methods in the Integrated Assessment of Climate Change: Implications for IA Practitioners," *Socio-Economic Planning Sciences* 37 (2003): 289–316; and B. Hobbs and P. Meier, *Energy Decisions and the Environment: A Guide to the Use of Multi-Criteria Methods* (Dordrecht: Kluwer Academic, 2000).
5. K. Arrow and L. Hurwicz, "An Optimality Criterion for Decision-Making under Ignorance," in C. Carter and J. Ford (eds.), *Uncertainty and Expectations in Economics: Essays in Honour of G. L. S. Shackle* (Oxford: Basil Blackwell, 1972). More recently, see R. Woodward and

R. Bishop, "How to Decide when Experts Disagree: Uncertainty-Based Choice Rules in Environmental Policy," *Land Economics* 73, 4 (1997): 492–507; and V. Bier, Y. Haimes, J. Lambert, N. Matalas and R. Zimmerman, "A Survey of Approaches for Assessing and Managing the Risk of Extremes," *Risk Analysis* 19, 1 (1999): 83–94.

6. Union of Concerned Scientists, *Energy Security: Solutions to Protect America's Power Supply and Reduce Oil Dependence* (Cambridge, Mass.: Union of Concerned Scientists, 2000); A. Lovins, E. Datta, O.-E. Bustness, J. Koomey and N. Glasgow, *Winning the Oil Endgame: Innovation, Profits, Jobs and Security* (Snowmass, Colo.: Rocky Mountain Institute, 2004).

7. This approach addresses many issues, but I restrict my discussion here to its relevance to my objective of defining, selecting and pursing a sustainable energy system. For a broader background, see R. Nelson and S. Winter, *An Evolutionary Theory of Economic Change* (Cambridge, Mass.: Harvard University Press, 1982), and O. Williamson, *The Economic Institutions of Capitalism* (New York: Free Press, 1985). Looking further back, evolutionary economists pay tribute to the seminal work of J. Schumpeter, *The Theory of Economic Development* (Cambridge, Mass.: Harvard University Press, 1934), and Z. Griliches, "Hybrid Corn: An Exploration in the Economics of Technological Change," *Econometrica* 25, 4 (1957): 501–522.

8. See, for example, P. Mulder, H. De Groot and M. Hofkes, "Economic Growth and Technological Change: A Comparison of Insights from a Neo-Classical and an Evolutionary Perspective," *Technological Forecasting and Social Change* 68 (2001): 151–171; J. van den Burgh and J. Gowdy, "Evolutionary Theories in Environmental and Resource Economics: Approaches and Applications," *Environmental and Resource Economics* 17 (2000): 37–57; and P. Stoneman, *The Economics of Technological Diffusion* (London: Blackwell, 2002).

9. See A. Grubler, *Technology and Global Change* (Cambridge: Cambridge University Press, 1998).

10. Key studies include the following. J. Goldemberg (ed.), *World Energy Assessment: Energy and the Challenge of Sustainability* (New York: United Nations Development Programme, 2000); J. Goldemberg and T. Johansson (eds.), *World Energy Assessment: 2004 Update* (New York: United Nations Development Programme, 2004); Intergovernmental Panel on Climate Change, *Climate Change 2001, Third Assessment Report* (Cambridge: Cambridge University Press, 2001); Intergovernmental Panel on Climate Change, *IPCC Special Report on Carbon Dioxide Capture and Storage* (Cambridge: Cambridge

University Press, 2005); J. Gale and Y. Kaya (eds.), *Greenhouse Gas Control Technologies: Proceedings of the Sixth International Conference on Greenhouse Gas Control Technologies* (Oxford: Elsevier Science, 2003); R. Sims, H.-H. Rogner and K. Gregory, "Carbon Emission and Mitigation Cost Comparisons between Fossil Fuel, Nuclear and Renewable Energy Resources for Electricity Generation," *Energy Policy* 31 (2003): 1315–1326; E. Tzimas and S. Peteves, "The Impact of Carbon Sequestration on the Production Cost of Electricity and Hydrogen from Coal and Natural Gas Technologies in Europe in the Medium Term," *Energy* 30 (2005): 2672–2689; D. Kammen and S. Pacca, "Assessing the Costs of Electricity," *Annual Review of Environment and Resources* 29 (2004): 301–344.

11. C. Green, "Potential Scale-Related Problems in Estimating the Costs of CO_2 Mitigation Policies," *Climatic Change*, 44 (2000): 331–349.
12. For the latter example see J. Ogden, R. Williams and E. Larson, "Societal Lifecycle Costs of Cars with Alternative Fuels/Engines," *Energy Policy* 32 (2004): 7–27.
13. M. Fung and T. Macyk, "Reclamation of Oil Sands Mining Areas," in R. Barnhisel, R. Darmody and W. Daniels (eds.), *Reclamation of Drastically Disturbed Lands* (American Society of Agronomy, Agronomy series 41, 2000), 755–774.
14. See D. Goodstein, *Out of Gas: The End of the Age of Oil* (New York: Norton, 2004); V. Vaitheeswaran, *Power to the People* (New York: Farrar, Straus and Giroux, 2003); R. Heinberg, *The Party's Over: Oil, War and the Fate of Industrial Societies* (Gabriola Island, B.C.: New Society Publishers, 2003); P. Roberts, *The End of Oil: On the Edge of a Perilous New World* (New York: Houghton Mifflin, 2004); A. Lovins, E. Datta, O.-E. Bustness, J. Koomey and N. Glasgow, *Winning the Oil Endgame: Innovation, Profits, Jobs and Security* (Snowmass, Colo.: Rocky Mountain Institute, 2004).
15. See International Energy Agency, *Oil Crises and Climate Challenges: 30 Years of Energy Use in IEA Countries* (Paris, International Energy Agency, 2004).
16. J. Dooley, *US National Investment in Energy R&D: 1974–1999* (Washington, D.C.: Battelle Memorial Institute, 2001).
17. G. Unruh, "Understanding Carbon Lock-in," *Energy Policy* 28 (2000): 817–830.
18. Goodstein, *Out of Gas,* 39.
19. J. Turner, "Sustainable Hydrogen Production," *Science* 305 (2004): 972–974.

20. A. Lovins, E. Datta, T. Feiler, K. Rabago, J. Swisher, A. Lehmann and
     K. Wicker, *Small is Profitable: The Hidden Economic Benefits of
     Making Electrical Resources the Right Size* (Snowmass, Colo.: Rocky
     Mountain Institute, 2002). The general argument is associated with E.
     Schumacher, *Small is Beautiful: A Study of Economics as if People
     Mattered* (London: Blond and Briggs, 1973).

8 | *Sustainable energy policy: how do we get there?*

BOOKS on the global energy system are replete with utopian visions: the nuclear future, the solar future, the efficiency future, the hydrogen future, and the "small-scale energy technologies are beautiful" future. All too often, these visions are described in detail, but the path for getting there is left vague. This reminds me of the cartoon of two mathematicians at the blackboard gazing in satisfaction at a complex set of equations on the left, the simple elegant solution on the right, and an incomprehensible jumble of equations and symbols in the middle to link both sides, all of which are crossed out except for the statement "somewhere about here a miracle happens."

I too have presented a vision of a future, desirable energy system. In developing this vision, however, I have taken into account key real-world constraints on the potential for shifting away from current trends. These include the strong penchant for humans to use substantially more energy as population and wealth increases, public attitudes to extreme event risks that are especially challenging for nuclear power, wide-ranging concerns for the geopolitical risks associated with oil import dependence or the global spread of nuclear weapons, the difficulties of attaining a rapid scale-up of modern renewables-based technologies, and the path dependence advantages of fossil fuels. In combining these constraints in a choice evaluation that involves both prescription and prediction, I have outlined the energy forms, technologies, costs and international developments for achieving a more sustainable energy path.

But this is not enough. Even though my vision incorporates these real-world constraints, the transition to a low impact and low risk energy system requires profound technological changes that represent a dramatic shift from our current path, and these will not occur without substantial policy intervention.

In this chapter, I identify key challenges for sustainable energy policy-making, then survey and evaluate the policy options, and conclude by proposing a portfolio of feasible policies entailing national and international initiatives. These policies are purposely shaped to overcome the real-world constraints facing those who seek to motivate global and national policies that drive profound technological change. While these policies have already proven their effectiveness in specific real-world applications, I present here the rationale and design requirements for their wider-scale application.

8.1 The challenges of sustainable energy policy

In discussions about achieving a cleaner energy system, one common source of confusion is the failure to distinguish between actions and policies. An *action* is "a change in the choice of equipment, buildings, infrastructure and land use, or in operating and management practices, or in lifestyles that leads the energy system to evolve differently than it otherwise would have." Acquiring a new type of stove or light bulb is an action, as is choosing facilities and equipment that capture and store emissions instead of venting them to the atmosphere. Actions are as diverse as expanding a public transit system, constructing a hydrogen distribution network, building a nuclear plant, rezoning urban land use for greater mixed use or higher residential density, and using a personal vehicle less.

A *policy* is "an effort by public authorities to induce actions by consumers, businesses and perhaps other levels of government." Policies include things like information provision, regulation, taxation, subsidies, and the decision to take direct action in those cases where government itself owns equipment, buildings and infrastructure, and manages land and water resources.

The distinction between actions and policies is not trivial. We love to talk about actions. People will drive their cars less. Households will buy more efficient appliances. Industry will develop fuel-cell vehicles and successfully market them. Renewable electricity production will replace fossil fuel generation plants. And so on.

What we have trouble discussing, however, are the policies that will make these actions happen. What would lead people to drive less than they otherwise would have? What would motivate industry to reallocate R&D funds to the development and commercialization of lower emission technologies? What would spur businesses and households to change their behaviors and investment choices from what they otherwise would have been?

These are policy questions. They are not much fun. They require hard-nosed realism about the psychology of consumer behavior, the market realities of the business world, and the potential ineffectiveness of government. They require difficult trade-offs in which there are winners and losers, and real short-term pain for intangible long-term gain. No wonder that so many visionaries prefer to focus on the vision and leave its realization to others – in effect, to no one.

Greenhouse gas abatement is the prime contemporary example. Over the last fifteen years I have reviewed untold numbers of studies for regions, countries and the planet (and participated in too many as well I must confess) that identify and sum up the actions to reduce carbon emissions by X percent over Y years, leading to stabilization of atmospheric CO_2 concentrations at level Z. A recent example presenting a set of actions (called wedges in this case) to stabilize global emissions over the next fifty years has no discussion of policies, admits that costs are ignored, and combines actions which are contradicted by real-world evidence.* In one action the planet's projected two billion cars would have twice today's fuel efficiency, while in a simultaneous action these cars would be driven half as much as today (5,000 miles per year instead of 10,000). There is no mention of what policy could possibly induce people to pay extra for high efficiency cars that they hardly ever use. In the real world of the past ten years, drivers in North America bought less efficient vehicles (sport utility vehicles, vans and trucks) and yet drove them more per year than ever; vehicle use rose even in Europe with its high fuel prices. Somewhere about here a miracle happens.

This wide-scale fixation on actions at the expense of policy has led me to a dangerous place – I am starting to express sympathy for politicians. Increasingly, I see politicians as the nexus of our own contradictions. We want the world to be better. We want a cleaner

* See S. Pacala and R. Socolow, "Stabilization Wedges: Solving the Climate Problem for the Next 50 Years with Current Technologies," *Science* 13 (2004): 968–972. I do not mean to be overly critical of this particular study. As noted, I have been responsible for similar studies myself, especially in the 1990s.

energy system that endures and is not expensive. We do not want trade-offs. Because of this, we put politicians in the impossible position where they must support all of the things we desire, yet dare not tell us about the trade-offs we do not want to see and the costs we do not want to bear.

If we really want to move toward a sustainable energy system, we need to be more realistic about these constraints facing politicians. We need to think carefully about our objectives and the trade-offs they imply, and then apply ingenuity to the design of policies that make the trade-offs more palatable in some way, that garner sufficient support so that politicians are not faced with career-ending decisions if they are committed to the objectives.

To help politicians, we must be clear about just what our objective is. It is to transition toward an energy system that is enduring and has low impacts and risks. Preferably, the transition would not be traumatic and its achievement would not dramatically increase the costs of key energy services. To ensure its endurance, the system would need to be flexible and thus adaptable to changing circumstances.

Our objective is not a specific penetration of renewable energy or efficiency or nuclear power. These are only means to an end. Like fossil fuels they are simply primary forms of energy that we have as options in the construction of our sustainable energy system. We measure the sustainability of that system not by the contribution of one of these means (such as by the percentage of renewable energy) but rather by that system's ability to satisfy the components of our sustainability objective. Those components are endurance and cleanliness.*

The rationale for endurance policy

Although it is no less important as an objective, the endurance component may present less of a challenge from a policy perspective. Market economies have a built-in mechanism to trigger substitution from inputs that are becoming scarce toward inputs that are less scarce. The scarcity of one input creates a seller's market in which

---

* Many studies that purport to indicate national sustainability performance have accounts for greenhouse gases and other emissions but also an account for the percentage of energy that is produced from renewables. This is a confusion of means and ends.

higher prices are demanded and paid. These higher prices trigger efforts to find more of the scarce resource and to develop and market substitutes. I described this process in chapter 5 with reference to the apparent scarcity of conventional oil. As long as substitutes of comparable cost can be developed, the system endures.

If there are ready substitutes and the market system works well, there may be no role for the policy maker when it comes to endurance. Indeed, the most important decision for the politician is to resist acting even when action seems required. Rising prices are an important signal in the economy. They provide an expectation of positive returns to investments in substitutes. That expectation is removed if politicians succumb to the clamor of the public, media pundits and opposition politicians for price controls every time energy prices spike. Market intervention that prevents the price signal exacerbates a temporary imbalance by delaying the needed adjustments that would bring supply and demand back into balance at a price that reflects long-run production costs.

If such price swings result from market manipulation by oligopolies, international cartels or foreign governments, a policy response may be warranted.* But price changes usually reflect market imbalances resulting from the inherent uncertainties in energy markets, whether caused by unforeseen surges or reductions in demand, pack mentality of investors leading to oversupply or shortfalls, technical failure of existing facilities, or real shifts in costs of production.

Selling people on the benefits of volatility is not easy. Dramatic price increases, which are often exhibited by commodity markets like oil and natural gas, create real hardship for the more vulnerable members of society. It is difficult to explain that, like democracy, the market system is horribly flawed, but just happens to be better than the alternatives. As an expert involved in energy policy issues in my corner of the world, I have come to accept strong public reactions to market volatility as inevitable, so vigilance is required to prevent politicians from bowing to the pressure to mute price signals at the wrong time.†

---

* It may also be warranted to correct a previous government intervention, as in the case of the California electricity reform that created a highly volatile and manipulated electricity market.

† I was commissioned in 1996 by my provincial government in Canada to head a public inquiry into competition in gasoline prices, and I was surprised at the level of competitiveness I found. After many in the media and public would not

Even if we accept that markets are pretty effective at input substitution in general, we might decide that they will not perform well in a specific circumstance, such as during the depletion of high quality conventional oil. Businesses and consumers in the marketplace might be like passengers earnestly playing cards for money on the *Titanic*, focused intently on maximizing their short-term benefits and unaware that their individual decisions have no effect on their ultimate fate. If this threat to endurance were seen to be the case, this too would warrant policy intervention. An example would be an intensive policy effort to develop low-cost renewable or nuclear energy in response to the peaking of conventional oil production.

A key element of my analysis in chapters 5, 6 and 7 was to assess the extent to which the endurance objective might justify policy intervention in the energy system. In general, the evidence does not support substantial intervention. The earth has a lot of energy available for humans to exploit. There are still a lot of fossil fuels. There is enough renewable energy that humans will be able to shift in this direction as they exhaust the economically accessible portion of the earth's non-renewable, fossil fuel endowment. Humans can also develop nuclear power as a replacement – fission today, perhaps fusion tomorrow. As long as this substitution is not forced to occur at an unnecessarily rapid pace, the transition should not lead to dramatically higher energy costs. Policy can help in modest ways to increase the chance of a smooth transition by making sure that substitutes like renewables and nuclear are available when the time comes. But there is no need for policy to plan, and then try to force, the exact timing and precise character of any transition that is required. This is best left primarily to markets.

---

believe my findings, I sought an explanation for this disbelief from a psychologist who offered *cognitive bias* as the reason people notice only price increases. They focus on changes for the worse (price increases) from an instinctual guardedness against being cheated by others, but unconsciously absorb changes for the better (price decreases) as somehow related to their good luck or deserving character. The media may be partly to blame. I do many interviews when energy prices rise, but as I complained to my media counterpart, "When the prices fall, I wait by the phone and I scan e-mail – but you never call or write."

The rationale for cleanliness policy

In contrast, the other main objective – an energy system with low impacts and risks – often does require policy intervention, although even here there may be instances where the best option is for government to do nothing. Externality is the main justification for action, which I explained in chapter 7 as uncompensated damages or risks that are not accounted for in the price of a good or service. Each of the impacts and risks I characterized as unsustainable in previous chapters can be considered from the externality perspective – indoor air pollution, urban air pollution, regional acid precipitation, global climate change risk, and direct impacts and risks to land and water.

The history of industrialized and rapidly developing countries indicates that households automatically devote part of their rising incomes to technologies and energy forms that provide domestic energy needs without compromising indoor air quality. Energy-related policy can undoubtedly help to guide technology and energy choices toward those that are best from an indoor air quality perspective, and to ensure access to clean secondary forms of energy, but most of the benefits occur naturally as incomes rise. This is explained in part by the fact that indoor air quality is less of an externality; the negative impacts are internalized to the household and not to third parties. It is also explained by the serendipity between cleaner indoor air and the greater convenience of switching from solid fuels (mostly biomass) to liquid and gaseous fuels. The critical determinant of this switch is income, so policies fostering economic growth and more equal income distribution are most important when it comes to improving indoor air quality.

The other key energy-related impacts are true negative externalities. Urban air quality is significantly affected by the emissions generated by nearby electricity plants, industrial facilities, vehicles and other modes of transport, and domestic energy consumption for cooking, space heating and water heating. The challenge is that, without public awareness of the link between local activities and poor urban air quality, effective policies that regulate or financially penalize these activities have difficulty mustering sufficient support to be enacted and enforced. Technological advances have ensured that black smoke coming from vehicle exhaust is now a rarity in most cities, but the ongoing unseen emissions of nitrogen oxides and tiny

particulates pose substantial impacts and risks for the local ecosystem
and humans.

A similar concern exists with acid precipitation. The emissions are
invisible and their impact involves processes that are difficult to
understand. To this is added the complication of distance; impacts
can occur hundreds, even thousands, of kilometers from the emission
source. Nonetheless, governments have come to accept the importance
of controlling acid emissions, and great progress has been made in
industrialized countries, with the resulting technologies spreading to
developing countries.

Reducing greenhouse gas emissions is in a special category in terms
of the policy challenge. For one thing, the link between our actions
as consumers and the resulting GHG emissions is not readily apparent to most people. For another, the degree to which GHG emissions
place ecosystems and people at risk is highly uncertain, and likely to
remain so. Policy makers wanting to reduce GHG emissions find
themselves in the unenviable position of possibly imposing significant near-term costs on consumers and businesses for hazy and poorly
understood benefits in the future, benefits mostly realized by future
generations on the other side of the planet. Politicians who prefer
minimal effort can use this uncertainty to their advantage. The rejection of the Kyoto Protocol in 2001 by US president George W. Bush
was explained by former advisor Paul O'Neil as, "The base [President
Bush's Republican political base] likes this and who the hell knows
anyway."[1]

While externality provides an initial rationale for policy intervention, some skeptics note that this is a necessary but not sufficient
condition. There needs to be a reasonable expectation that policy
intervention will make an improvement from what would otherwise
happen.

Some opponents of policy intervention for a cleaner energy system
argue that economies naturally evolve toward service and information
activities as incomes rise, and that this evolution reduces environmental impacts and risks. In support of their argument, they point to
evidence of pollutants that decreased as countries got wealthier. There
is disagreement, however, over the extent to which this trend results
from the unfettered market decisions of individuals and firms or
from a combination of these decisions and increasingly stringent environmental policies that reflect rising demands for environmental

improvement in step with growing affluence.* In the former case, there is no need for policy. Government steps aside and allows the energy system, indeed the entire economy, to evolve toward dramatically lower impacts and risks. In the latter case, policy intervention is a key driver, resulting from the changing aspirations of society. This second interpretation seems more plausible. Certainly, there is an autonomous decline in the energy and material intensity of economic output; yet total use of energy and materials per capita still rises with affluence. Where this trend is associated with increases of environmentally harmful byproducts, policies have been required – as is clear from my earlier description of the history of fossil fuel pollution control over the last centuries.

A second reason for reluctance to pursue policy intervention is that even where there is agreement that current trends are undesirable, government intervention might fail to improve the overall situation because of the real-world imperfections of the political process. Policies to improve the collective well-being can be captured or manipulated by narrow interest groups. This is because the costs of policy can be concentrated on one or a few interests while much larger benefits are diffused over amorphous groups or even the entire population. Those facing concentrated costs have a great incentive to mobilize against the policy, perhaps preventing it, perhaps deflecting it from its initial aims to the extent that "the cure may be worse than the disease."† While this perspective leads policy skeptics to conclude that no policy is often the best response, it can instead inject a healthy

---

* For an overview of the issue, see M. Bernstam, *The Wealth of Nations and the Environment* (London: Institute of Economic Affairs, 1991). The general phenomenon is depicted as an inverted U-shaped curve showing rising pollution as incomes rise above a minimum level but then declining pollution as they continue to rise past a wealth threshold. This is sometimes referred to as the *environmental Kuznets curve*, in honor of the economist S. Kuznets, who postulated a similar inverted U-shaped relationship between wealth and equity. For a survey of recent evidence and analysis, see D. Rothman and S. de Bruyn (eds.), "Probing into the Environmental Kuznets Curve Hypothesis," special issue of *Ecological Economics* 25 (1998).

† *Public choice* theory explores the extent to which the policy process can be captured or manipulated by groups furthering their own interests at the expense of the collective interest. For overviews see M. Olsen, *The Logic of Collective Action* (Cambridge: Cambridge University Press, 1965); and D. Mueller, *Public Choice II* (Cambridge: Cambridge University Press, 1989).

dose of realism to policy design – challenging the policy advisor to
devise ways of placating or countering narrow interests without losing sight of the major policy objective of increasing society's overall
well-being.

A third obstacle to policy intervention is the argument that it is too
difficult or expensive to change the course we are on. This has been
heard recently in relation to greenhouse gas emissions and climate
change, but it has been used in the past to resist policies to reduce
acid emissions and other pollutants. The basic argument in the case of
climate change is that CO_2 emissions and economic output are inex-
tricably linked, as indicated by a relatively constant CO_2/GDP ratio
over the past 200 years. This fixed ratio is presented as evidence that
significant deviation in future is impossible, meaning that CO_2 emissions can only be decreased by reducing economic output proportion-
ately – an 85% reduction in CO_2 emissions implies a catastrophic
85% implosion of the economic system. Viewed in this light, it
appears preferable for humanity to bear the costs of human-induced
climate change rather than the costs of preventing it.

This logic was used in the past to argue against policies to curb acid
emissions. Until thirty years ago, acid emissions had mostly grown in
step with economic activity in industrialized countries, certainly in the
US. But starting in 1970 the US government launched the first of
several increasingly stringent policies to reduce acid emissions, especially sulphur dioxide (SO_2). Between 1970 and 2000, the SO_2/GDP
ratio fell at an average rate of 9% per year.* The formerly steady SO_2/
GDP ratio was clearly a misleading indicator of the policy potential to
reduce acid emissions.

The stable CO_2/GDP ratio of previous centuries is similarly misleading if it is interpreted as indicating an inability to change. Instead of
blindly assuming that the past is also the future, we need to carefully
assess the best evidence available. The latest evidence, as I summarized
it in chapters 6 and 7, suggests that even if we sustain our dependence
on fossil fuels we can break the link between CO_2 emissions and GDP.

---

* US SO_2 emissions were 31 million tons in 1970 and 16 in 2000, while GDP was
$1 and $10 trillion ($US 2000). The SO_2/GDP ratio thus fell from 31 to 1.6, an
annual decline of 9%. See US Environmental Protection Agency, *National
Emission Inventory Emission Trends Data* (Washington, D.C.: Environmental
Protection Agency, 2003).

Even if they agree that breaking the CO_2/GDP link is technically possible, there are people who argue that the costs of reducing GHG emissions exceed the benefits – that money for reducing a GHG like CO_2 is misspent. This could be true. We cannot know for sure because there is, and will continue to be, enormous uncertainty about the full human and environmental impacts of rising atmospheric concentrations of GHGs over this century. But we have a decision to make. Do we want to take the risk? Or is the cost of avoiding the risk worth incurring? The evidence from chapters 6 and 7 is that breaking the link of CO_2 to GDP will cost us energy price increases of about 25–50% over the next half-century or so. This might seem like a lot. But such an increase would still leave energy service costs cheaper than they were 100 years ago in wealthy countries, and the rate of real price increase would be less than 1% per year over this time span – a long-run trend that would be unnoticeable amid the noise of short-term price fluctuations. I believe that most people in wealthier countries at least would be willing to bear this cost of risk avoidance, although the trade-off has rarely been presented to them in this way, so it is difficult to know. (Most polling surveys ask people if they want to prevent climate change, and of course they say yes.) In developing countries it is a more difficult choice, given all of the valuable alternative uses of scarce investment resources. An important consideration, however, is that the clean energy technologies that reduce and eliminate energy-related GHGs also can provide clean air for cities and prevent acid emissions – so the benefits are more than just reduced risk of climate change.

Even if there is not complete agreement on the need for policies to reduce GHGs, there is agreement that any such policies should be cost-effective. To this end, the reduction of CO_2 and other GHG emissions presents special challenges related to the inertia I noted when describing the concept of path dependence. First, it is extremely costly to convert to alternative capital stocks of equipment, buildings and infrastructure more rapidly than the "natural rate of capital stock turnover" – the rate at which equipment stocks would normally require retirement and replacement. Second, new, higher cost technologies face the conundrum of needing market dissemination today in order to lower their costs in future, but needing lower costs today in order to achieve market dissemination. Third, new technologies are inherently riskier, and perceived that way by businesses and consumers, again requiring market penetration and greater use to reduce perceived and real risk. Fourth, to the extent that technologies require longer pay-back periods to show a profit, even though they may be more profit-able over their expected lifespan, businesses and consumers will be reluctant to adopt them.

Policy design must address these special challenges to cost-effective-ness. It must provide signals that motivate businesses and consumers to innovate and adopt new zero-emission technologies at the time of capital stock turnover. But it must not shock the economic system with a dramatic increase in energy prices or loss of competitive position with unregulated trading partners in a short time period, which can lead to premature obsolescence of what otherwise was productive capital equipment.

Another contribution to cost-effectiveness, in a situation of extreme uncertainty such as climate change, is to design policies that allow flexibility as experience provides updated information on the costs and benefits of policy intervention. Thus, a well-designed climate change policy would send a strong signal to drive innovation and adoption of new technologies at the margin, but it would not commit rigidly to a specific technological path or timetable that was not adaptable as new information became available about the benefits and costs of alternative energy options, alternative rates of GHG emission abatement, and alternative policy designs.

As this discussion of endurance and cleanliness suggests, I believe that the greatest policy challenge for a sustainable energy system is the need to address environmental impacts and risks rather than endur-ance. I now turn to the policy options that can be applied to this end, and then evaluate these and assemble them into my policy portfolio for achieving a sustainable energy system.

8.2 Policy options for a cleaner energy system

In their comprehensive survey of research into the relationship be-tween environmental policy and technological change, A. Jaffe, R. Newell and R. Stavins find considerable empirical support for the argument that the cost of environmental improvement is sensitive to the timing and choice of policy instrument.[2] Some policies better match the pace of technological change to the natural rate of capital stock turnover, reducing compliance costs. Others are better at inducing private R&D for technological innovations that reduce the cost of environmental improvement in the long run. Some policies are better at influencing the preferences of businesses and consumers, and thus at achieving political acceptance.

Policy design must trade off potentially conflicting objectives. On the one hand, it must provide strong long-run signals to motivate technological innovators, companies commercializing cleaner technologies, and consumers interested in greener lifestyles. On the other hand, those strong signals should be designed to avoid unnecessary economic cost in the short run, which also improves the prospects for political acceptance.

To assess performance in addressing these trade-offs, policy analysts have developed policy evaluative criteria. Four common criteria are:

- environmental effectiveness;
- administrative feasibility;
- economic efficiency; and
- political feasibility.

While the first three criteria are self-evident, the fourth requires elaboration. Political feasibility indicates the extent to which a policy has "attributes that enable the negotiation of an acceptable balance among clearly defined interests." This criterion is sometimes referred to as negotiability or equity in that it highlights the reasons why some policies may score well against the first three criteria and yet politicians who want to implement them dare not.[3] As I discuss below, greenhouse gas taxes provide an example of a policy that has great difficulty achieving political feasibility even though it performs well in terms of environmental effectiveness, administrative feasibility and economic efficiency. I refer to all four criteria in presenting and evaluating the major policy options.

Command-and-control regulations

Command-and-control regulations (sometimes called *prescriptive regulations*) mandate specific emission levels, energy efficiency standards, or other technology characteristics, with non-compliance incurring stringent financial or legal penalties. This approach dominated environmental policy in the 1970s and is still prevalent today. Early on, economists criticized regulations because they can be economically inefficient where they require identical equipment choices or management practices by participants whose costs of compliance differ considerably, and they usually provide no incentive for companies to innovate beyond the legal requirement.[4] While corporate leaders and economists have convinced politicians and even some environmentalists that many prescriptive regulations inflict an unnecessary economic burden, these are still appropriate in certain circumstances. This includes cases in which even trace releases of a pollutant are unacceptable, where each source of a pollutant needs to meet specific obligations because of local conditions, where administrative feasibility of alternative policies is low, and where the loss of economic efficiency caused by a regulation is likely to be small.[5]

Regulations are prominent in the nuclear power industry, ranging from technically detailed safety requirements to an outright moratorium on nuclear plants in some jurisdictions. With renewables, regulations relating to land and water use are already important and will undoubtedly increase in significance as the contribution of renewable energy grows. As for combustion of fossil fuels (and some biomass), regulations on point emission sources are still significant throughout the world, even where some jurisdictions have augmented these with more flexible, market-oriented policies. Regulations on mobile emission sources (vehicles and other transportation equipment) remain the norm as other types of policies face administrative and political feasibility challenges.

While some energy-related regulations have focused directly on emissions, a common alternative has been to regulate energy efficiency. Since most energy use in industrialized countries is associated with fossil fuel combustion, reduced energy use equates to reduced emissions. Also, the oil price shocks of the 1970s motivated governments to implement energy efficiency regulations in order to reduce oil import dependency. These regulations were often highly prescriptive, stipulating minimum efficiency levels for appliances, industrial equipment, buildings and vehicles. However, some regulatory policies allowed for flexibility. The Energy Policy and Conservation Act in the US in 1975 set Corporate Average Fuel Economy Standards that allowed automobile manufacturers a range of vehicle efficiencies as long as the total set of vehicles sold by each corporation achieved the efficiency target on average.

Although they are widely used, efficiency regulations have been controversial for several reasons. One argument is that price is more responsible for reductions in energy use.[6] In the 1980s vehicle efficiencies improved in part because most people assumed that energy prices would continue to rise. As energy prices trended downward in the 1990s, consumers circumvented efficiency regulations on standard automobiles by switching to vans, trucks and sport utility vehicles. Another argument is that by focusing on energy efficiency instead of energy emissions, regulations may have perverse effects in terms of the emission objective. As noted earlier, energy efficiency reduces operating costs, which can stimulate a rebound effect of increased vehicle use that offsets some of the emission reduction gains. A third critique is that efficiency regulations have negative equity effects by increasing the up-front capital costs of equipment and buildings and thereby reducing access to these goods for lower income households. Counter evidence suggests that modest efficiency regulations – affecting, say, the least efficient third of available equipment for a given end-use – can be designed with negligible welfare effects. Some recent research shows that most consumers who purchased moderate to low efficiency appliances say that they would have purchased a more efficient appliance when provided with more information on the full range they could have chosen from.[7]

Community energy management, which I described in chapter 3, combines urban zoning regulations that promote nodes of higher density with mixed land-use and investments in public transit. While advocates argue that this type of land-use regulation is win-win in providing financial gains and lifestyle improvements, some research suggests that it overlooks the considerable value many urbanites place on low density, single-use suburbs.[8]

Similar controversies to those with energy efficiency have permeated most applications of regulations to achieve environmental goals. Some theorists have countered the argument that regulations are economically inefficient by citing evidence that strong environmental regulations can give a country a competitive edge in a future world of ever more stringent constraints on pollution, as its firms are forced to develop and adopt innovations that will eventually be sought after by firms in other countries. The counter argument is that regulations nonetheless foreclose options and raise costs, and it is risky to presume that the government has better foresight than others into which regulations will come into force in other countries.[9]

My own position is somewhere between. While I believe that regulations have a role to play in the transition to a lower impact and lower risk energy system, I also have substantial caveats. I fear that overly prescriptive regulations will result in much higher costs than necessary for a given environmental objective, so I prefer flexible instruments. I believe that energy efficiency regulations could have perverse effects in reducing the costs of energy services so that humans consume more, so I prefer regulations that are aligned closely to the environmental objective – which is impact and risk reduction, not energy efficiency. I find that all-encompassing regulations are often ineffective and politically infeasible for driving the profound technological change that is needed in the energy system, so I prefer applications of command-and-control regulations that seek to consolidate technological gains rather than force them. Energy-related regulations should usually be restricted to modest emission requirements that constrain perhaps one quarter to one third of technologies that otherwise would compete to provide a given energy service.

There are instances, however, when firm regulations are justified. An example is a phased-in requirement on manufacturers that all household and office appliances and equipment not consume energy when not in use – eliminating what experts refer to as "plug-load" and "pilot-light load." There are also instances where regulations can be designed so that their economic costs are minimized because of flexibility provisions. In the section below on market-oriented regulations, I describe this alternative to conventional command-and-control regulation.

Financial disincentives (taxes)

Starting with A. Pigou in 1920, economists have argued that the appropriate response to negative externality is to apply a unit tax equivalent to the monetary value of uncompensated damages.[10] This approach has not been widely used, but in recent decades it has garnered support from environmentalists and even politicians in some countries. The policy is often referred to as an *emissions tax*, but the potentially broad scope is better reflected by a term like *financial disincentives*. These can include charges, levies, fines and other financial penalties, and can apply to emissions, effluents, solid wastes, land-uses, water consumption and other activities.

Financial disincentives, if set to reflect incremental environmental damages, are assumed to promote economic efficiency. They avoid involving governments in judgments about technological choice or individual behavior; each business or consumer pays charges based on the amount of pollution they cause, but they are not prohibited from these pollution-causing activities. In this way, the policy is sensitive to the diversity of industry pollution reduction costs and consumer preferences. The total cost to society of achieving an aggregate environmental improvement is minimized if each plant or household pursues its self-interest in reducing pollution only to the point where additional reductions cost more than paying the tax. (Economists call this the *equi-marginal principle*.) Furthermore, this policy provides a continuous impetus for pollution-reducing innovations, since even the smallest levels of pollution incur the tax. Financial disincentives can be economically efficient, environmentally effective, and in most cases administratively feasible if they are integrated with existing mechanisms for setting prices and collecting taxes.

In terms of political feasibility, however, financial disincentives present a challenge. In requiring either tax payment or an action to reduce emissions, this policy is often portrayed as an instrument of intrusive and coercive government, associated with the suspicion that the charges reflect government revenue needs rather than a legitimate attempt to correct prices to reflect environmental harms and risks. If proposed taxes imply significant energy price increases, some consumer advocates point to the equity impacts; lower income groups often have the least efficient cars, houses and appliances and cannot afford to upgrade these. Governments recognize these sources of antagonism – or soon learn from painful experience – and so tend to be reluctant to use this policy approach other than for modest tax adjustments.* Another major challenge is the inherent uncertainty in

---

* Among industrialized countries, Europeans and Japanese have exhibited a greater willingness than citizens of the US to accept financial disincentives reflecting environmental costs, but even in this case the shift toward environmental taxes has rarely entailed substantial price changes; already high fuel taxes in some countries were simply shifted from low-emission to high-emission fuels with little change in the revenue flowing to government. For a survey, see

the monetary value of the energy system's impacts and risks. There is little chance of broad agreement on the value that best reflects environmental and other externalities.

One effort to make financial disincentives more palatable, called environmental fiscal reform, involves recycling the revenue from environmental taxes as rebates to those who paid the taxes or as reductions in other taxes or fees – in effect combining financial disincentives and incentives. Modest initiatives include deposit-refund schemes and vehicle feebates (low sales tax for low-emission vehicles and high sales tax for high-emission vehicles), while more ambitious proposals under consideration involve the application of greenhouse gas tax revenue to reduce government payroll charges, income taxes or other unpopular levies. Analysis of the application of greenhouse gas taxes often turns on the question of how governments should recycle the tax revenue, with some studies suggesting the potential for an additional benefit (referred to as a *double dividend*) if this step reduces other taxes that have a dampening effect on economic growth.[11]

Still, this is a difficult sell. Those who might benefit from environmental fiscal reform are generally less aware and less well mobilized to support such a change prior to its occurrence. New companies that might stand to gain are in their infancy while existing high-emission industries are well established, with communities and regions dependent on their survival. It is more difficult to motivate individuals with low-emission technologies and lifestyles to support a policy that promises vague future gains than to mobilize resistance from people who fear that a policy will raise their cost of living or eliminate their jobs. In spite of claims of revenue neutrality, there remains considerable suspicion among the public and media, even in countries with a well-educated populace, that governments tinker with the tax system only to reap more revenue.

As an economist, my instinct is to prefer financial disincentives and especially environmental fiscal reform for the transformation of our

Organization for Economic Cooperation and Development, *Economic Instruments for Pollution Control and Natural Resources Management in OECD Countries: A Survey* (Paris: OECD, 1999). See also H. Hammer, A. Lofgren and T. Sterner, "Political Economy Obstacles to Fuel Taxation," *The Energy Journal* 25, 3 (2004): 1–17.

energy system. Prices are an effective and efficient way to signal to firms and households the impacts and risks of their current energy system. My years of advising politicians, however, have made me sympathetic to the real constraints under which they operate, and have led me to understand the low probability for solitary reliance on this policy because it performs so poorly against the political feasibility criterion. As one politician said to a group of advisors, "If I am going to announce this new pollution tax, I want you economists in the room standing between me and the public on that day." The more likely scenario is that, like regulations, financial disincentives will play a consolidating role in support of other leading-edge policies that drive the profound technological change that is required. Use of this policy instrument will be modest, at least in the near future.

Financial incentives (subsidies)

If financial disincentives have political feasibility problems, then an alternative way of fostering actions that provide cleaner energy is to offer *financial incentives* in the form of grants, low interest loans, tax credits, insurance guarantees, publicly funded infrastructure and public R&D. Governments have a long history of funding R&D for energy supply, especially for nuclear power. Even when unacknowledged, governments are compelled by media pressure to provide final recourse insurance for nuclear power, large hydropower and any other form of energy that might pose extreme event risks to the environment and human health. Governments also support oil and natural gas exploration and extraction through various tax credits such as resource depletion allowances and accelerated depreciation on capital. In recent years, some of these tax benefits have been extended to renewables and energy efficiency. On the energy demand side, governments provided businesses and consumers with grants and low interest loans to shift consumption away from oil during the 1970s, electric utilities applied these to promote electricity efficiency in the 1980s, and governments turned to them again in the 1990s in their ongoing slate of policies for greenhouse gas abatement. The infrastructure grants that senior levels of government provide to local government have also been linked at times to energy conserving actions such as expansion of public transit.

Government largesse is obviously popular with recipients, so this policy appears to score well in terms of political feasibility. In practice, however, the use of financial incentives faces substantial constraints. First, the policy requires funds that governments mostly acquire through unpopular taxes, and subsidies to energy-related investments must compete against other unquenchable claims on the government's budget, including health care, education, social support and public security. Subsidy programs by energy utilities have likewise decreased in recent years as non-participants have convinced utility regulators of the inequity of taxing all electricity consumers in order to subsidize participants of efficiency programs. Second, it is inherently difficult to design subsidy programs to satisfy the effectiveness criterion because of the free rider problem I discussed in chapter 3. The goal of a subsidy is to get someone to do something they would not otherwise have done. Yet how do we separate those who would have purchased an efficient light bulb from those who would not? Some hindsight studies of subsidy programs detect evidence of free riders as high as 80%, meaning that only 20% of the "actions" observed in the market can be attributed to the subsidy program.[12] Third, many types of subsidy programs are costly to administer, requiring adjudication of applications, monitoring of performance and hindsight evaluations.

Once these factors are included, financial incentives can fare poorly in terms of both effectiveness and economic efficiency, and with their magnitude limited by competing demands on public funds they are unlikely to drive the profound technological change that is required. Nonetheless, politicians will remain attracted to this policy instrument for obvious reasons, so I offer some suggestions to improve its performance in terms of effectiveness and efficiency.

The essential first step is to reduce and eliminate existing subsidies to those conventional energy technologies and projects that are responsible for the impacts and risks that render our current energy system unsustainable. Global subsidies of this nature were estimated to be US $150 billion per year in the 1990s, although the figure can be lower or higher depending on how subsidy is defined. These subsidies have decreased over the past decade because of several factors. The demise of the planned economies of the former Soviet bloc and the transition toward a market economy in China have led to reductions by half to two thirds in Russia, China and Eastern Europe.[13] India has enacted similar pricing reforms to reduce energy subsidies, albeit at a slower pace. The move toward liberalized energy markets in industrialized countries has also reduced public subsidies, especially in the electricity sector, and governments have used the stagnation of nuclear power as an excuse to decrease R&D support.

If governments are to provide modest subsidies toward a cleaner energy system, the chances for political feasibility are enhanced if revenues issue from environmental fiscal reforms – where a supplementary gasoline tax funds public transit and initial hydrogen refueling stations, or a carbon tax on electricity is earmarked for windpower purchases and development of a carbon capture and storage demonstration project. Public funds for infrastructure and for energy R&D should be leveraged by joint ventures or special R&D credits in order to maximize the risk sharing by private investors.

For improving the energy efficiency of end-use equipment, subsidies should be targeted at equipment manufacturers rather than final consumers. As noted earlier, manufacturers have considerable flexibility at the design stage to decide how much electricity or fuel a given product will require, including when not in operation. A financial incentive to appliance manufacturers to develop higher efficiency models (sometimes called a *golden carrot*) has a greater impact than a similar amount offered to influence the choices of final consumers, again because of the free rider problem. When matched with other policies, such as modest regulations that remove the least efficient models, this approach can be somewhat effective even without energy price increases.

Governments can provide revolving funds for certain energy efficiency investments that help businesses and consumers overcome high up-front costs of these devices. This support would be repaid from operating cost savings, with the only costs to government being program administration and its share of financial risk from misinvestments.

In developing countries, where the goal is to expand services of electricity and other forms of clean commercial energy, subsidies should support access, not consumption. Subsidies on the consumption of energy commodities can spiral out of control as incomes and demand increase and, in any case, these do not reach the poorest members of society. In Bangladesh, electricity subsidies in the late 1990s, which only assisted the relatively wealthier 16% of households with electricity service, were estimated at US $100 million per year, exceeding the government's entire health budget.[14] Where electric grid extension is socially beneficial, subsidies would provide one-time assistance for the grid extension investment but not electricity price relief. In situations where the development of a local energy system would not entail connection to the grid, subsidies would still only provide access, such as assistance with the initial investment but not with the operating costs of local photovoltaic, small hydro, or biomass energy systems. In all cases, competitive bidding for the subsidy increases its cost effectiveness, as developments with grid-extension policies in rural areas of Argentina have shown.[15]

Finally, governments can bear extra costs in their own energy-related decisions, acquiring low-emission vehicles, zero-emission electricity, energy efficient equipment, and constructing new public buildings to high efficiency designs. This can help new technologies achieve the market thresholds that reduce production costs.

Voluntarism and information

Voluntarism combines information and moral suasion campaigns in an effort to convince businesses and consumers of the ethical and self-interest benefits of actions to reduce energy and material use, and the resulting pollution. Voluntary policies include advertising, labeling, information brochures, awards, demonstration projects, sponsorship of conferences and coordination of collective efforts by industry associations, consumer groups, community organizations and local governments.

In contrast with other environmental policies, voluntary programs cast government in the role of information provider, facilitator, role model and cheerleader, while letting individual firms and households determine their level of effort for environmental protection and improvement. Popular new catchphrases such as *natural capitalism, eco-efficiency, eco-effectiveness, the natural step* and *triple-bottom-line* suggest that companies can increase profits and individuals save money by voluntarily adopting technologies and management practices that are more efficient in their use of energy and materials.[16] Over the past decade, governments, industry and environmentalists have shown a growing interest in the design and implementation of information programs that explain these benefits.

However, while the growth of government voluntary policies has been dramatic and participants offer much anecdotal evidence of voluntary actions to improve the environment, the effectiveness of such programs is difficult to determine. Achievement of a given voluntary environmental target does not confirm the effectiveness of the policy, for it could be that even without it the desired environmental improvement would have been achieved. In a recent survey of voluntary approaches to environmental protection, M. Khanna noted that only a few empirical studies have tried to estimate the actual environmental impact of such programs, and these have detected little effect. Similarly, the OECD recently concluded that the "environmental effectiveness of voluntary approaches is still questionable," and, "The economic efficiency of voluntary approaches is generally low."[17]

These discouraging results should hardly be surprising. As I noted in my earlier discussion of energy efficiency, there is a significant gap between how proponents of efficiency see the world and the actual options facing businesses and consumers. Efficiency advocates simply list all of the investment and behavior changes that could reduce energy use and increase financial returns relative to the status quo, without asking if there are also new profitable investment opportunities and lifestyle changes that would continue to use air, water and land as a free waste receptacle. While some firms and households might opt for increased efficiency, others will just as easily make an energy-intensive, pollution-intensive choice if it provides a competitive advantage or lifestyle benefit. If industry, government and the media highlight only the cases where greater efficiency is profitable, our view of reality is distorted – only to be rudely awakened when we examine the aggregate trend of an emission like greenhouse gases and see that it continues to rise in spite of a litany of emission-saving proclamations.

Why, then, is voluntarism still so often pursued as a policy for environmental improvement? Households and firms obviously prefer voluntarism to prescriptive regulations or higher taxes, both of which impose costs that affect their bottom line. Voluntarism also allows firms to look like good corporate citizens, protecting the environment "because they care." Governments like voluntarism because it is politically feasible; they are seen to be taking the initiative in addressing a policy challenge, and it is impossible to prove in advance that a new voluntary program will be environmentally ineffective and economically inefficient. These programs can even be supported by those environmental lobbyists who want to believe that a more sustainable energy system, like other environmental objectives, can be achieved without trade-offs. As long as both industry and environmentalists are onside, government dare not question this approach. Once again, government is the nexus for our contradictory views of the world.

My own view is that we will continue to have voluntary policies in the energy sector even if these are largely ineffective in terms of the profound technological changes that are needed. This approach is just too attractive to corporations, individuals and government, and when we are unsure of whether or not some environmental goal requires significant trade-offs, this may be a legitimate first response. Once indicators start to reveal that voluntarism is not progressing toward a given objective, however, more effective policies like regulations and financial instruments should take the lead – even while voluntary policies are retained. In fact, coercive policies might still be portrayed as voluntarism in some cases.[18] The "voluntary environmental covenants" between industry and the government in the Netherlands in the 1990s were undertaken with a clear understanding that strong mandatory policies would otherwise be applied (what one industrialist termed "gun-to-your-head voluntarism"). Even where more forceful policies are being pursued, voluntary policies can raise the overall awareness of the issue among industry and the public, which in turn can help build support for the stronger policies.

Market-oriented regulations – emissions cap and tradable permits

In 1968, J. Dales first showed how the allocation of tradable property rights to pollute could minimize the costs of pollution reduction.[19] Government sets a maximum level for emissions (effluents, solid wastes, etc.), then allocates tradable emission permits (also called allowances) to all emitters covered by the program so that the total allowed by the permits equals the emissions cap – hence the term *emissions cap and tradable permits* (ECTP). Usually the permits decrease in number or value over time, gradually lowering the aggregate emissions cap. The ECTP is a form of regulation in that the aggregate emissions cap cannot be exceeded, participation is compulsory, and penalties for non-compliance are substantial. Unlike traditional command-and-control regulation, however, the ECTP has similarities to environmental taxes in that it allows participants to determine what actions if any they take to reduce emissions and whether, as a consequence, they buy or sell in the emissions permit market. This means that the policy should be economically efficient as long as each participant only acts to reduce emissions where this costs less than the permit trading price. Because it combines regulation at the aggregate level with individual market flexibility, this type of policy is sometimes referred to as a *market-oriented regulation* or a *quantity-based market instrument*.

Economists have generated a large literature debating the relative merits and most appropriate applications of ECTP and financial disincentives – what is sometimes called the "quantities versus prices" debate.[20] In theory, both approaches should cost about the same to achieve a given level of emission reduction. But ECTP provides greater certainty about the emissions outcome, which is key when the pollutant is one we are willing to pay a great deal to reduce (if even trace amounts are highly toxic) or we are fairly confident in our cost of abatement estimates. Environmental taxes provide greater certainty about maximum cost (no one pays more than the tax), which may be important when we are not certain of the environmental harm or the cost of abatement, and are unwilling to incur high costs until we learn more.

The most noteworthy application of ECTP began with an amendment to the US Clean Air Act in 1990, which has inspired a growing number of policy experiments in the US and elsewhere. Sulphur emissions from specified electricity generation plants were subject to ECTP in exceedingly stringent five-year phases starting in 1995. The policy produced substantial reductions in emissions with costs that were estimated to be 50% lower than would have been incurred by a command-and-control approach.[21]

Depending on the number of participants and their level of experience with market trading instruments, application of the ECTP faces hurdles in terms of administrative feasibility. Also, in terms of political feasibility, the allocation of permits involves a delicate balancing of interests; auctioning all permits would concentrate costs on heavy emitters whereas awarding all permits according to base-year emissions (*grandfathering*) could have the opposite effect, even generating considerable wealth for heavy emitters if they have the lowest incremental abatement costs or can partly manipulate the market for permits. The greatest challenge for ECTP is where the cost of emission reduction is uncertain but possibly very high in the near term. Governments are reluctant to set stringent emissions caps in case these cause high costs to the economy (perhaps especially during the typical four to five year political mandate). In a compromise proposal, suggested initially in the mid-1970s by M. Weitzman, M. Roberts and M. Spence, the government would offer to sell an unlimited number of permits at a fixed price.[22] This guarantees a ceiling (*safety valve*) for the ECTP cost, but accordingly reduces confidence in achieving the environmental outcome.

Adding a permit price ceiling to the ECTP effectively converts it into a *hybrid price-quantity* policy. Because of the cost, benefit and timing uncertainties associated with emissions abatement, and the resulting political feasibility challenges for implementing effective policy, the ECTP with permit price ceiling has lately attracted a great deal of research interest for the design of GHG abatement policy.[23] Analysts assess where the cap should be set (upstream on the carbon content of fuels production or downstream on end-use carbon emissions), the level at which the price ceiling should be set initially (to reduce cost anxieties and limit premature retirement of capital stock), whether it should include a schedule for increasing over time (to provide the appropriate long-term signals for innovation and new capital investment), and how it could work as part of an international permit trading system.

The ECTP with a scheduled declining emissions cap – and rising emission permit price ceiling in the case of a price-quantity hybrid – has attractive features. It minimizes the risk of short-term economic disruption while providing a long-term signal to stimulate R&D and dissemination of new technologies; this should help with political feasibility and economic efficiency. Also, its permit trading flexibility provides a uniform price signal throughout the economy, depending on how widely the policy is applied, which should improve the prospects for economic efficiency.

The ECTP therefore seems likely to make a contribution to the control of global, regional and even local emissions because of its appropriateness for dealing with large point sources that offer cost-savings from permit trading. This value has already been demonstrated with acid emissions and with local air pollutants from point sources in the Los Angeles basin. With greenhouse gas emissions, a key uncertainty for the ECTP is the delicate balance between the magnitude of the economic signal necessary to provoke profound technological change and the political feasibility of higher energy and product prices resulting from the cost of purchasing permits or undertaking investments. While I have provided evidence that energy commodity costs in a cleaner energy system need not be more than 25–50% higher than today's prices, I have also argued that substantial technological change requires strong signals in order to overcome the inertia of business investment patterns and consumer behavior.

Market-oriented regulations – artificial niche market regulation

The ECTP controls emissions, but the principles of market-oriented regulation have also been applied to regulating market outcomes at a technology or energy level. The purpose is to establish *artificial niche markets* for critical new technologies that might not otherwise gain a foothold in the economy, a foothold that helps launch the typical cycle of initial product diffusion, production cost reductions through learning and economies-of-scale, initial consumer feedback and product improvement. Once new technologies have reached this market-recognition stage, policy-makers should find it easier to intensify environmental taxes or ECTP because businesses and consumers would have available alternatives to their conventional high-emission technologies. Noteworthy applications of niche market regulations involve the energy sources for electricity generation and the emission levels for automobiles.[24]

The *renewable portfolio standard* (RPS) emerged in the 1990s as an instrument to force greater generation of electricity from renewables. Electricity providers (or consumers in some jurisdictions) are required to ensure that a minimum percentage of electricity in their portfolio is generated by renewables. Each provider must comply or take advantage of flexibility provisions that allow for purchasing of credits (called green certificates in Europe) from those whose renewables generation exceeds the minimum requirement; non-compliance results in exclusion from the market or substantial penalties. Thus, the RPS forces an aggregate market outcome, but supports economic efficiency by encouraging only those with the lowest generation costs to provide electricity from renewables to the market.

Governments have traditionally supported renewables with R&D subsidies, investment or production tax credits, production or consumption price subsidies, and information and voluntary programs. In recent years, however, the RPS has been adopted by Australia, almost twenty states in the US and several countries in Europe, and is under development in many other jurisdictions, including at the federal level in the US and Europe. The RPS in Texas was implemented in 1999 and stimulated the installation of 900 MW of windpower in just a few years, well in advance of interim targets.

Four characteristics help explain the emerging interest in the RPS.[25] First, ongoing competition for the renewable market share maintains an incentive for renewables producers to reduce costs, thereby enhancing economic efficiency. Second, because the supply portfolio blends a small share of high-cost renewables with a large share of low-cost conventional electricity, the policy's impact on consumer prices is small (as long as bidding and price setting in the two markets are segmented), which helps with political feasibility. Third, the policy can be directly linked to environmental targets given that renewables have zero emissions (except for local air emissions from combusting biomass). Fourth, the policy minimizes government budgetary involvement because customers pay producers directly for the extra financial cost of renewables, and the selection of renewables can be left to market forces through a competitive bidding process. In contrast, the Danish government paid over 100 million Euros in 1998 alone in annual subsidies to wind generators.[26]

The *vehicle emission standard* (VES) is another form of niche market regulation that requires automobile manufacturers to guarantee a minimum percentage of vehicle sales in one or more categories according to emission levels. Historically, manufacturers claimed that low- or zero-emission vehicles would be too expensive to build and, in any case, would not satisfy consumer demands for acceleration, horsepower, range and safety. Then, in 1990, the California Air Resources Board, a quasi-judicial environmental regulatory agency under state legislation, established a VES that set deadlines in future time periods for minimum percentage sales of vehicles in low- and zero-emission categories, creating artificial niche markets for these new technologies. Vehicle manufacturers are allowed to work together so that the total California fleet meets the standard even if individual manufacturers fall short.

The California VES seems to have played a pivotal role in the development of new options for vehicle power platforms, including gasoline-electric, battery-electric and fuel-cell platforms.[27] The California legislation has been adopted by twelve other states in the US, with provisions in New York, Massachusetts, Vermont and Maine to adjust automatically their standard to any changes made in California (together with California, these account for about 20% of the US automobile market). It has also had a significant effect on technology developments in Europe and Japan, although no other country has yet matched the policy.

The VES was not implemented without difficulties, especially in the debates, negotiations and legal challenges surrounding the zero-emission vehicle (ZEV) category. The initial ZEV requirements were for 2% in 1998 and 10% in 2003 (measured as a percentage of 1992 new vehicle sales). However, the California Air Resources Board reduced these requirements and added flexibility provisions in a negotiated agreement with automobile manufacturers in 1996 because of setbacks in the development and commercialization of battery-electric vehicles, which were initially assumed to be the favored ZEV technology. With emerging evidence that fuel-cell vehicles might triumph over battery-electric for meeting the ZEV mandate, albeit in the more distant future, and the realization that gasoline-electric hybrid vehicles might achieve widespread diffusion, the Board agreed that extra sales of hybrids could compensate for missing the ZEV targets, with equivalencies calculated on the basis of emissions of local pollutants and CO_2.

California's VES has been described both as a huge failure and a huge success. Critics claim that it failed to produce a zero-emission vehicle in the intended timeframe and wasted public and private money in the process. Supporters claim that it pushed automobile manufactures worldwide to design and commercialize a technological transformation that is providing real benefits in terms of commercially attractive low-emission vehicles. They argue that California's regulators demonstrated foresight in first pushing for different categories of low and zero-emission vehicles, and then adaptability in recognizing the potential for gasoline-electric hybrid vehicles to meet the short-term emission goal while allowing time to ascertain if battery-electric or fuel cell vehicles will prevail in fulfilling the long-tem zero-emission goal.

These recent experiences with the renewable portfolio standard and the vehicle emission standard illustrate the possible strengths of market-oriented regulation that focuses on creating artificial niche markets for specific end-use technologies or forms of energy.[28] First, the policy sends a regulatory signal that pushes manufacturers to innovate and commercialize new low-emission technologies without significantly impacting vehicle or energy prices. In order to meet their minimum sales requirements, producers will either capture higher revenue from those consumers willing to pay more for low-emission technologies, or subsidize these technologies from their sales of conventional electricity (RPS) or conventional vehicles (VES). Because the niche market for the low-emission technology is initially small, any cross-subsidy has a minimal effect on the price of these conventional products. By allowing technological change to occur at a pace that matches the natural rate of capital stock turnover, a carefully designed policy can avoid huge economic costs from premature capital stock retirement or retrofit.

Second, by forcing innovation and commercialization efforts, the policy provides policy makers with critical information about the future production costs and consumer acceptance of low-emission technologies, which can inform subsequent decisions about the timing and ambition of energy-environment targets. We will not know if the battery-electric, gasoline-electric hybrid or fuel-cell vehicle is a realistic possibility until we make a serious R&D and commercialization effort to assess its long-run production cost and the likelihood of acceptance by consumers. The minimum market share generates critical information on how economies-of-learning and economies-of-scale are likely to influence the long-run production cost, and about the likely success of mass marketing efforts. Even if battery-electric vehicles never achieve a substantial market breakthrough, R&D and commercialization expenditures will have been worthwhile if the regulator adjusts the VES in a timely manner once critical cost information emerges. In terms of equity, the cost of acquiring this information is appropriately borne by the purchasers of conventional vehicles who cause the externality impacts and risks in the first place, instead of by general taxpayers, some of whom might not own or use personal vehicles.

Third, the market niche policy incorporates the other positive features of the ECTP policy. Market-share requirements can be scheduled to rise gradually over time, signaling the long-term objective to industry and consumers without short-term disruption to productive capital stocks. Trading between participants reduces the cost of compliance. The penalty for non-compliance can be set to perform like the cost ceiling that transforms the ECTP into a hybrid price-quantity policy, which reduces the risk to policy makers. The California vehicle emission standard has a $5,000 penalty per vehicle shortfall, and most renewable portfolio standards have penalties that provide a safety valve for policy costs.

The major critique of regulating artificial niche markets is that this approach could be economically inefficient in that by stipulating specific energy or technological outcomes, the regulator may overlook lower cost ways of achieving the environmental target. The renewable portfolio standard may cause unnecessarily high costs if it turns out that zero-emission fossil fuels, nuclear or some combination of these can achieve low impact and low risk electricity production at much lower costs than renewables. A policy that targets emissions instead of the energy form, as with the California vehicle standard, reduces this risk within a sector, but fails to address the potential for dramatically different emission reduction costs in different sectors. Perhaps the renewable portfolio standard costs one fifth per unit of local air emission reduction as the vehicle emission standard. Perhaps all of our effort should therefore be in the electricity sector initially. Moreover, because it focuses on an environmental target in one sector of what is an integrated energy system, the vehicle emission standard could have perverse effects in encouraging low-emission vehicles that use electricity or hydrogen generated by a technology or energy form that causes higher net global or local impacts. A vehicle with low end-use emissions might end up having lower emissions than a zero-emission vehicle, once emissions over the full fuel cycle from primary to end-use energy are tabulated.

My own view is that regulated niche markets are likely to play a substantial role as part of a comprehensive package of policies if the goal is to achieve profound technological transformation. They score well in terms of political feasibility, so it is no accident that they are rapidly increasing in popularity among policy makers. The policy approach does pose economic efficiency risks, however, so it must be applied cautiously. Ideally, it would be applied to energy end-uses and energy conversions where the prospects for developing profound technological change at a reasonable long-run cost are good, and where such change would otherwise be extremely difficult to launch, most likely because of path dependence and the political infeasibility of alternative policies. It would focus as closely as possible on the environmental target while generally avoiding detailed prescriptions about technologies and energy forms. Low-emission cars are the objective, not necessarily fuel-cell cars. Low-emission electricity generation is the objective, not necessarily windpower or PV generation. Market niche policies in individual sectors should therefore be coordinated. This can be difficult prior to initial implementation because of cost uncertainty, but as cost information is generated by the policy, additional coordinated adjustment of market niche targets can be undertaken. Finally, the policy should be applied in concert with other policies. This policy, would drive technological change in key sectors and end-uses but overarching policies, like an economy-wide ECTP or environmental tax, are necessary to provide a unitary economic signal across the economy that will consolidate the technological advances into wide-scale diffusion of low impact and low risk technologies and energy forms.

8.3 Proposed policy portfolio for energy system sustainability

This survey suggests that policies have different strengths when applied to the pursuit of a cleaner energy system. Table 8.1 assesses the policy approaches against the four policy evaluative criteria I presented at the

Table 8.1. Policy evaluation summary

	Environmental effectiveness	Economic efficiency	Administrative feasibility	Political feasibility
Command-and-control regulations	Good	Poor	Good	Medium
Financial disincentives	Medium	Good	Good	Poor
Financial incentives	Medium	Poor	Medium	Good
Voluntarism and information	Poor	Poor	Good	Good
Emissions cap and tradable permit	Good	Good	Medium	Medium
Niche market regulation	Good	Medium	Medium	Good

outset. No approach performs perfectly against all four criteria, and only the two market oriented regulations – ECTP and artificial niche market regulations – escape a strong negative assessment. When it comes to inducing profound technological change, the other four each have at least one weakness. Command-and-control regulations and financial incentives perform poorly against economic efficiency, financial disincentives perform poorly against political feasibility, and voluntary and information programs perform poorly against environmental effectiveness and economic efficiency.

The table provides only a crude indication, however, of how the policies might perform in practice. First, each policy can be modified in various ways to incorporate elements of the others, so the table is really only a caricature of the alternatives. The real world is much messier.[29] Second, individual policies are often applied in concert, as a portfolio. This is not always a good idea. Sometimes governments try to look busy by assembling a potpourri of uncoordinated policies that overlap and even work at cross-purposes. At the same time, there are certainly applications where a combination of policies can be more effective at meeting all policy criteria than a single policy.

In the remainder of this chapter, I present my proposal for a policy portfolio to drive our energy system to a more sustainable path. I focus initially at the national level, presenting a portfolio that could be developed by one country, or a group of countries coordinating their policies to act as one. I refer mostly to the US for this example. I then briefly present proposals for international coordination of efforts where the energy sustainability objective is global in scale. The policy goal of greenhouse gas abatement is the focal point in this case.

National level energy policy

Governments at national and local levels continue to pursue voluntarism and information policies in my portfolio. Political acceptability makes these too appealing to eliminate, even if they are not highly effective. Indeed, initial efforts at voluntarism and information provision for greenhouse gas reduction in industrialized countries are increasingly seen as ineffective, setting the stage for more aggressive policies over the coming decade. But voluntarism may still be effective for those environmental objectives that do not involve substantial trade-offs.

Prescriptive regulations also have a role in my policy portfolio. The regulations that currently control energy-related activities in industrialized countries – establishing safety standards for workers and nearby residents, determining mineral rights and other land uses, and controlling water use and quality – would remain much as they are, with continuation of the trend toward tighter standards. With emissions that are toxic in even trace amounts (mercury, lead, radiation), stringent standards are appropriate. With other types of emissions, for which the benefits increase gradually with emission reduction and the exact location of the emitting source is not critical, regulations should only be used to consolidate technological improvements that have occurred voluntarily or as the result of some other policy instrument. Thus, energy efficiency regulations would establish minimum efficiency standards. My policy portfolio differs little in this regard from the current regulatory practices of most industrialized countries, although as noted earlier it would include a prohibition on "plug-load" on most household devices (my personal pet peeve). In developing countries, internal household emissions of gaseous, liquid and eventually solid-fuel cooking stoves available on the market would be regulated. The relationship between rising incomes and access to cleaner secondary energy will remain the main driver for reducing emissions from these domestic devices for cooking and heating.

While some application of financial disincentives (emission taxes) would be part of the policy portfolio, any GHG tax that was implemented would initially be at a low level. In order to improve the prospects of political feasibility, the modest revenues from financial disincentives would be redistributed as financial incentives to promote information programs about climate change, public and private R&D collaboration, expansion of public transit infrastructure, some niche market commercialization of low impact and low risk technologies, and, in developing countries, access to cleaner forms of commercial energy. The political acceptance of taxes as an environmental policy instrument differs by society; many US citizens appear to be less accepting of this use of taxes than their European counterparts, although this may evolve.[30] But specific design elements can also be critical in determining political acceptance. In the 1990s, Norway successfully enacted a $50 per tonne CO_2 tax which included exemption provisions for industries whose competitive position vis-à-vis foreign firms would be put in jeopardy by the tax. As noted in chapter

6, this tax motivated the Sleipner project, in which captured CO_2 is injected for permanent storage in a deep saline aquifer under the North Sea.

In terms of reducing emissions, my policy portfolio is dominated by market-oriented regulations, especially the emissions cap and tradable permit. The ECTP would be applied to address local air pollution (especially in large urban centers with significant point sources), regional acid emissions and greenhouse gas emissions. The ECTP approach would also combine with command-and-control regulations and some direct financial disincentives, especially for small, non-point emission sources. Where profound technological change is desirable and appears feasible, selective niche market regulations would spearhead the ECTP policy. These include the vehicle emission standard, the renewable portfolio standard and a carbon capture and storage requirement.

The US provides an example for the national application of my energy policy portfolio. Some key changes are needed to shift its energy system over the next century toward a more sustainable trend. The US policy portfolio would include an ECTP applying to greenhouse gas emissions just as the country has already implemented an ECTP to address acid gas emissions. The ECTP would likely include the following elements.[31]

After its first decade, the cap would not be more than 5–10% below the forecast level of GHG emissions for those activities to which it applies, but over the ensuing decades it would decline at a rate that forces an increasingly significant decoupling of economic activity and greenhouse gas emissions across the US economy, at a pace consistent with economic growth and the natural rate of capital stock turnover. The cap, which would apply to all GHG emissions in accordance with their CO_2 equivalence, would require that total emissions fall below their 1990 level by 2035, and would include a tentative schedule for much greater emission reductions in the period 2035–2060. It would apply not to upstream carbon content as this would result in politically infeasible fuel price increases in the short-term, but instead to large downstream emission sources, such as steel, cement, pulp and paper, petrochemicals, mining, and energy sector activities in electricity generation, oil refining, natural gas processing, and oil and gas extraction and transportation. The cost of gaseous and liquid hydrocarbon fuels would increase only slightly, because only the emissions from oil and gas production plants would require permits, not the carbon content in the fuel products themselves. In contrast, the price of electricity would have greater upward pressure, especially in regions of the US in which most electricity is produced by thermal processes from coal combustion (the emissions of the coal-fired plants would require permits).

More important than the magnitude of the ECTP cap in the early years would be the size of its associated permit price ceiling (safety valve). Government would offer unlimited permits at a price that would be modest initially, but scheduled to rise steadily over the next few decades: for example, from \$50US/tC (\$14/tCO$_2$) in 2015 to \$200/tC (\$55/tCO$_2$) in 2035. The schedule would also indicate the timing for extending the ECTP to the end-use emissions of smaller industry, the commercial sector and eventually households. For example, gasoline retailers would be required to purchase permits (at or below the safety valve price) for the fuel they acquire, and they would pass these permit costs on to final purchasers of the gasoline; permit costs would be identified separately on receipts with an identifier such as "atmosphere user permit fee." This schedule is important to ensure that the initial application of the ECTP to electricity generation but not final emissions from home heating units does not result in fuel switching that must later be reversed.

Perhaps 75–90% of ECTP permits would be allocated based on initial emissions (grandfathering) in a base year like 2000 with the rest allocated by auction. Auction revenues should be recycled in ways that help individual regions and industries adjust to changing costs, especially in providing modest assistance with acquisition of zero- and low-emission technologies.

The ECTP designed and applied in this way would provide substantial impetus for technological innovation and commercialization, even though its short-term economic impacts would be negligible. Its early implementation is especially important because the rising price of natural gas since 2000 has driven a revival of interest in coal-based electricity generation, with US companies poised for major new investments.*

* In 2004, the US Department of Energy identified 106 new coal plant proposals totaling 65,000 MW of capacity. It is uncertain what percentage of these plants will actually be constructed. See US Department of Energy, *National Energy Technology Laboratory Report on Proposed Capacity Additions* (Washington, D.C.: US Department of Energy, 2004).

Before the complete transition from an industry-focused ECTP to an economy-wide ECTP, zero-emission technologies and processes need to be developed to the point where consumers and businesses perceive these as legitimate options. Thus, the ECTP would be applied in concert with the application of a few key niche market regulations that strategically target areas where profound technological change has great potential but faces high transitional costs. These regulations would focus on vehicles, electricity generation and the fossil fuel chain.

Either by continued adoption by individual states, or by federal legislation, the US would nationally apply the California vehicle emission standard. The low-emission component of the VES would aggressively push the widespread commercialization of low-emission vehicles. The VES would also continue to include a zero-emission requirement, which would involve ongoing setting and revisiting of targets as the automobile industry and regulators learn about the long-run prospects for producing and successfully marketing a given quantity of zero-emission vehicles. California might retain a leadership role since it has a strong motive for improving local air quality, but the function could also pass to the federal government, especially because of the explicit inclusion of greenhouse gas emissions in the VES.

The definition of the zero-emission vehicle may need adjustment as R&D and commercialization experiences provide new information on the alternative technology paths for vehicles, and as the focus expands from reducing local pollutants (in the Los Angeles airshed for example) to include the reduction of GHG emissions from the full fuel cycle – not just the emissions from the vehicle but also upstream emissions in the production of electricity, hydrogen or possibly other fuels (such as biomass) used by the vehicle. For example, a plug-in hybrid that has computer controls to verify that it is powered by combustion of hydrocarbon fuels less than a certain distance per year might be allowed to compete with hydrogen fuel-cell and battery electric vehicles inside the zero-emission niche, as long as its full fuel-cycle emissions were below a certain threshold. Likewise, the definition of low-emission vehicles may need adjustment to allow some use of biofuels for climate change objectives, provided that these fuels are relatively clean-burning in terms of local air quality objectives.

As it grew in national importance, the VES would supplant energy efficiency regulations (the CAFE standard) as the principal regulatory means of developing a low-emission transportation system. While improvements in vehicle energy efficiency are still the cheapest means of reducing emissions over the medium term, over the long term these are continually at risk of being swamped by the growing number of vehicles in the US (and worldwide) and by the rebound effect that the extremely low operating cost of super-efficient vehicles would have on vehicle use rates. Super efficient vehicles would provide an irresistible incentive for Americans to load the kids in the car and drive across the country for their next vacation, or to realize the dream of life in a semi-rural setting far from their place of work. Zero emission vehicles are not subject to the countervailing effect of increased use, and given that so much of the growth in the vehicle stock will occur in developing countries over the next decades, they also provide a means for technology transfer that will help prevent deteriorating urban air quality in these countries and reverse the rising trend in greenhouse gas emissions.

The second niche market regulation in my proposed policy portfolio for the US is the renewable portfolio standard in electricity generation. Like the VES, the RPS would be extended to nationwide application either by its adoption by those states that have not yet done so, or by federal legislation. The RPS should push renewables, not counting existing large hydro, to a 10–15% share of national electricity generation over the next two to three decades. A trading mechanism would ensure that the national requirement is realized even though some regions may do less and some more. Once they reach this level, continued expansion of renewables will depend on how they fare relative to other energy options under the ECTP. In other words, the objective of the RPS is to guarantee a large enough market niche for the most economically attractive renewables so that they realize significant cost reductions from economies-of-learning and economies-of-scale. Their market share will grow beyond that niche only if they are able to outcompete other energy options as the ECTP (and its safety valve) imposes increasingly higher costs on all electricity generation technologies that emit greenhouse gases. This ensures that nuclear and zero-emission fossil fuels are not excluded arbitrarily from a growing contribution to the electricity system. The RPS would not stipulate market shares for individual forms of renewables within the regulated market niche. In the interests of economic efficiency, it is preferable that market competition make this determination, and there is no inherent reason to favor one renewable over another – although some will face more onerous regulatory constraints because of conflicts over land, water and other resources, with large hydro being a salient example.

Unlike the first two, the third proposed niche market regulation in my policy portfolio has not yet been applied anywhere. This is a carbon capture and storage standard (CCSS) mandating that the fossil fuel industry sequester a minimum percentage of the carbon it extracts from the earth each year. The mandate would be as flexible as possible. It would apply to the coal, oil and natural gas industries together, meaning that all of the CCSS mandate might be fulfilled by actions in just one of these sectors, such as generation of electricity from coal, hydrogen production in oil refineries, hydrogen production in oil sands plants, enhanced oil recovery, coalbed methane production, or in association with H_2S as part of acid gas injection in geological strata. All fossil fuel producers would be subject to penalties unless they take actions themselves or pay credits to those whose actions are sufficient to meet the CCSS requirement – meaning that there could be many small projects or just a few large ones, but the costs would be averaged across all fossil fuel producers on the basis of their share of carbon extraction from the earth. Sequestration can be in any form in any medium, as long as other permitting requirements have been met – meaning that geological storage of the CO_2 gas might be augmented or even replaced by solid carbon storage, ocean CO_2 storage or something else depending on research, engineering, economics, public acceptance and regulatory approval.

There already is a natural niche market for CCSS in cases where injecting CO_2 into mature oil and natural gas wells is a profitable means of enhanced recovery, and where pumping CO_2 into deep coal seams is an economical means of extracting coalbed methane. In the past, however, such activities were not conducted with the goal of permanent CO_2 storage, so the long-term stability of critical components such as well caps was not carefully pursued; producers were unconcerned with eventual leaks of the CO_2. The goal of the CCSS is to create an incentive for the pursuit of additional niche markets, as there are some cases in which a modest change in financial incentives would make carbon capture and storage desirable. The CCSS should be sized to avoid acute increases in energy production costs while at the same time ensuring that carbon capture and storage is incorporated into major new fossil-fuel related investments. The initial effect on fuel costs will be small. Its ultimate impact will depend on the scheduled increase in the requirement and the ultimate costs of carbon capture and storage. According to the cost estimates in chapters 6 and 7, the achievement of 90% CCSS by the middle decades of the century would increase the cost of producing electricity by 25–50%.

If the ECTP were relatively aggressive from the start (low cap and high permit price ceiling) and if it applied to all GHG emissions (instead of just industrial emissions) the CCSS would not be needed; an economy-wide ECTP would motivate carbon capture and storage investments just as the carbon tax in Norway motivated the Sleipner project. However, economy-wide application of the ECTP is unlikely to be politically and administratively feasible in the initial phases, and a high ECTP permit price ceiling would also not be politically feasible. The role of the CCSS, therefore, is to provide a parallel impetus for innovation and technology diffusion in the fossil fuel chain that the RPS provides for renewable electricity generation. As the ECTP permit price ceiling rises, the need for the CCSS and the RPS diminishes.

Like the ECTP, the three artificial niche market regulations would include a safety valve in order to improve political feasibility. The VES would include California's penalty of $5,000 per vehicle in non-compliance, creating an upper limit for industry's costs. The RPS would have an upper cost for renewables of 10 ¢/kWh, which could be applied in the form of unlimited sales of green electricity certificates at this price by government – similar to some of the European RPS programs. For the CCSS policy, the government would provide unlimited carbon capture credits at a price of $200/tC ($55t/CO_2) in the early phases. This is much higher than the early ECTP price ceiling in order to ensure that early carbon capture and storage projects are undertaken, since the objective is to lower their cost and reduce the uncertainty for ongoing policy development.

This long-run policy design includes the eventual phase-out of all three niche market regulations as the permit price ceiling of the ECTP rises (and its cap falls) and as the ECTP is extended to the rest of the economy or matched by a parallel carbon tax for final consumers. In other words, the niche market regulations ensure the early development and cost reduction of technologies that offer low-emission alternatives to businesses and consumers as they prepare for the rise in the cost of emitting greenhouse gases, as indicated by the scheduled rise in the ECTP permit price ceiling. At the same time, the early emergence of this cost information will provide government with an indication of the economic impacts of sustaining the initial schedule for a rising ECTP permit price ceiling or for adjusting it if need be. This information will also enable comparison of incremental emission reduction costs in each key sector (vehicles, electricity production, fossil fuel extraction), which may lead to niche market share adjustments in order to minimize total costs of achieving a given level of GHG reduction.

This portfolio of policies for the US illustrates the essential character of the approach I propose, although a comprehensive strategy would require additional elements. One key policy area is the design of regulations and institutions for energy facility siting. Some people would like to see these regulations so strict as to prohibit any large energy facilities, ushering in an era of small-is-beautiful energy technologies. Others believe that regulations are already too tight and will prevent the needed development of new sites for nuclear plants, coal mines, oil and gas exploration, coal polygeneration plants, large windfarms, biomass plantations, and transmission rights of way for oil, natural gas, electricity, hydrogen and CO_2. Holders of this latter position essentially argue that regulations are often tilted too far in favor of the "not in my back yard" (NIMBY) attitude to energy projects and that this allows small interest groups to prevent developments that would benefit society as a whole.

Given the significant externalities associated with our production and use of energy, and the great potential to develop a low impact and low risk energy system, I tend to believe that NIMBY can sometimes be a good thing.* It forces energy system developers to gravitate toward projects that do not have large negative impacts and risks, especially at the local level. Of course, society must ensure that a few people do not hold it to ransom for spurious reasons, but we generally have the political, regulatory and legal means of exercising this right while allowing the expression of substantive NIMBY concerns through media, political action and legal processes. Local powers are increasing in strength in industrialized and developing countries alike,

---

* Although the concept did seem to get out of hand when I once heard a conference speaker also refer to NIMTOO – not in my term of office, BANANA – build absolutely nothing anywhere near anyone, and NOPE – not on planet earth.

and I see this general trend as positive. It will temper the development of large energy facilities but will not prevent these altogether. It might force coal polygeneration plants to develop initially at the sites of previous coal electricity plants or near existing coal mines. It might hinder the development of new nuclear sites, favoring redevelopment of existing sites. It might push large windfarms to offshore sites and isolated regions. It might hinder the development of new electricity transmission lines, which will improve the prospects for cogenerated electricity which increases energy efficiency and is usually small scale. It might push geological storage of CO_2 away from urban areas, which seems prudent anyway.

At the same time, the NIMBY phenomenon also works against small-scale energy projects. It can hinder some small hydro and wind-power projects, as society faces the trade-off between developing 100 small facilities versus one or two large ones. It can hinder smaller cogeneration projects, where these increase air emissions in sensitive areas. Issues in facility siting will play a key role in shaping the choice and scale of energy technologies – but NIMBY alone does not guarantee a small-is-beautiful energy system.

My proposed policy portfolio would lead a country like the US toward a significantly different path in terms of the impacts and risks of its energy system. Local air emissions and acid emissions would continue their decreasing trend of recent decades. Greenhouse gas emissions would decouple from economic output and begin to follow a similar downward trajectory.* The already extremely low risks of radiation leaks would decline slightly with continued safety refinements at existing nuclear facilities. Land use impacts would diminish significantly, in part through more complete rehabilitation of defunct facilities. Safety for employees and the general public would improve.

---

* With a detailed energy-economy model that I have developed and applied for the past fifteen years, I recently simulated the impact in Canada of a similar portfolio – focused on greenhouse gas policy – for an independent policy institute. Because the simulation only covered the period 2000–2035, the full effect of these policies on the century-long evolution of the energy system is not estimated, but key trends emerge over the period showing a substantial decoupling of greenhouse gases from economic output, and falling costs of greenhouse gas abatement with the commercialization and further development of new technologies. See M. Jaccard, N. Rivers and M. Horne, *The Morning After: Optimal Greenhouse Gas Policies for Canada's Kyoto Obligations and Beyond* (Toronto: CD Howe Institute, 2004).

Renewables would be favored that have the smallest impacts on land use. Geopolitical risk due to oil imports from unstable regions would decline as energy supply for countries like the US diversified toward greater use of domestic renewables, domestic coal, and natural gas from North American suppliers as well as a diversity of offshore suppliers of liquefied natural gas. At the same time, the long-run average cost of energy supply would not increase by more than 25–50%, and perhaps by much less. This rising price signal would lead to a steady but not dramatic improvement in energy efficiency, augmented by both conventional and market-oriented regulations.

My policy portfolio is designed to fit a wide range of situations, but its application would vary from country to country. Some countries may prefer emission taxes to the ECTP. NIMBY in most developing countries is not yet as effective as it is in wealthier countries, but this situation is changing. Many developing countries are unwilling, at this point, to make serious efforts at reducing greenhouse gas emissions until industrialized countries take substantial actions, which inhibits the introduction of ECTP and niche market regulations for this particular objective.

International policy initiatives for sustainable energy

International policy initiatives related to sustainable energy are currently dominated by greenhouse gas emissions, which is to be expected given the global nature of this risk, the fairly recent awareness of it, the high degree of uncertainty, the difficult equity challenges it poses, and the fundamental changes it requires of the energy system. But for other reasons, energy has long been at the forefront of international relations and even international conflict. In recent decades, crude oil trade and nuclear power have been of particular concern, and this is reflected in the development of existing international institutions.

In 1960, major oil exporting countries formed the Organization of Petroleum Exporting Countries (OPEC) in an effort to negotiate a better price for their crude oil exports. While the dramatic oil price increases in 1973 and 1979 are commonly attributed to the OPEC cartel's restriction of output, they actually resulted from the oil embargo by Arab members of OPEC in 1973 in support of Arab countries at war with Israel, and from the sudden disruption of Iranian exports during its revolution in 1979–1980. Many industrialized countries formed the International Energy Agency (IEA) in Paris in 1974 initially to coordinate their efforts to stockpile oil and protect themselves in others ways (energy efficiency, alternative supplies) from oil supply disruption. Over the decades, the relationship between OPEC and the IEA has evolved from adversarial to mostly cooperative, as both sides pursue stable oil prices and coordinate their research into oil markets and policies. While OPEC tries to support strong oil prices, it also tries at times to dampen oil price instability from geopolitical events. An increasing global reliance on OPEC oil exports would sustain the important policy role for these two agencies, while the greater development of domestic coal resources by countries like the US, China and India would have the opposite effect.

The International Atomic Energy Agency, located in Vienna, was created in 1957 initially as Atoms for Peace at the initiative of the US and other countries developing domestic nuclear industries. Its mandate includes monitoring the nuclear power programs of individual countries to ensure that facilities and expertise are not diverted to nuclear weapons proliferation. The importance of this responsibility was illustrated during the critical period before the US-led invasion of Iraq in 2003. It is likely to grow in importance in future, as the intensified security concerns of the US and other major powers lead them to demand a greater right to monitor and intervene if necessary in the nuclear power programs of countries that might pose risks.

Renewables are not associated with international policy issues although this could change as their share of the global energy system increases, especially if this is associated with energy trade. There already is an extensive history of bilateral coordination of major hydropower development of river systems that straddle international borders, as between the US and Canada on the Columbia River.

The massive needs of developing countries for investment in clean energy systems is a concern for international agencies like the World Bank, the International Monetary Fund, the United Nations Development Programme, the United Nations Environment Programme and the International Energy Agency. These entities try to improve the flow of energy investment funds toward developing countries, but the aggregate level of such investment remains woefully inadequate.[32]

I described the international effort to curb greenhouse gas emissions in chapter 6. The Intergovernmental Panel on Climate Change (IPCC) was created by the United Nations in 1988. It assembles international experts on climate change and has issued major reports with successively stronger statements about the link between human-produced greenhouse gases and climate change. The Framework Convention on Climate Change (FCCC), signed by 165 states in 1992, relies on IPCC information in negotiating agreement on an aggregate abatement target, the allocation of this among individual countries and the design of international policies to achieve it. Years of negotiations culminated in the signing of the Kyoto Protocol in 1997 by eighty-four countries, which allotted different abatement targets to individual and groups of countries, mostly the industrialized countries called Annex I, to be achieved by the 2008–2012 time period. The protocol included various flexibility mechanisms – emissions trading, augmentation of domestic carbon sinks like forests, credit for advancing abatement in other countries inside and outside the protocol – and set procedures for ongoing negotiations about disputed definitions, penalties and targets for future time periods. The protocol became binding after ratification by Russia in 2005, but the US, China, India and many smaller emitters have no protocol commitments to reduce GHGs. Negotiations have begun for the post-Kyoto period with the hope of encompassing the entire global community in the next agreement.

The Kyoto Protocol has generated a great deal of popular and academic literature, with criticisms from many quarters for many different reasons. These can be grouped into problems with the magnitude and timing of the Kyoto target and problems with the design and coverage of the Kyoto policy mechanisms. I briefly present salient critiques and their counter-arguments.

First, the magnitude of greenhouse gas abatement attributable to Kyoto actions will not appreciably reduce the long-run increase in global emissions, so the benefits of Kyoto are negligible. Supporters reply that Kyoto is but the first step in a process of intensifying the effort of the global community over several decades. Second, it is premature to act while so much scientific uncertainty about climate change exists. Supporters of Kyoto reply that we are very close to a scientific consensus, that media attention on skeptics misrepresents their importance, and that humans must frequently make decisions under uncertainty in which acting and not acting both entail risks. Third, the imminent Kyoto deadline is too close to allow for capital stock turnover that lowers the cost of emission abatement. In response, supporters note that some abatement actions involve short-lived capital stocks or no stock turnover at all, although countries that delay action will indeed face substantially higher costs for meeting their targets. Fourth, the long-run costs of greenhouse gas abatement will be lower if the world delays action until R&D has developed technologies that can reduce emissions at lower costs.[33] Supporters of early action counter that technological innovation is induced by price and policy signals, which a strategy of waiting fails to provide. The trick is to provide these signals without forcing the premature retirement of still-effective capital stocks, and this is the intent with the initially modest Kyoto target and with national policies like modest carbon taxes, modest ECTP systems and niche market regulations. Without the policy initiative by California's air quality regulators in 1990, it is unlikely that a new technology like the hybrid vehicle would be commercially available today.

Additional criticisms focus on the design and coverage of the Kyoto mechanisms. First, major emitters like China and India do not have abatement commitments under the protocol, so reductions by Annex I countries will be offset by emissions growth from these countries. Kyoto supporters respond that all countries should be included in subsequent phases of what is a multi-decade global effort, but that industrialized countries needed to demonstrate their willingness to bear the initial costs before financially constrained countries would follow. Being an international member of the China Council for International Cooperation on Environment and Development for much of the 1990s, I noticed a significant change in the views of senior Chinese energy officials and the resulting Chinese policies after Kyoto was signed. Motivated in part by the desire not to be left behind as the industrialized world shifted to zero-emission technologies, China responded after Kyoto was signed in 1997 by cutting its coal subsidies and intensifying its efforts to advance coalbed methane, coal gasification, natural gas exploration and imports, energy efficiency, and a domestic renewable portfolio standard.*

---

* A renewable portfolio standard was listed as a component of China's tenth Five-Year plan, as described in M. Jaccard, H. Chen and J. Li, "Renewable Portfolio Standard: A Tool for Environmental Policy in the Chinese Electricity Sector," *Energy for Sustainable Development*, special issue on China, 5, 4 (2001): 113–121.

Second, the protocol's flexibility mechanisms have various design flaws that will prevent cost-effective allocation of the international abatement effort and perhaps cause the collapse of the entire agreement.[34] Supporters counter that these mechanisms will continue to evolve as we learn more about what works best. While a global trading mechanism will be difficult to negotiate and enforce, subsidiary permit trading systems encompassing sub-groups of countries might provide the building blocks for eventual international frameworks in the same way that multi-national trading agreements sometimes develop from an initial pact between a subset of countries. In its effort to comply with the Kyoto Protocol, the European Union enacted in 2005 a CO_2 ECTP applying to about 12,000 large final emitters in twenty-five member states: sectors include electricity generation, petroleum refining, cement, iron and steel, glass and ceramics, and pulp and paper. This international agreement between a subset of Kyoto signatories could provide valuable experience for future policy design and for linking other groups of countries.[35]

In contrast with my set of policies for national governments, I do not have as firm a vision for the international policy initiatives that would drive the planet toward a sustainable energy system. For many clean energy challenges, national initiatives are almost sufficient. But where global common property resources are involved, international action is required. One area where progress has been made is in the prevention of ocean oil spills. These have been substantially reduced and even greater risk reduction is possible with only a minimal effect on the cost of fuels transported by sea. International action is still required, however, because unnecessary ocean dumping of oily ballast continues. Other energy-related international issues, such as controlling transborder acid emissions, monitoring nuclear power facilities, and coordinating and managing hydropower developments on international rivers, likewise require the ongoing development of institutions and procedures that bring scientific knowledge and a fair assessment of competing values to negotiating and decision-making processes. In some areas, we have made significant progress, but much remains to be done.

Greenhouse gas emissions, however, represent a uniquely intractable clean energy challenge for the international community. In an ideal world, the international community would reach an agreement on greenhouse gases that improved on the Kyoto Protocol with the following elements. It would include all major emitters. It would have a firm timetable for emission reductions consistent with the rate of innovation and capital stock turnover. It would establish a global ECTP with a permit ceiling price (or a global carbon tax) set to drive technological innovation without causing short-run economic hardship. It would create an independent and trusted agency to supervise compliance, resolve disputes and administer the international permit trading mechanism of the ECTP. And it would allocate initial permits in a manner that all countries – industrialized and developing, large emitters and small – agreed to.

Unfortunately, this prescriptive vision needs to be balanced with predictive realism. There are enormous difficulties in negotiating most global accords, and the climate change challenge is fraught with uncertainty about the magnitude and location of costs and benefits, entailing potentially huge equity impacts between countries. This leaves me more than a little dismayed at those who take great pleasure in pointing to the flaws of the Kyoto Protocol. The first cut at an international agreement on climate change will inevitably be flawed when viewed from a single dimension such as economic efficiency or equity. I also find it surprising to hear that humanity needs to be more certain before acting. In the real world, we must always make decisions under uncertainty. Arguments to delay policy implementation while we develop lower cost technologies presumes that innovation arrives like manna from heaven. Of course we should avoid premature replacement of capital stock, we should not force technological change at a pace that is too rapid for the cost-effective development of key innovations, and we should minimize irreversible decisions in order to maximize flexibility when facing a highly uncertain future. But regulations and financial policies have a role to play in inducing innovation, so policies are needed today that recognize the extent to which necessity is the mother of invention.[36]

Various approaches have been offered for the post-Kyoto phase of international negotiations on GHG emissions. Some of these focus on the design of international permit trading mechanisms, so that an ECTP in one country or bloc of countries allows for cost-effective permit trading with the ECTP system of other countries. Some focus on equity mechanisms to ensure that developing countries have commitments under the next protocol while ensuring that they do not bear the same costs as industrialized countries. Some focus on international revenue mechanisms, like a $1/tCO_2$ universal carbon tax, to fund internationally sponsored and monitored R&D into zero-emission technologies. Some focus on technology protocols and technology exchange mechanisms to accelerate the development and transfer of zero-emission technologies and know-how between countries.[37]

Research of these and other proposals is critical if we are to achieve a coordinated global effort to curb greenhouse gas emissions. At the same time, we should be willing to explore and embrace bilateral and multi-lateral initiatives that even if sub-optimal from a global perspective might be the best we can hope for initially in a less-than-ideal world. I have already noted the example of the Europeans with their collective policy approach to acid emissions and more recently to greenhouse gases. There are hints that Europe might eventually pursue with Russia a broad energy-environment accord dealing with oil and gas development, energy supply security, greenhouse gas policy, safety at nuclear power facilities and zero-emission development of fossil fuels.

Because of my policy advisory work in China, I have been especially interested in the idea of a bilateral clean energy pact between the US and China. These two countries are major trading partners whose economies are increasingly interdependent. Together accounting for almost half of global CO_2 emissions, they face international pressure to adopt stronger abatement policies. US politicians from both ends of the political spectrum have stated an unwillingness to do so unless major emitters like China are also taking action. Both countries are also increasingly concerned about a growing dependence on oil imports and yet both have enormous, low cost coal resources. If the international crude oil price were to stabilize above $40 a barrel, both countries face the choice of producing synthetic gasoline from coal (resulting in major greenhouse gas emissions in the production of the gasoline and its final consumption in vehicles) or instead investing in zero-emission conversion of coal into electricity, hydrogen and a much smaller share of synthetic fuels. If the US and China were to jointly implement an ECTP policy combined with coordinated niche market regulations for renewables in electricity, zero-emission vehicles and carbon capture and storage, this would present a powerful impetus for shared innovation, joint investments, technology transfers and even political cooperation between these two powers, influencing many other countries and perhaps providing a framework for the negotiation of a post-Kyoto global agreement.

Energy policy at the global level might never seem as logical and coherent as some would wish, but this is no reason for despair. The realities at this level simply require creative thinking, a willingness to compromise, and an ability to seize opportunities as they arise. Rising incomes in developing countries provide such an opportunity because of the enormous energy investments that will occur over the coming decades. Likewise, if current high oil prices are sustained, the energy market will attract substantial investment in industrialized countries. These two developments create an unprecedented opportunity to shape the character of the future global energy system, an international policy opportunity that we cannot afford to miss.

8.4 Policy overview

While much is written on the actions that can produce a more sustainable energy system, the policy domain is often neglected. This is unfortunate because while energy system endurance is usually well served by the operation of energy markets unfettered by political interference, much innovation is needed to help policy makers with the formidable challenge of energy system cleanliness, especially the need to reduce the risk of climate change from GHGs emitted during fossil fuel combustion.

When assessing policy options, it is important to understand that environmental effectiveness and economic efficiency are only two criteria among several and that administrative feasibility and especially political feasibility loom large in the calculus of politicians – by necessity. This means that straightforward, economically efficient policies like emission taxes are rarely an acceptable option for politicians, who must instead find ingenious ways of providing an immediate and strong long-run signal to innovators, manufacturers and consumers without inducing economic havoc and major political resistance in the short run.

If information and voluntary programs are largely ineffective for substantial GHG reduction, if conventional command-and-control regulations are often economically inefficient, if financial incentives in the form of consumer subsidies are mostly captured by free riders and therefore ineffective, and if financial disincentives in the form of emission taxes are politically untenable, what options do policy makers have? This conundrum has led researchers and policy makers to explore hybrid approaches that combine elements of various policies. Of particular note are market-oriented regulations that operate like regulations in requiring a specific, aggregate market outcome, but like financial instruments in providing a price signal in the economy and allowing flexibility among those being regulated to trade among themselves in achieving aggregate compliance at minimal cost.

An emissions cap and tradable permit system has good prospects for economic efficiency and for political acceptance if it is accompanied by a permit price ceiling by which the government guarantees that the cost of permits will not exceed a specified threshold. This ceiling should be scheduled to climb over time in conjunction with a reduction in the cap so that environmental effectiveness of the policy increases at a pace consistent with the time needed for innovation and commercialization of new technologies, and the natural turnover rate of equipment, buildings and infrastructure. For reasons of administrative and political feasibility, the emissions cap policy might only be applied to large industrial emitters in the early years, thus requiring complimentary policies in the household sector. These would include a small financial disincentive (emissions tax), modest efficiency regulations for equipment and buildings, and clear communication that the emissions cap would eventually apply economy-wide and increase in its stringency.

A modest but intensifying emissions cap and trade instrument would be the prime policy, but its effectiveness would be enhanced by additional market-oriented regulations that motivated technological developments in the critical areas of renewables electricity generation, zero-emission vehicles and carbon capture and storage. These policies would ensure niche markets for new technologies so that they achieved the threshold production levels necessary for substantial cost reductions via economies-of-scale and economies-of-learning. For market penetration that surpasses these niche markets, the success of any particular technology would depend on its ability to compete with other options as the emissions cap was tightened and extended to the rest of the economy over a pre-set schedule. Thus, the relative contribution of efficiency, nuclear, renewables and zero-emission fossil fuels to a clean energy system would ultimately result from their relative advantages with respect to decision factors like long-run cost, extreme event risk and geopolitical risk.

At the international level, these proposed national policies for GHG emission abatement have attributes that enable their extension from one country to a bloc of countries and eventually the entire planet. Permits can initially be traded between a subset of countries, as the Europeans are demonstrating with their greenhouse gas permit system, with more countries joining over time and with extensions to non-energy sources of GHG emissions. Individual countries can levy a nominal carbon tax for R&D with the revenues submitted to an international agency that allocates research funds and monitors performance. Technology protocols affecting equipment efficiency and emission levels can be applied to an initial bloc of countries and then extended to others through trade-related negotiations. Niche market regulations in one jurisdiction can be adopted by other jurisdictions along with an automatic adjustment mechanism in the same way that the state of New York links its vehicle emission standard to that of California.

While comprehensive international agreement on a planetary GHG abatement target with a consistent portfolio of international policies for achieving it is a laudable ideal, reality is likely to be more complicated. Acceptance of this should increase the prospects for early progress that can later be improved upon.

Notes

1. In R. Suskind, *The Price of Loyalty: George W. Bush, the White House, and the Education of Paul O'Neil* (New York: Simon and Schuster, 2003).
2. A. Jaffe, R. Newell and R. Stavins, "Environmental Policy and Technological Change," *Environmental and Resource Economics* 22, 1–2 (2002): 41–69.
3. See R. Hahn and R. Stavins, "Economic Incentives for Environmental Protection: Integrating Theory and Practice," *American Economic Review* 82, 2 (1992): 464–468.
4. S. Millman and R. Prince, "Firm Incentives to Promote Technological Change in Pollution Control," *Journal of Environmental Economics and Management* 17, 3 (1989): 247–265.
5. D. Cole and P. Grossman, "When is Command and Control Efficient? Institutions, Technology, and the Comparative Efficiency of Alternative Regulatory Regimes for Environmental Protection," *Wisconsin Law Review* 5 (1999): 887–938.

6. See J. Kwoka, "The Limits of Market-Oriented Regulatory Techniques: The Case of Automotive Fuel Economy," *Quarterly Journal of Economics* 98, 4 (1983): 695–704; and D. Greene, "CAFE or Price? An Analysis of the Effects of Federal Fuel Economy Regulations and Gasoline Price on New Car MPG, 1978–1989," *The Energy Journal* 11, 3 (1990): 37–57. This latter study estimated that efficiency regulations made twice the contribution of fuel prices in causing efficiency improvements to the US vehicle fleet in the period 1978–1989.

7. For contrasting views, see R. Sutherland, "Market Barriers to Energy Efficiency Investments," *The Energy Journal* 12, 3 (1991) 15–34; and E. Moxnes, "Estimating Customer Costs or Benefits of Energy Efficiency Standards," *Journal of Economic Psychology* 25, 6 (2005): 707–724.

8. For a discussion of the potential benefits of changes to urban form, see W. Anderson, S. Kanaroglou and E. Miller, "Urban Form, Energy, and the Environment," *Urban Studies* 33, 1 (1996): 7–35. For a discussion of the potential costs of land-use zoning, see P. Cheshire and S. Sheppard, "The Welfare Economics of Land-Use Planning," *Journal of Urban Economics* 52 (2002): 242–269.

9. For two sides, see M. Porter and C. van der Linde, "Toward a New Conception of the Environment-Competitiveness Relationship," *Journal of Economic Perspectives* 9 (1995): 97–118; and K. Palmer, W. Oates and P. Portney, "Tightening Environmental Standards: The Benefit-Cost or the No-Cost Paradigm?" *Journal of Economic Perspectives* 9 (1995): 119–132.

10. A. Pigou, *The Economics of Welfare* (London: Macmillan, 1920).

11. See I. Parry, W. Williams, C. Roberton III and L. Goulder, "When Can Carbon Abatement Policies Increase Welfare? The Fundamental Role of Distorted Factor Markets," *Journal of Environmental Economics and Management* 37, 1 (1999): 52–84.

12. See, for example, D. Loughran and J. Kulick, "Demand Side Management and Energy Efficiency in the United States," *The Energy Journal* 25, 1 (2004): 19–43; and J. Farla and K. Blok, "Energy Conservation Investments in Firms: Evaluation of the Energy Bonus in the Netherlands in the 1980s," *Industrial Energy Efficiency Policies: Understanding Success and Failure*, Proceedings of Workshop by the International Network for Energy Demand Analysis in the Industrial Sector (Utrecht: University of Utrecht, 1998); and K. Train, "Incentives for Energy Conservation in the Commercial and Industrial Sectors," *The Energy Journal* 9, 3 (1988): 113–128.

13. J. Goldemberg (ed.), *World Energy Assessment: Energy and the Challenge of Sustainability* (New York: United Nations Development Programme, 2000), 425.

14. World Bank, *Energy Services for the World's Poor* (Washington, D.C.: World Bank, 2000), 71.

15. Ibid., 76.

16. See P. Hawken, A. Lovins and H. Lovins, *Natural Capitalism: Creating the Next Industrial Revolution* (Boston: Little, Brown, 1999); and K.-H. Robert, B. Schmidt-Bleek, J. Aloisi de Larderel, G. Basile, J. Jansen, R. Kuehr, P. Price Thomas, M. Suzuki, P. Hawken and M. Wackernagel, "Strategic Sustainable Development – Selection, Design and Synergies of Applied Tools," *Journal of Cleaner Production* 10 (2002): 197–214.

17. Organization for Economic Cooperation and Development, *Voluntary Approaches for Environmental Policy: Effectiveness, Efficiency, and Usage in the Policy Mixes* (Paris: OECD, 2003), 14; and M. Khanna, "Non-Mandatory Approaches for Environmental Protection," *Journal of Economic Surveys* 15, 3 (2001): 291–324. See also C. Carraro and F. Levesque (eds.), *Voluntary Approaches in Environmental Policy* (Dordrecht: Kluwer Academic, 1999).

18. See P. Karamanos, "Voluntary Environmental Agreements: Evolution and Definition of a New Environmental Policy Approach," *Journal of Environmental Planning and Management* 44, 1 (2001): 67–84.

19. J. Dales, *Pollution, Property and Prices* (Toronto: University of Toronto Press, 1968).

20. See M. Weitzman, "Prices vs. Quantities," *Review of Economic Studies* 41, 4 (1974): 477–491. For an overview of issues, see R. Kemp, *Environmental Policy and Technical Change: A Comparison of Technological Impact of Policy Instruments* (Cheltenham: Edward Elgar, 1997).

21. D. Ellerman, P. Joskow, R. Schmalensee, J.-P. Monetero and E. Bailey, *Markets for Clean Air: The US Acid Rain Program* (Cambridge: Cambridge University Press, 2000). For applications to this and other pollutants in the US see D. Ellerman, P. Joskow and D. Harrison, *Emissions Trading in the US: Experiences, Lessons and Considerations for Greenhouse Gases* (Washington, D.C.: Pew Center on Global Climate Change, 2003).

22. Weitzman, "Prices vs. Quantities," and M. Roberts and M. Spence, "Effluent Charges and Licenses under Uncertainty," *Journal of Public Economics* 5 (1976): 193–208.

23. See W. McKibbin and P. Wilcoxen, *A Better Way to Slow Global Climate Change* (Washington, D.C.: Brookings Institute, 1997); H. Jacoby and D. Ellerman, "The Safety Valve and Climate Policy,"

Energy Policy 32 (2004): 481–491; W. Pizer, "Optimal Choice of Policy Instrument and Stringency under Uncertainty: The Case of Climate Change," *Resource and Energy Economics* 21 (1999): 255–287; and R. Nordhaus and K. Danish, *Designing a Mandatory Greenhouse Gas Reduction Program for the US* (Washington, D.C.: Pew Center on Global Climate Change, 2003).

24. See M. Jaccard and Y. Mao, "Making Markets Work Better," in T. Johansson and J. Goldemberg (eds.), *Energy For Sustainable Development: A Policy Agenda* (New York: United Nations Development Programme, 2002); and M. Jaccard, "Policies that Mobilize Producers Toward Sustainability: The Renewable Portfolio Standard and the Vehicle Emission Standard," in G. Toner (ed.), *Building Canadian Capacity: Sustainable Production and the Knowledge Economy* (Vancouver: University of British Columbia Press, 2005).

25. For an overview, see M. Jaccard, "Renewable Portfolio Standard," in C. Cleveland (ed.), *Encyclopedia of Energy*, Volume 5 (New York: Elsevier, 2004): 413–421.

26. P. Menanteau, D. Finon and M.-L. Lamy, "Prices versus Quantities: Choosing Policies for Promoting the Development of Renewable Energy," *Energy Policy* 31 (2003): 799–812.

27. See R. Kemp, *Zero Emission Vehicle Mandate in California. Misguided Policy or Example of Enlightened Leadership?* (University of Maastricht: MERIT, 2003).

28. See Jaccard and Mao, "Making Markets Work Better," and T. Jackson (ed.), *Mitigating Climate Change: Flexibility Mechanisms* (London: Elsevier Science, 2001).

29. This challenge for policy comparison and policy design is discussed in W. Harrington, R. Morgenstern and T. Sterner (eds.), *Choosing Environmental Policy: Comparing Instruments and Outcomes in the United States and Europe* (Washington, D.C.: Resources for the Future, 2004).

30. G. Svendsen, *Public Choice and Environmental Regulation: Tradable Permit Systems in the United States and CO_2 Taxation in Europe* (Cheltenham: Edward Elgar, 1998).

31. For an overview and assessment of design alternatives, see Nordhaus and Danish, *Designing a Mandatory Greenhouse Gas Reduction Program.*

32. See International Energy Agency, *World Energy Investment Outlook* (Paris: International Energy Agency, 2003).

33. For a survey of issues and perspectives, see G. Heal and B. Kristrom, "Uncertainty and Climate Change," *Environmental and Resource Economics* 22 (2002): 3–39, and M. Grubb, "Technologies, Energy

Systems, and the Timing of CO_2 Emissions Abatement," *Energy Policy* 25 (1997): 159–172.

34. See, for example, D. Victor, *The Collapse of the Kyoto Protocol and the Struggle to Slow Global Warming* (Princeton, N.J.: Princeton University Press, 2001).

35. J. Kruger and W. Pizer, *The EU Emissions Trading Directive: Opportunities and Potential Pitfalls* (Washington, D.C.: Resources for the Future, 2004).

36. Estimates of the contribution of regulation, energy prices and other factors to energy-related innovations are provided by R. Newell, A. Jaffe and R. Stavins, "The Induced Innovation Hypothesis and Energy-Saving Technological Change," *Quarterly Journal of Economics* 114 (1999): 941–975, and D. Popp, "Induced Innovation and Energy Prices," *American Economic Review* 92, 1 (2002): 160–180.

37. See J. Aldy, S. Barrett and R. Stavins, *Thirteen Plus One: A Comparison of Global Climate Policy Architectures* (Washington, D.C.: Resources for the Future, 2003); B. Bodansky, *International Climate Efforts Beyond 2012: A Survey of Approaches* (Washington, D.C.: Pew Center on Global Climate Change, 2004); B. Bucher and C. Carraro, "Economic and Environmental Effectiveness of a Technology-Based Climate Protocol," *Climate Policy* 4 (2005): 229–248; and B. Sanden and C. Azar, "Near-Term Technology Policies for Long-Term Climate Targets – Economy Wide versus Technology Specific Approaches," *Energy Policy* 33 (2005): 1557–1576.

9 | *Broadening the definition: is sustainable energy sustainable?*

9.1 Energy system sustainability

THERE is considerable evidence that our current energy system is on an unsustainable path. A significant percentage of humanity still combusts solid fuels in open, indoor fires for cooking and heating, resulting in widespread respiratory and other illnesses and several hundred thousand premature deaths each year. Fuel combustion for electricity generation, transportation, industrial production, and in commercial and residential buildings causes region-wide acid precipitation and localized air pollution with substantial harm to humans and ecosystems. Combustion of carbon-based fuels releases greenhouse gases into the atmosphere with potentially disruptive risks to the global climate. In addition to these combustion-related effects, other impacts and risks from the energy system include radiation leaks from nuclear power facilities, releases of crude oil and refined petroleum products on land and in water, health and safety concerns for energy industry workers and adjacent residents, and land and water despoliation from energy extraction activities.

If current trends continue, some of these unsustainable conditions will worsen. Although rising incomes allow more poor households to acquire commercial forms of energy that will improve indoor air quality and save lives, increasing wealth also leads to a dramatic increase in energy use and especially greater combustion of fossil fuels. This leads to growth in local air pollutants, regional acid precipitation and atmospheric concentrations of greenhouse gases.

To shift our energy system toward a sustainable path, we need a clean and enduring combination of greater efficiency, nuclear, renewables and zero-emission uses of fossil fuels, in concert with a shift in secondary energy toward greater use of electricity, hydrogen and some cleaner burning hydrocarbons, many of these produced from biomass feedstocks. We need to vigorously constrain impacts and risks to land

315

and water from the exploitation of these primary sources and from our use of secondary forms of energy. While it is impossible for any energy system to be impact and risk free, it is technologically and economically possible for us to achieve a profound transformation of the energy system in this direction over the next century. At the end of this transition, energy services will cost the average person no more than 10% of their annual budget and more likely not much above the 6% that they currently absorb in industrialized countries.

I prescribe these characteristics as a goal that humanity should adopt for its energy system. In achieving this goal, my evaluation of the primary energy alternatives leads me to predict that fossil fuels will not be abandoned and indeed will sustain their dominant role through this century and perhaps well beyond.

Energy efficiency will be vigorously pursued. However, the use of energy per person is still so low in much of the developing world and its linkage to improvements in living standards so strong that the global energy system will expand about three-fold over this century – which is still much slower growth than its sixteen-fold expansion over the last one.

Because of its association with extreme event risk to environmental and human health, and with geopolitical risks of nuclear weapons proliferation, nuclear power needs a significant cost advantage if it is to outstrip fossil fuels and renewables as the global energy system expands. The evidence suggests that this is unlikely. Nuclear may expand significantly from its current status, but this will not result in a much greater share of the expanded global energy system. This leaves renewables and zero-emission fossil fuels to compete for dominance of this system.

Fossil fuels are likely to remain dominant through this century. Their high energy density and capacity for storage gives them a significant cost advantage, and evidence from existing technologies suggests that zero-emission uses of fossil fuels will not cause dramatically higher secondary energy costs. Inertial forces of path dependence are also on their side, with investment capacity and technological expertise already concentrated in the fossil fuel sector. While conventional oil is perceived to have geopolitical risks for countries like the US and China, development of plentiful domestic coal resources provides a means for these and other countries to mitigate this risk. Natural gas is also widely distributed around the globe, and there is considerable evidence that the amount of this resource that will be available to human use with modest technological developments is many times larger than the reserve estimates we currently rely on. Finally, while renewables in some situations can be cost-competitive with zero-emission fossil fuels, this is likely more the exception than the rule, at least in the earlier decades of the century. As the highest quality fossil fuel resources are depleted, however, the relative balance should shift in favor of renewables. Most likely this will not happen until the second half of this century, and perhaps much farther in the future given the potential for unconventional oil, unconventional natural gas and coal to replace conventional oil and natural gas in the production of clean secondary energy. Even with sustained rapid growth rates, renewables will not supplant fossil fuels in this century.

I see no reason to act rashly in banishing fossil fuels from our energy system, even though so many experts and non-experts are calling for this. If the high quality energy of fossil fuels allows for their conversion to zero-emission, low impact and low risk energy, while costing less than the alternatives, this enables humanity to allocate more resources to social development goals of adequate and nutritious food, clean drinking water, quality housing, essential health services, education, security and basic infrastructure. With much of the planet's population growth slated to occur in poorer countries, even incremental reductions in the cost of energy services will be important for pursuing these other goals. A continued role for fossil fuels does not preclude the development of energy efficiency, nuclear power and renewable energy, and can be complementary – allowing these to develop at a pace consistent with R&D, technological change, capital stock turnover, wealth creation, improved security measures and relative cost evolution. Indeed, my scenario of a sustainable fossil fuel future presumes that efficiency gains are achieved more rapidly than during the past 100 years and that renewables sustain a tremendous growth rate throughout this century.

This cleaner, lower risk global energy system is unlikely to be significantly more decentralized than our current system. The conversion of fossil fuels to cleaner forms of secondary energy involves substantial economies-of-scale, as does the production of nuclear power, especially when we include the costs of land acquisition, regulatory approvals and safety systems. Although some advocates of renewables link these forms of energy with a decentralized energy system, human demands for reliable and convenient energy will create pressures for technological developments and facilities that concentrate and store energy. Some of these technologies will benefit from economies-of-scale, which will in turn promote centralized production facilities (extensive windfarms with high voltage transmission, biomass energy processing plants, and large-scale energy storage). Advances in structurally integrated photovoltaic systems might generally work in favor of decentralized production while advances in biotechnology might have the opposite influence. If a dramatically more decentralized energy system is to occur, it will be because of deliberate choices, not because of the growing role for renewables.

The transition toward a more sustainable energy system will not happen on its own. Policies are required that address the costs and other difficult trade-offs when the objective is profound technological transformation. While my analysis of long-run costs suggests that the low impact and low risk energy system will not be significantly more expensive than today's, there are substantial hurdles in overcoming the inertia of our existing system. We reduce these transitional costs by not banishing fossil fuels prematurely and unnecessarily. But the shift from today's combustion of fossil fuels to their zero-emission development will require well-crafted policies that provide the correct long-run signal to innovators, manufacturers and consumers, without inflicting high short-run costs on some groups or regions that would in turn engender intransigence and ultimately political stalemate.

Voluntary and information policies may help but are not sufficient. Subsidies can play a role, but they are constrained by competing claims on government fiscal resources, and it is difficult to ensure that they actually change long-run behaviour. Traditional command-and-control regulations are problematic in that they cast government in an unpopular, coercive role and can lead to higher than necessary costs for a given environmental improvement. Their role is more likely limited to consolidating technological change than to driving it. Taxes and other financial disincentives place policy-makers in a similar dilemma in that only modest application is likely to be politically feasible, relegating these policies also to the role of reinforcing but not driving technological change. The most promising policy approach involves some combination of all of these with other newly emerging market-oriented regulations. The emissions cap and tradable permit has already been applied in a few jurisdictions for regional control of acid emissions and local control of air quality-related pollutants. It will also be applied over the next decade in Europe and elsewhere for GHG emission reduction.

A promising use for market-oriented regulation is to create niche markets by requiring, for instance, minimum levels of renewable electricity generation, zero- and low-emission vehicle drive-trains, and the zero-emission transformation of fossil fuels into electricity, hydrogen, and low-emission synthetic fuels. These niche market regulations require substantial technological transformation, but have negligible upward effect on short-run energy prices or the costs of conventional technologies. They unleash market forces to stimulate R&D and commercialization of desired technologies, reducing the need for governments to pick winning technologies, something they often do poorly. The regulated niche markets also allow time for learning both about technology costs and about energy system impacts and risks. If, over the next decade or so, we learn that one technological path is more promising than another (hydrogen fuel cell versus battery versus plug-in hybrid vehicles), we can divert our resources without having made a wholesale transformation of capital stock in the wrong direction. If, over the next twenty years, we learn that our climate science has missed some important countervailing factor, we can ease up on our greenhouse gas reduction effort – although we are likely to continue the pursuit of zero-emission fossil fuels because of the other benefits in terms of local and regional air quality. Finally, as the niche market regulations develop and disseminate zero- and low-emission alternatives for businesses and consumers, this policy approach can be gradually supplanted by economy-wide taxes or tradable permit instruments that provide a consistent price signal throughout the economy. This offers the best chance of an economically efficient investment path.

9.2 A broader definition of sustainability

My analysis points to a conclusion that few people believe today – that we can achieve a dramatically lower impact and lower risk energy system while fossil fuels retain their dominant role through this century and beyond. Even more disturbing perhaps, I further conclude that such an energy system be called sustainable in that it would provide a substantially expanded level of energy services indefinitely,

with little increase in energy service costs, and eventually with a
smooth transition – as smooth as can be expected in a commodity
market with its share of spikes and crashes over the decades – to other
forms of energy and greater efficiency as the depletion of fossil fuels
increases the costs of developing the remaining resources.

But is my use of the word sustainable broad enough? Is this "sustainable energy system" truly sustainable if I expand my definition
beyond energy?

The World Commission on Environment and Development, headed
by G. H. Brundtland, defined sustainable development in 1987 as
"development which meets the needs of the present without
compromising the ability of future generations to meet their own
needs."[1] This term caught the world's imagination, but it also ignited
a vigorous debate and an enormous literature about what guidance it
provides to today's policy makers. Given our uncertain knowledge of
the future impacts of our decisions, not to mention uncertainty about
our current impacts on the earth, and given our inability to know what
future generations might want, how can we possibly determine the
criteria by which to judge our current actions? Responses to this
question range widely.

One thrust focuses on *biogeophysical sustainability*, what is sometimes called the *natural carrying capacity* of the earth.[2] Essentially, this
says that human activity is unsustainable if it exceeds or otherwise
disrupts the natural cycles of energy and materials in the biogeosphere.
One approach to determining sustainability according to this criterion
is to identify indicators of the integrity of the biogeophysical system.
Increasing acid precipitation or concentration of greenhouse gases in
the atmosphere would be obvious indicators, as would be decreases in
biodiversity as the Amazon rainforest is reduced in South America,
loss of arable land to desertification in Sub-Saharan Africa, or the
shrinking of the Aral Sea in Asia.

Some analysts have attempted to develop a single, comprehensive
indicator. The *ecological footprint* compares the resource use of a
particular region (or the entire planet) with the natural rate of bioproductivity from photosynthesis, and the region's material and energy
wastes with the assimilative and recycling ability of the region's (or the
planet's) natural system.[3] This position is especially associated with
concerns that humans are destroying *natural capital* (the earth's
existing biogeophysical system) that will be highly valued by future

generations. For some, it even suggests that any loss of natural capital is unsustainable, even if compensated by human-produced capital in the form of infrastructure, buildings, equipment and technological know-how. According to H. Daly, natural capital and human-produced capital are essentially complements with only slight substitution capability over time – an approach that has been referred to as *strong sustainability*.[4]

This contrasts with an approach, commonly associated with J. Hartwick and R. Solow, which posits that ongoing substitution between natural and human-produced capital can be consistent with sustainability – what has been referred to as *weak sustainability*.[5] From this perspective, a concept like sustainable development cannot provide us with detailed guidance about what we can and cannot do in order to protect the interests of future generations. Instead the concept simply expresses a moral obligation under extreme uncertainty to act in accordance with our best guess at what future generations would have preferred us to do. This would mean, for example, that our use of exhaustible resources like fossil fuels would be acceptable if we re-invest the net benefits from resource exploitation into human-produced capital that might better the lives of people in ways that lead to wealthier and healthier future generations (clean water supply and sewage infrastructure in developing countries, advances in medical knowledge). Under this conception, society's choice can legitimately range from allowing a decline in some forms of natural capital, like biodiversity, to a vigorous effort to preserve all forms of natural capital even though the economic and social trade-offs are large. Except in extreme situations of ecological imperative, this preservation of natural capital is more likely a moral choice in which we guess at the preferences of future generations when trading off environmental, economic and social objectives today.[6]

This latter perspective especially finds illogical the argument that we should abstain from the use of non-renewable resources like fossil fuels in case future generations might value them more highly than ourselves. How can any past or future generation escape this same argument? No generation can know if the resource would be more valuable to future generations. But if all generations assume this, humanity forgoes in perpetuity the high quality energy from fossil fuels even if their use could better the lives of needy people today and improve the human condition for generations to come.

This perspective also suggests that a concept like the ecological footprint is unlikely to be helpful in determining if our actions are sustainable. It sets planetary bioproductivity as an indicator of the sustainable limit for human energy use (directly and in producing goods and services), even though ongoing technological innovations allow humans to exploit ever more of the incoming solar radiation in the form of the mechanical energy of wind and hydropower, and in converting solar energy directly into electricity with photovoltaic panels on rooftops or covering an expanse of desert. Also, if we only focus on the natural ability of the biosphere to absorb the CO_2 from fossil fuel combustion, we exclude our technological capability to augment this capacity by capturing and storing carbon in oil and gas reservoirs, deep saline aquifers, and perhaps elsewhere in the earth's crust or on its surface.[7]

J. Simon epitomized the optimistic extreme of the weak sustainability position, claiming that human ingenuity is the only resource that really matters.[8] Humanity's problem-solving capacity, notably its ability to devise substitutes for anything, can enable the perpetual improvement of the human condition, even as we exhaust non-renewable resources like fossil fuels. More recently, B. Lomborg argued that a look at key indicators lends support to Simon's claim that humans are improving their own well-being without causing significant harm to themselves or the integrity of the biogeophysical system.[9]

This optimism about human ingenuity basically implies that we can focus on fostering economic growth as the best way of meeting the goals of sustainable development, that the technological capacity to master natural capital that inevitably accompanies economic growth is the best legacy we can leave to future generations. Not surprisingly, there is much criticism of these assumptions. Human history includes periods of steady progress in bettering our conditions, but also evidence of catastrophic collapse of fairly sophisticated societies. Studying these events can yield insights into what can go wrong and why we should temper our optimism with caution.[10] Natural history tells a similar story of periods of stability and equilibrium, and then periods of instability with catastrophic effects on ecosystems and species. Studying these developments can provide insights into where and how a cautionary approach can reduce the risk of destabilizing the biogeophysical system – by paying attention to properties like ecosystem resilience and limits in our interactions with natural systems.[11]

Understanding the thresholds beyond which species or ecosystems might slip from resiliency into vulnerability motivated the concept of *safe minimum standard* for endangered species and the broader term *precautionary principle* for wide-ranging decisions about human interference with the biogeophysical system.[12] The basic argument is that we should err on the side of keeping ecosystems well back from thresholds at which they might become destabilized and perhaps collapse to a new, less desired equilibrium.

The precautionary principle might suggest that dramatic conservation of fossil fuels should begin immediately since we do not know what value they might have to future generations, whether for use as an energy source or as a feedstock for valuable goods in the petrochemical industry, for example. But one challenge with the precautionary principle is that it usually focuses on only one side of the ledger.[13] If our desire to be cautious leads us to do less of something, we need to know what we are giving up for that. If the precautionary principle suggests reducing fossil fuel use in rural parts of India, will this accelerate deforestation in areas where biodiversity is threatened? Should we not simultaneously apply the precautionary principle to deforestation when we apply it to fossil fuel use reduction?

Obviously, we want to be cautious in how we use the resources of this earth – seeking to anticipate the preferences of future generations. Obviously, we can do much better in terms of resource conservation. But the decision of how much to conserve and how much to use cannot be reduced to a one-dimensional application of the precautionary principle. We will have to make trade-offs between the benefits and risks implied by our choices.

9.3 The wider risks of sustainable energy

Although I know that trade-offs are always present, I find the arguments compelling that we should worry a great deal about the impacts of our inevitably expanding global energy system. This is why I define at the outset a sustainable energy system as one that has negligible impacts and risks now and in the future. My constraints on the energy system are severe, including not just emission controls, but also a continued tightening of controls on all energy-related activities presenting impacts and risks to land and water. Fortunately, the evidence suggests that over this century the total costs of this approach are not unreasonable, implying that the trade-offs are acceptable. Nonetheless, we should not accept greater costs than absolutely necessary in our drive for a clean and enduring energy system.

I am also ready to accept that our current use of some fossil fuels be moderated by concern for the possibility that these might have high value to future generations. However, a lower quality fossil fuel like coal is unlikely to be extremely valuable to future generations, given what we already know about our advancing technological potential to reap relatively low impact and low risk secondary energy from renewables and perhaps nuclear in the future. In contrast, a willingness to forgo some consumption of conventional oil today simply means that the share of coal in the fossil fuel mix gets a bit larger earlier in the century. Such an application of the precautionary principle could involve a difficult trade-off. When deciding to preserve conventional oil and natural gas for future generations, we need to understand the slowing of economic growth in developing countries that might be implied by this decision. This can have real repercussions for the well-being of the poorer people on this planet today and for those yet to be born during this century.

Like most economists, I have sympathy for the argument that our ability to develop substitutes to meet our needs is greater than most people suspect – and far greater than foretold by today's prophets of doom. I believe that a static view of resources can lead to the wrong decisions if we are seeking a balance between improving the lives of poorer people today and preserving options for future generations. On the other hand, I also worry about the risks of ardent techno-optimism. Because of this concern, the technological options I focus on for achieving zero-emission fossil fuels are already used in industry today, which provides greater confidence in their capabilities and costs. In this sense, I refer to my analysis as "techno-realist" in contrast to the "techno-optimists" like J. Simon. The optimists are less interested in the technological details because their conclusions are drawn from an inherent faith in the ability of humans to innovate in the face of constraints. The realists want careful thermodynamic and engineering analysis at a minimum, and prefer technological capability that has already seen real-world demonstration – as is the case with the technologies I have identified and characterized for providing zero-emission fossil fuels.

From a policy perspective, I have no illusions that society will naturally evolve toward the widespread dissemination of these more environmentally benign technologies. In this case, optimists focus on the ways in which reductions in energy and material use will increase profits for businesses and improve lifestyles for consumers, and they overlook all the ways in which increased energy and material consumption might benefit businesses and consumers when use of the environment as a free waste receptacle is still permitted. If we are serious about reducing the impacts and risks of our activities, then forceful, effective policies are an immediate necessity.

Finally, what ultimately might happen if I am right? What if we can and do achieve a relatively clean and inexpensive energy system over this century? Does this mean that we will also satisfy the broader definition of sustainability?

Unfortunately, it does not. The impacts and risks to the earth from human activity are so much more than just those directly associated with our energy system. Indeed, a cornucopia of cheap and clean energy unshackles humanity to continue, if it wants, the appropriation of more and more of the earth's surface. We can already see what cheap energy means where wealthy people in wealthy countries can realize their dreams for luxurious, spacious and mobile lifestyles without feeling constrained by energy costs. Rich people use a great deal more energy per capita than poor people, in spite of having more energy efficient devices. They also use more of the earth's surface – land and water – for living space, recreation, and the production and disposal of materials.

Our efforts toward a more sustainable energy system do not ensure sustainability in a holistic sense, but they can make an important contribution. The goal of sustainability requires profound changes to the material and energy flows associated with humanity in that these flows cannot result in the accumulation of disruptive substances or excessive waste heat in the biogeophysical system. The technologies and resource uses that achieve this objective for the energy system could be equally applicable to controlling material flows related to agriculture, mining, forestry, fisheries and the inputs and waste outputs from urban areas. Human economies will need to evolve toward closed-loop principles that are currently identified with concepts such as *industrial ecology, biomimicry* and *environmental life-cycle management*. All of these imply that the inputs and outputs of human activity are designed and controlled to ensure that these flows are non-disruptive to the earth's biogeophysical system, including the maintenance of biodiversity.

The policy designs for a more sustainable energy system are equally applicable to the broader sustainability objective. Just as the energy system requires tighter controls over the uses of land and water, and the rehabilitation of these where activities entail some degree of unavoidable disruption, so too will other activities require this. In some locations, this will involve severe restrictions on any human activity whatsoever – in effect, allowing natural systems to evolve as they would without human interference. Just as the energy system requires special policies like niche market regulations to induce profound technological change, so too will these types of policies be required for a broad range of activities in which energy use is but a small part of the equation. Manufacturers of consumer products, for example, may be required to ensure that a small but growing percentage of their sales are comprised of products that are either completely biodegradable or 100% recycled, including the packaging. Some of these policy objectives and designs are already being pursued in various jurisdictions, but the widespread dissemination of these ideas and efforts is still ahead of us.

Big challenges of sustainability are indeed still to come. In this pursuit, however, the evaluation of our energy alternatives suggests that the simple characterization of options as good or bad is unhelpful. Even a non-enduring and potentially harmful resource like fossil fuels can be part of a sustainable energy system if we guard against confusing our objectives with the options for achieving them. Viewed according to their attributes, as we currently know them, fossil fuels are an undesired input that calls for rapid banishment. Viewed according to their quality and quantity, and the technological potential to use them differently than we currently do, fossil fuels can play a key role over this century and beyond as we pursue an enduring, benign and affordable energy system.

Notes

1. World Commission on Environment and Development, *Our Common Future* (New York: Oxford University Press, 1987).
2. M. Munasinghe and W. Shearer, *Defining and Measuring Sustainability: The Biogeophysical Foundations* (Washington, D.C.: World Bank, 1995).
3. M. Wackernagel and W. Rees, *Our Ecological Footprint: Reducing Human Impact on Earth* (Stony Creek, Conn.: New Society Publishers, 1996).
4. H. Daly, "Operationalizing Sustainable Development by Investing in Natural Capital," in A. Jansson, M. Hammer, C. Folke and R. Costanza

(eds.), *Investing in Natural Capital: The Ecological Economics Approach to Sustainability* (Washington, D.C.: Island Press, 1994).

5. J. Hartwick, "Intergenerational Equity and the Investing of Rents from Exhaustible Resources," *American Economic Review* 66 (1977): 972–974; R. Solow, "On the Intertemporal Allocation of Natural Resources," *Scandinavian Journal of Economics* 88 (1986): 141–149.

6. See R. Solow, "Sustainability: An Economist's Perspective," in R. Dorfman and N. Dorfman (eds.), *Economics of the Environment: Selected Readings* (New York: Norton, 1993), 179–187, and W. Beckerman and J. Pasek, *Justice, Posterity, and the Environment* (Oxford: Oxford University Press, 2001).

7. R. Costanza, R. Ayres, R. Herendeen, I. Moffatt, H. Opschoor, D. Rapport, W. Rees, C. Simmons, K. Lewis, P. Templet, J. G. van Kooten, E. Bulte, M. Wackernagel and J. Silverstein, "Forum on the Ecological Footprint," *Ecological Economics* 32, 3 (2000): 341–394.

8. J. Simon, *The Ultimate Resource II* (Princeton, N.J.: Princeton University Press, 1996).

9. B. Lomborg, *The Skeptical Environmentalist: Measuring the Real State of the World* (Cambridge: Cambridge University Press, 2001).

10. J. Tainter, *The Collapse of Complex Societies* (Cambridge: Cambridge University Press, 1988); J. Diamond, *Collapse: How Societies Choose to Fail or Succeed* (New York: Viking Penguin, 2005).

11. C. Holling, "An Ecologist View of the Malthusian Conflict," in K. Lindahl-Kiessling and H. Landsberg (eds.), *Population, Economic Development and Environment* (Oxford: Oxford University Press, 1994), and E. O. Wilson, *The Future of Life* (New York: Knopf, 2002).

12. Safe minimum standard was originated by S. Ciriancy Wantrup, *Resource Conservation* (Berkeley: University of California Press, 1952). The precautionary principle is elaborated in C. Perrings, "Reserved Rationality and the Precautionary Principle: Technological Change, Time, and Uncertainty in Environmental Decision Making," in R. Costanza (ed.), *Ecological Economics: The Science and Management of Sustainability* (New York: Columbia University Press, 1991).

13. R. Hahn and C. Sunstein, "The Precautionary Principle as a Basis for Decision Making," *The Economists' Voice* 2, 2, article 8 (2005): 1–10.

Bibliography

Adelman, M. "Comment on: R. W. Bentley. 'Global Oil and Gas Depletion,'" *Energy Policy* 31, 4 (2003): 389–390

"Mineral Depletion with Special Reference to Petroleum," *Review of Economics and Statistics* 72, 1 (1990): 1–10

Adelman, M., and M. Lynch. "Fixed View of Resources Limits Creates Undue Pessimism," *Oil and Gas Journal* 95, 14 (1997): 56–60

Adelman, M., and C. Watkins. "Oil and Natural Gas Reserve Prices 1982–2002: Implications for Depletion and Investment Cost," Working Paper 03–016, MIT Center for Energy and Environmental Policy, 2003

Aldy, J., S. Barrett and R. Stavins. *Thirteen Plus One: A Comparison of Global Climate Policy Architectures* (Washington, D.C.: Resources for the Future, 2003)

Allard, P., D. Djlevic and C. Delarue. "Origin of Carbon Dioxide Emanation from the 1979 Deng Eruption, Indonesia: Implications for the Origin of the 1986 Nyos Catastrophe," *Journal of Volcanology and Geothermal Research* 39 (1989): 195–206

Anderson, S., and R. Newell. "Prospects for Carbon Capture and Storage Technologies," *Annual Review of Environment and Resources* 29 (2004): 109–142

Anderson, W., S. Kanaroglou and E. Miller. "Urban Form, Energy, and the Environment," *Urban Studies* 33, 1 (1996): 7–35

Arrow, K., and L. Hurwicz. "An Optimality Criterion for Decision-Making Under Ignorance," in C. Carter and J. Ford (eds.), *Uncertainty and Expectations in Economics: Essays in Honour of G. L. S. Shackle* (Oxford: Basil Blackwell, 1972)

Atmosphere, Climate & Environment Information Programme. "History of Air Pollution," *Encyclopedia of the Atmospheric Environment* (Manchester: Manchester Metropolitan University, 2002)

Ayres, R. "The Second Law, the Fourth Law, Recycling and Limits to Growth," *Ecological Economics* 29 (1999): 473–483

Azar, C., K. Lindgren and B. Andersson. "Global Energy Scenarios Meeting Stringent CO_2 Constraints – Cost-Effective Fuel Choices in the Transportation Sector," *Energy Policy* 31 (2003): 961–976

Bachu, S., and W. Gunter. *Characteristics of Acid Gas Injection Operations in Western Canada*, Report PH4/18 to the Greenhouse Gas R&D Programme (Paris: International Energy Agency, 2003)

Beckerman, W., and J. Pasek. *Justice, Posterity, and the Environment* (Oxford: Oxford University Press, 2001)

Bell, M., B. Hobbs and H. Ellis. "The Use of Multi-Criteria Decision-Making Methods in the Integrated Assessment of Climate Change: Implications for IA Practitioners," *Socio-Economic Planning Sciences* 37 (2003): 289–316

Bentley, R. "Global Oil and Gas Depletion: An Overview," *Energy Policy* 30, 3 (2002): 189–205

Bentzen, J. "Estimating the Rebound Effect in US Manufacturing Energy Consumption," *Energy Economics* 26 (2004): 123–134

Bernstam, M. *The Wealth of Nations and the Environment* (London: Institute of Economic Affairs, 1991)

Berry, G. "Present and Future Electricity Storage for Intermittent Renewables," in *Proceedings of the Pew Center Workshop 'The 10–50 Solution: Technologies and Policies for a Low-Carbon Future'* (Washington, D.C.: Pew Center on Global Climate Change, 2004)

Berry, L. "A Review of The Market Penetration of US Residential and Commercial Demand-Side Management Programmes," *Energy Policy* 21, 1 (1993): 53–67

Besenbruch, G., L. Brown, J. Funk and S. Showalter. "High Efficiency Generation of Hydrogen Fuels Using Nuclear Power," paper presented at the OECD/NEA Information Exchange Meeting on the Nuclear Production of Hydrogen, Paris, 2000

Bier, V., Y. Haimes, J. Lambert, N. Matalas and R. Zimmerman. "A Survey of Approaches for Assessing and Managing the Risk of Extremes," *Risk Analysis* 19, 1 (1999): 83–94

Bockris, J. *Energy: The Solar-Hydrogen Alternative* (New York: Halstead Press, 1975)

Bodansky, B. *International Climate Efforts Beyond 2012: A Survey of Approaches* (Washington, D.C.: Pew Center on Global Climate Change, 2004)

Bradley, R. *The Increasing Sustainability of Conventional Energy*, No. 341 (Washington, D.C.: Cato Institute, 1999)

Brilhante, O. "Brazil's Alcohol Programme: From an Attempt to Reduce Oil," *Journal of Environmental Planning and Mangement* 40, 4 (1997): 435–450

British Petroleum. *BP Statistical Review* (London: British Petroleum, 2004)
Energy in Focus: Statistical Review of World Energy 2004 (London: British Petroleum, 2004)

Statistical Review of World Energy 1998 (London: British Petroleum, 1998)

Brookes, L. "The Greenhouse Effect: The Fallacies in the Energy Efficiency Solution," *Energy Policy* 18, 2 (1990): 199–201

Brown, L. *Eco-Economy: Building an Economy for the Earth* (New York: Norton, 2001)

Brown, M., M. Levine, J. Romm, A. Rosenfeld and J. Koomey. "Engineering-Economic Studies of Energy Technologies to Reduce Greenhouse Gas Emissions: Opportunities and Challenges," *Annual Review of Energy and the Environment* 23 (1998): 287–385

Bryce, R. "More Precious than Oil," *Texas Monthly,* February 1991: 109

Bucher, B., and C. Carraro. "Economic and Environmental Effectiveness of a Technology-Based Climate Protocol," *Climate Policy* 4 (2005): 229–248

California Air Resources Board. *On Road Activity,* Emissions Inventory Series (Sacramento: California Air Resources Board, 2002)

Campbell, C., and J. Laherrere. "The End of Cheap Oil," *Scientific American* 278, 3 (1998): 78–84

Carraro, C., and F. Levesque (eds.). *Voluntary Approaches in Environmental Policy* (Dordrecht: Kluwer Academic, 1999)

Cheshire, P., and S. Sheppard. "The Welfare Economics of Land-Use Planning," *Journal of Urban Economics* 52 (2002): 242–269

Ciriancy Wantrup, S. *Resource Conservation* (Berkeley: University of California Press, 1952)

Cole, D., and P. Grossman. "When is Command and Control Efficient? Institutions, Technology, and the Comparative Efficiency of Alternative Regulatory Regimes for Environmental Protection," *Wisconsin Law Review* 5 (1999): 887–938

Costanza, R., R. Ayres, R. Herendeen, I. Moffatt, H. Opschoor, D. Rapport, W. Rees, C. Simmons, K. Lewis, P. Templet, J. G. van Kooten, E. Bulte, M. Wackernagel and J. Silverstein. "Forum on the Ecological Footprint," *Ecological Economics* 32, 3 (2000): 341–394

Craig, P., A. Gadgil and J. Koomey. "What Can History Teach Us? A Retrospective Examination of Long-Term Energy Forecasts for the United States," *Annual Review of Energy and the Environment* 27 (2002): 83–118

Dales, J. *Pollution, Property and Prices* (Toronto: University of Toronto Press, 1968)

Daly, H. "Operationalizing Sustainable Development by Investing in Natural Capital," in A. Jansson, M. Hammer, C. Folke and R. Costanza (eds.), *Investing in Natural Capital: The Ecological*

Economics Approach to Sustainability (Washington, D.C.: Island Press, 1994)

Dasgupta, P., and G. Heal. "The Optimal Depletion of Exhaustible Resources," *Review of Economic Studies* 41 (1974): 3–28

DeCanio, S. *Economic Models of Climate Change – A Critique* (New York, Palgrave Macmillan, 2003)

DeCarolis, J., and D. Keith. "The Cost of Wind's Variability: Is There a Threshold?" *The Electricity Journal,* January/February 2005: 69–77

Deffeyes, K. *Hubbert's Peak: The Impending World Oil Shortage* (Princeton, N.J.: Princeton University Press, 2001)

Deutch, J., and E. Moniz (co-chairs). *The Future of Nuclear Power: An Interdisciplinary MIT Study* (Cambridge, Mass.: MIT Press, 2004)

Dewey, S. *Don't Breathe the Air* (Texas: Texas A&M University Press, 2000)

Diamond, J. *Collapse: How Societies Choose to Fail or Succeed* (New York: Viking Penguin, 2005)

Dixon, R., J. Winjum, K. Andrasko, J. Lee and P. Schroeder. "Integrated Systems: Assessment of Promising Agroforests and Alternative Land Use Practices to Enhance Carbon Conservation and Sequestration," *Climatic Change* 30, 1 (1994): 1–23

Dooley, J. *US National Investment in Energy R&D: 1974–1999* (Washington, D.C.: Battelle Memorial Institute, 2001)

Downing, R., R. Ramankutty and J. Shah. *RAINS-ASIA: An Assessment Model for Acid Deposition in Asia* (Washington, D.C.: World Bank, 1997)

Drennen, T., A. Baker and W. Kamery. *Electricity Generation Cost Simulation Model,* report No. SAND 2002–3376 (Albuquerque: Sandia National Laboratories, 2002)

Drolet, B., J. Gretz, D. Kluyskens, F. Sandmann and R. Wurster. "The Euro-Québec Hydro-Hydrogen Pilot Project [EQHHPP]: Demonstration Phase," *International Journal of Hydrogen Energy* 21, 4 (1996): 305–316

Dunbar, R., M. Stogran, P. Chan and S. Chan. *Oil Sands Outlook: Potential Supply and Costs of Crude Bitumen and Synthetic Crude Oil in Canada 2003–2017* (Calgary: Canadian Energy Research Institute, 2004)

Dunn, S. *Hydrogen Futures: Toward a Sustainable Energy System* (Washington, D.C.: Worldwatch Institute, 2001)

Ellerman, D., P. Joskow, R. Schmalensee, J.-P. Monetero and E. Bailey. *Markets for Clean Air: The US Acid Rain Program* (Cambridge: Cambridge University Press, 2000)

Ellerman, D., P. Joskow and D. Harrison. *Emissions Trading in the US: Experiences, Lessons and Considerations for Greenhouse Gases* (Washington, D.C.: Pew Center on Global Climate Change, 2003)

European Commission. *ExternE: Externalities of Energy* (Luxembourg: Office for Official Publications of the European Communities, 1995)
External Costs: Research Results on Socio-Environmental Damages Due to Electricity and Transport (Brussels: Director-General for Research, European Commission, 2003)

Farla, J., and K. Blok. "Energy Conservation Investments in Firms: Evaluation of the Energy Bonus in the Netherlands in the 1980s," *Industrial Energy Efficiency Policies: Understanding Success and Failure*, Proceedings of Workshop by the International Network for Energy Demand Analysis in the Industrial Sector (Utrecht: University of Utrecht, 1998)

Fetter, S. *Climate Change and the Transformation of World Energy Supply* (Palo Alto, Calif.: Center for International Security and Cooperation, Stanford University, 1999)

Fickett, A., C. Gellings and A. Lovins. "Efficient Use of Electricity," *Scientific American* 263, 3 (1990): 64–75

Fischoff, B., A. Bostrom and M. Quadrel. "Risk Perception and Communication," *Annual Review of Public Health* 14 (1993): 183–203

Fung, C. "Clean Air for Hong Kong," in G. Haq, W. Han, and C. Kim (eds.), *Urban Air Pollution Management and Practice in Major and Megacities of Asia*, Proceedings of Workshop, Air Pollution in the Megacities of Asia Project, Seoul, Korea (Seoul: Korea Environment Institute, 2002)

Fung, M., and T. Macyk. "Reclamation of Oil Sands Mining Areas," in R. Barnhisel, R. Darmody and W. Daniels (eds.), *Reclamation of Drastically Disturbed Lands* (American Society of Agronomy, Agronomy Series 41, 2000): 755–774

Gale, J., N. Christensen, A. Cutler and T. Torp. "Demonstrating the Potential for Geological Storage of CO_2: The Sleipner and GESTCO Projects," *Environmental Geosciences* 8, 3 (2001): 160–166

Gale, J., and Y. Kaya (eds.). *Greenhouse Gas Control Technologies: Proceedings of the Sixth International Conference on Greenhouse Gas Control Technologies* (Oxford: Elsevier Science, 2003)

Garwin, R., and G. Charpak. *Megawatts and Megatons: A Turning Point in the Nuclear Age?* (New York: Knopf, 2001)

Geller, H. *Energy Revolution: Policies for a Sustainable Future* (Covelo, Calif.: Island Press, 2003)

Georgescu-Roegen, N. "The Crisis of Resources: Its Nature and Its Unfolding," in G. Daneke (ed.), *Energy, Economics and the Environment* (Lexington, Mass.: Lexington Books, 1982), 22
The Entropy Law and the Economic Process (Cambridge, Mass.: Harvard University Press, 1971)

Global Environmental Facility. *Renewable Energy: GEF Partners with Business for a Better World* (Washington, D.C.: Global Environmental Facility, 2001)

Goeller, H., and A. Weinberg. "The Age of Substitutability," *American Economic Review* 61 (1978): 1–11

Gold, T. *The Deep Hot Biosphere* (New York: Copernicus Books, 1999)

Goldemberg, J. (ed.). *World Energy Assessment: Energy and the Challenge of Sustainability* (New York: United Nations Development Programme, 2000)

Goldemberg, J., and T. Johansson (eds.). *World Energy Assessment: 2004 Update* (New York: United Nations Development Programme, 2004)

Goldemberg, J., T. Johansson, A. Reddy and R. Williams. *Energy for a Sustainable World* (New Delhi: Wiley-Eastern Limited, 1988)

Goodland, R. "Environmental Sustainability in the Hydro Industry: Disaggregating the Debate," in T. Dorcey (ed.), *Proceedings of the Workshop on 'Large Dams: Learning from the Past, Looking in the Future'* (Washington, D.C.: IUCN, World Conservation Union, and World Bank Group, 1997)

Goodstein, D. *Out of Gas: The End of the Age of Oil* (New York: Norton, 2004)

Green, C. "Potential Scale-Related Problems in Estimating the Costs of CO_2 Mitigation Policies," *Climatic Change* 44 (2000): 331–349

Greene, D. "CAFE or Price? An Analysis of the Effects of Federal Fuel Economy Regulations and Gasoline Price on New Car MPG, 1978–1989," *The Energy Journal* 11, 3 (1990): 37–57

Greene, D., J. Kahn and R. Gibson. "Fuel Economy Rebound Effect for US Household Vehicles," *The Energy Journal* 20, 3 (1999): 1–31

Greening, L., and S. Bernow. "Design of Coordinated Energy and Environmental Policies: Use of Multi-Criteria Decision-Making," *Energy Policy* 32 (2004): 721–735

Greening, L., D. Greene and C. Difiglio. "Energy Efficiency and Consumption – the Rebound Effect – a Survey," *Energy Policy* 28 (2000): 389–401

Griliches, Z. "Hybrid Corn: An Exploration in the Economics of Technological Change," *Econometrica* 25, 4 (1957): 501–522

Grimston, M., and P. Beck. *Double or Quits: The Global Future of Civil Nuclear Energy* (London: Earthscan, 2002)

Grubb, M. "Energy Efficiency and Economic Fallacies," *Energy Policy* 18, 8 (1990): 783–785

"Technologies, Energy Systems, and the Timing of CO_2 Emissions Abatement," *Energy Policy* 25 (1997): 159–172

Grubler, A. *Technology and Global Change* (Cambridge: Cambridge University Press, 1998)

Häfele, W. *Energy in a Finite World: A Global Systems Analysis* (Cambridge, Mass.: Ballinger, 1981)

Hahn, R., and R. Stavins. "Economic Incentives for Environmental Protection: Integrating Theory and Practice," *American Economic Review* 82, 2 (1992): 464–468

Hahn, R., and C. Sunstein. "The Precautionary Principle as a Basis for Decision Making," *The Economists' Voice* 2, 2, article 8 (2005): 1–10

Hammer, H., A. Lofgren and T. Sterner. "Political Economy Obstacles to Fuel Taxation," *The Energy Journal* 25, 3 (2004): 1–17

Haq, G., W. Han and C. Kim (eds.). *Urban Air Pollution Management and Practice in Major and Megacities of Asia,* Proceedings of Workshop, Air Pollution in the Megacities of Asia Project, Seoul, Korea (Seoul: Korea Environment Institute, 2002)

Haq, G., W. Han, C. Kim and H. Vallack. *Benchmarking Urban Air Quality Management and Practice in Major and Megacities of Asia* (Seoul: Korea Environment Institute, 2002)

Harrington, W., R. Morgenstern and T. Sterner (eds.). *Choosing Environmental Policy: Comparing Instruments and Outcomes in the United States and Europe* (Washington, D.C.: Resoures for the Future, 2004)

Hartwick, J. "Intergenerational Equity and the Investing of Rents from Exhaustible Resources," *American Economic Review* 66 (1977): 972–974

Hawken, P., A. Lovins and H. Lovins. *Natural Capitalism: Creating the Next Industrial Revolution* (Boston: Little, Brown, 1999)

Heal, G., and B. Kristrom. "Uncertainty and Climate Change," *Environmental and Resource Economics* 22 (2002): 3–39

Heinberg, R. *The Party's Over: Oil, War and the Fate of Industrial Societies* (Gabriola Island, B.C.: New Society Publishers, 2003)

Hirst, E. "Actual Energy Savings after Retrofit: Electrically Heated Homes in the Pacific Northwest," *Energy* 11 (1986): 299–308

Hitchon, B., W. Gunter, T. Gentzis and R. Bailey, "Sedimentary Basins and Greenhouse Gases: A Serendipitous Association," *Energy Conversion and Management* 40 (1999): 825–843

Hobbs, B., and P. Meier. *Energy Decisions and the Environment: A Guide to the Use of Multi-Criteria Methods* (Dordrecht: Kluwer Academic, 2000)

Hoffert, M., K. Caldeira, G. Benford, D. Criswell, C. Green, H. Herzog, A. Jain, H. Kheshgi, K. Lackner, J. Lewis, H. Lightfoot, W. Mannheimer, J. Mankins, M. Mauel, L. Perkins, M. Schlesinger, T. Volk and T. Wigley.

"Advanced Technology Paths to Global Climate Stability: Energy for a Greenhouse Planet," *Science* 298 (2002): 981–987

Hoffert, M., K. Caldeira, A. Jain, E. Haites, L. Harvey, S. Putter, M. Schlesinger, S. Schneider, R. Watts, T. Wigley and D. Wuebbles. "Energy Implications of Future Stabilization of Atmospheric CO_2 Content," *Nature* 395, 29 (1988): 881–884

Hoffman, P. *Tomorrow's Energy: Hydrogen, Fuel Cells and the Prospects for a Cleaner Planet* (Cambridge, Mass.: MIT Press, 2001)

Hohmeyer, O. *Social Costs of Energy Consumption* (Berlin: Springer-Verlag, 1988)

Hohmeyer, O., R. Ottinger and K. Rennings (eds.). *Social Costs and Sustainability: Valuation and Implementation in the Energy and Transport Sector* (Heidelberg: Springer, 1997)

Holdren, J. (chairperson). *Report to the President on Federal Energy Research and Development for the Challenges of the Twenty-first Century* (Washington, D.C.: President's Committee of Advisors on Science and Technology, Panel on Energy Research and Development, 1997)

Holling, C. "An Ecologist View of the Malthusian Conflict," in K. Lindahl-Kiessling and H. Landsberg (eds.), *Population, Economic Development and Environment* (Oxford: Oxford University Press, 1994)

Holloway, S. "Safety of Underground Disposal of Carbon Dioxide," *Energy Conversion and Management* 38 (1997): S241–245

Hubbert, M. "National Academy of Sciences Report on Energy Resources: Reply," *Bulletin of the American Association of Petroleum Geologists* 49, 10 (1965): 1720–1727

Intergovernmental Panel on Climate Change. *Climate Change 1995, Second Assessment Report* (Cambridge: Cambridge University Press, 1996)

Climate Change 2001, Third Assessment Report (Cambridge: Cambridge University Press, 2001)

IPCC Special Report on Carbon Dioxide Capture and Storage (Cambridge: Cambridge University Press, 2005)

Revised 1996 IPCC Guidelines for National Greenhouse Gas Inventories, Volume 3: *Reference Manual* (Paris: IPCC/OECD, 1997)

Special Report on Emissions Scenarios (Cambridge: Cambridge University Press, 2000)

Summary for Policy Makers, Synthesis Report, Climate Change 2001: Third Assessment Report (Cambridge: Cambridge University Press, 2001)

International Energy Agency. *Energy Balances of non-OECD Countries 1998–1999* (Paris: OECD, 2000)

Key World Energy Statistics 2004 (Paris: International Energy Agency, 2004)

Oil Crises and Climate Challenges: 30 Years of Energy Use in IEA Countries (Paris: International Energy Agency, 2004)

Photovoltaic Power Systems Programme, Trends in Photovoltaic Applications in selected IEA Countries between 1992 and 2001 (Paris: International Energy Agency, 2002)

Renewables in Global Energy Supply: an IEA Factsheet (Paris: International Energy Agency, 2002)

The Prospects for CO_2 Capture and Storage (Paris: International Energy Agency, 2004)

World Energy Investment Outlook (Paris: International Energy Agency, 2003)

World Energy Outlook (Paris: OECD, 2002)

Jaccard, M. "Renewable Portfolio Standard," in C. Cleveland (ed.), *Encyclopedia of Energy*, Volume 5 (New York: Elsevier, 2004), 413–421

"Policies that Mobilize Producers Toward Sustainability: The Renewable Portfolio Standard and the Vehicle Emission Standard," in G. Toner (ed.), *Building Canadian Capacity: Sustainable Production and the Knowledge Economy* (Vancouver: University of British Columbia Press, 2005)

Jaccard, M., A. Bailie and J. Nyboer. "CO_2 Emission Reduction Costs in the Residential Sector: Behavioral Parameters in a Bottom-Up Simulation Model," *The Energy Journal* 17, 4 (1996): 107–134

Jaccard, M., H. Chen and J. Li. "Renewable Portfolio Standard: A Tool for Environmental Policy in the Chinese Electricity Sector," *Energy for Sustainable Development*, special issue on China, 5, 4 (2001): 113–121

Jaccard, M., L. Failing and T. Berry. "From Equipment to Infrastructure: Community Energy Management and Greenhouse Gas Emission Reduction," *Energy Policy* 25, 11 (1997): 1065–1074

Jaccard, M., J. Nyboer, C. Bataille and B. Sadownik. "Modeling the Cost of Climate Policy: Distinguishing between Alternative Cost Definitions and Long-Run Cost Dynamics," *The Energy Journal* 24, 1 (2003): 49–73

Jaccard, M., J. Nyboer and A. Fogwill. "How Big is the Electricity Conservation Potential in Industry?" *The Energy Journal* 14, 2 (1993): 139–156

Jaccard, M., N. Rivers and M. Horne. *The Morning After: Optimal Greenhouse Gas Policies for Canada's Kyoto Obligations and Beyond* (Toronto: CD Howe Institute, 2004)

Jaccard, M., and Y. Mao. "Making Markets Work Better," in T. Johansson and J. Goldemberg (eds.), *Energy for Sustainable Development: A Policy Agenda* (New York: United Nations Development Programme, 2002)

Jackson, T. (ed.). *Mitigating Climate Change: Flexibility Mechanisms* (London: Elsevier Science, 2001)

Jacoby, H., and D. Ellerman. "The Safety Valve and Climate Policy," *Energy Policy* 32 (2004): 481–491

Jaffe, A., and R. Stavins. "The Energy-Efficiency Gap: What Does it Mean?" *Energy Policy* 22, 10 (1994): 804–810

Jaffe, A., R. Newell and R. Stavins. "Environmental Policy and Technological Change," *Environmental and Resource Economics* 22, 1–2 (2002): 41–69

Jansson, A., M. Hammer, C. Folke and R. Costanza (eds.). *Investing in Natural Capital: The Ecological Economics Approach to Sustainability* (Washington, D.C.: Island Press, 1994)

Jochem, E. (ed.). "Energy End-use Efficiency," chapter 6 in J. Goldemberg (ed.), *World Energy Assessment: Energy and the Challenge of Sustainability* (New York: United Nations Development Programme, 2000)

Johansson, T., B. Bodlund and R. Williams (eds.). *Electricity: Efficient End-Use and New Generation Technologies, and Their Planning Implications* (Lund: Lund University Press, 1989)

Johansson, T., H. Kelly, A. Reddy and R. Williams (eds.). *Renewable Energy: Sources for Fuels and Electricity* (Washington, D.C.: Island Press, 1993)

Joskow, P. "Utility-Subsidized Energy-Efficiency Programs," *Annual Review of Energy and the Environment* 20 (1995): 526–534

Joskow, P., and D. Marron. "What Does a Negawatt Really Cost? Evidence from Utility Conservation Programs," *The Energy Journal* 13, 4 (1992): 41–74

Kammen, D., and D. Hassenzahl. *Should We Risk It? Exploring Environmental, Health, and Technological Problem Solving* (Princeton, N.J.: Princeton University Press, 1999)

Kammen, D., and S. Pacca. "Assessing the Costs of Electricity," *Annual Review of Environment and Resources* 29 (2004): 301–344

Karamanos, P. "Voluntary Environmental Agreements: Evolution and Definition of a New Environmental Policy Approach," *Journal of Environmental Planning and Management* 44, 1 (2001): 67–84

Keeney, R., and H. Raiffa. *Decisions with Multiple Objectives: Preferences and Value Tradeoffs* (New York: Wiley, 1976)

Kemp, R. *Environmental Policy and Technical Change: A Comparison of Technological Impact of Policy Instruments* (Cheltenham: Edward Elgar, 1997)

Zero Emission Vehicle Mandate in California. Misguided Policy or Example of Enlightened Leadership? (University of Maastricht: MERIT, 2003)

Khanna, M. "Non-Mandatory Approaches for Environmental Protection," *Journal of Economic Surveys* 15, 3 (2001): 291–324

Khazzoom, D. "Energy Savings Resulting from the Adoption of More Efficient Appliances," *The Energy Journal* 8, 4 (1987): 85–89

Kraushaar, J., and R. Ristinen. *Energy and the Problems of a Technical Society* (New York: Wiley, 1993)

Krautkraemer, J. "Non-renewable Resource Scarcity," *Journal of Economic Literature* 36, 4 (1998): 2065–2107

Kruger, J., and W. Pizer. *The EU Emissions Trading Directive: Opportunities and Potential Pitfalls* (Washington, D.C.: Resources for the Future, 2004)

Kwoka, J. "The Limits of Market-Oriented Regulatory Techniques: The Case of Automotive Fuel Economy," *Quarterly Journal of Economics* 98, 4 (1983): 695–704

Leggett, J. *The Carbon War: Global Warming and the End of the Oil Era* (New York: Penguin Books, 1999)

Leggett, J., W. Pepper and R. Swart. "Emissions Scenarios for IPCC: An Update," in J. Houghton, B. Callander and S. Varney (eds.), *Climate Change 1992: The Supplementary Report to the IPCC Scientific Assessment* (Cambridge: Cambridge University Press, 1992)

Levine, M., E. Hirst, J. Koomey, J. McMahon and A. Sanstad. *Energy Efficiency, Market Failures, and Government Policy* (Berkeley, Calif.: Lawrence Berkeley Laboratory, 1994)

Lomborg, B. *The Skeptical Environmentalist: Measuring the Real State of the World* (Cambridge: Cambridge University Press, 2001)

Loughran, D., and J. Kulick. "Demand Side Management and Energy Efficiency in the United States," *The Energy Journal* 25, 1 (2004): 19–43

Lovins, A. "Energy Savings Resulting from the Adoption of More Efficient Appliances: Another View," *Energy Journal* 9, 2 (1988): 155–162

  "Negawatts: Twelve Transitions, Eight Improvements, and One Distraction," *Energy Policy* 24, 4 (1996): 331–343

  "Saving Gigabucks with Negawatts," *Public Utilities Fortnightly* 115, 6 (1985): 19–26

  Soft Energy Paths: Toward a Durable Peace (San Francisco: Friends of the Earth International; Cambridge, Mass.: Ballinger Publishing, 1977)

Lovins, A., E. Datta, O.-E. Bustness, J. Koomey and N. Glasgow. *Winning the Oil Endgame: Innovation, Profits, Jobs and Security* (Snowmass, Colo.: Rocky Mountain Institute, 2004)

Lovins, A., E. Datta, T. Feiler, K. Rabago, J. Swisher, A. Lehmann and K. Wicker. *Small is Profitable: the Hidden Economic Benefits of Making*

Electrical Resources the Right Size (Snowmass, Colo.: Rocky Mountain Institute, 2002)

Lovins, A., L. Lovins, F. Krause and W. Bach. *Least-Cost Energy: Solving the CO_2 Problem* (Andover, Mass.: Brick House Publishing, 1981)

Lovins, A., J. Neymark, T. Flanigan, P. Kiernan, B. Bancroft and M. Sheppard. *The State of the Art: Drivepower* (Snowmass, Colo.: Rocky Mountain Institute, 1989)

Lyman, E., and S. Dolley. "Accident Prone," *Bulletin of the Atomic Scientists* 56, 2 (2000): 42–46

Lynch, M. *Facing the Elephant: Oil Market Evaluation and Future Oil Crises.* (Boulder: International Research Center for Energy and Economic Development, 1998)

Maddison, A. *The World Economy: A Millennial Perspective* (Paris: OECD, 2001)

Marchetti, C. "Hydrogen and Energy," *Chemical Economy and Engineering Review* 5, 1 (1973): 7–25

Marland G., T. Boden and R. Andres. "Global, Regional, and National CO_2 Emissions," in *Trends: A Compendium of Data on Global Change* (Oak Ridge, Tenn.: Carbon Dioxide Information Analysis Center, Oak Ridge National Laboratory, 2001)

McKibbin, W. and P. Wilcoxen. *A Better Way to Slow Global Climate Change* (Washington, D.C.: Brookings Institute, 1997)

McNeill, J. *An Environmental History of the Twentieth-Century World* (New York: Norton, 2000)

Menanteau, P., D. Finon and M.-L. Lamy. "Prices Versus Quantities: Choosing Policies for Promoting the Development of Renewable Energy," *Energy Policy* 31 (2003): 799–812

Metcalf, G., and K. Hassett. "Measuring the Energy Savings from Home Improvement Investments: Evidence from Monthly Billing Data," *Review of Economics and Statistics* 81, 3 (1999): 516–528

Millman, S., and R. Prince. "Firm Incentives to Promote Technological Change in Pollution Control," *Journal of Environmental Economics and Management* 17, 3 (1989): 247–265

Morgan, M., and M. Henrion. *Uncertainty: A Guide to Dealing with Uncertainty in Quantitative Risk and Policy Analysis* (New York: Cambridge University Press, 1990)

Moxnes, E. "Estimating Customer Costs or Benefits of Energy Efficiency Standards," *Journal of Economic Psychology* 25, 6 (2005): 707–724

Mueller, D. *Public Choice II* (Cambridge: Cambridge University Press, 1989)

Mulder, P., H. De Groot and M. Hofkes. "Economic Growth and Technological Change: A Comparison of Insights from a Neo-Classical and an Evolutionary Perspective," *Technological Forecasting and Social Change* 68 (2001): 151–171

Munasinghe, M., and W. Shearer. *Defining and Measuring Sustainability: The Biogeophysical Foundations* (Washington, D.C.: World Bank, 1995)

Nadel, S. *Lessons Learned: A Review of Utility Experience with Conservation and Load Management Programs for Commercial and Industrial Customers*, Report no. 1064-EEED-AEP-88 (New York: American Council for an Energy-Efficient Economy, 1990)

Nakicenovic, N. (ed.). "Energy Scenarios," chapter 9 in J. Goldemberg (ed.), *World Energy Assessment: Energy and the Challenge of Sustainability* (New York: United Nations Development Programme, 2000)

Nakicenovic N., and A. Grubler. "Energy and the Protection of the Atmosphere," *International Journal of Global Energy Issues* 13, 1–3 (2000): 4–56

Nakicenovic, N., A. Grubler and A. McDonald (eds.). *Global Energy Perspectives* (Cambridge: Cambridge University Press, 1998)

Nanduri, M., J. Nyboer and M. Jaccard. "Aggregating Physical Intensity Indicators: Results of Applying the Composite Indicator Approach to the Canadian Industrial Sector," *Energy Policy* 30 (2002): 151–163

Nelson, R., and S. Winter. *An Evolutionary Theory of Economic Change* (Cambridge, Mass.: Harvard University Press, 1982)

Newell, R., A. Jaffe and R. Stavins. "The Induced Innovation Hypothesis and Energy-Saving Technological Change," *Quarterly Journal of Economics* 114 (1999): 941–975

Nichols, A. "Demand-Side Management: Overcoming Market Barriers or Obscuring Real Costs," *Energy Policy* 22, 10 (1994): 840–847

Nordhaus, R., and K. Danish. *Designing a Mandatory Greenhouse Gas Reduction Program for the US* (Washington, D.C.: Pew Center on Global Climate Change, 2003)

Nordhaus, W. "The Allocation of Energy Resources," *Brookings Papers on Economic Activity* (1973/74): 529–570

Northwest Power Planning Council. *Columbia River Basin Fish and Wildlife Program: A Multi-Species Approach for Decision Making* (Portland, Ore.: Northwest Power Planning Council, 2000)

Nuclear Energy Agency. *Projected Costs of Generating Electricity* (Paris: Nuclear Energy Agency, 1998)

Odell, P. "Dynamics of Energy Technologies and Global Change," *Energy Policy* 27, 13 (1999): 737–742

Oil and Gas: Crises and Controversies 1961–2000 (Brentwood, UK: Multi-Science, 2001)

Why Carbon Fuels Will Dominate the 21st Century's Global Energy Economy (Brentwood, UK: Multi-Science, 2004)

Ogden, J. "Prospects for Building a Hydrogen Energy Infrastructure," *Annual Review of Energy and the Environment* 24 (1999): 227–279

Ogden, J., and R. Williams. *Solar Hydrogen: Moving Beyond Fossil Fuels* (Washington, D.C.: World Resources Institute, 1989)

Ogden, J., R. Williams and E. Larson, "Societal Lifecycle Costs of Cars with Alternative Fuels/Engines," *Energy Policy* 32 (2004): 7–27

Olivier, J., A. Bouwman, K. Van der Hoek and J. Berdowski. "Global Air Emission Inventories for Anthropogenic Sources of NO_x, NH_3 and N_2O in 1990," *Environmental Pollution* 102 (1998): 135–143

Olsen, M. *The Logic of Collective Action* (Cambridge: Cambridge University Press, 1965)

O'Neill, B., F. L. MacKellar and W. Lutz. *Population and Climate Change* (Cambridge: Cambridge University Press; Laxenburg, Austria: IIASA, 2001)

Organization for Economic Cooperation and Development. *Economic Instruments for Pollution Control and Natural Resources Management in OECD Countries: A Survey* (Paris: OECD, 1999)

Outlook 2000 – Perspectives 2000 (Paris: OECD, 2000)

Voluntary Approaches for Environmental Policy: Effectiveness, Efficiency, and Usage in the Policy Mixes (Paris: OECD, 2003)

Ottinger, R., D. Wooley, N. Robinson, D. Hodas and S. Babb. *Environmental Costs of Electricity* (New York: Oceana, 1990)

Pacala, S., and R. Socolow. "Stabilization Wedges: Solving the Climate Problem for the Next 50 Years with Current Technologies," *Science* 13 (2004): 968–972

Paffenbarger, J., G. Lammers and C. Ocaña. *Electricity Reform: Power Generation Costs and Investment* (Paris: International Energy Agency, 1999)

Palmer, K., W. Oates and P. Portney. "Tightening Environmental Standards: The Benefit-Cost or the No-Cost Paradigm?" *Journal of Economic Perspectives* 9 (1995): 119–132

Palmgren, C., M. Morgan, W. Bruine de Bruin and D. Keith. "Initial Public Perceptions of Deep Geological and Oceanic Disposal of Carbon Dioxide," *Environmental Science and Technology* 38, 24 (2004): 6441–6450

Panwar, T. "Air Pollution Management in India," in G. Haq, W. Han and C. Kim (eds.), *Urban Air Pollution Management and Practice in Major and Megacities of Asia*, Proceedings of Workshop, Air Pollution in the Megacities of Asia Project, Seoul, Korea (Seoul: Korea Environment Institute, 2002)

Parry, I., W. Williams, C. Roberton III and L. Goulder. "When Can Carbon Abatement Policies Increase Welfare? The Fundamental Role of Distorted Factor Markets," *Journal of Environmental Economics and Management* 37, 1 (1999): 52–84

Patterson, M. "What is Energy Efficiency?" *Energy Policy* 24, 5 (1996): 377–390

Perrings, C. "Reserved Rationality and the Precautionary Principle: Technological Change, Time, and Uncertainty in Environmental Decision Making," in R. Costanza (ed.), *Ecological Economics: The Science and Management of Sustainability* (New York: Columbia University Press, 1991)

Peterson, C., S. Rice, J. Short, D. Esler, J. Bodkin, B. Ballachey and D. Irons. "Long-Term Ecosystem Response to the *Exxon Valdez* Oil Spill," *Science* 302 (2003): 2082–2086

Pigou, A. *The Economics of Welfare* (London: Macmillan, 1920)

Pindyck, R. "Irreversibility, Uncertainty and Investment," *Journal of Economic Literature* 29, 3 (1991): 1110–1152

Pitzer, K. *Thermodynamics* (New York: McGraw-Hill, 1995)

Pizer, W. "Optimal Choice of Policy Instrument and Stringency under Uncertainty: The Case of Climate Change," *Resource and Energy Economics* 21 (1999): 255–287

Popp, D. "Induced Innovation and Energy Prices," *American Economic Review* 92, 1 (2002): 160–180

Porter, M., and C. van der Linde. "Toward a New Conception of the Environment-Competitiveness Relationship," *Journal of Economic Perspectives* 9 (1995): 97–118

Rabl, A., and J. Spadaro. "Public Health Impact of Air Pollution and Implications for the Energy System," *Annual Review of Energy and the Environment* 25 (2000): 601–627

Radetzki, M. "Coal or Nuclear in New Power Stations: Political Economy of an Undesirable but Necessary Choice," *The Energy Journal* 21, 1 (2000): 135–147

Ramesohl, S., and G. Boyd. "Advances in Energy Forecasting Models Based on Engineering Economics," *Annual Review of Environment and Resources* 29 (2004): 345–381

Raskin, P., T. Banuri, G. Gallopin, P. Gutman, A. Hammond, R. Kates and R. Swart. *Great Transition: The Promise and Lure of the Times Ahead* (Stockholm: Stockholm Environment Institute, 2002)

Rasmussen, N. (ed.). *Reactor Safety Study: An Assessment of Accident Risks in US Commercial Nuclear Power Plants* (Washington, D.C.: Nuclear Regulatory Commission, 1975)

Reddy, A. "Energy Technologies and Policies for Rural Development," in T. Johansson and J. Goldemberg (eds.), *Energy for Sustainable Development: A Policy Agenda* (New York: United Nations Development Programme, 2002): 115–136

Rhodes, J., and D. Keith. "Biomass Energy with Geological Sequestration of CO_2: Two for the Price of One," in J. Gale and Y. Kaya (eds.), *Greenhouse Gas Control Technologies*, Proceedings of the Sixth International Conference on Greenhouse Gas Control Technologies (Oxford: Elsevier Science, 2003), 1371–1377

Rifkin, J. *The Hydrogen Economy: The Creation of the Worldwide Energy Web and the Redistribution of Power on Earth* (New York: Tarcher/Putnam, 2002)

Robert, K.-H., B. Schmidt-Bleek, J. Aloisi de Larderel, G. Basile, J. Jansen, R. Kuehr, P. Price Thomas, M. Suzuki, P. Hawken and M. Wackernagel. "Strategic Sustainable Development – Selection, Design and Synergies of Applied Tools," *Journal of Cleaner Production* 10 (2002): 197–214

Roberts, M., and M. Spence. "Effluent Charges and Licenses under Uncertainty," *Journal of Public Economics* 5 (1976): 193–208

Roberts, P. *The End of Oil: On the Edge of a Perilous New World* (New York: Houghton Mifflin 2004)

Rogner, H.-H. "An Assessment of World Hydrocarbon Resources," *Annual Review of Energy and the Environment* 22 (1997): 217–262

Rogner, H.-H. (ed.). "Energy Resources," chapter 5 in J. Goldemberg (ed.), *World Energy Assessment: Energy and the Challenge of Sustainability* (New York: United Nations Development Programme, 2000)

Romm, J. *The Hype About Hydrogen: Fact and Fiction in the Race to Save the Planet* (New York: Island Press, 2004)

Rothman, D., and S. de Bruyn (eds.). "Probing into the Environmental Kuznets Curve Hypothesis," special issue, *Ecological Economics* 25 (1998)

Ryan, J. "Hubbert's Peak: Déjà Vu All Over Again," *International Association of Energy Economics Newsletter*, 2nd Quarter, 2003

Ryan, M. "Fuel Costs Taking More of O&M Budget: Even as Costs Drop, Efficiency Rises," *Nuclear Fuel* 24, 14 (1999): 1–10

Sanden, B., and C. Azar. "Near-Term Technology Policies for Long-Term Climate Targets – Economy Wide Versus Technology Specific Approaches," *Energy Policy* 33 (2005): 1557–1576

Sanstad, A., and R. Howarth. "Normal Markets, Market Imperfections, and Energy Efficiency," *Energy Policy* 22, 10 (1994): 811–818

Schafer, A., and D. Victor. "The Future Mobility of the World Population," *Transportation Research Part A* 34 (2000): 171–205

Scheer, H. *The Solar Economy: Renewable Energy for a Sustainable Global Future* (London: Earthscan, 2002)

Scheraga, J. "Energy and the Environment: Something New under the Sun?" *Energy Policy* 22, 10 (1994): 811–818

Schipper, L. (ed.). "On the Rebound: The Interaction of Energy Efficiency, Energy Use and Economic Activity," *Energy Policy* 28, 6–7 (2000): 351–354

Schipper, L., S. Meyers and H. Kelly. *Coming in from the Cold: Energy-Wise Housing in Sweden* (Santa Ana, Calif.: Seven Locks Press, 1985)

Schmidt-Bleek, F. *MIPS and Factor 10 for a Sustainable and Profitable Economy* (Wuppertal: Wuppertal Institute, 1997)

Schumacher, E. *Small is Beautiful: A Study of Economics as if People Mattered* (London: Blond and Briggs, 1973)

Schumpeter, J. *The Theory of Economic Development* (Cambridge, Mass.: Harvard University Press, 1934)

Sebold, F., and E. Fox. "Realized Savings from Residential Conservation Activity," *The Energy Journal* 6, 2 (1985): 73–88

Shackley, S., C. McLachlan and C. Gough. *The Public Perceptions of Carbon Capture and Storage* (Manchester: Tyndall Centre for Climate Change Research, 2004)

Sharp, J., M. Jaccard and D. Keith. *Public Attitudes Toward Geological Disposal of Carbon Dioxide in Canada*, Report to Environment Canada and the Alberta Ministry of Environment (Vancouver: Simon Fraser University, 2005)

Shell International Inc. *Exploring the Future: Energy Needs and Possibilities* (London: Shell International Inc., 2001)

Simon, H. "Prediction and Prescription in Systems Modeling," *Operations Research* 38, 1 (1990): 7–14

Simon, J. *The Ultimate Resource* (Princeton, N.J.: Princeton University Press, 1981)

The Ultimate Resource II (Princeton, N.J.: Princeton University Press, 1996)

Sims, R., H.-H. Rogner and K. Gregory. "Carbon Emission and Mitigation Cost Comparisons between Fossil Fuel, Nuclear and Renewable Energy Resources for Electricity Generation," *Energy Policy* 31 (2003): 1315–1326

Skinner, R., and R. Arnott. *The Oil Supply and Demand Context for Security of Oil Supply to the EU from the GCC Countries* (Oxford: Oxford Institute for Energy Studies, 2005)

Slovic, P. "Perceived Risk, Trust and Democracy," *Risk Analysis* 13 (1993): 675–682

Smil, V. *Energy at the Crossroads* (Cambridge, Mass.: MIT Press, 2003)
  "Energy in the Twentieth Century: Resources, Conversions, Costs, Uses, and Consequences," *Annual Review of Energy and the Environment* 25 (2000): 21–51

Smith, S., H. Pitcher and T. Wigley. "Global and Regional Anthropogenic Sulphur Dioxide Emissions," *Global and Planetary Change* 29, 1–2 (2001): 99–119

Soderholm, P., and T. Sundqvist. "Pricing Environmental Externalities in the Power Sector: Ethical Limits and Implications for Social Choice," *Ecological Economics* 46 (2003): 333–350

Solow, R. "The Economics of Resources or the Resources of Economics," *American Economic Review* 64 (1974): 1–14
  "On the Intertemporal Allocation of Natural Resources," *Scandinavian Journal of Economics* 88 (1986): 141–149
  "Sustainability: An Economist's Perspective," in R. Dorfman and N. Dorfman (eds.), *Economics of the Environment: Selected Readings* (New York: Norton, 1993), 179–187

Stavins, R. "The Costs of Carbon Sequestration: A Revealed Preference Approach," *American Economic Review* 89, 4 (1999): 994–1009

Stirling, A. "Science and Precaution in the Appraisal of Electricity Supply Options," *Journal of Hazardous Materials* 86 (2001): 55–75

Stoneman, P. *The Economics of Technological Diffusion* (London: Blackwell, 2002)

Suskind, R. *The Price of Loyalty: George W. Bush, the White House, and the Education of Paul O'Neil* (New York: Simon and Schuster, 2003)

Sutherland, R. "The Economics of Energy Conservation Policy," *Energy Policy* 24, 4 (1996): 361–370
  "Market Barriers to Energy Efficiency Investments," *The Energy Journal*, 12, 3 (1991): 15–34

Svendsen, G. *Public Choice and Environmental Regulation: Tradable Permit Systems in the United States and CO_2 Taxation in Europe* (Cheltenham: Edward Elgar, 1998)

Sweeney, J. *The California Electricity Crisis* (Stanford, Calif.: Hoover Institution Press, 2002)

Tainter, J. *The Collapse of Complex Societies* (Cambridge: Cambridge University Press, 1988)

Thomas, C., B. James, F. Lomax and I. Kuhn. "Fuel Options for the Fuel Cell Vehicle: Hydrogen, Methanol or Gasoline?" *International Journal of Hydrogen Energy* 25 (2000): 551–567

Train, K. "Incentives for Energy Conservation in the Commercial and Industrial Sectors," *The Energy Journal* 9, 3 (1988): 113–128

Turkenburg, W. (ed.). "Advanced Energy Supply Technologies," chapter 7 in J. Goldemberg (ed.), *World Energy Assessment: Energy and the Challenge of Sustainability* (New York: United Nations Development Programme, 2000)

Turner, J. "Sustainable Hydrogen Production," *Science* 305 (2004): 972–974

Turton H., and L. Barreto. "Automobile Technology, Hydrogen and Climate Change: A Long-Term Modeling Analysis," *International Journal of Energy Technology and Policy* (forthcoming, 2005)

Tzimas, E., and S. Peteves. "The Impact of Carbon Sequestration on the Production Cost of Electricity and Hydrogen from Coal and Natural Gas Technologies in Europe in the Medium Term," *Energy* 30 (2005): 2672–2689

Union of Concerned Scientists. *Energy Security: Solutions to Protect America's Power Supply and Reduce Oil Dependence* (Cambridge, Mass.: Union of Concerned Scientists, 2000)

United Nations. *Millennium Ecosystem Assessment Synthesis Report* (New York: United Nations, 2005)

   World Urbanization Prospects: The 2001 Revisions, Data Tables and Highlights (New York: Population Division, Department of Economic and Social Affairs, United Nations Secretariat, 2002)

Unruh, G. "Understanding Carbon Lock-in," *Energy Policy* 28 (2000): 817–830

US Congressional Record, 1875

US Department of Energy. *National Energy Technology Laboratory Report on Proposed Capacity Additions* (Washington, D.C.: US Department of Energy, 2004)

US Energy Information Administration. *Annual Energy Review 2002* (Washington, D.C.: US Department of Energy, 2003)

   International Energy Annual 2001 (Washington, D.C.: US Department of Energy, 2002)

   International Energy Outlook 2004 (Washington, D.C.: US Department of Energy, 2004)

US Environmental Protection Agency. *Achieving Clean Air and Clean Water: The Report of the Blue Ribbon Panel on Oxygenates in Gasoline*, EPA420-R-99-021 (Washington, D.C.: Environmental Protection Agency, 1999)

   AP-42: Compilation of Air Pollutant Emission Factors, Volume II: *Mobile Sources*, 5th edition (Research Triangle Park, N.C.: US Environmental Protection Agency, 2001)

National Air Pollutant Emission Trends Report, 1900–1995 (Research Triangle Park, N.C.: US Environmental Protection Agency, 1996)

National Emission Inventory Emission Trends Data (Washington, D.C.: Environmental Protection Agency, 2003)

US General Accounting Office. *Acid Rain: Emissions Trends and Effects in the Eastern United States* (Washington, D.C.: General Accounting Office, 2000)

Vaitheeswaran, V. *Power to the People* (New York: Farrar, Straus and Giroux, 2003)

van den Burgh, J., and J. Gowdy. "Evolutionary Theories in Environmental and Resource Economics: Approaches and Applications," *Environmental and Resource Economics* 17 (2000): 37–57

van der Zwaan, B. "Nuclear Energy: Tenfold Expansion or Phase-Out?" *Technological Forecasting and Social Change* 69 (2002): 287–307

Victor, D. *The Collapse of the Kyoto Protocol and the Struggle to Slow Global Warming* (Princeton, N.J.: Princeton University Press, 2001)

Viklund, M. "Energy Policy Options – From the Perspective of Public Attitudes and Risk Perceptions," *Energy Policy* 32 (2004): 1159–1171

Violette, D. *Evaluating Greenhouse Gas Mitigation through DSM Projects: Lessons Learned from DSM Evaluation in the United States* (Boulder: Hagler Bailly Consulting, 1998)

Von Weiszacker, E., A. Lovins and L. Lovins. *The Factor Four – Doubling Wealth, Halving Resource Use* (London: Earthscan, 1997)

Wachs, M., and D. Beal. "Taxing our Highways," *Westways*, November/December 2000

Wackernagel, M., and W. Rees. *Our Ecological Footprint: Reducing Human Impact on Earth* (Stony Creek, Conn.: New Society Publishers, 1996)

Walsh, M. "Global Trends in Motor Vehicle Use and Emissions," *Annual Review of Energy and the Environment* 15 (1990): 217–243

Watkins, C. "Oil Scarcity: What Have the Past Three Decades Revealed?" *Energy Policy* (forthcoming, 2005)

Weidou, N., T. Johansson, J. Wang, Z. Wu, Y. Mao, Q. Zhu, F. Zhou, Z. Li, B. Anderson, U. Farinelli, M. Jaccard and R. Williams. "Transforming Coal for Sustainability: A Strategy for China," *Energy for Sustainable Development* 7, 4 (2003): 21–30

Weitzman, M. "Prices vs. Quantities," *Review of Economic Studies* 41 (1974): 477–491

Williams, R. "Nuclear and Alternative Energy Supply Options for an Environmentally Constrained World: A Long-Term Perspective," in P. Leventhal, S. Dolley and S. Tanzer (eds.), *Nuclear Power and the*

Spread of Nuclear Weapons: Can We Have One Without the Other? (Washington, D.C.: Brassey's Inc., 2002)

Williamson, O. *The Economic Institutions of Capitalism* (New York: Free Press, 1985)

Wilson, E. *The Future of Life* (New York: Knopf, 2002)

Wirl, F. *The Economics of Conservation Programs* (Boston: Kluwer Academic, 1997)

   "Lessons from Utility Conservation Programs," *The Energy Journal* 21, 1 (2000): 87–108

Woodward, R., and R. Bishop. "How to Decide when Experts Disagree: Uncertainty-Based Choice Rules in Environmental Policy," *Land Economics* 73, 4 (1997): 492–507

World Bank. *Energy Services for the World's Poor* (Washington, D.C.: World Bank, 2000)

World Commission on Environment and Development. *Our Common Future* (New York: Oxford University Press, 1987)

World Energy Council. *Survey of Energy Resources 2001* (London: World Energy Council, 2001)

World Health Organization. *World Health Report 2002: Reducing Risks, Promoting Healthy Life* (Geneva: World Health Organization, 2002)

Worrell, E., S. Ramesohl and G. Boyd. "Advances in Energy Forecasting Models Based on Engineering Economics," *Annual Review of Environment and Resources* 29 (2004): 345–381

Yamashita, K., and L. Barreto. "Energyplexes for the 21st Century: Coal Gasification for Co-producing Hydrogen, Electricity and Liquid Fuels," *Energy* 30 (2005): 2453–2473

Zittel, W., W. Weindorf, R. Wurster and W. Bussmann. "Geothermal Hydrogen – A Vision?" Paper presented at European Geothermal Energy Council's 2nd Business Seminar, European Geothermal Energy Council 2001, Altheim, Austria

Synopsis and chapter reading guide

Synopsis

More and more people believe we must quickly wean ourselves from fossil fuels to save the planet from environmental catastrophe, incessant oil conflicts and economic collapse. This view is epitomized by the claim in one of many recent anti-fossil-fuel books that "Civilization as we know it will come to an end sometime in this century unless we can find a way to live without fossil fuels."[1]

This view is misguided. This book explains why.

Those who argue that the end of fossil fuels is nigh usually start with evidence that we consume conventional oil faster than we find it, and then link this to the latest energy price spike and geopolitical conflict. What they overlook is that a peak in the production of "conventional oil" is unlikely to be of great significance given the potential for substitution among the planet's enormous total resources of conventional and unconventional oil, conventional and unconventional natural gas, as well as coal. Refined petroleum products like gasoline and diesel can be produced from any of these other fossil fuels, and indeed are produced today from unconventional oil in the form of oil sands (Canada), natural gas (Qatar) and coal (South Africa). The planet has perhaps 800 years of coal at today's use rate and an even longer horizon for natural gas if we exploit untapped resources like deep geopressurized gas and gas hydrates. While this substitution potential does not mean that energy supply markets will always operate smoothly – prices can oscillate, sometimes dramatically, from one year or decade to the next – it suggests that we should not misinterpret periods of high prices as indicating the imminent demise of our still plentiful fossil fuel resources.

---

[1] D. Goodstein, *Out of Gas: The End of the Age of Oil* (New York: Norton, 2004), 123.

When it comes to fossil fuels, those worried about resource exhaustion find common cause with those worried about environmental impacts. But we can use fossil fuels with lower impacts and less risk.

Fossil fuels are a high quality form of stored solar energy – the result of millions of years of photosynthesis that grew plants and the animals that fed upon them, the decomposing remains of both of which were trapped in sediments and eventually transformed through subterranean pressures into natural gas, oil and coal. When humans are ignorant or uncaring about the impacts of using this source of energy, they can create great harm to themselves and the environment. Open pit coalmines destroy mountains and valleys. Oil spills soil coastlines and harm wildlife. Uncontrolled burning pollutes the air in homes and cities, acidifies lakes and forests, and risks major climate disruption.

This litany of impacts and risks presents a black image for fossil fuels. However, the history of fossil fuel use is also one of humans detecting and then successfully addressing its environmental challenges. Industrialized countries are the most dependent on fossil fuels, and yet in these countries indoor air quality is excellent compared to all of human history since the discovery of fire (with a huge benefit for life expectancy), urban air quality is better in many cities than it was 100 years ago, and acid emissions have fallen in some regions by over 50% in the past 30 years.

The latest challenge is CO_2 emissions from fossil fuel combustion, the most significant of the human-produced greenhouse gases that threaten to raise global temperatures and disrupt weather patterns and ecosystems. But in the decade or so that researchers have grappled seriously with this challenge many promising solutions have appeared. Fossil fuels can be converted to clean forms of energy – electricity, hydrogen and cleaner-burning synthetic fuels like methanol and dimethyl ether – through gasification processes that enable the capture of carbon and its safe storage, most likely deep in the earth's sedimentary formations.

There are costs. Estimates from independent researchers suggest that zero-emission fossil fuel production of electricity would increase final electricity prices by 25–50% were this technology to become universally applied. Researchers also suggest that the cost of vehicle use would increase by about the same percentage as we shifted from gasoline and diesel to primarily hydrogen, electricity and some biofuels for personal mobility. This increase, which is less than recent price jumps of electricity, gasoline, heating oil and natural gas in many jurisdictions, implies that the cost of energy would climb over the next century from its current level of 6% to about 8% of a typical family's budget in an industrialized country – remaining much lower than it was 100 years ago and than it is today for a poor family in a developing country. Thus, to shift our use of fossil fuels to these zero-emission processes over the course of this century would result in real energy price increases of much less than 1% per year during the next three to five decades.

Even if we can use fossil fuels cleanly, however, we might prefer to switch to other options sooner in order to ensure that our energy system is not a house of cards that collapses when we deplete our lower cost fossil fuels. But this decision requires careful consideration of the difficulties and costs involved in forcing the switch quickly versus allowing it to occur gradually as the cost of fossil fuels trends upward in the distant future. We need to have a realistic view of the other options – the "usual suspects" of energy efficiency, nuclear power and renewable energy.

Energy efficiency has great potential according to physicists, engineers and environmentalists. There are, however, significant countervailing factors that will hinder efforts to make dramatic efficiency gains. First, efficiency gains lower the cost of energy services and therefore incite some greater use of existing technologies, and especially the innovation and commercialization of related energy-using technologies, a feedback effect that has caused energy consumption in industrializing countries to grow almost as fast as economic activity over the past two centuries. Ambitious increases in energy efficiency require a dramatic rise in the cost of energy in order to prevent the widespread adoption of the myriad of energy-using innovations commercialized every year. But, as noted, the shift to zero-emission energy supplies, whether from renewables, nuclear or fossil fuels, is unlikely to increase final energy prices by more than 25–50% from current levels. Second, the energy system itself will consume increasing amounts of energy in the process of converting lower quality and less accessible primary energy sources (unconventional oil, unconventional gas, coal and renewables) into higher quality and cleaner secondary energy (electricity, hydrogen and synthetic fuels). The net effect is to decrease the overall efficiency of the global energy system. Third, the more than 50% increase in the world's population over this century will happen mostly in poorer regions of the world, where energy use is minimal. Even a marginal increase in energy use by people in these countries to provide the most basic services has a profound implication for aggregate energy use at the global scale. Thus, while we should pursue energy efficiency, it is likely that the global energy system will still expand three- or four-fold over this century, especially as people in developing countries use their rising incomes to enjoy energy services that most people in wealthier countries take for granted.

Nuclear power is potentially inexhaustible, but it must overcome public fears about radiation leaks from operational accidents, waste storage and even terrorist attacks, as well as superpower concerns about nuclear weapons proliferation. To make significant advances, therefore, nuclear must be substantially cheaper than its competitors for providing zero-emission energy. Most cost estimates, however, suggest that it will be cost-competitive at best and perhaps more expensive when the full costs of facility decommissioning, waste disposal and insurance liability are accounted for. The use of nuclear will grow in some regions, but for the next 100 years its share of the global energy system is unlikely to expand much beyond its current 3%. In the more distant future, developments in fusion technology or other non-radiating nuclear alternatives may expand its opportunities.

Renewable energy is seemingly inexhaustible and environmentally benign, yet many of its manifestations are characterized by low energy density, variability of output and inconvenient location. This will often require dedicated facilities for energy concentration, storage and transmission, and these can cause significant environmental and human impacts depending on their character and scale. The dams and reservoirs of large hydropower projects flood valuable valley bottoms and impede migratory fish and animals, windpower farms can conflict with scenic, wildlife and other values, and biomass energy plantations compete for fertile land with agriculture and forestry. As the contribution of renewables grows in scale, the associated energy concentration and storage costs will become more of an issue. Even when helped by strong policies, it takes time for renewables-using innovations to achieve the commercialization and expanded production that is necessary to lower costs. Starting from the negligible market share of renewables today, and in a growing global energy system, it will be an enormous and likely very expensive endeavor to force the wholesale replacement of fossil fuels with a renewables-dominated system in the course of just one century.

In anticipating the relative contribution of each of these energy options over this century, it is important not to confuse means and ends. The end is not an energy system dominated by renewables or nuclear or fossil fuels. The end is a low impact and low risk energy system that can meet expanded human energy needs indefinitely and do this as inexpensively as possible, without succumbing to cataclysmic forces at some future time. With this sustainable energy system as the goal, it is unjustifiable to rule out fossil fuels in advance of a holistic comparison that considers critical decision factors. These factors include cost, of course, but also the general human desire to minimize the risk of extreme events (like a major nuclear accident), to ensure adequate and reliable energy supplies free from geopolitical turmoil, and to sustain values, institutions and lifestyles.

Even though it will perhaps triple in size over this century, the global energy system should nonetheless reduce its environmental impacts and risks. If the costs are not too great – and they appear not to be – it can become in effect a zero-emission energy system with negligible impacts on land, air and water. And any residual, unavoidable hazards can be ones from which the system could recover within a reasonable time, either from natural processes alone or in concert with human remediation efforts.

This sustainability objective for the global energy system is achievable, and indeed we have several options. But when all of these options are compared without prejudice, fossil fuels – the "unusual suspect" – are likely to retain a significant role in the global energy system through this century and far beyond, and the transition toward renewables and perhaps eventually nuclear will be gradual. Deliberately diverting from this lowest cost path by prematurely forcing fossil fuels out of the energy supply mix may not mean as much for wealthy countries, but for the poorer people on this planet this arbitrary requirement would divert critical resources that could otherwise be devoted to essential investments in clean water, health care, disease prevention, education, basic infrastructure, security, improved governance and biodiversity preservation.

Ironically, however, clean energy – whether relying on fossil fuels or some other option – does not ensure a sustainable human presence on earth. Indeed, if the eventual, long-term costs of developing a clean energy system are as low as some of the evidence suggests, the challenges to sustainability may be even greater as humans use energy to satisfy their basic needs and seemingly inexhaustible desires for materials and living space.

Chapter reading guide

This chapter guide provides a summary of each chapter and suggests key pages for those readers who, although they currently lack the time for a full reading, wish to grasp its key theses, arguments and evidence after reviewing about 100 pages.

Chapter 1: What is energy sustainability?

Our energy system appears unsustainable because it is 85% based on fossil fuels, which are both non-renewable and polluting. A sustainable energy system should meet humanity's essential energy needs indefinitely, cleanly and hopefully at a reasonable cost. Even with major efficiency efforts, the essential needs for the expanding population of the developing world imply a three- to four-fold expansion of the global energy system over this century. While nothing lasts forever, energy supplies must be plentiful and, if they are depletable, must offer a relatively smooth transition to an enduring substitute – which renewables and perhaps nuclear can one day provide for fossil fuels. While all human activity has impacts on the natural world, a sustainable energy system must have negligible impacts and risks of extreme events, and any negative effects that occur should be ones from which natural systems can fully recover in a reasonable time. This book looks at whether fossil fuels can be part of the energy system according to this definition of sustainability. It addresses secondary energy choices – electricity, hydrocarbons, hydrogen – but especially focuses on the critical supply options – increased efficiency, nuclear, renewables and fossil fuels. *(See pages 1–6 and 11–12.)*

Chapter 2: Is our current energy path sustainable?

A current trends projection indicates that over this century global population could reach 10.5 billion while income grows seven-fold. Undesirable environmental and human impacts of the energy system would intensify, especially in urban areas of developing countries and at the global level in terms of climate change risk. The global energy system needs to change its current trajectory. Because there is nothing unique about this trajectory – the literature is full of projections indicating our system's unsustainability – the chapter is not essential reading. *(See page 53.)*

Chapter 3: The prospects for clean secondary energy

Recent books extol the virtues of hydrogen, but it is not widely understood that hydrogen is not a source of energy – it is a secondary form of energy, like electricity, that needs to be produced from a primary source, like fossil fuels, nuclear power or renewables. A sustainable energy system will require that secondary energy forms be produced with near-zero emissions and low impacts on land and water. Electricity should see its share grow to at least 30% of secondary energy by 2100. Hydrocarbons (refined petroleum products, natural gas, biofuels) and hydrogen will vie for the remaining 70%, but hydrogen will need to capture at least 30% of the total, and biofuels a significant part of the remaining hydrocarbon share, if emissions from secondary energy are to be at sustainable levels for both urban air quality and climate change risk. The relative shares of electricity, hydrogen and hydrocarbons will depend on the interplay of these emission constraints with key technological developments (and the resulting energy service costs) of fuel cells, hydrogen storage, biomass fuel production, and plug-in hybrid cars that rely on electricity from non-emitting sources. *(See pages 56–60 and 69–76.)*

Chapter 4: The usual suspects: efficiency, nuclear and renewables

Advocates of energy efficiency emphasize its role in reducing our need for primary energy, with the resulting sustainability benefits. Unfortunately, these advocates tend to ignore rigorous research showing that gains in efficiency make energy more attractive to businesses and consumers for satisfying new needs and perceived wants. This explains the close connection between economic growth and energy consumption of the past two centuries, and the difficulty of disconnecting these two for long periods of time without recourse to politically unpopular policies like strict regulations and significant energy tax increases. In the absence of such aggressive policies, worldwide energy use will grow substantially to meet urgent needs in the developing world and to provision energy-using innovations in industrialized countries. Nuclear power provides virtually clean energy but poses limited risks of radiation exposure from accidents and waste handling. It must overcome, however, the aversion of many people to extreme event risk, which makes plant siting increasingly challenging, especially in wealthy, democratic societies. The technology's link to nuclear weapons also hinders its prospects for worldwide dissemination. Renewable forms of energy are enduring and emission free, but their wide-scale development must overcome low energy density, intermittency and inconvenient location. Addressing these constraints – providing large-scale energy storage for example – can be costly and even cause significant environmental impacts. Advocates tend to underestimate these challenges because renewables have such small impacts today when they represent only a fraction of global energy supply. Much time and effort is required before renewables can fully supplant conventional energy supplies. *(See pages 136–138.)*

Chapter 5: The unusual suspect: how long can fossil fuels last – and does it matter?

When coal is included, there are perhaps 1,000 years of fossil fuels remaining at today's use rates and almost 500 years if consumption grows as in the current trends projection. If the appraisal includes gas hydrates and geopressurized gas, the estimated fossil fuel resource more than doubles. Gasoline is currently produced from oil sands and coal at production costs that are competitive when the conventional crude oil price is at \$35/barrel. This reality belies the recent wave of books suggesting that a peak in global production of "conventional oil" will lead to astronomical energy prices and economic cataclysm. Even when these other fossil fuel alternatives to conventional oil are depleted centuries hence, it will matter little if there are ready substitutes to which the global energy system can make transition without great difficulty over an extended period of decades or even centuries. Renewables and perhaps nuclear offer that long-run substitution potential for fossil fuels. *(See pages 152–166.)*

Chapter 6: Can we use fossil fuels cleanly – and what might it cost?

Although fossil fuels have long been associated with various types of pollution, humans have had substantial success in reducing the negative impacts and risks. But there are still large challenges ahead as a growing energy system threatens to swamp previous gains. Motivated by these concerns, technologists are assessing the prospects for zero-emission uses of fossil fuels, in which natural gas, plentiful coal and perhaps oil are converted without combustion into electricity, hydrogen and cleaner-burning synthetic fuels, while potentially harmful byproducts like acid compounds, toxins and greenhouse gases are separated and safely stored in geological formations. Since the required technologies are already applied in fertilizer production, refineries, electricity generation, enhanced oil and gas recovery, and coal-to-liquid-fuel conversion, this zero-emission fossil fuel strategy appears to be technologically and economically feasible, although scale-up would face various challenges. *(See pages 188–204.)*

Chapter 7: Sustainable energy choices: comparing the options

Visions and assessments of the global energy future are mostly provided either by advocates of one particular option, or by multi-disciplinary teams (like the Intergovernmental Panel on Climate Change or the World Energy Assessment) who are hindered from suggesting that some options will fare significantly better than others, or by engineers and economists who focus only on estimated cost. However, when societies make energy choices they trade-off cost with at least two other factors – the risk of an extreme event like a nuclear accident or an oil spill, and the geopolitical risks we associate with various energy supply options, like nuclear weapons proliferation or dependence on politically unstable regions. Another key consideration is the advantage that one option has because of its ability to mesh with our current technologies, industrial structure, institutional arrangements, investment attitudes and consumer preferences. When these additional factors are included, the zero-emission development of fossil fuels performs well, making it highly unlikely that civilization would want to "find a way to live without fossil fuels" before the end of this century. Indeed, the most affordable sustainable energy future may well be one in which fossil fuels gradually lose market share to renewables through the century, but still account for almost 60% of primary supply by 2100. While nuclear may grow enough to retain its current market share in a larger global energy system, its achievement of a more dominant role is unlikely in the absence of a major technological development or unexpectedly higher costs for zero-emission fossil fuels and renewables. *(See pages 216–222, 233–242 and 245–254.)*

Chapter 8: Sustainable energy policy: how do we get there?

Shifting to a more sustainable energy path at the primary and secondary energy level will require profound technological change over the coming decades, and this in turn requires a substantial policy effort. But most energy sustainability research tends to ignore policy, emphasizing technological and economic capability instead. Policy suggestions are sometimes offered by those who are naïve about the trade-offs involved in inducing profound technological change – and who therefore emphasize information and voluntaristic approaches alone – or naïve about the political constraints facing government – and who therefore tell politicians to apply politically unacceptable emission taxes alone. When political and administrative feasibility are seriously considered, it is apparent that we need carefully crafted policies that meld regulation with market incentives, namely emission cap and trade systems and niche market regulations, the latter guaranteeing a minimum market share for desired forms of energy (renewables in electricity generation) or categories of technologies (zero-emission vehicles, carbon capture and storage). These kinds of policies can set the stage for a greater reliance on price instruments like emission taxes as alternative technologies develop, especially if a growing reliance on emission taxes is pursued only gradually over several decades. *(See pages 259–261, 271 and 308–310.)*

Chapter 9: Broadening the definition: is sustainable energy sustainable?

Once we set aside pre-conceived notions about fossil fuels, and instead assess our options for a sustainable energy system based on criteria that reflect much of humanity's objectives and values, the argument that we should phase out their use during this century is difficult to support. Indeed, the more likely outcome in the quest for a clean and enduring energy system is that fossil fuels will retain a dominant role throughout this century and perhaps well beyond. Unfortunately, however, clean energy is a necessary but not sufficient condition for a sustainable global economy. Indeed, clean and low cost energy would free people to live and travel where they want, and consume as much as they want, which could intensify the pressure on valued ecosystems and the depletion of other non-renewable resources. A sustainable fossil fuel future does not guarantee a sustainable human presence on this shrinking planet. *(See pages 315–319 and 323–326.)*

Index

Italicized page numbers indicate figures and tables. Page numbers followed by "n" indicate footnotes.